Sociological
Thinking
A **New** Introduction

John T. Pullinger

Printed and bound in the United Kingdom by
4edge Ltd, 7a Eldon Way Industrial Estate, Hockley, Essex, SS5 4AD.

Contents

*To my wife Suzanne, for her
unremitting patience.*

*Thanks to Mick Bull for some
pointers on the use of apostrophes*

Preface to the text

In writing this new introduction, the author has remained faithful to the aims of the previous volume that was published in 2008 and which are identified below. The new volume has tracked some subsequent developments and reorientations in the subject which reflect social changes. As a result, the content of each chapter has been broadened and expanded. In updating the earlier volume, a decision was made to retain and rework the sections covering founding theory and early research since one of the aims of the book remains to provide a sense of how the subject has developed historically as a mirror of social change.

Compared to the previous volume, the author has integrated a range of selective quotations. Also, to assist the reader in following up a broader range of resources, the original list of recommended books has been expanded into a short bibliography and key referencing has been provided.

The author has approached this work with the aim of providing a manageable length and accessible introduction to sociology. The text concentrates more heavily than standard A level texts on guiding the reader to develop the psychological and intellectual qualities that are necessary to effectively approach the subject. It is pitched at GCE A Level and is aimed at the sociology student or general reader who is looking for an alternative to the standard texts. This text is different to the latter, however, in that, as the title suggests, it focuses more on guiding the reader into thinking sociologically than providing an encyclopaedic grounding in the academic content of the subject. The idea for this type of text originated from a perceived need for such an alternative which came from teaching Access to Higher Education students and is modelled on an approach that has been applied successfully in working with such groups.

The approach adopted by the author guides the reader to develop a critical and open-minded outlook on society. With this aim in mind, readers are led to examine and deconstruct their preconceptions about society and then reconstruct an understanding through the reflective use of sociological concepts and theories.

Based on this approach, the text caters for the following needs of sociology students and the general reader. It:

offers an inroad into the subject at an introductory level which makes no assumptions about the reader's prior knowledge in the subject;

guides students / the reader through the process of breaking down preconceptions on the way that they view society and their own lives;

leads the reader into appreciating the challenges that sociological thinking poses;

provides a clear introduction to sociological concepts and theories and offers a challenging learning curve in constructing sociological approaches and insights.

This volume concentrates on guiding the reader to raise essential questions about society and use sociology to develop reflective insights. It does not aim to be comprehensive in terms of academic content or breadth within the topic areas covered. Instead, the work focuses more on the task of guiding the reader in the development of intellectual qualities necessary to think sociologically. To assist this process, the approach adopted in the text:

introduces the terrain of the subject and alerts the reader to a range of challenges that it offers (Chapter 1);

prefaces each chapter with an abstract to orientate the reader to the forthcoming chapter content;

starts chapters by highlighting typical preconceptions that need to be confronted in making a successful transition from layperson to sociologist;

guides this transition by developing sociological understanding of social phenomena.

Definitions of key terms are integrated into the text to help the reader acquire a sound conceptual grounding in the subject. A historical chronology is built into each of the chapters to assist the reader in acquiring a feel for historical developments in the subject. Each chapter can be approached independently but the text also takes the form of a building process. For example, contemporary theory is briefly introduced toward the end of chapter two. It is then built on at the end of each topic chapter three to eight and taken to a more detailed level in chapter nine.

Although the theories considered in the text are broadly, sometimes even globally, applicable, the main geographical target audience is a British one and the data and research included reflects this. Audiences who would benefit from the text include:

those looking for an accessible text which can help them make the transition from GCSE to GCE A Level thinking in the subject;

A Level students who are looking for a reflective alternative which can be used to complement the standard texts;

mature students who are looking for an unintimidating text which can nevertheless guide them to a challenging level of study;

students in higher education who are new to the subject area and are looking for an introductory text in sociology which has less the feel of an A Level textbook than the more traditional ones;

the general reader who is interested in contemporary issues such as those surrounding globalisation and who is looking for an approachable text.

Finally, the author hopes that in this work he has been able to make a contribution to a rewarding intellectual venture for the reader.

1 // Sociology – The Terrain and the Challenge

Abstract

This chapter introduces a number of key sociological concepts. It emphasises the complexity of the subject, goes on to chart some of its key dimensions, and alerts the reader to a number of difficulties that a newcomer to the subject is likely to experience. This complexity and these difficulties necessitate the development of certain intellectual qualities to successfully tackle this area of study. The chapter also attempts to allay and reverse some of the negative preconceptions that commonly abound regarding the subject.

It is a prerequisite that those embarking on the subject should have a curiosity and open mindedness to view society anew. The sociologist needs to be able to question their everyday knowledge and assumptions about society which may be shaped by general conceptions of common sense. This requires a certain distancing of oneself from society and a heightening of critical awareness toward unquestioning preconceptions regarding it that we are socialised into.

Through the definition of some key sociological concepts, an introductory examination is made of the forces of social constraint that bear down on individual action. Upon this is introduced the idea of a two way relationship between the individual and society in the formation of each other, locating purposeful individual action within the context of social constraint.

A fundamental distinction is made between animal behaviour, which is largely instinctive and pre-programmed, and human action which is reflective, purposeful, self-conscious and conducted within the context of linguistic communication. The nature (inbuilt characteristics) and nurture (environmental influences) debate is also touched on and the reader is alerted to being on guard against the master justification that is sometimes used to encourage acceptance of certain ways of behaving as being beyond question – 'it is human nature'. Instead, action should be viewed sociologically as both shaped by society and consciously reflected on by purposeful individuals.

The concept of 'life chances' is introduced and contrasted with that of random chance. It is explained in terms of the influences of socially structured inequalities of opportunity that surround individuals during their lives.

An essential quality required of the sociologist is to be able to develop an understanding of the social and global picture as the broader context of our personal experiences. This is initially illustrated by reviewing what C. Wright Mills has referred to as 'The Sociological Imagination', which includes the capacity to recognise the relationship between the experience of personal troubles and broader public issues. Following some examples provided by the author, the reader is encouraged to pause and attempt such analysis of their own.

Finally, the importance and difficulties of making the transition from layperson to sociologist are confronted and the issue of sociology providing an academic basis for enlightened social intervention is briefly raised.

Sociology – not a pushover

Sociology has often faced image problems. There are those who doubt the academic credentials of the subject and others who dismiss it as merely subversive. It is hoped that in following this and other sociology texts, the reader will agree with the author that sociology is not an academically lightweight discipline. Indeed, sociologists face problems of great complexity. As for the subversion criticism, if this amounts to a distorted expression of 'encourages critical awareness', then the author would argue that the rephrasing should be taken as a compliment to the capacity of the subject.

To the newcomer, sociology is likely to appear to be a bewildering subject. Students often initially experience confusion and frustration in trying to get onto the wavelength of the subject. Why is this so? Firstly, it is a discipline of great magnitude which studies highly complex phenomena by using a broad range of technical concepts that require precise understanding and careful application. This takes time and requires patience. Secondly, there is no single indisputably correct theory, but rather rival perspectives that require rigorous evaluation in their competition to explain this complex reality. Developing the ability to move between and compare alternative theories and explanations and use them selectively will therefore be necessary. Thirdly, to pursue the subject effectively requires certain psychological and intellectual qualities. The sociology student must be prepared to suspend and re-examine much that they may have taken for granted about society. This requires the development of mental flexibility and a predisposition of open-mindedness to unexpected findings. The budding sociologist needs to be motivated by curiosity, to nurture a scepticism regarding common sense outlooks and to be prepared to patiently embark on a long voyage of intellectual discovery. As Ken Browne clearly and succinctly explains

'Sociology is concerned with studying many things which most people already know something about. Everyone will have some knowledge and understanding of family life, the education system, work, the mass media, and religion simply by living as a member of society. This leads many people to assume that the topics studied by sociologists and the explanations sociologists produce are really just common sense: what 'everyone knows'. This is a very mistaken assumption. Sociological research has shown many widely held 'common-sense' ideas and explanations to be false. Ideas such as that there is no real poverty left in modern Britain; that the poor and unemployed are inadequate and lazy; that everyone has equal chances in life; that the rich are rich because they work harder; that men are 'naturally' superior to women; that it is obvious that men and women will fall in love and live together – these have all been questioned by sociological research. The re-examination of such common-sense views is very much the concern of sociology' (Browne, 2006, pp.1-2).

In analysing sociologically the society of which he / she is a part, it is not adequate for the sociologist to expect to engage in a more subtle and disciplined portrayal of what we already 'know'. The student must be open-minded to new insights and prepared to make qualitative leaps in thinking which may lead to findings that fly in the face of widely held common sense knowledge.

The aim of this chapter is to indicate the scope and nature of sociology, introduce a number of the defining concepts, raise some important implications regarding the subject, and alert the reader to key difficulties and challenges which lay ahead.

The meaning of concepts

All academic subjects have their own concepts. The purpose of concepts is to offer ways of conceiving reality. They help us to make sense of reality, structure our observations, communicate our understanding with others and assist our analysis. A number of sociological concepts such as socialisation, culture and role will shortly be introduced. The reader should be aware, however, and will see later, that as sociological concepts need to correspond as closely as possible to reality, new ones may need to be devised as society changes. Indeed, some of the concepts and theoretical foundations upon which the subject was developed have increasingly come into question as being inadequate for the task of understanding contemporary times and sociologists are struggling to develop improved alternatives.

Key concepts of sociology – society as constraint and control

Human behaviour is sometimes compared to animal behaviour to justify it as somehow 'natural'. However, an important starting point for the sociologist is the realisation that instinctive pre-programming of behaviour is an extremely small element of the human condition compared to that of animals and that our capacity for learning is much superior. Nature locks the range of animal behaviour into narrow channels. This behaviour is highly stimulus and response based and the capacity for passing on any learning is very limited. By contrast, humans are able to engage in abstract thinking and symbolic communication, making sophisticated understanding and communication in the form of written and spoken language possible, along with the passage of learning to successive generations to build on. We are able to contemplate the consequences of our own and others' action, consider and weigh up options available and engage in conscious decision making. Throughout the world we have developed a diversity of social and cultural environments, belief systems and institutions in response to problems encountered. Human capacities thus liberate our behaviour from the narrow constraints of the animal world and enable choice of action. But as individual behaviour is largely not predisposed into narrow channels by the constraints of instinct, something else must be responsible for co-operative co-existence to be possible. This realm is the subject matter for sociology in the understanding of human action – it is 'society'.

As individuals, we are born into pre-existing society. As we awaken to society, we encounter an environment which we tune into through our senses and adjust to through experience. In so doing, we learn and internalise features of this environment and respond to it. The extent to which the individual engages in a relatively active or passive relationship with the social environment has been much debated within sociology and will vary from individual to individual. However, sociologists emphasise that **socialisation** – the influence on individual consciousness and identity of culture, social values, norms, social roles, moral pressures and laws etc. - will be profound during our early years (referred to at this stage as **primary socialisation**) and accompany us throughout our lives. Let us briefly define some established sociological concepts which comprise the mainstays of the social environment.

As used in sociology, the term **culture** has a rather different meaning from the judgement of sophistication with which it is more commonly associated. In sociology, culture refers to the beliefs and values that make up a common way of life. It becomes internalised through our capacity to learn the meaning of sounds, gestures and symbols in the form of language. Culture also includes commonly recognised ceremonies, dress, rituals, traditions and artefacts which may substantially pre-date the lives of individuals in any contemporary society. It may be bound up with belief systems about the supernatural which we refer to as religion. Whilst socialisation into culture is a universal feature of human life, there is much diversity of culture between societies. However, through socialisation, at a general level individuals tend to take their own culture as their universal reference point.

The term **subculture** has been used to refer to social groups who share a set of values which are distinct from and may be in opposition to the values of the dominant culture. For example, dominant social values in contemporary western societies emphasise the importance of individual application and material success. In the context of school culture, these values promote academic application and striving for exam success. However, sociological research has shown that subcultures have emerged within schools (sometimes referred to as counter cultures) which hold academic success in disdain and powerfully influence the poor academic performance of group members.

Cultural diversity refers more to the degree of co-existence within a society of different cultural groups, usually distinguished by their own religious and ethnic cultural traditions. There is strong evidence that through migration contemporary western societies are becoming internally more culturally diverse. This growing diversity can on the one hand enhance tolerance between cultural communities or on the other promote intolerance.

Social **values** are a part of culture. They relate to belief systems which offer general guidelines by which action is judged as desirable or undesirable. Despite their multi-cultural diversity, societies tend to have dominant overarching value systems. For example, contemporary western societies value highly opportunities for individual achievement based on personal merit. A society which operates in accordance with these values is referred to as a 'meritocracy'. Evidence, however, may indicate that institutions and action which depart from dominant values are quite widespread. Regarding meritocratic values, some sociologists point to significant disparities between these values and what happens 'on the ground', particularly in the spheres of educational and occupational opportunity and achievement, where it appears that some people have far greater opportunities than others with little reference to individual merit. In sociology, social values which provide a systematic distortion of reality are referred to as **ideology**.

Norms relate to values but provide more clearly defined expectations of behaviour in regard to conventions. They specify what is deemed to be normal and acceptable within society. Thus, norms regarding family life in Britain in the 1950s emphasised a uniform model of a married male and female partnership for the upbringing of children, with primary financial support provided by the male breadwinner and domestic chores and childrearing the responsibility of the housewife. These norms were powerfully supported by **moral pressures** upholding separate and clearly defined male and female roles, stigmatising against cohabitation, illegitimacy and divorce, and imposing sanctions against offenders. Norms of contemporary household life indicate the acceptability of much greater diversity of lifestyle and arguably reflect a liberalisation of social and moral values of a more tolerant society.

In a formal sense, **social roles** are social niches which specify to individuals who occupy them standard expectations and constraints on their action vis-à-vis the occupants of other roles. Thus, the action of individuals is structured through role reciprocity. The relationships between people in different roles, when mutual expectations are shared, integrates the action of the participants. **Task orientated role relationships**, such as between managers and workers within the workplace, may be set within highly formalised and hierarchical organisational power structures, in which entitlements and responsibilities of participants are prescribed by job descriptions and backed up by legally binding contractual obligations. By contrast, **leisure roles**, such as between a host and visitors at a dinner party, are likely to be much more informal, but could include subtle expectations regarding etiquette.

Individuals live their lives within externally imposed social roles. As Peter Berger explains

'A role, then, may be defined as a typified response to a typified expectation. Society has predefined the fundamental typology. To use the language of the theatre, from which the concept of role is derived, we can say that society provides the script for all the *dramatis personae.* The individual actors, therefore, need but slip into the roles already assigned to them before the curtain goes up. As long as they play their roles as provided for in this script, the social play can proceed as planned' (Berger,1974, p.112).

This conformity may be superficial though, perhaps out of perceived necessity. Furthermore, individuals may actively adopt roles to engage in image manipulation. However, Berger goes on to show that by acting out roles, these roles come to enter the internal constitution of the individual.

'Roles carry with them both certain actions and the emotions and attitudes that belong to these actions. The professor putting on an act that pretends to wisdom comes to feel wise. The preacher finds himself believing what he preaches. The soldier discovers martial stirrings in his breast as he puts on his uniform' (Berger, 1974, p.113).

The characteristics of social roles, which exist external to the individual, become to some extent internalised through the process of acting them out.

Overall, individuals occupy many roles, which engage them in a variety of social relationships, each comprising reciprocal expectations. Therefore, within some situations, individuals may face conflicting role requirements, such the expectations associated with the role of employee and wife, which can be difficult to resolve. Key roles, such as those linked to domestic and work life, were relatively fixed for individuals in the post-war decades. Now, arguably, society is more rapidly changing and people have to develop the skills to navigate their way through many role changes throughout their lives.

Institutions also structure social action. They may take the form of formal organisations which can prescribe the roles of participants and impose rules and regulations through authority structures. At one extreme are institutions within which, through choice or compulsion, individuals find their lives confined. These would include mental hospitals, prisons, monasteries and boarding schools. Such institutions are referred to as 'total institutions' through which the capacity for control of the individual can be extreme. Other formal institutions would include educational establishments (excluding the above) and various workplaces. However, institutions can govern behaviour in a broader sense when they uphold traditions, such as 'the institution of marriage'.

The **law** formalises sanctions and imposes controls which tend to uphold dominant social and moral values and norms, but in a codified form. Changes in the law are often associated with parallel changes in social norms and values. For example, in Britain and many western societies, a liberalisation of norms and values regarding family life has been accompanied by a liberalisation of divorce laws and more liberal sexual morals has led to changes in the law whereby homosexuality ceased to be a crime and, more recently, same sex civil partnerships and marriage have become possible through legislation. The enactment of legislation can also be fuelled by a response of moral outrage to the infringement of social norms and values, as in the case of public response to the reckless behaviour behind the banking crisis of 2008 and its subsequent economic consequences.

Individual compliance may not always be embraced but sometimes pursued, even grudgingly, out of **practical necessity**. Thus, the need to work to obtain an income is for many a necessity so that bills can be paid to provide at least food, shelter and a degree of comfort as well as acquiring a standard of living and quality of life that we (are encouraged to) aspire to. To some extent, the need for this type of compliance may be born out of our inability to extract ourselves from being victims of enticed material aspiration in which the mass media may have a powerful controlling effect.

The above mainstays structure the actions of individuals within society. The degree to which they are synchronised with each other provides a framework of consistency that orders the behaviour of individuals. We have now reached the position where the problem is not that of explaining how social action is ordered, but explaining levels of individual freedom, choice of action and diversity, as well as conflict and disorder encountered in modern societies. We will later see that emphasising the importance and explaining the basis of social order or conflict in society was a fundamental dimension of dispute between the different founding theoretical perspectives of functionalism and Marxism respectively.

The individual and society

That society is possible at all is based on human capacity for intelligent communication, co-operation and organisation. It is thus a phenomena which emerges from the capacities of humans living in aggregates. However, society reacts back on its participants through the constraints and opportunities that the social world brings. We have identified above some of the social influences and constraints that shape individual action. These influences operate externally to individuals. Customs, moral values, institutions and laws etc. exist outside of individuals in the sense that they predate our existence, will continue to operate long after we are gone, and for most of us, whether we were ever here or not will make little difference to them. We are swept along by them, often unaware of their influences because we live in a social world where we take much for granted. These external social influences are internalised through the process of socialisation.

However, it would be far too strong to say that these processes precisely 'determine' individual behaviour. Although it shapes action, society does not just call forth socially regulated responses from individuals. If it did so, the effect of society on humans would be much like that of nature in animals. By contrast to animals, the human condition includes the capacity for reflection, attribution of meaning and symbolic communication and conscious decision making which enable in individuals a degree of free thought and action. Therefore, viewed sociologically, the action of individuals is a delicate balance between social constraints and individual choice. The effect of choice by an individual on society as a whole is usually infinitesimal, but multitudinous effects of individual choices can react back into society which will change as a consequence. One of the founding social theorists, Max Weber, contended that despite the constraining effect of social institutions, society was ultimately the outcome of purposive action of individuals.

For Emile Durkheim, another founding social theorist, individuals need to accept social constraints as the price to pay for a greater freedom. The great gift **of** society is to enable human kind to realise its potential and exist above the brutal state of nature. Social co-existence and co-operation enables the creation of an environment which bestows on individuals protection from life dominated by the wild forces of nature. It makes civilisation possible and for this individuals must be prepared to play their part in sustaining society. For example, the necessity to work and in the workplace conform to institutional requirements provides economic resources that enable a certain standard of living and participation in a range of leisure activities to be possible.

However, an alternative view would place more emphasis on the importance of socially patterned differences in constraints and opportunities that exist **within** society. These differences reflect patterned inequalities in the distribution of power and privilege which impact on the lives of individuals through the social structure, providing some with far more freedom and advantages than others.

Society is extremely complex and there may be much in each view. The first position tends to be taken up by functionalist theorists such as Durkheim who adopt a consensus view of society and the second by conflict theorists such as Weber and Marx.

Some important implications

A number of implications can be summed up at this point to help provide guidance for the prospective sociologist:

1. Use theories critically and selectively

The scope and complexity of sociology is massive, ranging from the study of the smallest social environments of friends, families and partners, through to broader communities and right up to the societal and global level. No single all embracing theory holds a monopoly of understanding, but a number of theories compete for plausibility and demonstrate strengths and weaknesses in different areas. In this text, a number of theoretical perspectives will be reviewed, from those of the founding fathers through to the ideas of more contemporary thinkers. Using theory can have a liberating effect against the intellectual constraints of conventional wisdom and common sense dogma. A key capacity for a sociologist is to use theories critically and selectively to develop insights into the workings of society. It is therefore important to remain vigilant that the potential intellectual liberation that theory entails is not itself closed down by one's dogmatic adherence to a particular perspective.

2. Consider environmental explanations, even when genetic explanations may seem to be obvious

Sociologists challenge the view that social action is largely the outcome of innate and fixed capacities residing within individuals – the 'nature' argument. Rather, it is primarily viewed as a product of socialisation and the restrictions and opportunities that derive from the social environment – the 'nurture' argument. Consider, for example, evidence which may suggest that levels of intelligence run in families. A simple nature interpretation, once emphasised by psychologists of the eugenics movement, is that such evidence is proof that intelligence levels are genetically inherited. Sociologists, in emphasising nurture explanations, do not deny that people are born with different intellectual capacities and potentials. However, the same evidence on intelligence would be studied more in terms of the influence of the social environment on the development of intellectual potential. Interest would focus on a different type of inheritance - the inheritance of different socially constructed 'life chances' that people are born into, affording varying opportunities for intellectual success, rather than explanations emphasising fixed and genetically transmitted intellectual qualities.

3. Question explanations of behaviour that are put in terms of human nature

We should beware of explanations of 'behaviour' couched in terms of 'human nature'. This term can be, and has been, used as a largely vacuous justification for almost any particular type of behaviour. When behaviour is explained in terms of human nature, it tends to be assumed that the latter is a narrow and fixed innate human capacity, determining certain behaviour as inevitable. However, even a casual survey across societies and history would reveal a very broad and varied range of human behaviour, influenced by different social and cultural contexts.

Viewed sociologically, human nature provides a very broad canvas of behaviour potentials, the outcome of which society shapes.

As a single example, to say that it is human nature to be materialistic and individually competitive is to: a) ignore the evidence of cultural diversity – many cultures have held more communal based values, b) apply a fatalistic attitude to possible alternatives, and c) ignore the key message of sociology that human nature is malleable through socialisation within different social environments. To say that materialism and individual competition are fundamental values of contemporary western society that we are socialised into and therefore strongly influence behaviour is much nearer to the mark. To put this more provocatively, when people's minds become the receptacles of the trash of contemporary advertising and celebrity culture, the sociological question is not what is human nature but what have we become by the type of society that we (and who are the we here?) have created.

Although we are biological beings, our actions are not, as in the case of animals, narrowly determined by our biology. Although we have instincts, our actions are not just instinctive. And although we may refer to our human nature, this provides a propensity for a very broad range of action. Our action is largely the outcome of a mixture of constraints and influences from our social environment and individual reflection on potential courses of action.

4. Think about life profiles in terms of socially structured life chances and opportunities

As individuals, sociologists or otherwise, we may occasionally reflect on the profile that our lives have taken. Perhaps they could have gone, to some extent, in one direction or another based on circumstances and decisions made at different points in time. How can we best analyse this? The major influences on our lives are likely to include a mixture of individual innate capacities, chance and social environment.

Sociologists do not deny that to some extent our path in life may be influenced by our innate makeup, for example in the form of personality characteristics and physical and intellectual capacity. Without ability, a person cannot become a university professor. Further, a mixture of chance encounters, lucky decisions and the personal ability and learning aptitude to take advantage of situations can be important factors in the way that our lives unfold. Indeed, the idea of chance or luck may itself act as a motivating factor, keeping dreams alive of winning a fortune in such competitions as the National Lottery in the face of otherwise limited or bleak life alternatives that many people face. In this case, chance is random and the entrants all face equal and extremely thin odds of winning a fortune.

However, chance and luck are clearly not equally distributed in society. Lottery type luck finishes at or before birth. Sociologists emphasise that from birth our individual course of life is powerfully influenced by the social environment. It can shape our personality and nurture or impede the development of our intellectual capacity. The types of inequality that the social structure imposes can influence the type of education that we may have access to, the type of people that we are likely to associate with and the chances of living a healthy, rewarding and successful life. These chances are socially loaded in favour of some and against others through the effects of the social structure. This reality is expressed in sociology by the concept of 'life chances' – socially structured differences in, for example, material and cultural resources within the backgrounds that people are born into and come from and which continue to influence the opportunities that they are likely to have access to.

A key area of debate within sociology is the extent to which individuals can overcome unfavourable circumstances of the social environment that they have been brought up in. To put it another way, how strong is the influence of these life chances in determining our opportunities and course of life or to what extent are we alternatively able to create our own life chances, opportunities and outcomes, by, for example, overcoming disadvantage through individual ability and determined action? And, very important sociologically, which institutions may enhance or impede this process?

People sometimes view their life experiences in terms of fate. Bound up with belief in fate is often the idea that society is an impenetrable mystery and even that there are mysterious forces at work that we cannot understand but should resign ourselves to. In any society where people experience restricted opportunities, belief in fate can provide consolation; our fortune is in the lap of the gods. But such an outlook is likely to be debilitating. One of the tasks of sociology is to reveal through analysis the degree to which societies, including the one that we live in, offer equality of opportunity for individual achievement.

5. Stand back and be prepared to question common sense views of society, especially your own

As members of society, our everyday worlds comprise our outlooks based on the social influences and experiences that we have been exposed to. However, given the diversity of societies and cultures, as well as groups within society, it is clear that our world view is only one of many. Difficult as a previous section implies that it may be, we must make every effort to suspend what we take for granted about people and society if we are to attempt to understand this diversity in an open minded way and become effective sociologists.

Sociology is not likely to appeal to those who fear stepping outside of conventional wisdom, who place a mental block on ways of thinking that they are unfamiliar with, or who find it difficult to relate personal experiences to a far larger social canvas. It will not appeal to those who expect to find singularly right or wrong answers to the questions that it raises.

The purpose of this text is to encourage the reader to make a transition in thinking about society from that of the common sense and often restricted thinking of the layperson to that of the analytical approach of a sociologist. This may not be a simple task. It is not uncommon for newcomers to the subject to find the early stages of their studies to be disorientating. The subject seems to click for different people at different stages. In anticipation of these early difficulties, the reader is alerted to the need for patient commitment to this subject.

The sociological challenge

1. Developing your sociological imagination

In his work of that title, first published in 1959, C Wright Mills referred to 'the sociological imagination'. What did Mills mean by this term? For Mills, developing the sociological imagination is a creative intellectual process in which the practitioner becomes liberated from preoccupation with a restricted and everyday view of the self and society shaped by conventional thinking and the limited viewpoint of immediate social encounters. Mills argued that cultivating the sociological imagination is about developing an awareness of how immediate experiences relate to the broader social structure and society as it moves through history. It is about developing the intellectual capacity to move between different social levels, topic areas and perspectives to generate new insights into the relationship between our restricted world of immediate experiences and broader structural influences.

Mills went on to emphasise the intellectual, consciousness raising and practical implications of applying the sociological imagination by distinguishing between 'personal troubles' and 'public issues'. Regarding the former, people often individualise their experiences and problems. As such, they tend to look to themselves and known others for blame or remedy, and examine experiences in terms of individual abilities or shortcomings. This may sometimes be an appropriate level of analysis for viewing and tackling problems. However, by itself this viewpoint may also sometimes be misplaced and debilitating and indicate a lack of sociological imagination.

For Mills, to become an effective sociologist, one must develop an awareness of the broader social context to the lives of individuals (including themselves) and how social structures impact on our small worlds and private lives. For the individual who has cultivated the sociological imagination, this awareness can have an enlightening effect. Developing the capacity to move between the small picture view of our personal lives and the influence of the wider social structure enables us to relate personal experiences to extensive social forces and translate our personal troubles into broader public issues. The following section is an abridged and paraphrased version of an account from Mills in which he develops these ideas.

> A most productive distinction which the sociological imagination works between is that of the immediate environment, in which people experience 'personal troubles', and 'public issues', which relate to the broader social structure. The ability to apply the sociological imagination to working between these levels is an

essential tool for sociologists and was commonly practiced by the classical sociological theorists.

Personal troubles are a feature of the character of the individual and relate to experiences within one's immediate social environment. Viewed at this level alone, to explain and resolve troubles lies within the individual and the close social setting which is directly experienced and to some extent open to one's influence. A trouble is experienced as a private matter which poses a threat to one's closely held values.

By contrast, viewing experiences at the level of public issues enables one to transcend the viewpoint of the immediate world and recognize that the institutions and history of society as a broader social structure comprise many overlapping personal environments. As an issue is a public matter, its context is that of broader public values which are felt to be threatened. Public values and challenges to them arouse public debate, but this debate and the issues may lack focus as they are more detached from immediate social environments and experiences.

The benefit of applying the sociological imagination to working between the levels of personal experiences and society's broader structure can be illustrated in a number of examples.

If in a city of 100,000 people, only one person is unemployed, this is a personal trouble. The focus of solving that trouble would rightly be on the character of that individual, their skills and the opportunities available. If in a nation of 50 million employees 15 million people are unemployed, at one level this is experienced as 15 million personal troubles. However, it should be viewed as a public issue and analysed at the level of a social structure within which opportunities for employment have collapsed. The range of solutions then remains within an analysis of society's economic and political institutions, not just the personal characteristics or circumstances of a large number of unemployed individuals.

In times of war, a variety of personal problems may be experienced including one's very survival, promotion within the military apparatus to a level of safety, and making money. However, looked at from a structural point of view raises issues to do with the causes of war in the first place in the context of a world of irresponsible nation states.

Within marriage, partners may experience problems which can be addressed within their small environment of personal troubles. But when divorce rates within society as a whole spiral to the level of 250 per 1,000 marriages within the first four years, this becomes a broader issue regarding the institution of marriage and family life itself and the impact of other institutions upon them.

Whilst the broader economy remains arranged in such a way that slumps occur, the problem of unemployment cannot be solved at the personal level. To the extent to which the nation state system gives rise to war, the individual is powerless to solve the personal troubles that this situation imposes on them. And if the institution of the family forces women into domestic slavery and men into being their providers, the mass of unsatisfactory marriages cannot be resolved just at the private level.

The origin of personal troubles which affect us and our immediate worlds can often be found in the broader social structure. To understand this, we need to look at the bigger picture of the social structure and its institutions. To move our viewpoint between the experiences of our personal world and the broader social structure is to use the sociological imagination (Mills, 1975, pp.14-17).

What was Mills' central message? Mills was emphasising that a preoccupation with explaining action in terms of individual characteristics or the little picture of our immediate environment is likely to blind us to asking more searching questions and raising social issues. These only become evident when we develop the ability to relate immediate experiences to broader structural influences. This is not to deny individuals responsibility for their actions, but to generate insight into the reasonable limits of that responsibility given the broader constraints (which now may be taking an increasingly global dimension) operating on people and the options available to them. Analysis may then lead to the broader practical option of pressing for social reform to improve people's lives.

Developing the sociological imagination remains a process of creative but disciplined sociological insight by which problems experienced at a personal level can be effectively related to the influence of the broader social structure and posed as public issues. Taking up Mills' reference to unemployment, one view often encouraged by certain sections of the mass media is that people who are out of work are lazy and develop dependence of benefit when they should do more about remedying their situation. Indeed, individuals may know of particular instances where they believe this to be so and individual case studies have been used within the media to try and substantiate the view that this is very general phenomena. The focus of the problem is then fixed on the moral nature of a large number of individuals.

Using the sociological imagination raises new vantage points on the problem of unemployment. If individual laziness is essentially at the heart of the problem, the question arises as to why there are so many more inherently lazy people when 3,000,000 people are unemployed than when 1,000,000 people are unemployed? Raising this simple question shifts the focus of attention to the relative powerlessness of individuals in the face of a malfunctioning economy. The broader public issues related to an immense number of personal troubles would then be to do with questioning how the economy is run and why certain sections of society prefer to focus attention on individual shortcomings instead.

Other examples can be provided to show how using the sociological imagination can elevate troubles viewed at a personal level to that of public issues. For example, a growing number of people in Britain in the early 1990s experienced the personal troubles of mortgage arrears and repossession. Although many had originally made far from reckless decisions when taking out mortgages, an increase in these personal troubles can be related to the broader issue of social policy that was designed to expand the private housing market and ultimately left many individuals relatively powerless in the face of a substantial rise in interest rates.

Another problem and issue area is that of job insecurity. Although directly experienced as a personal trouble by very many individuals, analysing job insecurity sociologically would place it in the context of government policy and this in the yet broader context of the need to attract inward investment in conditions of highly mobile global capital investment by encouraging a flexible labour market. Analysis here must be of the range of national policy options and the forces of global capitalism. It may also raise issues about conditions of employment in other parts of the world and that of ethical trading.

Personal financial insecurity provides a further example of troubles and issues. A fall in the value of private pensions by 30% in the three years leading up to October 2011 had been experienced as a personal financial trouble for many people approaching retirement at this time. However, when viewed as a broader public issue, questions arise as to the decision made by British governments from the 1980s to reduce the value of state pensions and encourage people to invest in private pensions whose value is related to stock market performance.

Likewise, threats to individual savings with the collapse of a number of financial institutions between 2007 and 2008 (and major threats to the entire global banking system in 2008) can be viewed at the level of personal troubles to many individual savers. Millions of people in many countries also faced a decline their standard of living for years afterwards. The extent to which these personal troubles were a consequence of light touch banking regulation and perverse risk incentives within a globally interconnected financial industry requires the phenomena to be analysed at the level of public issues within both national and global contexts if the possibility of mass personal trouble of this type is to be avoided in the future.

There are many other areas in which the experience of personal troubles can be studied in the context of public issues and new insights gained and issues raised. It would be a valuable exercise for the reader to pause and in pursuing other examples, some of which may relate to their own personal experiences, develop their sociological imagination.

2. Making the transition from layperson to sociologist

What does making the transition from the vantage point of layperson to that of sociologist entail? It essentially requires a person to be prepared to examine their taken for granted assumptions about society and contemplate whole new social panoramas. Accepting a common sense outlook may offer the comfort of familiarity and easy answers, but such a viewpoint can provide illusions which sociology is able to penetrate. Comfort in illusion is the easy option, but in taking this option, we may be unwittingly conspiring against ourselves since sociology can reveal much that the powerful would prefer to remain hidden. The subject can therefore expect no favours from these quarters.

To achieve this critical stance, it is necessary to adopt a mental position as if standing outside of the very society that a person has been brought up in and feels so familiar with. For the sociologist, the layperson's familiarity with society through their everyday life assumptions may be misleading compared to the findings of academic sociology. For the layperson initially studying sociology, the experience of stepping outside of a taken for granted world may, at least at first, feel disconcerting. But to be an effective sociologist, this step needs to be made. A key aim of this text is to offer guidance in this process.

Why, then, is everyday knowledge likely to be inadequate for purposes of sociological analysis? There are many reasons. Perhaps the first question to ask is where does the lay observer of society obtain his or her working knowledge of society from? This knowledge is likely to come from a variety of sources including mass media information, the opinions and experiences of others that we converse with and our own personal experiences. It may often be adequate for everyday purposes, but would not stand up to the criteria of scrutiny required in academic sociology. Knowledge of society gained in the above ways is likely to be biased, unsystematic, and unrepresentative, and, in the light of sociological scrutiny, the self-evident may turn out to be misleading.

Consider, for example, how one may relate to the tabloid press. The everyday reader may be susceptible to such newspapers shaping what they believe to be important and influencing their opinions and common sense outlook. The tabloid press may also be of interest to the sociologist. However, the purpose will be a different one. By stepping back and studying how the tabloids attempt to manipulate common sense through the use of stereotypes, emotional language, positioning of articles etc., and raising broader questions of whose interest this serves, the sociologist adopts a more detached and analytical posture.

One way of gaining analytic distance on society is through the vantage point of historical distance. This can help us to gain insights into society that may have eluded contemporaries. For example, think of the dominant values behind the American Declaration of Independence of 1776. The writers of this tract based their reasoning on the Enlightenment view that all men are created equal and that citizens have the right to throw off a tyrannical government. In this day and age, we may be astounded to learn that some of those who professed adherence to these values were also slave owners. From our outside vantage point, we can easily spot what appears to be a clear contradiction between professed values and social institutions. However, during their time, this incongruity did not seem so apparent to many.

Being encapsulated in the everyday thinking of our society and age may blind us to what may be seen by the outsider as logical inconsistencies. Unless we can gain a similar analytic distance from contemporary society, future others may look back at us with similar amazement that we failed in our everyday lives to recognise the contradictions of our own time. We must therefore find some way of distancing ourselves from our taken for granted world. The theories and concepts of sociology can assist us in making detached and critical evaluations. On the other hand, governments, not always great supporters of subjects like sociology, may have a vested interest in promoting that common layman activity of not engaging in joined up thinking on social issues.

Sociology is not just an academic exercise, but sociological analysis can be a prerequisite for intelligent intervention is society. However, it does not offer us solutions for the creation of a perfect society. If this was once the aim of some early social theorists, who by the way differed fundamentally in their images of an ideal society, the disappointments of the twentieth century and the social complexity and relentless change of the contemporary world have curbed such expectations. For those who are dissatisfied with everyday knowledge of society, sociology offers new insights and a more exacting level of analysis to help us formulate a broadly considered and academically based view of society. It is the aim of the following chapters to assist the reader in this direction.

2 // Sociological Perspectives

Abstract

This chapter explains what is meant by sociological concepts and theories and introduces the reader to some founding theoretical perspectives in sociology. It does not attempt a critical evaluation of these theories, but rather locates them as responses to the challenge of radical social transformations which were taking place from the late eighteenth century.

The founding perspectives provide an underpinning to sociology as it emerged in the context of nineteenth century modernisation. 'Modern' sociological theory is thus explained to date from this period.

Some key features of French and English of modernisation, in terms of the French and Industrial Revolutions respectively, are sketched to provide a contextual background to pioneering attempts to develop sociological theory. The early theoretical responses to the process of modernisation – St.Simon's and Comte's positivism, Spencer's evolutionism, and Marxism being included here – are presented as attempts to provide an understanding of a much changed social environment to that of traditional society by offering rational and scientific explanations of social change. It is shown that each of these theoretical approaches claimed that society operated in terms of social scientific laws and that understanding of these laws would explain the transition from traditional to modern society as well as anticipate the features of the type of society that would emerge in the future. It is further argued that these theorists were delineating their own future social utopias.

The key characteristics of functionalist theory are introduced with reference to the ideas of Emile Durkheim. Growing out of the French positivist tradition, this perspective retains faith in the possibility of social scientific intervention to improve society through 'social engineering'.

Weber's social action theory is presented as a perspective which emphasises the importance of understanding behaviour at the micro (small scale) level as well as the macro (large scale) level. The author shows Weber to be critical of various aspects of the pioneering approaches. Weber attempted to counter what he felt to be an overemphasis on explaining society in terms of economic factors (Marxism) and an inappropriate application of science to study social life (positivism). Social action theory paves the way for a more 'subjective' approach to sociology which emphasises that a full understanding of action must take the perceptions of actors into account.

The perspectives of Spencer, Marx and Weber are briefly taken up as broad frameworks to see what light they might shed on a more contemporary issue - the financial and economic crises following 2007.

Micro orientated theoretical perspectives with a subjective emphasis are taken up next. One such approach that is introduced is symbolic interactionism. This perspective originated through the works of Mead, relatively independently from the influence of Weber's social action theory. From this perspective, the distinguishing feature of social life is the human capacity to communicate meaning through the use of symbols and the author picks up on the important insight of the shaping of self-identity through social interaction with others.

An introduction to phenomenology and ethnomethodology is included. These perspectives offer a radical challenge to the assumption of conventional sociology that society is a structure in its own right which exists external to individuals and can be understood scientifically. They argue that a sense of social order is actively constructed by people in their everyday life engagements and that sociology should focus solely on how this is achieved.

The author reiterates that the main purpose of sociological theory is to act as a guide in the insightful understanding of society. It is therefore important to remember that developing sociological understanding should remain a live activity in which theories act as touchstones but not as fixed and final explanations. Indeed, the idea of the need to rejuvenate the subject as a result of far reaching changes in contemporary society is introduced. Postmodern and high modern perspectives, to be reviewed in more detail throughout the text, are identified as contemporary responses.

A multiple choice exercise with answers is provided at the end of the chapter. The aim is to give the reader an opportunity to assess their recollection of the main features of the perspectives introduced in the chapter and to backtrack over any areas of uncertainty.

Introduction

Compared to the insights generated by sociological thinking, non sociologists may appear to be either in a state of sleepy acceptance or if critical of society ill equipped to develop penetrating insights and analyses of society and social issues. However, sociology does not offer a single infallible alternative viewpoint. Instead, it offers various theoretical perspectives. Theories are made up of logically interconnected concepts. A concept is an abstract idea which stands for something in the real world. For example, in sociology, social class and political power are concepts which explain social layering (stratification) and influence respectively in the real world. Concepts are combined in sociological theories which can be tested through the findings of research. A theoretical perspective is broader than a theory. Perspectives offer different vantage points from which to view society and act as interpretive and filtering devices through which to see and understand society. The plurality of competing theoretical perspectives reflects the near infinite complexity of society which can be plausibly represented in many different ways. Theories and perspectives are also likely to relate to the different values and vantage points of theorists themselves.

The process of utilising different theoretical perspectives can be likened to that of trying on different pairs of glasses, each of which equips the wearer with an alternative view of society. Each perspective, through its interconnected concepts, offers a filter through which the observer is equipped with a simplified view of society. Each simplified view offers its own patterned understanding. It is through working with a number of sociological perspectives that new windows of awakening on society can be developed and the transition from lay person to sociologist made. The aim of this chapter is essentially to delineate a number of sociological perspectives, whilst alerting the reader that they should ultimately be applied reflectively, selectively and critically.

Before reviewing the major founding perspectives of sociology, it is important to pause and consider the social context of their origin which made the quest for a new understanding of society so necessary.

Modernisation as the context for founding social theory

The major perspectives comprising the early theoretical foundations of sociology were developed during the nineteenth and early twentieth centuries. The impulse for social theorising came from rapid and far-reaching social, political and industrial change, which, related to the advance of rational and scientific thinking, was challenging the traditions and religious outlooks upon which the old social order was based. The idea of social progress – the belief in on going betterment, accompanied by optimism in its continuation into the future – was taking root.

In France, eighteenth century Enlightenment thinkers applied rational scrutiny to traditional ideas and institutions. This helped to undermine the legitimacy of the remnants of an old feudal order of fixed social ranks, privileges and duties and contributed toward the dramatic events of the Revolution of 1789. The revolutionary values of liberty, equality and fraternity were now associated with the idea of progress toward a new type of society where reason would prevail at the expense of religion. However, liberation from the old social constraints brought protracted social and political turmoil and instability.

In England, Enlightenment thinking focussed more on economic matters, explaining how the advance of science and technology would be applied to new ways of working and producing for a free market. New machinery and sources of power were introducing new types of work specialization and early mass production. In concentrating workers in ever larger numbers in factories, these changes were setting in motion large scale rural to urban migration and the unprecedented growth of towns and cities. England's late eighteenth century revolution was an industrial one but the changes were also very much social. In promoting urbanisation and the factory system, it undermined the ways and traditions of rural life and enhanced the wealth and power of factory owners.

Throughout the nineteenth century, advances in science – especially geological – were increasingly throwing the literal interpretation of creation derived from the Bible into question. Fatalistic religious attitudes toward illness were being challenged within learned circles as medical science grappled to eradicate contagious diseases which ravaged populations living in overcrowded and squalid urban environments.

During the nineteenth century, these forces of modernisation were bringing about a new type of society in which the power and values of the old landed elite were being challenged by the growing power of industrialists. For the latter, power in the new order should be based on economic wealth derived from industriousness rather than inherited privilege. But the new society was also spawning a mass urban working class and generating problems of mass poverty, disease, social polarisation, economic destabilisation, and social unrest. How could these problems be addressed? As science and rational thinking were at the centre of progress, it was reasonable to be optimistic that science and rational thinking should have the capacity to tackle the problems that progress had brought.

In such modernising societies, there had emerged a context of both belief in and need for the capacity of man to rationally understand and control the conditions of modernisation. The term 'modern' sociological theory is thus used to refer back to theory originating in this context and those who retain faith in its quest. Unlike their more common everyday use, modern theory and modern society are not usually used in sociology as synonymous with 'contemporary'. Indeed, some theorists believe that the most advanced contemporary societies have more recently undergone changes every bit as profound as those associated with the earlier revolutions and entered a 'postmodern' era for which a new postmodern approach to social theory is necessary.

Founding social theorists: scientific laws of social change toward utopian futures

By the early nineteenth century, social theorists were struggling to understand the nature and causes of the social and intellectual conditions of change touched on above. Given the protracted upheaval of the French Revolution, was a return to the past possible or desirable? Could past levels of social order be re-established? How could we know what form a society of the future might take? Some key ideas of two French pioneers in the history of sociology who attempted to answer such questions, Henri St.Simon and Auguste Comte, will be tackled shortly.

The works of these pioneering social theorists often took the form of social philosophy rather than sociology. Their theoretical schemes were very broad ranging and not grounded in their own empirical research. A common theme of these theorists was the belief that society operated in a causal way and was thus amenable to scientific understanding. This faith in science led these founding theorists to gaze back through history in an attempt to extract laws of social change which they believed explained the durability and eventual collapse of the old feudal order, elucidated the problems of the new emerging society, provided a compass bearing for the transition to a future stable society, and would assist in guiding social reconstruction in that direction. Their ideas began to establish some of the important themes of what in sociology would become the functionalist perspective.

The belief that scientific laws of social change operated and provided certainty of future social stability may have been very appealing during times of social instability. However, pioneering theorists often held utopian images of ideal future societies. These acted as frames of reference against which social change could be judged as progressive (or otherwise). It could therefore be argued that each utilised the idea of social laws in such a way as to show that progressive social change would lead to a society of their future ideal. Although they claimed scientific credentials, it may be suspected that to some extent their desired societies of the future shaped their reading of history and laws of change which were enlisted to demonstrate the future certainty of their social utopias. In this sense, it is informative to contrast the future societies envisaged by Comte, Spencer and Marx, their contrasting evaluations of what constitutes progress, and the forces of change that each believed would bring their ideal society about. Some of the key points are sketched in box 1 on utopianists and elaborated in the text.

Box 1: Utopianists

	Auguste Comte 1798-1857	Herbert Spencer 1820-1903	Karl Marx 1818-1883
Social Theorist			
Family Background	Catholic family background. Father orderly government official	Family of religious nonconformists who questioned social conventions	Father Jewish lawyer and influenced by Enlightenment thinkers
Social Context of Works	Social instability in the wake of the French Revolution during the late eighteenth and early nineteenth centuries	The achievements of free enterprise capitalism in mid nineteenth century England following the Industrial Revolution	The ravages of free enterprise capitalism in mid nineteenth century England following the Industrial Revolution
Features of Utopian Future	Positivist society – interventionist form of capitalist industrial society regulated by social scientific technicians	Non-interventionist free enterprise, free trade capitalist industrial society, harmonised through enlightened individualism	Communist industrial society in which the means of production are commonly owned and co-operation replaces class conflict
Forces of Social Change	Intellectual progress determines social progress through law of three stages and the hierarchy of the sciences	Social and moral evolution follows the same formula as evolution throughout the rest of the natural world	Economic relations determine social relations. Economic based class conflict drives social progress

Early positivism and the problem of social order

In its simplest form, the term 'positivism' refers to the view that social phenomena operate according to laws which can be discovered through a rational and scientific study of society. This positivist quest gained impetus in French social thinking during the decades following the French Revolution of 1789. This section will look at the ideas of two French theorists of this period – Henri St.Simon and Auguste Comte – whose quest was to uncover laws of social change. The practical social purpose of this quest was to rationally guide the process of social rebuilding and reorganisation following the socially destructive effects of the Revolution.

Given the positivist view that society proceeds in terms of social laws and is therefore amenable to scientific analysis and understanding, certain interrelated questions follow, namely: 1) how is the condition of society explained, 2) what promotes social change, and 3) what is regarded as social progress and to where does it lead?

For Henri St.Simon, an appropriate diagnosis of the current social malaise of the protracted social and political turmoil experienced during the post French Revolution decades and the way forward was dependent on the study of social history. This study would have to adopt a high altitude vantage point to look at societies in the whole and detect their direction of change over long periods of time. In pursuit of this task, St.Simon adopted an 'idealist' approach. Idealism in this context (not to be confused with idealism as a value judgement which could also be applied to St.Simon, as well as Comte, Spencer and Marx) emphasises that the condition of intellectual and belief systems determines the condition of society. The study of changes in prevailing intellectual and belief systems would therefore explain changes in the condition of society. A single and widely shared world view which emphasises duty to society would be highly conducive to promoting the conditions of social harmony and integration. Ideas that are critical of a single and integrated world view, which promote fragmented belief systems and emphasise individual rights, would lead to social disruption, fragmentation and even possibly revolution.

Scanning history, St.Simon characterised the feudal social order of the

Middle Ages as a stable and integrated society with a clearly defined and established social hierarchy. He argued that Catholicism provided an integrated system of thinking and religious dogma that was a basis for moral authority, promoting social harmony and integration. St.Simon referred to this condition of stability as an 'organic' period in history, meaning that society exhibited conditions of organic unity.

However, from an idealist perspective, intellectual progress will lead to social disruption if new thinking was critical of established systems of thinking without offering a united and constructive alternative. St.Simon maintained that from the Middle Ages the church became a servant to the political powers and vested interests of the nobility. As such, it resisted intellectual change and fell behind the advances in science which increasingly passed into the hands of laymen. From the sixteenth century, the religious Reformation challenged the moral authority of Catholicism, and by the eighteenth century Enlightenment philosophers were developing systems of thinking which increasingly attacked religious dogma through rational scrutiny. These challenges had a corrosive effect on the dominant religious belief system of Catholicism and with it the legitimacy of the privileges of feudalism that it supported. This fomented an erosion of authority and the undermining of social harmony and for St.Simon provided the seedbed of social discontent which eventually culminated in the French Revolution.

The French Revolution liberated the majority from the suppression of feudal institutions which it swept away, but what had people been liberated to? St.Simon argued that a period of intellectual and therefore social anarchy had stretched beyond the Revolution. New ideas of liberty, equality and fraternity which had clashed with the ideas of duty upon which the old order was based could not provide a single constructive alternative around which to reintegrate and reorganise society. In contrast to the past organic period, this period of intellectual, social and moral breakdown was referred to as a 'critical' period. For social and individual well-being, the critical period needed to be terminated and a higher organic phase of social order and stability instituted. The direction to the future and the new type of stable society that would emerge needed to be discovered by the analysis of history which would reveal laws of intellectual and social progress to provide guidance to assist social reconstruction.

What, from his overview of history, were these laws of change and what did they reveal regarding the future? A key feature of change was the advance of science. This precluded a return to the religion of the past as a cohesive system of thinking and basis for a new social and moral order. St.Simon argued that a study of the advance of science in history revealed that, starting in the inorganic subject areas, it was advancing its methods and explanations into the life sciences. As society was viewed as the highest life form, science was destined to become the means by which society could be understood and regulated. This would require new elites with the appropriate expertise to do so. To drive progress, critical and rational philosophies had already performed the negative task of attacking religious dogma and undermining the old order. From the intellectual and social anarchy created, science now had to perform the positive task of supplying a new integrated belief system and the intellectual means of organisation to build the new social order.

What was to be the nature of this new social order and who were to be the new leaders? To answer these questions, St.Simon utilised a 'militant' and 'industrial' typology. A typology is a simplified model which assists the understanding of complex social phenomena by extracting their essential features. For St.Simon, militant type societies prevailed in the Middle Ages. They comprised social hierarchies that were politically dominated by the nobility who ruled the masses coercively. Such societies were organised primarily for warfare.

Industrial type societies, organised for peaceful productivity, would come to replace militant societies. This was because along with the advance of science, society was on the verge of witnessing industrial modernisation. In transition to the industrial society, science and industry would be applied to the pursuit of economic production which enabled the growth of wealth by peaceful means to replace wealth acquisition through the plunder of warfare. The new battle would be in utilising the resources of nature. To regulate such a society in an efficient way, scientific and industrial expertise, in the hands of scientists and managers, would be necessary. It was therefore fitting that in the new social order, scientists and industrialists would replace the nobility as the new elite. A key insight derived by St.Simon was that in the new industrial society, these elites would be appointed on merit as opposed to the principle of birthright under the old order.

In summary, for St.Simon, the study of history revealed that there were scientific laws of social change which demonstrated that science and industry were the only progressive basis for establishing a new social order. The reorganisation of society according to scientific principles required the administrative application of a 'social physics' in the hands of proven experts to replace the old politics which had taken the form of the coercion of the productive by the idle. Private property would be protected. The industrial society would be socialist in the limited sense of the need for central rational economic planning but anti-democratic in denying the masses, regarded as unworthy, access to power. A new social cohesion would emerge around the values of industry and science, with the masses being imbued in its culture and dogma as a type of this worldly religion to constructively replace the old religion of Catholicism, and with the new elites taking on the role of intellectual governance (Pullinger, 2015, Ch2).

Auguste Comte acted as secretary to St.Simon until their acrimonious breakup. Comte offered a similar diagnosis of the social and moral condition of post-Revolution France to that of St.Simon, whose ideas he developed, modified and systematised. He also shared St.Simon's idealism, arguing that the condition of society is essentially determined by the progress and state of intellectual thinking and belief systems.

Like St.Simon, Comte argued that post-Revolution France was suffering social instability associated with intellectual and moral chaos. Whilst large numbers of people had been consigned to great poverty, others lived unconcerned in considerable wealth. Comte viewed excessive and uncaring individualism as a negative consequence of the collapse of old moral constraints of traditional society with no new socially binding intellectual outlook and morality emerging. To re-establish a sound social and moral order required a new integrated system of thinking which would provide a basis for the moral binding of individuals in social obligation, much as in feudal times under the shared religious outlook of the Catholic Church.

Comte argued that he had discovered laws of intellectual and social change that anticipated the emergence of a new stable social order. This he referred to as the positivist era. In this society, widespread faith in science would provide the world view for integrating the masses, whilst scientific understanding of the laws by which society operated through the new science of 'sociology' would form the basis for scientifically informed social intervention by elites, enabling them to regulate society independently from any party and sectional interests. Comte's mission was to attempt to prove that from what he saw as the current chaos, the reintegrated and reconstructed positivist society was immanent. To this end, he argued that he had extracted from his overview of history two interrelated laws of progress which he referred to as the 'law of the three stages' and the 'hierarchy of the sciences'.

Comte's law of the three stages signalled a break from the militant and industrial typology that has been used by St.Simon. It posited that human understanding of phenomena passes sequentially through three stages. These Comte referred to as the theological, the metaphysical and the positivist. The theological stage represents the infancy of knowledge. At this stage, phenomena is viewed as created and controlled by divine beings and religious belief systems prevail. For Comte, the height of the influence of theological thinking in Europe was during the Middle Ages when the world view and precepts of the Catholic Church formed the basis for intellectual and moral integration. This system of thinking upheld social order but in time became an obstacle to progress. At the metaphysical stage, belief in forces operating within phenomena challenges theological thinking which explains phenomena through the influence of external divine powers. These forces may still be rather mysterious, but the effect of metaphysical thinking is to confront and dissolve theological belief systems. In so doing, this stage dismantles theological obstacles to social progress but in subverting an integrated system of beliefs comes to undermine social order. However, it provides a stepping stone enabling a transition to be made toward the establishment of science, which ultimately reveals the concrete laws by which Comte argued all phenomena operate in their own way.

So, Comte maintained that all phenomena are governed by laws which in time will be revealed when, by transition through the three stages of thinking, science will explain everything. To the law of the three stages, Comte added the hierarchy of the sciences to explain that the laws governing different phenomena become understood at different times. This law indicated the sequencing by which scientific knowledge of laws that operate for different levels of phenomena is uncovered. For Comte, this sequencing is dependent on the level of complexity and generality of the phenomena in question. Scientific understanding is first possible with reference to the least complex and most general of phenomena. This is the physical realm to which mathematical analysis may be directly applied to demonstrate the laws by which the physical world is governed. The last frontier of science is that of the most complex and least general phenomena of the life sciences of the biological and social world which are least reducible to mathematical analysis. The transition from theological understanding through metaphysical to positivist thus takes place in the subject sequence of mathematics, astronomy, physics, chemistry, biology and finally sociology, the scientific study of society.

As illustrated in the simplified chart in box 2, combining these two laws shows that throughout history scientific understanding has been making advances up the hierarchy of the subjects, but at any point in time different subject areas may have reached different stages of understanding in their progression through the law of the three stages. For example, the lower science of astronomy was entering the scientific stage by the seventeenth century, yet as late as the nineteenth century political economists were applying to social phenomena a metaphysical view of society when referring to the mysterious 'invisible hand' of free market forces. However, scientific understanding had by then moved up to the life science of biology, immediately below that of sociology on the hierarchical scale. For Comte, this showed that science was on the verge of application to understanding the most complex of phenomena and discovering the laws of society. When this transpires, all knowledge will have reached the scientific stage. Science will be able to explain all levels of phenomena, providing the foundation for a new integrated intellectual outlook and the means for a new level of social and moral integration and objective social intervention. In this positivist society, the application of social science by positivist sociologists will enable the intelligent regulation of society and science will form the basis for the highest social consensus (Pullinger, 2015, Ch3).

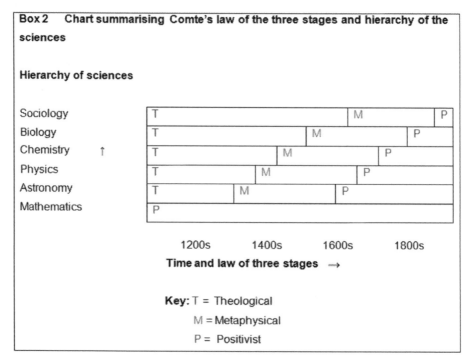

Box 2 Chart summarising Comte's law of the three stages and hierarchy of the sciences

Hierarchy of sciences

Sociology	T			M	P
Biology	T		M		P
Chemistry ↑	T		M		P
Physics	T	M		P	
Astronomy	T	M		P	
Mathematics	P				

1200s   1400s   1600s   1800s

Time and law of three stages →

Key: T = Theological

M = Metaphysical

P = Positivist

Both Comte and St.Simon argued that the future held the certain prospect of a highly regulated scientific and industrial society which would transcend what they viewed as the intellectual, moral and social chaos of the post-revolutionary period. For Comte, the positivist society would reunite order with social progress. The triumph of science in establishing the most highly ordered society would signify the end point in history. However, other writers in this era also claimed scientific credentials for their theories but with very different conclusions regarding the direction of social change and the type of society that would be its outcome. One such challenge came from the evolutionary theory of Herbert Spencer and another from the historical materialism of Karl Marx.

Spencer's science of evolutionism – social order through enlightened individualism

Although the Industrial Revolution in England had a profound effect on the way of life for many, England had not experienced in the eighteenth century the social and political turmoil of revolution, anarchy and political reaction that beset France in the late eighteenth and the early nineteenth century. By comparison at least, in England the social and political changes brought by the Industrial Revolution, though far reaching, were arguably less dramatic and extreme. Through these changes, an entrepreneurial class was emerging to challenge the social status, power and values of the aristocracy. This class were keen to establish a soundly based ethical justification for their new made wealth that would enhance their social standing – an ethical system which supported the institutions of free enterprise capitalism and the culture of individualism from which they were the main beneficiaries. Herbert Spencer proved to be a powerful intellectual advocate of such a justification.

For Spencer, the Enlightenment idea of progress as social improvement in terms of happiness maximisation could be found in the ideas of political economists such as Adam Smith. At the dawn of the Industrial Revolution, Smith analysed the conditions under which wealth creation and economic growth could be developed. He argued that a high division of workforce labour in terms of task specialisation would maximise efficiency of production and the creation of wealth. A high division of labour would necessitate production for exchange, as few people would be able to live just off the products that their labour contributed to produce. This would lead to the need for the extension of market exchange and competition between producers to achieve profitability and reinvestment. Such an environment would provide a catalyst for general economic growth – that is as long as production and markets remained free from government intervention. This model is referred to as 'political economy'.

Spencer took Smith's ideas on how a modern economy should run and broadened them out from an economic model into a model of a society of spontaneous co-operation framed by contractual obligations between free individuals. Smith's ideas were radicalised by Spencer to provide a model society of the future. What were the social forces that Spencer argued would move society in that direction?

Spencer did not adopt the idealist position of St.Simon and Comte. He strongly opposed the view that intellectual and belief systems determine the condition of society and provide a vehicle for progress. Instead, he argued that the range of workable social institutions is determined by the moral makeup of individuals as the units upon which the social fabric is built. Whilst this moral makeup can change through the impact of the social environment back on individuals, this change, he claimed, can only happen slowly as it takes the form of the inheritance of acquired characteristics. The slow rate and direction of social and moral change was explained by Spencer through his law of evolution.

Evolution refers to a process of growth in the form of the unfolding of an inbuilt potential. If a common evolutionary process could be demonstrated as the natural order of change operating in all phenomena, it could be argued that a natural direction of social change with a clear outcome could be scientifically established. Consequently, a model of the evolutionary high point of society could be provided as guidance for progressive social reform. Spencer's ultimate aim was to demonstrate that the superiority of a social and ethical system derived from political economy could be justified through his formula of evolution.

Through comparison of society with biological entities, otherwise known as the biological analogy, Spencer attempted to show that, as in organisms, likewise in society, the natural direction of evolutionary change could be established. He explained these parallel evolutionary processes in terms of structure and function. For Spencer, evolutionary advance takes the form of structural differentiation. In biological organisms, this refers to growing complexity and specialisation of organs as organisms grow from infancy toward maturity and as shown in more highly evolved types. Spencer argued that as societies modernise and evolve, a parallel process takes place as they grow in size and develop increasingly specialised and interconnected institutions which perform their precisely allocated functions within the social structure.

But how does change occur and what is the driving force? Central to the dynamics of evolution is the idea of adaptation. Structural and functional adaptation refers to the capacity of an organism to respond to the demands of the surrounding environment. Biological organisms must adapt to their environment to survive. Likewise, society must develop those institutions which will assist it to do so or it will go under. The effect of this surrounding social environment of other societies on adaptive capacity to survive can best be explained through reference to Spencer's use of the militant and industrial typology.

For Spencer, militant type societies (defined similarly to St.Simon) have dominated much social evolution. They are part of a broader hostile environment characterised by wars and conquests. Within this environment, societies that are highly regulated and have repressive political control mechanisms and rigid social hierarchies through which the powerful subjugate populations are best able to maximise the collective war effort in the battle for survival. The model of military hierarchy and political coercion impacts on other areas of the broader social structure. People living within such a barbaric social environment adapt a barbaric moral condition – given the freedom to do so, individuals would trample over the rights of others. Authoritarian control is thus necessitated to avoid anarchy. Such societies comprise simple authoritarian structures through which rulers rule by might and individual rights are little recognised or respected.

However, through compounding by military conquest and by natural growth, societies grow in size. With growth, an advance in structural differentiation takes place in the form of the emergence of a growing range of specialist institutions and occupations. Specialisation promotes commercial transactions and trading which enhances the free exchange of goods and services between individuals. As this mutuality accompanying industrial and commercial activities advances, the controls and suppressions of the militant society become impediments to the maximisation of wealth producing activity through free association. The evolutionary potential of large industrial societies is to develop a free social form of co-operating individuals in which the role of government retreats toward that of overseeing this process and restraining the declining number of recalcitrant members of society.

This change of social environment has a civilising effect on the moral nature of members of society. According to Spencer, through many generations of experience within this setting, the moral characteristics of responsible individualism become developed and acquired through inheritance. The moral nature of the individuals that constitute society gradually modifies and evolves from the condition of brutality within the barbaric conditions of militant society toward enlightened individualism in the industrial society. A particular form of industrial society (very different from the type envisaged by St.Simon) becomes the high point of social evolution and enlightened individualism becomes the correlative high point of moral evolution.

Spencer's image of the industrial society is one of pure free enterprise capitalism. It provides the highest level of individual specialisation and structural sophistication. Moral evolution to a state of enlightened individualism means that individual freedoms become mutually respected amongst members of society and external repressive control by the state becomes largely redundant. At this evolutionary high point, 'survival of the fittest' remains the driving force for innovation and change but becomes elevated from effectiveness in warfare to the capacity for efficient economic production. This is only possible through enlightened economic individualism within society and the broader context of peaceful trade between nations. The fabric of society will come to comprise a network of contractual relationships, agreements and co-operations freely entered into and honoured by individuals of high moral rectitude. Those societies that evolve in this way will have adapted to the natural conditions of competition between industrial societies.

Spencer characterised the fabric of such a society as follows:

> 'All trading transactions, whether between masters and workmen, buyers and sellers of commodities, or professional men and those they aid, are effected by free exchange..........This relation, in which the mutual rendering of services is unforced and neither individual subordinated, becomes the predominant relation throughout society in proportion as the industrial activities predominate. Daily determining the thoughts and sentiments, daily disciplining all in asserting their own claims while enforcing them to recognise the correlative claims of others........[such a society is] characterised throughout by the same individual freedom which every commercial transaction implies. The co-

operation by which the multiform activities of society are carried on, becomes a *voluntary* co-operation' (cited in Andreski, 1972, p.164).

Spencer's justification for minimal state intervention was related to the process of structural differentiation and growing social complexity leading to a delicate balance of finely interconnected free enterprise institutions and individuals. Within this type of society, to maximise both human happiness and wealth creation, a vastly contracted state should leave decision making to individuals who, in aggregate, would always make superior decisions, for example to satisfy their personal needs or invest profitably in enterprise, to those attempted on their behalf and imposed on them by the state. The latter is a cumbersome and inefficient mechanism of intervention in a complex industrial society. Moreover, Spencer argued that even if state intervention led to some planned desirable outcomes, the scope for unintended and often negative remote consequences in societies comprising highly complex and interconnected parts would outstretch the capacity of social scientific analysis to anticipate them and only require further intervention with its own unforeseen consequences to try and put right. Even state welfare intervention would therefore be counterproductive as well as an infringement of individual responsibility for self-support.

For Spencer, evolution to the industrial society presents a very different outcome to the future centrally regulated industrial society predicted by St.Simon and the positivist society of Comte. However, he counselled that the process was likely to be long and slow, with possible setbacks. The repressive and regulatory characteristics of militancy would re-emerge within industrial societies as a response of self-preservation if they became threatened by the emergence of a hostile external environment. Furthermore, although Spencer's future utopia of a deregulated capitalist industrial society was for him both the logical and desirable end product of history, for the maintenance of social order and stability, the retreat of state interventionism to make this possible should not run substantially ahead of the moral evolution of the population. Although the moral condition of populations is influenced by the social environment, Spencer argued that workable social institutions must ultimately reflect the stage of moral evolution of the individuals that make up society. As the latter can only evolve slowly, if state control retreats too quickly, the persistence of the moral traits of barbarism will mean that individual freedoms will be abused. In this situation, the only alternatives will be a retreat to greater regulation or the risk of growing social anarchy. Only when the moral nature of enlightened individualism is sufficiently widespread and advanced throughout society can the state safely largely withdraw its controls (Pullinger, 2015, Ch7).

Classical Marxism and the science of class conflict

Marxism, a theoretical perspective developed by Karl Marx and Frederick Engels at the height of English nineteenth century free enterprise capitalism, provides a radical theoretical alternative to Spencer's evolutionism. Marx placed economic forces at the centre of his social theory and provided a 'materialist' explanation of the causes of social change throughout history which took the form of a radical critique of capitalism.

Through a materialist interpretation of history, Marx emphasised that social change has as its driving force economic and material factors. This is in contrast to the view that changing intellectual and belief systems drive social and economic change in the idealism of St.Simon and Comte. From Marx's materialist perspective, changing belief systems emerge mainly as a response to economic change and take the form of justifications of social systems and hierarchies, benefiting the economically powerful in their control of a subject class. In the Manifesto of the Communist Party, Marx stated this precisely when he wrote

> 'What else does the history of ideas prove, than that intellectual production changes its character in proportion as material production is changed. The ruling ideas of each age have ever been the ideas of its ruling class' (Marx, 1973, p.85).

Related to this materialist position, classical Marxism is often interpreted as a form of 'economic determinism'. This means that the economy is the determining force around which the rest of society is organised. The economy and the distribution of wealth and power 1) structure society into relationships between social classes, arrangements which 2) are justified through dominant ideas and controlling institutions.

For Marx, work is the most fundamental social activity, without which society could not exist. Within society, therefore, the essential social relationships revolve around productive activity, and work relationships between social classes are central to the formation of social structures. In his analysis, Marx utilises the following concepts.

All production requires 'forces of production' which comprise levels of technology and machinery, production techniques, raw materials and labour power – all that makes production possible. Of the forces of production, the 'means of production' are those that take the form of legally owned productive property, therefore excluding workers in capitalist societies who are free to find alternative employment. For production to take place, there must exist social relationships. The term 'relations of production' refers to the form, shaped by duties and obligations between the parties, which social relationships that are necessary for production take. According to Marx, in all societies where the means of production are privately owned, these relationships mark out social class divisions. The fundamental feature of these social class divisions is that one class will own the means of production and also have at its disposal the only asset that the other class owns and has to sell – its labour power. The utilisation of workers' labour power is necessary for the owners of the means of production to create value and wealth, whilst the hiring out of labour power by workers is necessary to provide them with an income. Built into this relationship is conflict between the classes over the allocation of value created by the productive process.

The term 'mode of production' specifies how production is organised and refers to levels of advancement by which societies are differentiated as, for example, feudal, capitalist or communist modes of production. Historical materialism explains the forces that are at work which lead to changes in the dominant mode of production.

Private ownership of the means of production has been a feature of most of modern history. Indeed, when people were not free, such as slaves in slave societies, the entire forces of production were privately owned. For Marx, private ownership of the means of production is the source of social power for the owning class. Power derived from this economic source is the capacity that some people have to exert control over others. From this perspective, it is a fundamental characteristic of the relations of production which exist between the social classes.

Their power enables the owners of the means of production to extract an excessive appropriation of the value created in the productive process, which is only possible through the utilisation of the labour power of workers, for themselves. This means that those who have provided their labour are short changed in relation to the value it creates in terms of the products produced and the price at which they are sold. The relations of production when the means of production are privately owned therefore give rise to the 'exploitation' of a working class.

Under capitalism, workers (referred to by Marx as the 'proletariat') are obliged to provide their one asset, labour power, to capitalists (referred to as the 'bourgeoisie') in exchange for the wages that are necessary for their survival. But, Marx argued, as well as economic exploitation, this relationship leads to the degradation of the worker who feels like a powerless object performing meaningless tasks, with the employer, driven by the quest to maximise efficiency and profit, controlling the work process. An advance in the division of labour in the pursuit of efficiency heightens repetition of narrowly defined work tasks and renders work devoid of creative input and control from the worker. The resulting dehumanisation experienced by workers is referred to by Marx as 'alienation' – a malady deriving from the conditions of capitalist production. Marx characterised the alienating conditions experienced by factory workers under conditions of industrial capitalism in the following way:

> 'Owing to the extensive use of machinery and to division of labour, the work of the proletarians has lost all individual character, and, consequently, all charm for the workmen. He becomes an appendage of the machine, and it is only the most simple, most monotonous, and most easily acquired knack, that is required of him......[Workers] are daily and hourly enslaved by the machine, by the overseer, and, above all, by the individual bourgeois manufacturer himself' (Marx, 1973, p.74).

Given the vast numerical supremacy of the working class, why, then, is not open class conflict a common feature of this class relationship? An understanding of this question requires reference to the distinction made by Marx between the 'infrastructure' and the 'superstructure'.

Together, Marx refers to the means of production and the relations of production as the 'economic base' of society or the infrastructure. It is here where social class relationships are located and tensions generated. The term superstructure within the Marxist perspective refers to society's dominant social values, beliefs, laws and institutions. These operate as controls within the relations of production and as broader social controls. Whilst class conflict is built into the economic infrastructure, the dominant ideas and institutions of the superstructure serve to hide or suppress this conflict of interests and minimise the likelihood of actual open conflict emerging. Dominant ideas and institutions justify and support the unequal distribution of power within society and therefore primarily benefit the owners of the means of production by emphasising the normality and inevitability of the current situation. The laws of the land thus serve the needs of the dominant class, for example, for efficient and profitable production and the protection of private property, and workers are encouraged to accept the system and their position in it as natural.

Power and control can take the form of coercion. Coercion refers to the use or threat of the use of force. Within the superstructure, institutions of coercion, such as the armed forces, police, judiciary and prisons, impose social order and suppress discontent. But, for Marx, dominant social ideas also have a controlling effect. From Marx's power model, it follows that the prevailing ideas in society are the ideas conducive to the interests of the ruling economic class, i.e. the nobility under feudalism and the capitalist class under capitalism. They aim to give legitimacy to the existing social order by providing credible justifications for it and hiding or disguising the conflict of class interests. This can only be achieved via a systematic distortion of reality, referred to by Marx as 'ideology'. Through the process of socialisation, ideology induces a 'false consciousness' of reality into the subject class for the purpose of gaining its compliance.

A simplified illustration of the infrastructure and superstructure relationship is provided in box 3.

Box 3: The Marxist model of the generation and suppression of class conflict under capitalism

Superstructure
Institutions and ideas
Suppress class conflict. The armed forces, police, legal system and prisons enforce **coercive** control. The church and religious belief systems, the mass media and the values of consumerism, the educational system and the image of equality of opportunity and political parties and the view that the electorate have significant choice and power, all provide **ideological** distortions of reality for the purpose of manipulating conformity through creating false consciousness.

Infrastructure
Economic base
Forms exploitative social class relations in the productive process and generates class conflict.

Marx argued that the effectiveness of these controls cannot persist in the long term. This is because 'contradictions' (a term which has various applications!) exist at the heart of systems based on exploitation. For example, under capitalism the collective pooling of labour power that is necessary to create wealth and the private expropriation of a substantial proportion of that wealth is one such contradiction. Class exploitation, and the potential for conflict that it generates, can be hidden by ideological distortions, such as the notion of a contract freely entered into by both sides and a fair wage provided for a fair days work. For Marx, these distortions help govern the relations of production. However, the reality of exploitation cannot always remain hidden. Due to inbuilt competitive overproduction, the capitalist system cannot escape periodic economic recessions or depressions. At times of such great mass hardship, contradictions between ideology (fair wage) and reality (exploitation and unemployment) are very likely to become evident and the transparency of ideology could pave the way to mass opposition.

Contradictions can also emerge between the means of production, the corresponding relations of production and appropriate ideological justifications. The emergence of new means of production, for example the rapid growth of an urban located capitalist factory mass production processes and the decline of rural based agrarian production, will contradict old relations of production (between landowner and tied agricultural worker) and their supporting ideology (superiority through lineage and required deference from social inferiors) which were suited to the old means of production (pre-industrial low technology). As new relations of production emerge (contractual relationships between employer and free waged worker) which are appropriate to new means of production (factory technology), new ideological justifications for them become necessary (wealth as proof of industriousness, enterprise, and therefore merited). In the process, revolutionary social transformation takes place but the consequence for workers is that one form of class suppression will replace another all the time that the means of production are privately owned.

This process of transition from feudal to capitalist modes of production can be reviewed a little more closely. Feudal society, at its height in Europe during the Middle Ages, is pre-industrial and largely agricultural, typified by life in small rural communities. Religion and superstition are powerful sources of explanation and moral values. The means of production comprise land, agricultural buildings, machinery and implements of a low technological level (which may utilise wind and water power) and animals. Industrial production, conducted in small workshops, remains at a handicraft level, and working the land is the main basis for the generation of wealth. Land ownership is concentrated largely in the hands of the nobility and the church, who therefore comprise the ruling class. Various grades of commoner below the nobility and priesthood in the social hierarchy may own some property and land, but at the bottom of the social scale reside a large stratum of impoverished and landless agricultural labourers known as serfs. For Marx, the defining class relationship in this type of society is the exploitation of the labour of serfs by a landowning nobility and church. These agrarian relations of production, which are a potential point of fracture in the social hierarchy, are maintained by force where necessary and by an ideology which emphasises the importance of deference and loyalty of the lower orders toward their lords who claim for themselves the virtues of superior social breeding through tracing their noble lineage. This 'natural' social order is sanctified by the church in its religious teachings.

However, within the late feudal social order, new and more efficient means of production were being developed by enterprising artisans (craft workers) and inventors. In time, as industrial technology and machinery improve, industrial production expands but is restricted by feudal social relations. Both the feudal relations of production of serf bonded to master, based around land ownership, and the supporting ideology of superior social breeding of the nobility and deference and loyalty expected from serfs, begin to look antiquated. They are beginning to outlive their purpose. A point is eventually reached where, through private ownership and enterprising use of new technology, a capitalist class emerges to gain sufficient wealth and power to achieve social ascendancy. This industrial revolution is a bourgeois revolution, forcing the transition from feudal to capitalist society. Around the new means of factory mass production, new relations of production emerge which are appropriate to a dynamic capitalist economy. These are embodied in flexible wage labour contracts which benefit a new ruling class of capitalists employing waged workers.

This transformation from feudal to capitalist society requires correspondingly new ideological values to disguise worker exploitation and dissipate conflict. Changes in the economic infrastructure thus drive and shape necessary changes in the superstructure as the old institutions and ideologies of the feudal superstructure no longer match the requirements of the new infrastructure of industrial capitalism. The new ideological values are essentially those derived from the writers of political economy (and radicalised by Herbert Spencer) that the system is best left to self-regulate through forces of supply and demand and that workers are free to engage in contracts of employment with whom they wish. Moreover, position in society is now viewed as increasingly reflecting individual merit in a more open social structure.

The emergence of capitalism from feudalism simply replaces one form of class exploitation by another. Although the system has changed, private ownership of the means of production remains. Conflict of class interests over the allocation of value created in the production process therefore also remains and must in the long term come to the surface again. The potential under capitalism is for that conflict to bring into opposition a minority exploiting capitalist class and a majority exploited working class.

Marxists argue that free enterprise capitalism is essentially unstable since in the competitive quest between capitalists for profit maximisation through improving technological efficiency and suppressing wage levels, the overall long term inbuilt tendency is toward polarisation of wealth, overproduction, underconsumption and cyclical unemployment. It is particularly at times of downward pressure on wages and rising unemployment, that workers facing a common plight will be more likely to see through the ideological distortions that support capitalism and develop a common 'class consciousness' which recognises that capitalism is the cause of their plight. This possibility is enhanced through the conditions of production under which capitalism brings together workers into larger aggregates in both the workplace and in the urban environment. Such class consciousness is a prerequisite for revolution. Thus, in this system and productive process, capitalism has been assembling the troops of its own future destruction. The mechanics of capitalism therefore virtually impel, in the form of laws of change, the working class toward revolution.

Marx argued that the revolutionary overthrow of capitalism will be different from the revolution that brought the capitalist class to power. This is because the revolutionary class seizing power will now be the majority not a minority class. It will therefore take the means of production into common ownership, to be run in the common interest. Greed and selfishness, which appeared as universal features of human nature with life encapsulated in capitalist society, would give way within this new system to co-operation. The resulting communist society would be the product of the final revolutionary transformation of society since, as a classless society, it would resolve all class conflict and contradictions.

Early functionalism and the science of social engineering

Originating in Auguste Comte's more philosophical writings, which dated from the 1820s, functionalism in this French tradition found its sociological formulation from the late nineteenth century in the works of Emile Durkheim. These early functionalists were preoccupied in demonstrating the normality of social order whilst explaining the tribulations experienced by individuals in the modern age. For Comte, concern had been with terminating the social destabilisation of the post-Revolution decades. For Durkheim, it was the very nature of the new social order that had emerged which introduced new vulnerabilities for both society and individuals. For both thinkers, the development of social science held the practical usefulness of assisting policy makers to rationally intervene in society so as to promote social order.

Durkheimian functionalism used a biological or organic analogy to assist in the understanding of society. An analogy aids understanding through the process of comparison. Through analogy, the understanding of one area of knowledge can be enhanced by indicating similarities to another area which is already better understood. The biological analogy did not mean that society was literally viewed as an organism, but that the understanding of society could best be advanced by comparing it to that of a living body. Sociology could advance as a science of society on this basis because biology was also a science of life but a more advanced one. Sociology could haul itself up by the insights derived from the biological analogy – an observation derived from Comte's hierarchy of the sciences.

In what ways is it beneficial to view society as like an organism? To answer this question, the term function firstly requires definition. A function is a recurrent activity of a part of an integrated body which operates for the benefit of that body. For example, the beating of the heart is of crucial functional importance for the well being of the human body. In this sense, it is a 'functional prerequisite' – its operation is a pre-requirement for the very life of the body. Other organs play their own allocated functions. They are each interdependent, and the health and vitality of the entire human body relies on each organ performing its appropriate function effectively.

Formal institutions, especially those of business and the state, are the key functioning apparatus of society. Like the organs of the body, they need to be mutually integrated and synchronised for the whole entity, the bodily organism and society, to operate efficiently. Social institutions comprise structured frameworks within which individuals occupy roles which are interconnected. These roles specify and constrain the institutional activities of individuals.

Roles also govern individual activity outside of formal institutions, as do shared values, norms and obedience to rules and laws. For Durkheim, together, these various aspects of society are external to individuals and constrain their behaviour. Society is therefore viewed as more than an aggregate of individuals, but as an ordered entity in its own right with its history of change, its present and its future, preceding, superseding and succeeding the lives of its individual members. Individuals are absorbed into this social realm through socialisation.

The biological analogy can be suggestive of conditions of social good or ill health. Like the organs of a body, social institutions perform functions for the health and well being of the entire society. For example, the family rears the next generation and socialises them into the values and expectations of broader society, hence contributing to social harmony and order. As well as instilling academic knowledge, the education system imposes on pupils the need to abide by institutional rules and regulations, the habit of regularity, and the acquisition of work related skills, all of which are functional for efficient participation of individuals in the workplace. The workplace enables resources to be provided for society, incomes for families, and taxation for public services such as education. At the extreme, without social order and the routines of productive activity, modern society would soon cease.

A key implication of the biological analogy is that society should be viewed as a whole entity. By this, it is meant that the purpose of the parts of society – its various institutions which bring together individuals to structure and regularise their actions – can only be understood through firstly obtaining an overview of society in its entirety. Just as it would be insufficient to try and understand the workings of an organ within a human body in isolation from the whole body, so it would be insufficient to start with an analysis of individual institutions in an attempt to build up an understanding of the functioning of society. As in the case of the human body, an overview of society must first be acquired. From this, one is able to understand the functional workings of its different elements such as the family, educational institutions, the workplace, etc. and how they relate to each other. This vantage point is referred to in sociology as 'holism' and it makes functionalism a 'macro' theory – one which focuses on the broad dimensions of society. Furthermore, functionalism equated society with nation as a discrete entity of analysis.

Durkheim viewed societies as evolving like organisms. As societies grow and advance, they develop more complex forms of organisation. Like primitive organisms, primitive societies have simple structures - they exhibit a very low level of technological advance and little institutional specialisation. Communities tend to be segmented into small groups in the form of clans or tribes. With little specialisation and functional interdependence, as in a primitive organism, damage to one part of the community will have limited repercussions for the whole. Social integration, referred to by Durkheim as 'social solidarity', in societies of this type must take the form of the imposition of a binding collective identity (referred to by Durkheim as the 'collective consciousness'), powerful social sanctions against transgressions and the oppressive use of authority. Durkheim referred to these primitive societies as exhibiting 'mechanical solidarity'.

As societies evolve, they develop higher levels of technology and grow in size and dynamic intensity of life. Under these conditions, more specialised institutions will emerge along with specialist roles within them. These institutions perform increasingly specialised functions. They become integrated on a larger scale as the whole of society becomes one of exchange relationships. As institutions become increasingly interdependent, each is increasingly reliant of the others performing their necessary functions. In modern industrial societies, a new form of social integration is achieved. Sameness and suppression give way to an advance in the division of labour in a society which is interlocked by mutual dependence and exchange. Durkheim referred to societies of this type, characterised by the advance of individual diversity and freedom, as developing to a state of 'organic solidarity'.

For Durkheim, the specialisation, diversity and exchange that accompany modernisation bring a new form of societal precariousness. Given the complex interdependency of institutions in modern industrial society, it is more vulnerable to the widespread consequences of the malfunctioning of any of its institutions. This, and social conflict or factionalism, can be highly damaging to society. A faction ridden society is one where order and consensus have broken down and people put factional interests ahead of broader social needs. The effects of disruption to society through, for example, high levels of strike activity by workers, are likely to widespread. From a functionalist perspective, this would be a sign of social ill health which needs to be remedied. At the extreme, revolutionary change would be a condition of chronic ill health. The natural and healthy state suggested by the organic analogy is that societies grow and evolve through a process of gradual change and adjustment.

Any major social change can be socially destabilising and also dangerous for the well-being of individuals. In particular, there is the risk of the emergence of a disconnection between the individual and society within the more liberal environment which accompanies the development of organic solidarity in modern society. Durkheim pointed to the twin dangers of 'egoism' and 'anomie', especially during the period of early modernisation when old social structures and norms have broken down, new institutions are still emerging and social norms to guide individual behaviour appear uncertain. In this environment, egoism refers to the detachment of individuals from the constraints of social groups and an excessive preoccupation with the self. Anomie refers to loss of moral certainty and clear norms to guide behaviour. In a society of greater freedom and diversity, the constraints of social norms to guide behaviour can become so slackened that individuals can be left in a directionless state of aimlessness. This sense of loss which can form under the modern social condition bears some similarities within Durkheim's functionalist theory to the economic based malady of alienation in Marx's theory.

Functionalists maintain that social hierarchies are a natural and inevitable feature of all societies, although the principles around which they are organised change over time. They argue that in modern industrial societies, the functional importance of institutions provide the framework of the social hierarchy and that ability is the main criteria for the allocation of individuals to roles in their occupational capacity and position in the social hierarchy. This enables the efficient utilisation of a range of abilities available in society for the general social benefit. However, the prospect of individual achievement through merit, combined with the advancing capacity of society to generate wealth, can render individual expectations unbounded. Then, a heightening of egoism and anomie associated with the slackening of social constraints, can result in chronic levels of personal dissatisfaction and at the extreme suicide.

It needs to be remembered that the term 'analogy' in the biological analogy does not literally mean sameness between a biological organism and society. For example, society does not have the physical boundary of a body form – people can migrate between societies. So what is it that holds a modern society together and maintains order and regularity? Durkheim's answer to these questions was very different from that of Spencer. He argued that Spencer's model of an industrial society provided insufficient social fabric to constrain the disunity resulting from individual self-interest. It would rest on 'the vast system of particular contracts which link individuals as a unique basis ... Social solidarity would then be nothing else than the spontaneous accord of individual interests' (Durkheim, 1964, p.203). Durkheim went on to ask

> 'Is this the character of societies whose unity is produced by the division of labour? If this were so, we could with justice doubt their stability. For if interest relates men, it is never for more than some few moments......when the business has been completed, each one retires and is left entirely on his own....... For when interest is the only ruling force each individual finds himself in a state of war with every other since nothing comes to mollify the egos, and any truce in this eternal antagonism would not be of long duration. There is nothing less constant than interest. Today, it unites me to you; tomorrow, it will make me your enemy. Such a cause can only give rise to transient relations and passing associations' (Durkheim, 1964, pp. 203-204).

This classic functionalist statement argues that an enduring society cannot just be the sum total of freely entered into agreements between individuals. Society is something which exists external to individuals and must provide a fabric of its own to order and structure individual behaviour through the constraints of institutions, roles, rules, regulations, norms, moral pressures and laws etc. For Durkheim, society acts as an integrating force through imparting shared values via the processes of socialisation and education and by the pressures toward conformity imposed by moral constraints. Shared values promote broadly recognised norms of behaviour, social consensus and a degree of harmony which bind individuals to society. An integrated and smoothly functioning society represents a condition of social good health from which all, as members of society, benefit. By contrast, Durkheim argued that the industrial society envisaged by Spencer would be nothing more than an unstable aggregate of individual self-interest, in which individuals would suffer the despair of extreme egoism and anomie.

Bound up with functionalism in sociology has been the development of positivism – the view that society could ultimately be understood in scientific terms. If this were to be the case, sociologists would be able to act as 'social engineers', for Durkheim assisting policy makers in their reforms from a position of scientific neutrality as opposed to factional interest and bias. Policy interventions could then engineer institutions to promote social harmony, integration and consensus and counter the maladies of excessive egoism and anomie in a way analogous to a doctor or surgeon using scientific medical knowledge to promote the health of a patient.

It is also clear that functionalism (as consensus theory) and Marxism (as conflict theory) are diametrically opposed perspectives. But they do have one important characteristic in common. They are both macro perspectives which emphasise the downward impact of socialisation in moulding the consciousness and behaviour of individuals to the dominant norms and values of society. For Durkheim, this moulding process is positive, whereas for Marx, under capitalism, it is viewed negatively. However, they each offer little insight into the potential of individuals to act as free and purposive agents whose activities can have a feedback influence into shaping society itself. Max Weber's social action theory was an attempt to counter this imbalance.

Social action theory – social science and contingency

Max Weber was a German theorist and contemporary of Durkheim, producing his major works between the late nineteenth and early twentieth centuries. Weber developed a theoretical perspective which is more difficult to tie down than Marxism or Durkheimian functionalism because of its scope and relative openness. This perspective is referred to as social action theory, the key features of which can be summarised as follows.

Firstly, Weber was keen to emphasise the two way relationship which exists between the impact of society on the individual and the shaping of society by the interpretations and actions of individuals. He opposed approaches to sociology which 'reified' society. Reification of society is the view that society has a purpose and independent life of its own; a characteristic of both functionalist and Marxist theory.

Secondly, Weber recognised the importance of contingency in social change. The existence of chance events, inventions, and complex social interactions mean that the application of a scientific approach and prediction to society must be taken through painstaking research and with great caution. Social change could not be explained in terms of the types of scientific laws developed by positivist thinkers and through contingency and complexity the future remained uncertain.

Thirdly, Weber contested the Marxist view that social conflict and change are driven by economic and material factors and that belief systems are shaped by economic forces and social inequalities which they exist to justify. For Weber, cultural ideas can be more independent of economic forces and can themselves vitalise social and economic change.

Fourthly, Weber argued that for social action to be fully understood, the study of actors within micro environments and the apprehension of the subjective motives behind their actions is as important as recognising the influences of the broader social structure upon individuals.

For Weber, the study of social action can be approached as an academic venture and as a science of a sort. Here, though, Weber is critical of the positivist position which maintains that approaches relevant to the physical sciences can be adopted in (or even adapted to) the study of social action. For Weber, social 'science' is the systematic study of social action. But social action is the outcome of conscious decision making based on actors' meanings, interpretations and motives. These lie behind observed behaviour, rendering useless analysis of behaviour in strictly cause and effect terms. In emphasising the difference between causality in the physical realm (and the largely stimulus and response behaviour of the animal world), and conscious human choice, freedom of action and contingency within social action, Weber's approach to understanding society strongly departs from the positivistic emphasis in the works of Comte, Durkheim or Marx where individuals are seen as highly controlled and constrained by external social forces which operate in law like ways.

Although generally viewed as a conflict theorist, Weber's position is strongly at odds with the conflict approach of Marx. When viewing society at the macro level, Weber maintains that groups tend to compete for power and resources and that those who hold these assets will usually attempt to retain exclusive control through erecting barriers to access by others. However, whether and how this leads to conflict in particular societies and at particular times in history is regarded as a matter for analysis. It is therefore not appropriate to refer to either consensus or conflict as natural to societies in the way that functionalists and Marxists respectively do. For Weber, it is also misleading of Marxists to reduce social conflict primarily to that between economic classes and to use economic class defined in terms of relation to the means of production as the single key with which to explain the social structure, the distribution of power and motive force for social change.

In trying to explain social structures and social change, Weber argued that it is not the case that economic forces will necessarily have a determining effect. As he demonstrated in his comparative study of religions, belief systems and cultural values can sometimes be relatively independent and more important influences on the extent and direction of social change (or of social stagnation) than economic factors. Cultural values can indeed be the driving force behind peoples' actions and these can have economic consequences – a proposition which gives cultural values a potentially dynamic role to play in promoting social change and therefore potential prominence in analysis. It is ultimately for the analysis of particular societies and specific periods of history to uncover the complex and contingent influences on social conflict, consensus and social change.

In Weber's social action theory, cultural value systems provide an influential broader context for the motivations and actions of social actors. These systems form an important part of the social backdrop to action and can themselves change over time. Weber viewed the major change in cultural values associated with capitalist modernisation in the west in terms of the process of 'rationalisation'. To clarify this process, Weber employed the device of 'ideal types'. An ideal type is a pure intellectual construct. It models essential characteristics of a type of society in a pure and uncontaminated way. The pure type probably never exists in the highly complex real world but nevertheless it assists the analyst in understanding essential social features.

Weber distinguishes between two main ideal type cultural value systems which he refers to as the traditional and the rational. The traditional value system largely provided the broader framework for social action in much of western pre-capitalist society. In this context, action was guided largely by custom and tradition. Traditional ways tended to be justified as appropriate in their own right, without the rational appraisal of information regarding alternative and potentially more efficient courses of action. Customary ways were often continued relatively uncritically.

However, cultural values can change, providing a changing context guiding social action. Weber (1978) identified the emergence of certain religious belief systems (Calvinism and puritanism) as providing a challenge to the traditional outlook. These belief systems were able to germinate within the environment of relative religious tolerance in pre-industrial England. Calvinists felt it their duty to devote their energies exclusively to a life of hard work and application as their beliefs led them to conclude that achieving material success could be taken as a sign of their righteousness and salvation. These religious beliefs provided a powerful incentive to achieve economic and business success through weighing up different ways of working and introducing those which were likely to be more effective in producing economic reward. This religiously sanctioned rational evaluation of the means to efficiently achieve material ends, along with other fortuitous conditions that were present in England, was setting a dynamic in place whereby the utility of traditional ways would be questioned and upon which the values and material basis of modern western capitalism could grow. In contrast to Marx, therefore, Weber assigned a substantial role to the emergence of cultural and belief systems within traditional society that were conducive to rational calculation and focussed industrious action which were significant factors influencing the eventual emergence of a capitalist economy first in England.

Weber argued, though, that with the emergence of western capitalism, the work ethic and quest for rational efficiency would gradually detach itself from religious sanction. This is because rational thinking undermines religious superstition. Society would thus come to correspond more closely to Weber's ideal type in which rational calculation based on scientific and technical knowledge and practical rational action is applied to achieve profit maximisation. But through the self-destruction of the religious sanction behind materialistic aspiration and the advance of secularisation, the religious compass bearing of moral rectitude may be lost as the acquisition of wealth becomes an end in itself. To achieve this end, efficient organisational structures increasingly take the form of large, impersonal bureaucratic power hierarchies which progressively formalise social relationships. However, of course, in the real world, some remnants of traditional value systems and action are likely to remain in the mix.

Given Weber's academic caution and antipathy toward theories that refer to laws of change and the dominance of society over the individual, it is ironic that his studies led him to conclude that the real danger accompanying modern western capitalism is the bleakly inescapable march of rationalisation (rationally constrained thinking and action) and bureaucratisation (the spread of bureaucratic organisations throughout society) which he believed would constrain individual freedom and reduce individuals to little more than cogs within efficient social machinery. Worse than this, coldness and formality would crush the human spirit and technological dominance over nature would replace enchantment with the mysteries of the world with disenchantment with the world – a sense of spiritual loss which is a counterpart in Weber's theory to that of alienation in Marxist theory and the modern malaise of moral anomie in Durkheimian functionalism.

The analysis of action would however be one-sided and incomplete if it were only seen as being shaped by broad cultural and belief systems and social institutions. This emphasis tends to be a weakness of the functionalist approach which reifies society and its 'needs' to such a level that individuals seem to be just passing through it. For Weber, although society and its cultural systems and institutions exist outside of individuals, it is also the case that institutions are consciously planned, created and changed and value systems challenged through purposive action by individual actors.

Furthermore, the study and understanding of social action can only be complete if an analysis of the macro social dimension is complemented by micro studies using direct observation. To understand action in this setting, account must be taken of the meanings and motivations which reside behind it in the consciousness of social actors. These individual meanings and motivations may relate to broader cultural and belief systems. However, the difficulty facing the observer is that of being sure that they have correctly uncovered the subjective motives that lie in the minds of the actors and behind the observed action. To do so, the observer must attempt the challenging process of engaging in empathy – understanding the motives of the observed by putting oneself in their position. This process Weber referred to as 'verstehen' and is a reminder that to practice social science requires acknowledgement of the gulf that exists between the physical processes of the natural sciences and the subjective element in the study of social action.

Pause and reflection

The patience of the reader may well have been tried during this quite lengthy preamble through a number of the founding theoretical perspectives. In consideration of that likelihood, the author will now pause and consider the light that some of these perspectives would shed on a more contemporary phenomena; that of the financial crisis and economic recession following 2007. How would Spencerian, Marxist and Weberian perspectives provide alternative frameworks from which to view the events?

Regarding the crisis, some key points will be sketched first. In essence, various policies and circumstances conspired to bring about a precarious buoyancy in the housing market and consumer spending in the late twentieth and early twenty first centuries. Arguably, the main impetus for the collapse came from the United States, but the pursuit of similar policies in other countries such as Britain during this time period prior to the collapse and effects of global financial and economic interconnectedness assisted global contagion of events.

Following the economic stagnation of the 1970s and the recession of the early 1980s, a number of governments took the decision to deregulate financial institutions, enabling easier consumer access to credit and mortgages. Increased debt therefore provided an economic stimulus, but also led to an inflated and overvalued pricing of property assets. This deregulated financial sector became an expanding part of the economy. However, over time many financial institutions had put themselves in a vulnerable position through developing complex and high risk financial products incentivised by short term gain and overstretching themselves by providing speculative loans without sufficient capital reserve to cover potential losses.

When interest rates increased in the United States, more vulnerable mortgage holders defaulted, properties were repossessed and property prices collapsed. This precipitated the financial crisis of 2007-2008, in which it became clear that sub-prime loans (more risky mortgages to people on lower incomes) had been overvalued. Financial institutions faced self-reinforcing panics from investors who were keen to withdraw savings from banks that they feared might go bust. National governments had to bail out banks with insufficient capital to cover excessive withdrawals. Interest rates slumped, credit availability virtually dried up and the world stock markets fell dramatically. The contagion spread to much of the world economy with a steep recession in national output. Countries such as Greece hovered on the verge of national bankruptcy and had to be kept on life support through loans from international organisations which had conditions of severe austerity measures attached to them.

In sum, the millions of 'personal troubles' endured from this catastrophe have included: loss of homes, unemployment, a decline in wages and standard of living, delayed retirement, a decrease in public expenditure and an increase in the tax burden.

The reader is now encouraged to reflect on any insights into these events that may be derived from the above mentioned founding perspectives before reading the sketches in the following paragraphs.

One may recall that for Spencer a viable social structure is dependent on the (modifiable) moral nature of individuals, the social units comprising that structure. Applying a Spencerian approach, the damage to the financial sector and economy caused by the banking crisis cannot be explained in terms of the inherent weakness of capitalism as a system. Instead, it can be broadly viewed in terms of rapid financial deregulation running ahead of a necessary corresponding advance in the moral condition toward enlightened individualism. Without sufficient social constraint, individualism without enlightenment is likely to equate to purely self-serving action and self-centred greed without concern for the consequences of one's actions for others. Within this context, the existence of high financial incentives can lead to reckless risk taking. In a highly integrated global economy, any destructive consequences will be widespread. In Spencerian terms, the need for state intervention and regulation to put the banking system on life support and the introduction of control measures to help avoid irresponsible individualism in the future were retrograde but necessary steps to enable social institutions to become re-attuned to the reality of the prevailing moral condition of self-centred as opposed to enlightened individualism.

A very different viewpoint of the crisis stems from the Marxist perspective. Despite disagreements between Marxists on some specific matters, it is agreed that such crises are viewed as the inevitable product of capitalism as a system. In the competitive pursuit of survival and profit maximisation, private enterprises must innovate to increase productivity, steal a temporary advantage over their competitors, and reduce labour costs. Whilst of short term benefit, the overall and longer term consequences are a crisis of overproduction as, with a tendency toward rising unemployment and lower wages, there is a decline in the consumer spending power available to buy the surplus of goods produced. This will lead to economic depression, a crisis tendency which Marxists argue cannot in the long term be solved within capitalism (Smith, 26/11/2013).

However, governments and private enterprise will attempt to counter such crises and prop up the system. Credit can be made available to keep capitalism buoyant. Government spending, leading to an increased debt burden, can increase demand. Seductive advertising of products to consumers who are also given access to easy credit will also increase demand, but with it personal indebtedness increases. Large financial institutions, which themselves, from a Marxist perspective, do not create value, become a growing part of the economy, and should they malfunction the consequences are likely to be catastrophic for the 'real economy'. Measures of artificial buoyancy may prolong the life of capitalism, but the collapse is likely to be all the more dramatic, with one such crisis eventually leading to the overthrow of capitalism itself.

As working people have suffered the pains of the recent financial crisis and deep economic recession, public anger can be easily focussed on the greed of a few high profile individuals as the cause of the problem. Such personalisation, it is argued, distracts public attention away from recognising a systemic problem at the heart of capitalism. It therefore promotes a false consciousness of the problem.

From the broad contours of a Weberian perspective, a greater emphasis is placed on the importance of cultural values and rational social action.

It will be recalled that Weber argued that a powerful motive force behind the emergence of capitalism was a religiously sanctioned work ethic of sobriety, rectitude and austerity. For example, Barclays Bank was originally founded and run on principles of Quaker business integrity. However, Weber went on to argue that as the forces of rationalism that accompanied the advance of capitalism undermined religion and its sanctions, this would lead to a capitalism in which the pursuit of wealth, unbounded by religious ethical constraints, would become an end in itself. Within this context, deregulation of financial institutions would clearly run the risk of allowing the unbounded pursuit of material wealth.

Looking at social action a little more closely, Weber felt that the dividing line between action based on rational calculation and affective or emotional behaviour was not always clear. Thus, whilst it is easy to see rational action behind the pursuit of profit in a capitalist business enterprise, financial markets involve a greater degree of uncertainty regarding the future and a crowd psychology dimension which may induce irrational behaviour, especially during times of market turbulence of crisis. However, markets are now dominated by large financial institutions which have at their disposal substantial rational computer calculating power through which some will be able to derive benefit in crisis conditions (Gane, 2012, pp.65–69). Arguably, it is the speed and magnitude of this 'algorithmic' response which is the origin of market destabilisation rather than panic amongst the mass of small shareholders and despite massive overall losses, the most powerful institutions are most likely to benefit.

The emergence of micro perspectives

Although variations on the founding perspectives have retained an influence in sociology for much of the twentieth century, new perspectives were developed, some of which focussed wholly on explaining social action at the micro level. These perspectives – symbolic interactionism, phenomenology and ethnomethodology – are generally referred to as 'interpretive' sociology. At a general level, they hold in common the view that society is founded on shared meaning, that social action can only be understood through grasping the meanings that actors hold, and that the study of micro social environments is the more fruitful way for sociologists to approach an understanding of society.

1. Symbolic interactionism – social self-identity

Symbolic interactionism was a perspective developed in the United States during the early decades of the twentieth century and in this section some of the key ideas of the founding theorists, G.H. Mead and C.H. Cooley, will be explored.

Society, from the point of view of this perspective, is the product of purposeful actions of individuals and interaction with others in small scale situations provides the most important contexts in which individuals live their daily lives. Central to this perspective is the importance of symbols as a means of communication and shared understanding.

Despite this emphasis on purposeful social action and the micro dimension, symbolic interactionism developed relatively independently from the influence of Weber's social action theory. It was indebted more, both culturally and academically, to the tradition of American pragmatism (Ritzer, 2008, pp. 347-348). Briefly, this academic tradition held that ideas and actions relate to practical purpose. People understand situations in ways that are sufficient for practical action, and to engage in practical action, individuals must negotiate with others.

Central to Mead's interactionism is the emphasis that human capacity to think in terms of symbolic meaning separates human kind from animals and makes self-consciousness uniquely possible. Symbols include written and spoken language, gestures, signs and body language. They provide a medium for shared communication, making reflection and interpretation an on-going feature of social life. It is this constant monitoring of meaning which distinguishes reflective and purposeful social action from the automatic stimulus and response behaviour of animals who do not have the human capacity for sharing symbolic meaning. Far more than this, the social world provides an environment which has a profound effect on the individual sense of self. Self-identity is therefore not something which is biologically pre-determined.

Mead proposes a developmental model which locates self-identity within social processes and relates it to the maturation process. From early childhood, children learn social roles by copying the actions of 'significant others', especially parents and siblings, in their immediate environment.

Later, they come to develop the capacity to relate to other individual roles and eventually to people in multiple roles in larger organised settings. For example, the child needs to develop this awareness within the environment of the school. This is referred to by Mead as the development of an awareness of the 'generalised other' and through this a perception of the attitude of the group. By this process, the mature individual develops an awareness of how they are seen by others and the requirement for social compulsion.

Mead viewed the self as composed of the 'me' and the 'I'. The 'me' refers to the social self, built on the capacity that the individual has to see oneself through taking on the viewpoint and attitudes of others. This requires the capacity for 'representation' – the mental ability to step outside of ourselves to contemplate how others see us. Such self-consciousness is enhanced through our interaction with others. The formation of this aspect of the self is based on the appraisal of others and the values and expectations of the community. Through this process, the individual learns how to project a public image, shaped by the requirements of what others think about his or her actions and how they are likely to respond. This part of the self is both stabilised through the social environment and learns how to work that environment through the manipulation of self-image.

In distinction to the 'me', the 'I' element of the self refers to the more subjective inner self. It is that part of the self which retains spontaneity and the capacity to react back against society. An individual's angry outburst, despite knowledge of the rules of etiquette of a social situation, is a rather extreme example of the capacity of the ever lurking 'I' to at least momentarily overwhelm the 'me'. Individual action is therefore a combination of the 'me' and the 'I' and is: a) not biologically pre-determined and b) although socially shaped, not socially pre-determined.

Further insights within this perspective were developed by Charles Cooley, most notably his concept of 'the looking glass self' (Coser, 1977, pp. 305-307). For Cooley, the capacity for reflection enables individuals to view themselves through how they attribute others to see them. The components of this process are the imagination of how we appear to others, the imagined judgement of others based on that appearance, and the consequent positive or negative self-feeling. Rather than an imposing structure, society is the interweaving of such self-reflections and an environment in which individuals attempt to manage the promotion of their external self.

This perspective reveals potentially liberating practical implications. If we have been negatively viewed by others, this can lead to low self-esteem. We may act in confirmation of these views and retain the identity imposed by others. However, as symbolic interactionism reveals, social interaction is not just a one-way process of passive acceptance of others' judgements. We can initiate a change toward a more positive self-identity, but this is not just a private matter. By learning the changes that are necessary in the way that we project ourselves to convince others that we are not as they see us, we can assert to them a new image. If successfully carried off, through their modified responses to us, this new image can become stabilised and internalised in a changed sense of self as it is reflected back to us. Symbolic interactionism suggests that individuals have a degree of freedom and responsibility and an element of say in their self-identity through their capacity to manipulate their own image.

In sum, symbolic interactionists tend to view society as being in a state of flux. It is not a hierarchically imposed structure and overpowering identity moulding entity as portrayed in functionalist theory, but rather the creation of the actions of individuals, mutually orientated through the looking glass self. This is all possible through the medium of the shared understanding of symbols and the capacity for representation and it remains open as to whether social relationships are of co-operation or conflict between individuals or groups.

2. Phenomenology and ethnomethodology – the subjectivity of social structures

Phenomenology is a distinct and more radical theoretical approach to that of symbolic interactionism, but at a general level there are certain similarities between the two perspectives. They both emphasise the importance of understanding action through actors' subjective meaning and both focus on the centrality of symbolic communication between social actors. Both perspectives emphasise the importance of a micro approach to understanding social action and view social action essentially as a fluid process rather than the outcome of constraints originating in the social structure. Both perspectives are commonly referred to as 'interpretive' sociology – they adopt the view that an understanding of social action requires the study of the meaning frameworks adopted by actors.

In his development of phenomenology between the 1930s and the 1950s, Alfred Schutz built on the broader philosophical works of Edmund Husserl and the sociology of Max Weber. Weber recognised the importance of grasping the subjective meanings and motives of actors that lie behind and therefore give meaning to action for the observer. However, he did not provide a systematic theory of subjective meaning. In applying the philosophical insights of Husserl to social phenomena, Schutz attempted to construct a more systematic approach to subjective meaning to develop a foundation for sociology, one which would provide an understanding of the subjective processes involved whereby actors develop the perception of an ordered and structured social world.

A basic premise of phenomenology is that phenomena hold no intrinsic meaning, only that attributed by humans in their capacity to do so. In the social world, actors have to provide meaning to what their sensory perceptions reveal to make sense of their environment and enable them to engage in purposeful social action. The way that the social world is viewed is therefore actively as such defined by its participants. Meaning is assigned to behaviour through shared language and reality is structured through the classification of like labelled phenomena in the form of 'typifications'. A social typification assigns meaning to a category of behaviour, as for example that of a 'thief' or 'poet'. Such typifications provide the building blocks of a shared common sense view of a structured social world and enable assumptions to be made about how society works in a predictable way.

Working through the medium of shared common sense, the world of subjective meaning is intersubjective; subjective communication is able to take place on the reciprocal assumption that we all tend to view the world similarly. For Schutz, the 'life world' is an intersubjective and continuous flow of daily experience, framed by a shared common sense, in which each participant strives to make sense of the actions of others. The meaning framework provided means that this process often takes place quite automatically, but behaviour can be misunderstood and meaning is constantly open to change.

Subjectivity operates at various levels. Individuals have their own biographical profile of subjective experience. Subjective interchange takes place in close relationships which Schutz refers to as 'we' relationships. We may also subjectively relate to people in a more formal way or even anonymously, referred to by Schutz as 'they' relationships. The task of the sociologist from a phenomenological perspective is to understand the subjective meanings that people use in their daily lives. The aim of researchers is to apprehend the subjectivity of those observed to the extent of seeing the world as they do.

From a phenomenological viewpoint, society does not exist as a 'thing' in its own right. Although not intrinsic to the social world, the appearance of social structure is a consequence of the imposition of meaning onto behaviour through typifications and a common sense which in daily life become taken for granted. This sense of an external social structure is essentially an illusion, but is real to the extent that it is commonly believed and acted upon. Society thus comes to be seen as a thing in its own right by its creators.

For phenomenologists, functionalists mistakenly reproduce this viewpoint. They take this creation as an entity in its own right, thus reifying society. Society is taken as a starting point, providing the constraints of concrete structures, cultural consensus and socialisation to integrate individuals. Positivist approaches to sociology are guilty of viewing society in terms of its own intrinsic and independent structures and processes which can be analysed in terms of their own causes and effects with individuals comprising the data of solid facts.

The fundamental points are that for the phenomenologist, the social analyst needs to 1) suspend the common sense viewpoint and classificatory framework adopted by the lay person for everyday practical purposes and instead study the subjective processes involved by actors in arriving at the common sense viewpoint in the first place and 2) avoid the practice of functionalist / positivist sociologists of building on the common sense world and viewing structure and order as intrinsic to society. Action is not the product of the constraints of external structures but is guided by the conscious interpretations placed upon situations by actors.

Ethnomethodology shares the same philosophical terrain as phenomenology, but in making the transition from phenomenology to ethnomethodology, we are moving from a social philosophy to sociology. We have seen that Schutz's phenomenology theorised about the intersubjective creation of a sense of a structured world. Based on the same philosophical premises, the aim of ethnomethodology was to reveal the methods used by people (referred to as members) to build a sense of meaning and order through the activities of their everyday lives. This approach was pioneered in the late 1960s by Harold Garfinkle.

Following the outlook developed by Schutz, for Garfinkle members tend to share common understandings and mutual expectations which provide a framework for the routines of everyday life. When shared meanings and routines are undisturbed, members adopt a taken for granted stance; they are often hardly aware of them. It is only when disruption of the meanings and conventions which provide a sense of order takes place that awareness of them is raised and members engage in attempts to re-establish a sense of order.

As a very simple example, consider the following situation. Imagine that you have just moved into a neighbourhood and are getting to know local people. In the street, you acknowledge a person that you have come to recognise as a local, but find that your acknowledgment is sometimes returned and on other occasions you are completely ignored. This is not what you expect from the rules of etiquette in these everyday encounters. How do you respond to this apparently random behaviour? You will probably try to attribute sense to it by considering plausible reasons for the behaviour: perhaps he didn't hear me? perhaps he didn't remember me? perhaps he was preoccupied in thoughts or worries? If this behaviour should persist, there is likely to come a time when you will attempt to impose a new interpretation on the situation – this is an ill mannered person that I can not be bothered to acknowledge any more. You have actively resolved the ambiguity by interpreting behaviour and imposing meaning on it to make it understandable.

People actively strive to achieve a sense of order and structure in their daily lives. But given the taken for granted stance which commonly accompanies the routines of everyday life, how can this process be teased out? To study the process of the construction of meaning and a sense of order, ethnomethodologists set up experiments in natural settings. These often take the form of 'breaching experiments' in which the aim is to break the rules and conventions of certain situations. The purpose of this approach is to 1) bring into relief what was taken for granted within the situation in the first place and 2) especially to study the methods that actors employ to reconstruct meaning and a sense of order from the confusion caused so that they can make sense of the situation. Such experiments were pioneered by Harold Garfinkle (1984) and it may be helpful at this point for the reader to pause and review those referred to in the research methods chapter of this text.

Through constructing breaching experiments, ethnomethodologists are able to demonstrate how members play an active role in constructing a sense of social meaning and structure. From the findings of his experiments, Garfinkle developed concepts which he claimed reveal the processes by which members create a sense of order in their everyday activities. Through the 'documentary method', members select certain features from a mass of information and events to establish a sense of patterned meaning. Through 'reflexivity', an ongoing process of confirmation of this patterned meaning is established. Reflexivity works through a two way process. The established pattern helps the actor to select and make sense of further information and the meaning ascribed to this information provides confirming evidence of the pattern itself. Further, through 'indexicality', understanding of behaviour is influenced by the context within which the action takes place, with similar behaviour interpreted differently in different contexts.

Ethnomethodologists follow the criticisms of functionalist and positivist approaches that are made by phenomenologists. They argue that there are no social structures existing externally to and independently of people and imposing social conformity on relatively passive individuals. Sociologists who take these structures as real in their own right as the basis for sociological analysis are mistaken. They are ignoring what ethnomethodologists claim that sociology should be all about – a study of the methods by which a sense of structure is actively achieved by members.

Having mentioned the general similarities between symbolic interactionism and phenomenology at the beginning of this section, we are now in a better position to make a precise distinction between them. From a phenomenological and an ethnomethodological perspective, although symbolic interactionism adopts a subjectivist approach, in attempting to view the world as through the eyes of the participants in micro situations, it only builds its concepts on the common sense definitions provided by the actors. It does not reveal the active methods that they employ in the construction of a sense of order in the first place.

Structuration theory – combining purposive individual action and social structure

An enduring rift within sociological theory developed between macro and micro approaches. This rift has been between those theories through which society is viewed as an external constraining force, existing independently of individuals and operating as a system regulating and constraining their behaviour, and those which see it as the product of purposive individual action based on shared meaning and understanding. We have seen that the former approach is allied to the macro perspectives of both Marxism and functionalism and the latter to such micro approaches as symbolic interactionism, phenomenology and ethnomethodology. Weber attempted to combine both aspects in his social action theory, but others (see Slattery, 2003, pp. 274-275) have argued that the differences between the approaches are too fundamental to reconcile. In his theory of 'structuration', Giddens attempts this reconciliation by viewing social structures as constraining environments for but nevertheless modifiable through meaningful individual and collective action.

Society is ultimately made from the actions of individual human beings, without whom it clearly would not exist. However, society is ordered behaviour; it reacts back on individuals to restrict their freedom of action. Social institutions and structures comprise various rules, regulations and power relationships which are necessary to mobilise collective action in the productive process. In doing so, they constrain the range of free action open to individuals. Social structures develop over time, both pre and post existing the lives of individuals who make up society. As such, they can be experienced as if they are external regulatory forces with a life of their own. This is a form of 'reification' of society which corresponds quite closely to that portrayed in the classical functionalist perspective. Giddens challenges this degree of social structuralism in emphasising that societies carry individuals, who through their own or collective input can meaningfully modify systems and structures. Although they work within structures, individuals engage with them reflectively and ultimately have the freedom to challenge the legitimacy of even the most repressive political regimes. External to and overpowering of individuals as they may sometimes feel to be, social structures cannot exist independently of meaningful social action - they may restrict the scope of individual actions to varying extents but are always also the product of social action. People therefore, although having the range of their free action prescribed by the constraints of social structures, have the capacity to self-consciously control and shape those social structures by which they feel controlled. This is the duality of social life which Giddens explained as follows:

> 'By the *duality of structure* I mean that social structures are both constituted *by* human agency, and yet at the same time are the very *medium* of this constitution' (Giddens, 1976, p.121).

Sociological theory – the way ahead

Without the discipline of theory and evidence, the sociological imagination remains speculative and subjective. On the other hand, as mentioned at the beginning of this chapter, whilst theories equip the sociologist with the tools for perceiving and analysing society, being an effective sociologist is not just about uncritically applying theory to society. Instead, theory must be a living thing in the sense of being applied reflectively to society and modified whenever evidence suggests it necessary.

With this caution in mind, and without making any claim that the previous pages comprise anywhere near to a comprehensive history of sociological theory, this chapter will be concluded with brief reference to three main ways ahead for sociology. The first position refers to sociologists who still largely adhere to one or more of the founding perspectives, if in somewhat modified form. However, the basic viability of these perspectives to explain the social world early in the twenty first century has been increasingly called into question. How can functionalism adequately explain how societies function when through the processes of globalisation societies are no longer, if they ever were, clearly delineated and separately functioning entities? How can Marxist analysis, rooted in industrial capitalism with clear divisions between owners and non-owners of the means of production, explain the workings of post-industrial service and information based societies which have arguably undergone the reforms of becoming a widespread share and property owning form of popular capitalism? Can Weber's theory of bureaucratisation remain relevant to contemporary capitalism in which organisational structures need to be highly flexible and responsive to rapid change. And to what extent can the symbolic interactionist view of the development of self-identity remain a plausible model in a society where 'interaction' is increasingly mediated through technological communication?

A second and radical position is adopted by a range of theorists referred to as postmodernists, including writers such as Jean-Francois Lyotard and Jean Baudrillard. They define the 'modern' period as that emerging from the Enlightenment and now ending. This period was dominated by the discourse of science and the aspiration to use science and rational thinking as the method to achieve absolute truth and assist progress. Sociology itself emerged during this period to analyse society in scientific terms, in, for example the writings of Comte, Durkheim and Marx.

Postmodernists argue that the brutal track record of dominant science and the creation of a world devoid of emotional intelligence are leading to the abandonment of science as the quest for a single and absolute truth. In a society of competing belief systems, each of relative worth, it is becoming realised that neither founding social theory, nor in the extreme any social theory, is equipped to offer a single explanation of society which is superior to any other explanation. For postmodernists, 'truth' in the contemporary fast changing world of media created images is becoming illusive and with it sociology as a superior discipline for rationally understanding and organising society is becoming redundant.

Thirdly, are those such as Ulrich Beck and Anthony Giddens, who respectively view contemporary society as having reached a stage of second or high modernism. They maintain that major changes have taken place in contemporary society such as the erosion of the confines of traditional family life and the social class structure as well as the advance of rapid social change. Enhanced global interconnectedness has brought such new risks as global financial instability. For the individual, these changes can lead to the experience of greater uncertainty and insecurity. However, high modernists argue that it is still possible to intelligently guide practical intervention to protect societies and individuals from the negative consequences of these newly created risks. Indeed, guidance through sociological theory is much needed, but new approaches and concepts are required to reconnect sociology with a rapidly changing and globalised world.

Postmodernist and high modernist approaches will be explored further at the end of the topic chapters three to eight and developed in the concluding chapter nine.

Recap on the founding theories

The following exercise has been designed to assist the reader in gauging their recollection and understanding of the founding theories touched on in this chapter. For each statement presented, there is strictly speaking only one correct choice of theory. Phenomenology and ethnomethodology are coupled, as they are in the chapter, but a finer distinction within this choice is underlined in the answers. The statements are randomly ordered with regards to the theories to which they apply.

Using the coding system below, designate one of the following codes to each of the statements. The codes for the correct answers are given on the following page. It is hoped that this will assist the reader in establishing areas of strength and weakness and revisiting sections of the text to clarify understanding.

EP = Early positivism
SE = Spencer's evolutionism
DF = Durkheim's functionalism
M = Marxism
SAT = Social Action Theory (Weber)
SI = Symbolic interactionism
PE = Phenomenology / ethnomethodology

1   Social consensus is the normal and healthy social state.

2   Social change is viewed both in terms of progress and evolution.

3   Conflict is built into the social and economic structure of capitalism.

4   Social science is the key to the building of a new social order following the disorder of the revolution.

5   Social classes are identified in relation to the means of production.

6   Excessive social conflict indicates the ill health of society.

7   Social change is driven by class conflict.

8   The future high point is a society based on enlightened individualism.

9   Social classes are essentially in antagonism to each other.

10   Self-identity is influenced by the labelling process.

11   The model of the ideal industrial society is based on an extension of the ideas of political economy throughout society.

12   Taken for granted meaning is sufficient for people in their everyday worlds.

13   The new industrial society should be regulated by scientific and industrial elites.

14   The industrial society will ultimately be one of deregulated free enterprise.

15   The observer of social action needs to effectively engage in 'verstehen' to understand the action of others.

16   There are many contributory causes of broad social change, different ones being of greater significance in different societies at different times.

17   The conditions of survival of the fittest change through evolution from warfare to peaceful production.

18   The process of rationalisation is key to the development of modern capitalism.

19   Cultural values can be as important as economic factors in explaining social change.

20   Treated as productive objects, workers experience alienation under the conditions of capitalism.

21   It is of benefit to society that the individual is moulded and constrained by external social forces.

22   Personal identity is a product of the looking glass self.

23   The broad direction of social change cannot be understood by applying the causality of the physical sciences and the future cannot be predicted by laws of change.

24   Political power derives from economic power.

25   Efficient bureaucratic organisations proliferate in modern legal rational societies.

26   State intervention is fraught with unintended and remote consequences in highly complex industrial societies.

27   Social change is driven by economic forces.

28   This approach analyses how actors construct meaning and order in their everyday lives.

29   People both meaningfully create their society and are constrained by it.

30   Oppressive authority is necessary in societies in a state of mechanical solidarity.

31   Individuals can challenge the labelling process and negotiate their identity.

32   The history of thinking can be divided into three stages, the first two of which are the theological and the metaphysical.

33   As well as the social world impacting on the individual, individuals retain the capacity to change the social world.

34   Society is not intrinsically structured.

35   A full understanding of social action must complement macro and micro analysis.

36   With some regret, there is an increasing tendency for peoples' lives to become constrained by large impersonal institutions.

37   The purpose of the superstructure is to suppress inbuilt class conflict.

38   Systems of thinking govern the condition of society.

39   The advance of formality, bureaucratisation and rationalisation can lead to the experience of disenchantment with the world.

40   Private ownership of the means of production enables exploitation of the subject class.

41   The act of meaning construction can be best observed in the context of breaching experiments.

42   The decline in oppressive authority is a key feature of societies in a state of organic solidarity.

43   Economic life is the determining force around which the rest of society is organised.

44   Social inequality is not inevitable.

45   Shared values promote social integration.

46   The 'I' is the inner self which may react on the social environment.

47   The scientific understanding of society is at the pinnacle of the hierarchy of the sciences.

48   Self-identity is shaped in the process of interaction.

49   Anomie is an ailment of modern industrial societies, especially during times of major change.

50   Social communication and understanding is mediated by a shared understanding of symbols.

51   Capitalist society is organised primarily for the benefit of one class who will exploit another.

52   Society is beneficially structured by institutions, roles and rules to constrain individual behaviour.

53   Enlightenment thinking is responsible for undermining religious dogma and social order and precipitating revolution.

54   The 'me' is both a product of and manipulator of the social environment.

55   Understanding the meanings that people exchange in social interaction is as important as recognising the constraints of the broader social structure.

Answers can be found on the next page

Answers to multiple choice exercise

1	DF	19	SAT	37	M
2	SE	20	M	38	EP
3	M	21	DF	39	SAT
4	EP	22	SI	40	M
5	M	23	SAT	41	PE
6	DF	24	M	42	DF
7	M	25	SAT	43	M
8	SE	26	SE	44	M
9	M	27	M	45	DF
10	SI	28	PE	46	SI
11	SE	29	SAT	47	EP
12	PE	30	DF	48	SI
13	EP	31	SI	49	DF
14	SE	32	EP	50	SI
15	SAT	33	SAT	51	M
16	SAT	34	PE	52	DF
17	SE	35	SAT	53	EP
18	SAT	36	SAT	54	SI
				55	SAT

3 // Sociological Research Methods and Methodology

Abstract

This chapter begins by alerting the reader to the problem of the intrusion of personal bias into everyday knowledge about society and emphasises that sociology requires a methodical approach and a sound evidential base for the study of society which is able to justify claims to academically superior knowledge. It is also emphasised, however, that for a number of reasons, sociologists must be cautious about their findings. A limited number of key terms and concepts central to research methods are then introduced and clarified.

Research methods are the means by which sociologists obtain information about society. A simple classificatory framework is adopted to cover a range of research methods that sociologists have at their disposal. This framework classifies methods in terms of whether information is gained primarily through asking questions, through observation, or through utilising documents. However, it is also shown that, by their very nature or through their varied applications, methods may be located in other than just their primary category and that some methods may overlap with and even be used within other methods. The methods are explained in terms of how they are used and some of their strengths and weaknesses are considered. In these sections, reference is also made to the positivist or interpretive features of the methods outlined and a classification table is provided.

Research methodology is explained as something broader than just the practical use of research methods as research tools. It refers to approaches to establishing the truth and the guidelines for doing so. However, there are methodological disputes within sociology which are informed by differing theoretical and philosophical assumptions about how truth can be most effectively established when studying social phenomena. These assumptions signify different appropriate research procedures and these procedures tend to have affinities with particular types of method. The methodological differences between positivist, social action and interpretive approaches are reviewed. The issue of what the aims of sociology should be is also raised in this chapter.

Some more contemporary approaches to sociological research are introduced in the form of critical theory, feminism and postmodernism. These approaches raise a number of fundamental questions regarding established canons of sociological research including the questions of the certainty of knowledge, the nature of researcher and subject relationships, the possibility of value neutrality and the very status of sociology. The more extreme position of some postmodernists even dismisses the possibility of establishing the truth and challenges the traditional assertion that sociological knowledge is superior to any other knowledge about society. This claim is seriously questioned by the author.

The sociological challenge

In our daily situations, we all hold a stock of knowledge about the social world. This knowledge may seem to be self evidently correct and adequate for our everyday purposes. It may be only when events take place which challenge it that we are likely to engage in more thoughtful scrutiny of what we have previously taken for granted. In sum, in our everyday lives we are likely to hold a pragmatic view of society – what we take as true or adequate remains relatively unchallenged all the time that it gets us by.

But from where do we acquire our everyday knowledge about society? Its main sources will include our immediate experiences, hearsay information from other people, and information from the mass media; sources which vary in their impact, may overlap, and can complement or contradict each other. By such means, our attitudes and opinions are formed and influenced. We may be vulnerable to misrepresentation and manipulation but we are also likely to be conspirators in the process as we select information and interpret the world to confirm our beliefs through our choice of friends and associates, newspapers, television programmes and internet information.

Further consideration of the influences contributing to our everyday knowledge reveals how unreliable this may be as a basis for understanding society. For example, experiences vary from individual to individual and the world of our immediate social experiences is very small. How far, therefore, is it valid to generalise our knowledge of society from these limited experiences? They may be quite unlike the experiences of people of different gender, social class, ethnicity, age, and life chances, etc. Nevertheless, our immediate experiences help to form our attitudes and opinions and these in turn frame our interpretations of our experiences. We may share similar opinions and interpretations with those who we choose to be our friends and acquaintances. The potential for selective reinforcement of our attitudes and opinions can therefore be great, but these are the means through which we filter our understanding of broader society.

We also need to rely on the mass media for helping us frame the bigger picture – for example on global events. Even if we are cautious, suspecting that information is being distorted or that we are being manipulated, the key question to ask is how can we check the truthfulness of what we are being told? Is it enough to review alternative sources of media information when we cannot check hardly any of this information by direct experience? Furthermore, if the media is an important vehicle of agenda setting in the public domain, what can we know about issues or events that tend to remain off the agenda altogether?

Most sociologists would agree that as an academic subject, sociology can not be just an assemblage, even a well organised one, of the stock of everyday knowledge that exists about society. To be so would often be to reproduce everyday bias, subjectivity and selectiveness and it would not be possible to assess the relative worth of one person's viewpoint on society to that of another. Most sociologists adopt the position that sociology must generate its own superior findings through procedures which stand up to rigorous scrutiny even though these findings can never be taken as foolproof or undisputed or final truths. The findings may be of varying levels of interest for people in their everyday lives or even fly in the face of common sense knowledge or assumptions. However, it is the educative role of sociology to feed back its findings not just to its own academic community but to members of society and to encourage people to examine their taken for granted assumptions. Sociology therefore has a broader enlightening role to play.

So just where do we place sociology in providing a sound understanding of society? Having emphasised the superior academic credentials of sociological knowledge to common sense knowledge, some cautionary points need to be raised:

1. There is much debate within sociology over which aspects of rigour (for example, reliability or validity) are the most important as well as the uses and virtues of different methods of obtaining information.

2. Rarely is there any single method by which a particular area of study can be uniquely and conclusively researched.

3. In the study of any single topic area, different methods can provide different types of data and lead to different or contradictory findings. How can this be interpreted?

4. Often reality is multifaceted. Research may show that the reality of a situation is viewed differently by different groups of participants.

5. However well established and conclusive the findings of a piece of research may be at a particular point in time, the fact that society is constantly changing necessitates the need for ever new research and explanations.

6. A particular difficulty for sociology is that sociologists, as people, are deeply implicated in the subject of their studies. As well as sociologists, they are also lay members of society who hold their own values, attitudes and prejudices about society. These can intrude, possibly subconsciously, into the researcher's choice of topic area and various aspects of the research process including the choice of methods and how they are used and the evaluation of information. The claim to objectivity and superior academic credentials of the findings can thus be questioned.

The purpose of this chapter is to examine the approaches and methods that sociologists use to obtain information about and develop an understanding of society. This examination will indicate some of the strengths that sociological research offers in obtaining reliable and valid information compared to the epistemological (knowing) basis upon which everyday knowledge rests. It will also go further and encourage a critical assessment of the methods used by sociologists. Finally, consideration will be given of new approaches which question the traditional methodological assumptions that sociological research must aim for value neutrality and non-directiveness, and which even attack the possibility of sociologists achieving superior knowledge of society to that of the layperson.

Definition of main concepts

In sociology, a fundamental distinction in research methods can be made between whether the sources of information used are of a primary or secondary nature. **Primary** information is that which has been compiled by the researcher in the form required for the research. This may include, for example, information obtained through social surveys or participant observation. **Secondary** sources of information are those which have been compiled by others, often originally for non-sociological purposes. Official statistics, for example from HM Revenue and Customs, and personal documents, such as diaries, are examples of types of information which fall into this category.

Sociologists can use various forms of interviewing to elicit information from others. The terminology applicable to the participants is dependent on the style of interviewing. Some interviews follow a highly structured approach and the questions asked, listed on a standardised document in the form of a **questionnaire**, require just short answers. This approach to interviewing is typical of large scale **social surveys** in which formality is part of the process whereby the interview is organised for the purpose of focussing responses to questions deemed by researchers to be relevant to the research. In this style of interviewing, the term **interviewer** is applied to the person eliciting verbal feedback from another or others who are usually referred to as **respondent(s)**. The term respondent is also applied to those providing information in survey research which does not involve a verbal interview – for example, those who take away a questionnaire to fill in themselves or those who partake in mail or internet surveys. However, some styles of interviewing are less formal and allow the person(s) interviewed to more fully participate in elaborating their answers or even influencing the sequencing of the interview. For this approach to interviewing, the terms **interviewer** and **interviewee** are more appropriate. Sometimes, the interviewee is referred to as an **informant** when their role is one of guiding the interviewer toward other sources of information, as is more likely to be the case during the exploratory phase of research.

The technical terms 'population' and 'sample' are closely connected. In sociological research, the term **population** refers to a clearly defined category of people to which the research applies. Research into voting behaviour may take the 'British electorate' as the relevant population. Alternatively, a study of the causes of homelessness may define its population as 'those living without access to accommodation in Nottingham'. A **sample** is a small selection from an identified population for purposes of inclusion in the research. The aim of taking a sample is to make the research process efficient, or in many cases even possible at all, usually by aiming to obtain a precise fractional replication of the characteristics of the population for analysis. Two key points emerge from this: 1) the sample must be selected so that it is as representative as possible of the profile of the population from which it is drawn, and 2) the findings of the research based on the sample can then be legitimately generalised back to the population from which the sample was taken, but not beyond. In fact, there are a variety of approaches to sampling that have been used by sociologists and, dependent on the type chosen, are likely to lead to the selection of more or less representative samples.

In Chapter 2, a distinction was made between **positivist** and **interpretive** perspectives. A sociologist's orientation toward one of these perspectives may influence their methodology, research strategy and choice of methods used. The term **methodology** refers to theoretical assumptions upon which are based different research procedures and preferred methods. A connection between these different perspectives and the types of methods that are likely to be preferred will be indicated throughout this chapter. However, it should be appreciated that there can be some versatility in the use of specific methods and that sociologists often do not adopt a hard line methodological approach of exclusively positivist or interpretive orientated methods and research strategies.

Positivist methodology emphasises that society is little different from the natural world and can thus be analysed similarly in hard scientific terms. Sociologists who incline toward positivism will be looking to demonstrate that natural scientific method and precision has been undertaken in their research. Consequently, they will tend to devise precisely pre-planned and tightly controlled research strategies to obtain the type of information that they know they want. To assist in the precision of measurement, they will prefer to use methods which can supply **quantitative** information – that which is viewed as hard data and can be expressed in numerical form, often with the purpose of identifying trends, correlations and cause and effect relationships. Methods which can be used in this way and supply this type of information include the social survey, the experimental laboratory method and the analysis of official statistics.

When research procedures have been precisely specified and controlled, their use can be carefully **replicated** by others in further research. It is frequently suggested that this means that a researcher should be able to repeat the same controls and procedures on a similar sample of people and obtain the same results. This is an over simplistic and incorrect assertion. It would be more accurate and precise to say that positivist type methods such as the social survey or laboratory experiments should provide the same findings when repeated if it were possible that another researcher had used the identical method and procedures on the same participants at the same time. Consequently, confidence in the comparability of findings between different research projects can be high. Thus, if researchers apply the same methods and procedures at different times or places and obtain different results, it is likely that the difference is substantial (it may provide a reliable measure of social change or diversity) and not due to the vagaries of the method or the way in which it has been used.

Research which emphasises natural scientific procedures and the possibility of precise replication is considered to be high in **reliability**. This criterion of rigour is of primary importance to and viewed as a strength in positivist methodology and quantitative research.

By contrast, **interpretive methodology** is related to an approach to sociology which posits that understanding society can only be possible through a more subjective approach. Theorists who tend to identify with an interpretive stance will emphasise the importance of gaining insight into the meanings behind peoples' actions rather than attempting to measure behaviour in terms of causes and effects. Research will more likely be viewed as a continuous learning process. The methods and strategy used must therefore allow researchers to constantly review procedures and evidence and enable refinement of insight to take place. The preferred methods will tend to be those which generate **qualitative** information – that which is aimed at promoting quality of insight into the worlds of others and which may lend itself more to narrative than to quantitative expression. Methods particularly suitable for interpretive type research include participant observation, unstructured and in-depth interviewing and the study of personal documents.

Interpretive sociologists emphasise that in terms of rigour, priority should be placed on establishing certainty that the researcher is measuring what they claim to be measuring. Research procedures must therefore allow the researcher greater flexibility to engage in a learning process whereby closeness to the outlook of social actors can be established. If this is achieved, then rigour takes the form of establishing a high level of **validity** in the findings, which provides a key strength in interpretive methodology and qualitative research.

Positivist approaches tend to be weaker in establishing the validity of their findings. This is because they usually pre-structure research around researchers' meanings and adopt a greater clinical distance from the subjects of the research. By contrast, interpretive approaches, in prioritising validity, can be criticised for lacking sufficient reliability as each piece of research relies heavily on the subjective judgements and interpretations of the researcher and cannot be precisely replicated by others to provide a sound basis for the comparison of results.

The range of research methods

The methods of research used by sociologists are many and varied. It is rarely the case that any area of study can only be approached by using a single method which is deemed to be exclusively suitable. Various factors can influence the methods(s) used and the way in which they are used. These factors can include the amount of time that is available, the level of funding and manpower constraints and the ethical judgements of researchers. Another important area of influence relates to the researcher's theoretical and methodological leanings since certain methods can be seen to have affinities with particular methodological approaches adopted. The social survey or use of official statistics may be preferred by more positivist minded sociologists, whereas interpretivists may be more inclined toward such methods as in-depth interviewing or participant observation. Moreover, as all methods have their strengths and weaknesses, it is quite common for sociologists to utilise more than one method in a research project in an attempt to maximise overall rigor. This approach has been referred to as 'triangulation'.

The benefits of triangulation can be argued in different ways. For example, it can be emphasised that using a variety of methods enables the research to establish a closer and more subtle approximation to the truth than when using just one. Also, society may be viewed as a multi-layered and sometimes contradictory reality, the complexities of which are often only apprehended through the use of a rich variety of research methods.

Research methods themselves can be classified in various ways. One common approach has traditionally been to place them on a positivist – interpretivist scale. Although this dimension can rarely be completely ignored, other approaches have been adopted. For example, McNeill and Chapman (2005) comprehensively organise methods into the following chapters: social surveys, experiments and comparative method, ethnography, and secondary data.

The author of this text will apply two levels of organisation to a range of research methods. The first level will refer directly to the methods themselves as practical tools and the categories employed will be derived from answering the simple question 'how do the methods enable sociologists to obtain information?' The resulting categories used will be: through asking questions, through observing behaviour, and through utilising documents. Methods will be classified in terms of these above categories within which they can be primarily but not necessarily exclusively located. As research methods can be applied in a variety of ways, some will also require mention in more than one category. Methods may also overlap, or one method, for example participant observation, can encapsulate others, for example in-depth interviewing.

In this chapter, the theoretical and methodological positions of positivism, social action theory, symbolic interactionism, phenomenology and ethnomethodology, critical theory, feminism and postmodernism will be examined. The second level of organisation of research methods will relate them to these positions.

How do sociologists obtain information?

1. Primarily through asking questions

Most people have had experience of being interviewed, for example through participation in market research. Such an encounter is usually within the scope of a **social survey**, which is a highly pre-structured research method. By this is meant that the parameters of the research, the type of information elicited, the wording of questions, the size and type of sample selected, and the procedures employed by interviewers (when interviewing takes place) are precisely defined at the start by researchers. The questionnaire is a key tool which is invariably used within this method. A questionnaire comprises a standardised list of questions which are finely tuned to gain information on a particular topic area under investigation from a relatively large number of people. The focus of the research is usually designed to test a speculated explanation (hypothesis) and statistical analysis of data derived from the survey provides the means by which this can take place. However, it is important to be aware that in reality the process of designing the research and interpreting data is not just mechanical and always requires a degree of researcher insight, creativity and judgement.

Where face-to-face interviewing is used, the location of survey interview situations may vary with the nature of the research and could take place, for example, in the street, the respondent's home, the workplace or in an office of the interviewer. Much depends on the nature and sensitivity of the topic area. In the context of much survey research, the respondent is simply restricted to answering pre-set questions and the encounter is quite brief and formal. This enables a large number of people, usually constituting a sample, to be interviewed within the constraints of time and resources available, with the aim of generating a mass of information in the form of data which can be statistically analysed and conclusions drawn.

Supporters of the social survey point to statistical sampling, structuring, formality and standardisation as virtues of this method in the quest to obtain quantifiable and reliable information, with the possibility of generalising research findings from a sample to a broader population from which it was drawn. Within a social survey, questionnaires are designed as precision instruments for gathering focussed information on the area of interest. Care in the design of questionnaires is therefore crucial at a number of levels. The wording of questions must not be leading but must be clear, precise and absolutely relevant to the research. More than this, questionnaire design is of vital importance to encouraging the participation of respondents and eliciting honest and accurate information. To assist this process, most surveys include a pre-test of the questionnaire in which colleagues are invited to suggest improvements that can be made, for example in wording, style and sequencing of questions. This may be followed by a small-scale pilot survey, run in advance of the full survey, with the purpose of acquiring feedback on the clarity of the questions and instructions as well as information regarding the interview process itself as perceived from the viewpoint of both interviewer and respondent. The aim at this stage is therefore that of improving fine tuning rather than providing data from the answers. Interviewers themselves have to be carefully prepared to deliver the interview in a standardised and non-directive way - there should be no intimation to the respondent of preferred answers. If, in addition to the above preparations, the privacy and anonymity of respondents is guaranteed, respondents should feel that they are in a position to answer honestly, accurately and impartially – if they are so inclined!

Survey questions are not only delivered in the form of face-to-face interviews. Other approaches include allowing respondents to take away, fill in and return the questionnaire themselves, telephone interviewing, mail questionnaires, newspaper and magazine surveys, and e mail surveys. These alternative survey approaches may offer economical access to a broadly geographically spread sample of respondents compared to the option of using face-to-face interviewing, but they raise a range of other problems which could undermine the reliability of the research. For example, when respondents take questionnaires away for completion, there is a high risk that, unknown to the researcher, other people may influence the answers given. Furthermore, a significant proportion will not be returned, impacting on what is referred to as the 'response rate'. These are problems which are often exacerbated in the case of mail surveys. The problem is that however representative the original sample may have been of the population from which it was drawn, a low response rate may itself be unrepresentative of the sample, thus distorting the findings. For example, people holding strong views on the topic of the research may be more likely to be motivated to respond than others, thus underrepresenting information from those who hold moderate opinions. Moreover, without the presence of the interviewer, there is no opportunity for the respondent to ask for clarification of the questions (although this may be possible in the case of e mail surveys), and it cannot be certain that the selected person has filled in the questionnaire, or if so has answered the questions in the required order and with diligence.

Linked to the formality of this method and the quest for quantifiable data is the typical style of questioning. In many surveys, a large proportion of the questions take a closed ended form – they only offer the respondent choice from a range of pre-determined categories in selecting their answer(s). The purpose of such questions is to provide pre-coded data in which answers classified into categories can be structured for statistical analysis. This data, of course, will lack the subtlety of response which is the aim of open ended questions which ask the respondents to answer at greater length and in their own terms and in each answer provide detail which is unique to themselves. However, when used within the context of the social survey, open ended questions are still invariably part of a heavily pre-structured and often formally delivered method. Furthermore, the quality and diversity of information gained by this means is often at least partially compromised by the process of 'post-coding'. This is a procedure whereby, for purposes of assisting the quantification of the unique, rich and complex information, researchers look through the varied answers and construct a limited number of categories into which they can then be pigeon holed for a more statistical analysis.

Interviews used in social surveys can take the form of semi-structured encounters which offer the interviewee some feeling of control or, at the extreme, unstructured interviews even more so. However, logistically, interviews of the latter type are likely to be restricted to very small scale surveys within which both the size of the sample and type of information acquired would substantially diminish the scope for using statistical analysis. Most social surveys are of a large scale and standardised nature in the quest to obtain a mass of data. This requires the interview to remain a tightly focussed, efficient and strongly interviewer guided process.

An alternative approach to questioning which is sometimes employed within the social survey is the 'vignette technique' through which hypothetical situations in the form of cameo scenarios are presented to respondents to elicit their responses. The technique can be useful to measure attitudes and anticipated practical responses toward various specified social situations and can be a beneficial approach when it is suspected that a question may be interpreted in different ways by different respondents, thus invalidating question standardisation. For example, in their survey into family responsibilities, Finch and Mason (1993) employed this technique to help them compare participants' anticipated actions with norms of expected behaviour. The following is an example of a scenario from their research:

'Jane is a young woman with children aged 3 and 5. She has recently divorced. She wants to go back to work and she needs the money. But if she has a job she must find someone to mind the children after school. Her own family live far away but her former mother-in-law Ann Hill is at home all day and lives near by. Jane has always got on well with her former mother in law.
Should Ann offer to look after Jane's children?' (cited in Devine and Heath, 1999, p.50).

The answer to such a question could then be probed further with the use of closed and / or open ended questions to elicit more detail from the respondent.

The social survey is a well-established research method. It has been applied in various ways and across a broad range of topics. One form that it takes is the descriptive survey. The aim of such a survey is to measure the extent of social phenomena rather than to test sociological theory. The most comprehensive descriptive survey in terms of its numerical size is the government census which, once every ten years, aims to achieve a 100% response rate from the British population to provide demographic information (information about the makeup of the population) to assist government planning and social policy regarding such matters as educational and health service provision and road building. However, in 1991, more people were evading the census as those who were avoiding payment of the local authority community charge did not want their whereabouts to become known to the local authorities.

Poverty has been frequently studied through the social survey method. Although essentially descriptive surveys, the pioneering work of Charles Booth (accounts published 1889 - 1907) and Seebohm Rowntree (1899) provided compelling evidence of the widespread extent of absolute poverty in parts of England, challenged attitudes that blamed the poor for their plight, and provided an impetus for the introduction of social security reforms during the early twentieth century.

Social surveys usually take the form of cross sectional studies; they are one off pieces of research, gaining information from a sample of a population at a particular point in time. An interesting example of this type of survey for the issues that it raises was the National Survey on

Sexual Attitudes and Lifestyles, conducted by Wellings et al during 1990–1991, following the spread of the HIV virus. Given the sensitive nature of the topic area, the researchers had to be particularly careful in their choice of wording and sequencing of the questions. Pilot interviews were therefore an important prelude to the survey. Interviewers had to be carefully prepared in the way that they approached respondents so as to maximise the response rate and respondent honesty. The sample of nearly 30,000 people were initially supplied with briefing notes about the research and visited to ascertain their willingness to participate. Despite the care taken, under 20,000 people from the sample then went on to participate in the 40 to 60 minute face-to-face interviews. And all this transpired despite the fact that the government of the day attempted to stop the launch of the research by withdrawing its funding.

As cross sectional studies, standard surveys do not aim to track a particular group of people over a period of time. That approach is more specific to the longitudinal survey. Attempts to measure social change through the use of cross sectional surveys comprise a series of snap shot surveys, each taking a new sample. When surveys are repeated, the wording of all or a significant proportion of the questions is held constant so that direct comparisons of information can be made over time to measure social change. These surveys are referred to as **repeated cross sectional surveys**.

An example of such a survey of a descriptive type is the Crime Study for England and Wales which started as the British Crime Survey in 1982 and became conducted biannually. The survey now operates on a rolling basis, interviewing people throughout each year on their experiences of being the victims of crime during the previous twelve months, as well as on matters such as perceptions of and attitudes toward crime and the Criminal Justice System and their experiences of the police. In this survey, the victimisation section of the questionnaire has remained essentially unchanged but other sections have changed over time. A key aim of the survey has been to establish a more realistic measurement of the extent of different types of crime than official statistics based on reported and recorded crime can alone reveal.

For this survey, Royal Mail lists are used as a sampling frame from which addresses are randomly selected. A large main sample of approximately

35,000 households was chosen in 2013 for face-to-face interviewing of a randomly selected person from each household amongst those aged 16 or over. Also from the main sample, a smaller sample of 3,100 10 to 15 year olds was selected for inclusion for shorter interviews. The selected households received in advance a letter and leaflet providing information about the survey to enhance understanding and encourage voluntary co-operation. Response rates have usually attained close to 75%.

An example from the victimisation section of the 2012 – 2013 questionnaire, complete with instructions to the interviewer, is provided below in box 1 (Office For National Statistics, Crime Survey for England and Wales, 11/12/2013).

Box 1: Section from the questionnaire used from April 2012 in the 2012 – 2013 Crime Survey for England and Wales

5.5 CIRCUMSTANCES OF INCIDENT
VICTAREA [ASK ALL]
SL
Can I just check, did it happen in this area (within 15 minutes walk of here)?
1. Yes
2. No

WHERHAPP [ASK IF VICTAREA = NO OR DK/REF]
SL
Did it happen in England or Wales or did it happen somewhere else?
1. England or Wales
2. Elsewhere*

NOTE: If 'Elsewhere' and this is a Long victim form, it will switch to being a Short victim form. Other forms are unaffected.
RACEMOT [ASK ALL]
SL
Do you think the incident was RACIALLY motivated?
1. Yes
2. No
3. Don't Know

RACEPOSS [ASK IF RACEMOT = DON'T KNOW]
SL
Was there anything about the incident that made you think it might have been RACIALLY motivated?
1. Yes
2. No

YRACEMOA-
YRACEMOI [ASK IF RACEMOT = YES OR RACEPOSS = YES]
SL
Why do you think it [was/might have been] RACIALLY motivated?
DO NOT PROMPT CODE ALL THAT APPLY
1. Racist language used (comments, abuse, etc.)
2. Because of victim's race/country of origin
3. Because of offender's race/country of origin
4. Because offence only committed against minorities (e.g. doesn't happen to anyone else)
5. Because some people pick on minorities
6. Because it has happened before
7. Some other reason
VICTIMISATION MODULE 16/08/2012 51 of 266
HATEMT3A-
HATEMT3I [ASK ALL]
SL
WHITE SHOW CARD V1
Looking at the things on this card do you think the incident was motivated by the offender's attitude towards any of these factors?
CODE ALL THAT APPLY
1. Your religion or religious beliefs
2. Your sexuality or sexual orientation
3. Your age
4. Your sex
5. Any disability you have
6. Your gender identity (transgender)
7. Don't Know
8. None of these

The responses to questions are recorded on questionnaire tablets.

However, for very sensitive areas, such as section 19 which asks questions about sexual abuse and domestic violence, respondents are able to complete their own answers which then become hidden to the interviewer.

Although such descriptive surveys are not conducted originally for sociological purposes, the results, often in the form of official statistics, can be utilised, often with a degree of caution, as secondary information by sociologists for more analytical purposes.

A further example of the repeated cross sectional survey is the study of voting behaviour carried out in the British Election Studies which dates from 1964. The survey now uses a mixture of face-to-face interviewing, mail questionnaires and internet surveys to study why people vote the way that they do and to ascertain factors that have affected the outcome of elections. The aims of this survey therefore go somewhat beyond that of assembling descriptive data.

An example of primary research of a more analytical type is provided in Goldthorpe and Lockwood's (1969) classic social survey into changes in the class structure. The purpose of the survey was to test the validity of the 'embourgeoisement thesis' - the theory that modern societies are becoming increasingly middle class – in Britain. Within this survey, conducted in the Luton area, 229 married blue collar workers, who were purposely selected in income terms as affluent workers, and 54 white collar workers were interviewed. Lengthy interviews, which the relatively small sample size made possible, took place within the workplace regarding work related issues, and at home with reference to politics and leisure etc. Since the blue collar workers were not exhibiting strong signs of middleclassness, Goldthorpe and Lockwood argued that their evidence disproved the broader theory of embourgeoisement.

As a cautionary point, care should be taken not to over stereotype the survey approach. Surveys are likely, to a greater of lesser extent, to include ethnographic (study of everyday life) dimensions, especially if researchers live amongst the people that they are interviewing and conduct daily observations as part of their research. For example, living within the vicinity of the community that they were researching supplemented Young and Willmott's social survey research into family life in the East End of London (1957) with further insights. However, overall, survey procedures are claimed to match up to traditional canons of scientific objectivity and tend to be preferred by positivist orientated sociologists who strive to obtain factual data, either at a descriptive level or to test hypotheses and theories.

Longitudinal surveys differ from cross sectional surveys in that they return to the same people (if the participants are selected in terms of having a common birth period, the participants are referred to as a 'cohort') at key points over a protracted period of time, often many years, to acquire more information from them. Such surveys, like the cross sectional, tend to be large scale, work with mainly quantitative information and are generally seen, due to the continuity of participants, as superior to a series of surveys for the purpose of tracing processes that operate over lengthy time periods.

One example of a longitudinal survey is that conducted by the Office for National Statistics which, from 1971, took a 1% sample from census returns and followed up the information on these people with that obtained in subsequent censuses. The aim of this research was to study the relationship between social class, illness and death rates.

A further example is provided by the Labour Force Survey, which looks at employment, income, education and health etc. within families. In this survey, the questionnaire is revised annually. However, this is supplemented by interviews which take place at quarterly intervals and the same households are followed up on five occasions, firstly through face-to-face interviews and subsequently through telephone interviews.

Traditionally, the term **panel survey** originated in the study of political opinion, with the purpose of understanding why people change their attitudes over time or their vote from one election to another. For this research to be effective, the same people are interviewed at relevant periods of time, for example at successive elections. Anthony Heath et al (1994) have conducted extensive panel studies of this type in Britain.

On the theme of attitude change, de Vaus (1999, pp.37-40) has likened the panel survey to a type of incomplete experimental laboratory (see section 2) approach with the aim of measuring changes in attitude in a natural setting before and after an intervention to test the impact of that intervention. He has provided an example of such a survey in the following form. If one were to measure the religious beliefs of a new intake of university students and measure their beliefs again at the end of their studies, any measured decline may be deduced as attributable to the experience of university life having a 'secularising' influence on students. We will later identify weaknesses in making such a deduction.

One source of terminological confusion derives from the fact that the term panel survey has often become applied more generally to longitudinal surveys. For example The British Household Panel Survey, which was first established in 1991, was set up to look into social and economic change in people's lives. This research provides a good example of the dynamics of longitudinal samples. 5,500 households, comprising 10,264 individuals, participated in the first 35-60 minute face-to-face interviews in 1991. As many participants as possible were to be re-interviewed on an annual basis and contact in the meantime was maintained through letters, but within eight years the number of interviewees had fallen to 6,080 – this despite the fact that as the family was the unit of analysis, new members would be included. This problem of dropout rate, otherwise known as 'attrition', is characteristic of longitudinal research. It can be caused by losing people who move, who die and who refuse to continue their participation. From 2008, this survey was subsumed into the UK Household Longitudinal Study which comprised 40,000 households and looked at changing fortunes, attitudes and circumstances within families.

We have established that social surveys invariably require the use of questionnaires as a tool to gather structured information. When face-to-face interviewing is used, the encounter is likely to be experienced as a formal and highly structured one. However, alternative uses of interviewing may employ far more open approaches to interviewees. One could construct scale of interviewing in terms of structured to unstructured approaches as follows: 1) highly pre-structured, using closed ended questions only, 2) highly pre-structured, but also introducing some open ended questions, 3) semi-structured, employing mainly open ended questions and allowing some latitude to the input of the interviewee, 4) unstructured, comprising open ended questions and allowing the interviewee substantial personal input into the content and some influence on the direction of the interview, and 5) conversational, in which technically an interview may be taking place but the form that it takes is experienced by the 'interviewee' as if it were or very close to that of a spontaneous conversation.

Whilst the first two styles of interviewing tend to be characteristic of social surveys, types 3, 4 and 5 move increasingly into research which is likely to be undertaken on a smaller scale and from an interpretive perspective. From this perspective, the degree of pre-structuring of the social survey can be viewed as a barrier to understanding the world of the subject since the interests and definitions of researchers are imposed on the respondents from the start. If interviewing is to be used, interpretive sociologists are likely to prefer to engage in relatively unstructured interviewing (categories 4 and 5) which might be used alongside other methods as part of a broader ethnographic (studying peoples' lives through their first-hand accounts) approach or within the method of participant observation (see section 2 below).

Unstructured interviewing (often synonymous with in-depth interviewing) is usually far more time consuming per interviewee than formal style social survey interviewing. This is because the purpose is to acquire greater insight into the world of the interviewee. To assist in the process, it is important for rapport to be achieved between interviewer and interviewee. The interviewer allows the interviewee (or informant) far more input and scope in the answering of questions. Although the interviewer will be working within some degree of pre-specified areas of particular interest, the interview encounter will be far less formal and less obviously pre-structured than that experienced in a large scale social survey. Topic areas and general questions are likely to be formulated in advance of interviewing to assist research focus and achieve a limited degree of standardisation between the work of different interviewers, but these may be referred to by the interviewer more as a guide and not followed as a rigid sequential list. The interviewee may be offered significant scope in answering questions in ways that they see fit and even given some input into the order and direction of the interview.

In some cases, interviewing may appear to be so unstructured to the interviewee that it is experienced as if it were a spontaneous conversation. In fact, strictly speaking, this will rarely be the case as the 'conversation' is likely to be gently manipulated to the needs of the interviewer. If covert (undercover) research is being carried out, the interviewer is likely to have little other option than to disguise the interview within a conversational style. And unlike the social survey interview, which is likely to take place at an appointed time and place, through the conversational interview, the researcher may have to adapt their interviewing to the opportunities which arise spontaneously if it is part of a broader strategy of participant observation.

It is likely, furthermore, that interviewees may be interviewed numerous times at length as rapport is gradually built up and they are guided toward the interests of the research, whilst the interviewer becomes attuned toward the ideas that are emergent from the interviewees. This two way process of engagement between interviewer and interviewee is the basis for the development of what Strauss and Corbin (1998, pp.12-14) refer to as 'grounded theory'. Whilst early exchanges are likely to be of a highly conversational type, unstructured and even semi-structured interviews may follow as the interviewer is able to develop more refined questions.

A limited degree of structuring can also be enhanced through a 'structure layering technique' whereby at the start of an interview the interviewer summarises what he / she believes to be essential understandings from previous interviews. These understandings can be corrected if necessary by feedback from the interviewee and also provide a focus to build on in the forthcoming interview.

The interviewer in the unstructured interview situation will need to apply quite different qualities and skills to those of the survey interviewer. They will need to remain alert and open minded to the emergence of unexpected information and respond with appropriate questions, often off the cuff, as well as being able to retain an overview of the whole interview process whilst it is in progress to establish whether areas of importance to the research have been covered. Interviewers will need to decide on ways in which the interview may have to be shaped to bring the interviewee round to any areas which have been missed. And whilst remaining mindful of the theoretical issues and focal areas of the research, interviewers will need to translate these into everyday language to connect with the interviewee and elicit information from them at that level. Subtlety, sensitivity and flexibility are therefore key qualities required of the in-depth interviewer, qualities which can be enhanced through filmed role play interview training played back to the interviewer for analysis.

In contrast to the typical social survey interview, unstructured interviewing increases the potential for a rich flow of information, but also introduces the risk of the interview being too open and the interviewer developing a too close affinity with the interviewee. The interviewer can also be faced with certain dilemmas in recording information. Taking notes is likely to 1) interfere with the free flow of the interview and 2) lead to difficulty of keeping up with everything that is going on, with consequent loss of important detail. Making notes after the interview should overcome the first of these problems but would probably exacerbate the second due to selective memory recall and possible distortion. Using a recording device to capture the details may therefore be the preferred alternative. However, such devices are likely to be inhibiting for the interviewee who may take longer to feel relaxed, making a series of lengthy interviews necessary before much headway is possible. A methodological case can therefore be made for the covert recording of interviews, although this practice runs strongly counter to the ethical guidelines of the British Sociological Association regarding the acquisition of informed consent. Issues relating to the use of covert approaches will later be discussed under the broader method of participant observation.

Despite these dilemmas, research using a relatively unstructured approach to interviewing offers greater opportunity for the researcher to be open to the emergence of unexpected insights. Elizabeth Bott used in-depth interviewing of 20 London based married couples in her pioneering 1957 research into conjugal roles. Bott often made contact with couples through a person known to them. Field workers explained the general nature of the research and conducted between eight and nineteen interviews per couple. The interviews would usually begin with about 30 minutes of general talk before moving on to cover a broad range of pre-established topic areas, but in no particular order. Interviewers would raise topics to engage the couples in discussion, take notes in the process and if the couples wandered from the topic at hand, limited guidance to redirect them would be applied. Researchers also conducted observational studies of the families when the children were present at the weekends. Although the findings were of a qualitative nature and not amenable to statistical analysis, Bott discovered that the pattern of roles adopted by partners within the family related to the different types of friendship networks engaged in by the partners outside of the family.

A further advantage of unstructured interviewing is that it may be a more suitable way of engaging with groups who would shy away from the use of more formal methods that could be suggestive of officialdom, a classic example being Howard Becker's 1953 study of 50 subjects who used marihuana as a recreational drug (Becker, 1973). The sample comprised approximately 50% musicians and 50% from a broad range of other occupations. In probing into each interviewee's history of the drug use, Becker conducted most of the interviews himself and used the jargon of the users where he could. Although very little was said about the method used, it is clear from the detailed information provided that Becker used unstructured interviews to develop an understanding of the steps that users typically go through in their career of using the drug.

Another classic example of the use of unstructured interviewing is that of Ann Oakley's research into household task allocation and also the experiences of transition to motherhood. In the latter research, Oakley (1979) found that a collaborative approach resulted in a highly co-operative level of response from the interviewee. Four interviews of approximately two hours each, two before the birth and two after, were planned for each of the 66 women at the start of the interview process. Of these, 55 interviewees completed all four interviews and only one of the women who dropped out did so voluntarily (Oakley, cited in Lincoln and Denzin, 2003, p.255). The reasoning behind the method adopted by Oakley holds many similarities to that justified by interpretivists but with a particularly feminist twist which will be picked up on in a later section of this chapter.

Semi-structured interviewing is an approach which is more flexible than the pre-structured approach of survey interviewing. It is likely to employ a mixture of closed and open ended style questions. Although the interview will be steered by the interviewer in terms of a research framework established prior to the interview, some latitude will be available in the sequencing of the interview and the improvisation of more specific questions to follow up information which emerges in the course of the interview. Hence, the semi-structured interview attempts to combine some of the virtues of structured survey interviewing and unstructured in-depth interviewing by combining opportunities for qualitative insight with a degree of standardisation and comparability between interviews.

Although the boundaries between unstructured and semi-structured interviewing are not always easy to establish, the interviewing of the marriage and grammar school samples in Young and Willmott's 1955 research into family life in East London would seem to provide a good example of semi-structured interviewing. This sample was taken from their broader survey sample to add a qualitative dimension to their research. Such sampling from within samples is referred to as multi-stage sampling. In contrasting the interviewing approach in these smaller samples with that of the main survey, Young and Willmott state that

> 'the interviews with the marriage samples in both borough and housing estate and the grammar school sample......were relatively 'intensive'. They varied in length from one to three hours, and we called back for further interviews on a number of informants......We used a schedule of questions, but the interviews were much more informal and less standardised than those in the general survey. Answers had to be obtained to all the set questions listed (though not necessarily in the same order), but this did not exhaust the interview. Each couple being in some way different from every other, we endeavoured to find out as much as we could about the peculiarities of each couple's experiences and family relationships, using the set questions as leads and following up anything of interest which emerged in the answers to them as the basis for yet further questions. After each interview we wrote up, from our notes, a full interview report, including where possible people's verbatim remarks' (Young and Willmott, 1974, pp.206-207).

A particular form of unstructured interviewing is taken in the form of **oral histories**. In this case, the interviewee is recounting past events such as the experience of emigrating to and settling down in a new society or providing unofficial accounts of what life was like working within a particular institution. Such research provides a particularly valuable record of past events if a community is faced with a major change such as rehousing or the decline of an industry such as the coal mining industry. This method enables first-hand accounts of past experiences of people to be documented before getting lost along with the life of the interviewee. The method is of course highly subjective and in reality oral histories are usually prompted, contextualised and checked through the use of documents within the broader method of **life histories** which will be reviewed later under the heading of case studies.

The term **longitudinal research** has already been referred to within the context of social surveys. Since the key characteristic of this method is the tracing of change over long periods of time by periodically collecting more information from participants, the scale of the research does not necessarily have to be of social survey proportions. It may adopt a small scale and qualitative approach which uses a more open ended interviewing style. This was illustrated in '7 Up' – a television series commissioned in 1964. The study selected 21 seven year old children from a broad cross-section of social backgrounds but only focussed on 14 who filmed well. This process of selection, of course, would not be acceptable for sociological research purposes as those included were not likely to be a representative selection from the original 21. From the starting age of 7, returning at seven yearly intervals to re-interview those participants who were prepared to remain in the project, the series traced, through information provided from an open style of questioning, their experiences, outlooks and fortunes against the backdrop of their varied life chances in an attempt to document the long term effects of social class background on their lives.

An alternative approach to the on-going longitudinal method is found in retrospective longitudinal research which allows measurement to be taken at one point in time. The classic example of this is that of oral and life history methods mentioned elsewhere in this chapter where the longitudinal dimension comprises reflections on the past and the use of personal and public historical documents.

2. Primarily through observing behaviour

Methods which rely heavily on direct observation, of necessity tend to limit research to quite small scale dimensions. The classic sociological observational method is **participant observation**, a method which often incorporates the use of interviewing, either semi-structured or unstructured or that disguised as every day conversation. The purpose of participant observation is to capture the meanings of behaviour as it takes place rather than provide a mass of statistical data to study broader social patterns or processes. Participant observation therefore is a micro and interpretive type method which produces qualitative information that is rarely amenable to statistical analysis.

The method has been used in sociology in a variety of ways. One way of distinguishing different uses of the method has been with reference to a classificatory scale ranging from high involvement to complete detachment of the researcher from those being observed. Gold (cited in McCall & Simmons (ed.), 1969, pp.33-37) has constructed such a scale of researcher stances comprising the following: 1) complete participant, 2) participant as observer, 3) observer as participant and 4) complete observer. The extreme position of non-participant complete observer is, strictly speaking, not participant observation at all since the researcher has no involvement in the activities of those observed. This stance is one of the detached observer whose observations are likely to be unknown to the observed, and thus conducted 'covertly'. By contrast, the complete participant researcher would be so fully immersed in the activities of a group that he / she is able to pass themselves off as a group member. For Gold, this stance is also likely to require that the research is carried out covertly, as any knowledge by members of the group of the participant's true researcher role would be likely to invalidate the group's full acceptance and distort their behaviour. The more central positions on the scale involve research which is likely to be carried out overtly (with the knowledge of the group) and this tends to comprise the mainstream use of this method. Different issues arise for the researcher to confront dependent on the position adopted, but however used the essential feature of this method is that it attempts to study behaviour as it naturally takes place, and is hence referred to as 'naturalistic' approach.

Using participant observation raises a number of questions and difficulties. For example, if entry to a group is necessary, which it usually is, how does the researcher gain access? When access and entry are achieved, what type of stance or role can the researcher adopt? How is it possible to capture information which is constantly flowing, especially in hectic situations? And how can the researcher minimise the impact of their presence on the spontaneity of the behaviour observed? Such issues will be touched on throughout this section.

In sociology, participant observation has been particularly useful, and sometimes the only realistic approach available, to study life within social groups that engage in law breaking activities or are viewed as deviant by the majority in mainstream society. This method has thus been used to study, amongst other groups, street corner gangs (Whyte, 1955, Liebow, 1967), criminal gangs (Patrick, 1973), life on the wards of a mental hospital (Goffman, 1968), religious groups (Festinger, Riecken, and Schachter, 1956), the behaviour of prisoners (Kaminski, 2004) and fringe political organisations (Fielding, 1993). These groups would almost certainly be highly defensive against being studied by formal methods such as structured interviews which smack of officialdom. They may well refuse to co-operate, or if research is possible participants would be likely to be highly selective in what they are prepared to reveal. Furthermore, pre-structured surveys have proved to be of limited worth in providing detailed ethnographic (first hand study to understand cultural meaning) material and are of no use in attempting to understand behaviour as it takes place. Participant observation is a more naturalistic method in which the researcher usually blends in with the group and typically adopts a non-judgmental approach. Deviant groups may therefore be prepared to allow research of this type to be conducted if their anonymity and that of individual members is guaranteed. In this case, researchers can adopt an overt approach by revealing their research intentions to the group.

Before research can get under way, the difficult issue of gaining entry to the group has to be carefully considered. Groups may be more or less inviting to or suspicious of an outsider entering their midst to study them. On the matter of planning to enter a group, Schatzman and Strauss (1973, Ch.2) have provided important guidance. They suggest that careful preparatory research and hands of reconnaissance should be undertaken since there may be only one opportunity to make favourable contact. Reviewing similar research may give pointers to successful approaches, whilst low key preliminary reconnaissance (often adopting a total observation role) may reveal some of the routines of the group, key potential contacts and how the researcher might advantageously present themselves.

Initial contact with the group can sometimes be initiated by use of a trusted intermediary and the most advantageous entry point may be through a group leader or a prestigious group member. The priority of the initial contact would be to develop an amicable relationship and, with careful timing, float the idea of research to the contact person. Schatzman and Strauss point to the importance of providing a document which states in simple terms a request for research to be conducted and spells out the aims of the research, the fact that the researcher is a learner and will not be there to pass judgement, that anonymity will be guaranteed, and that the group will eventually be provided with feedback from the research. The intention would be for this document to be used by the contact person in discussion with group members to enable the research to be undertaken. However, even on gaining successful entry, researchers would need to recognise that this may be at the sufferance of the group and could be terminated at any point, making the research at times an exercise in treading on egg shells.

It must be recognised that given the nature of the target groups, gaining access to conduct research overtly may not always be possible. Where this is the case, an alternative strategy available is to infiltrate the group to be researched covertly. The British Sociological Association's ethical guidelines caution against such an approach which breaches the normal requirement of obtaining the informed consent of the subjects of research. Ultimately, the ethical decision lies with the researcher.

Planning for successful covert entry to a group will also need to be a painstaking task for the sociologist. This is because the very reason why covert research is necessary is likely to be due to the fact that the group may be engaging in activities that make them suspicious of infiltration by certain outsiders such as the police or journalists. A good example of the care that may be necessary to enter such groups is provided by the journalist Donal MacIntyre (1999), whose aim was to enter the world of the Chelsea Headhunters, a group of violent football hooligans.

For MacIntyre, preliminary archive research was necessary. Police files were studied to obtain the names and pictures of those who were to be 'befriended'. Research of newspaper articles provided names and information relating to past cases of violence implicating members of the group. The history of Chelsea Football Club also had to be carefully studied. Preliminary observations were undertaken. A general background on football hooligans was acquired through observations on the margins of their activities in bars and on the streets during the World Cup in France. And to be accepted into the group, conveying the right appearance was necessary. MacIntyre needed to learn how to smoke convincingly and had to acquire a Chelsea tattoo. Although he knew the locality of one of his key targets, MacIntyre had to hang around the streets to find out where he lived. He was able to move into the same block of flats and watch out for his target's routine. Designer clothes were worn, an expensive car was hired out for show and every effort was made to be seen about. Eventually, first contact was made at a fast food outlet.

Attempts to track down another member of the group took MacIntyre to Reading where he scanned local newspapers for background information on cases involving his target. This identified certain Reading pubs which were trawled but without success. However, a young accomplice who knew the target was befriended and further important information was obtained.

Through such careful preparation, MacIntyre was able to enter the group, became accepted, and was able to record by using a covert camera, the stories and activities of the participants. In such cases, the continuation of the research and the very safety of the researcher will require great vigilance in acting the required role to avoid one's cover being blown.

A further example of journalistic use of covert participant observation is provided by Jason Gwynne who gained access to British National Party meetings through a disillusioned Party member. His covert recording of speeches and conversations by leading figures in the British National Party provided both material for a television programme 'The Secret Agent' and evidence that was used as prosecution material.

Although covert participant observation may be used in virtually identical fashion by journalists and sociologists, it is important to distinguish between the aims. When journalists use this approach to attempt to uncover the actions and identities of those engaging in deviant or illegal acts, it is less likely to be guided by the quest to enhance sociological understanding and more for the purpose of raising moral questions, bringing about a public response or even the punishment of identified culprits. By contrast, when sociologists engage in covert participant observation, their aim is to provide information to test and develop theories which will advance sociological understanding of behaviour. The value judgements of the researcher need to be avoided or held in check and the anonymity of subjects guaranteed.

Covert sociological research can sometimes by carried out under cover of an officially designated role. Thus, research by Goffman (1968) into life on the wards of a psychiatric hospital, that was covert to the patients and most of the staff, was undertaken, with the agreement of the hospital authorities, under the guise of Goffman working in the official role of an Assistant Athletics Director.

Jacobs (1969) conducted covert participant observation under the cover of a case worker in a social welfare agency. His findings, in common with those of Goffman, reveal an important advantage of the method used. Through penetrating the veneer of conformity which inmates and workers respectively convey when they suspect that they are under the scrutiny of officialdom, the studies revealed to the covert observer the unofficial practices which take place within such formal organisations; practices which would have been unlikely to have been revealed by using more conventional methods such as social surveys.

Whether conducted overtly or covertly, the aim of participant observation is to accurately portray the lives of people and understand the meanings of their actions. Whether more fully participatory or detached observational stances are adopted may depend on the situations involved, the topic at hand and the subjects in question. A relatively detached observational role may be possible if the study is of people in public places such as libraries or railway stations. Indeed, within libraries, given the nature of the environment, the research could be conducted in a highly covert way. From such a stance, there is very little risk of the research becoming biased through one's subjective involvement. However, the problem with the highly observational role comes with the attempt to understand behaviour at a distance. Here, the problem of 'verstehen' arises – how can we be sure that the meanings that we attribute to the observed behaviour correspond to those in the minds of the participants since we are not able to engage with them to check?

To combat this problem, most researchers will prefer to adopt a more participatory stance. Those who advocate a highly participatory approach argue that via a high level of immersion in the group, empathy with the participants can be maximised and insights into their lives generated, often through the personal experiences of the researcher as a group member, which may not be accessible by other methods. But if the research is being undertaken covertly, it may necessary for the researcher to offer proof of their worthiness to be a group member through engaging in an initiation process and it will be virtually impossible to avoid taking a fully participatory role in a range of activities when participation is the expected behaviour of all group members. These issues will need to be carefully weighed up as much as possible in advance and the researcher will need to think carefully about where to draw the line on the type of behaviour he / she is prepared to be involved in. If situations arise where non-involvement is decided upon, great care must be taken to justify non-participation without arousing suspicion amongst group members and risk having one's 'cover blown', especially given the dangers that this could pose to the safety of the researcher. In this context, Howard Parker (1974) felt it necessary to engage in criminal activities to retain his cover in the covert study of a juvenile gang. By contrast, William Whyte (1955), who conducted overt participant observation of a street corner gang, was able to justify his non-participation in acts of violence.

A different type of risk from high participation is a methodological one. It is the negative side of the high level of subjective involvement invested by the researcher; he / she may become so close to the lives of the subjects of the research that a healthy degree of clinical detachment is lost and the research becomes value biased and distorted by the researcher's close identification with his / her subjects of study. When complete absorption into the group compromises researcher objectivity, this phenomena is referred to as 'going native' – a term which indicates the early origins of participant observation in the field work of anthropologists.

Cases where a highly participatory role is necessary may therefore require periodic extraction of the researcher from the group to 'cool off' and review information and experiences at a more objective distance. Ideally, it would seem that the judicious balance would be a form of participation in which the researcher is able to at times manoeuvre closer to the subjects to enhance insight and on other occasions stand back to ensure that a healthy degree of detachment is achieved to protect the objectivity of the research.

However employed, participant observation is not usually as tightly a pre-structured method and research strategy as are more positivist approaches such as the social survey or the shortly to be reviewed experimental laboratory approach. By contrast, the researcher could well start in the field with quite a loose focus on the research. Open minded as to what he or she might find, the early stages of the research are likely to be exploratory with the researcher acutely preoccupied in watching and listening. Part of the early tuning in process could involve overcoming a degree of culture shock if the culture of the group is substantially different from that with which the participant observer is familiar. Only over a period of time, as the researcher becomes sensitised to the life of the group, may relevant questions and categories of analysis become formulated. These will enable more focussed observation to take place. By this process, participant observation offers much more opportunity for the researcher to obtain a grounding in the reality of the group (providing grounded research) than if a rigid but alien framework of researcher pre-defined categories and structured analysis were imposed from the start. The fundamental aim of participant observation is to develop a sociological understanding and exposition of behaviour which the group members would themselves recognise as valid.

The participant observer is likely to need to use some form of interviewing as part of their method. During the early stages of the research, interviewing may be of a conversational or unstructured style to help the researcher to make sense of situations. However, in time, to test the validity of the researcher's understanding or acquire more precise and detailed information on areas of particular interest, a more focussed and semi-structured approach is likely to be more appropriate and possible if the research is being conducted overtly. The style of interviewing, nevertheless, is usually relatively informal and the form that the questions take is only likely to have emerged within the research process. For example, during his overt research into the activities of a street corner gang, William Whyte (1955), developed questions based on his observations and would interview members of the gang to help clarify his own understanding of their behaviour.

By contrast, when covert participant observation is used, such focussed questioning would be virtually impossible since it would be unnatural and reveal to the group the presence of a covert researcher whose cover would be blown. Anything approaching interviewing would need to be conducted in a carefully disguised and highly conversational style. This necessity is explained effectively by Riecken (1956, cited in McCall and Simmons (ed.), 1969, pp.39-42) in an article entitled 'The Unidentified Interviewer'. Riecken, Festinger and Schachter covertly infiltrated a small religious group who assembled at the house of a prophet of doom by presenting themselves as ordinary enquirers. To reduce the influence of their presence on the behaviour of others, they adopted a relatively low key role of 'sympathetic listeners' who were keen to learn. In fact, disguised in a casual and conversational style, they were covertly interviewing members of the group.

In summary, box 2 highlights some of the relative advantages and disadvantages involved in comparing overt and covert approaches in the use of participant observation.

Box 2: Participant Observation			
Overt Conducting research on and recording information openly to all participants.		**Covert** Researcher role in hidden to participants and information about their behaviour is recorded without their knowledge.	
Advantages	**Disadvantages**	**Advantages**	**Disadvantages**
1 No ethical dilemma	Takes a long time for participants to feel more comfortable in presence of observer	Careful preparation enables gaining of participants' trust	Ethical dilemma – professional and personal
2 Can avoid involvement in 'dubious activities'	Observer presence restricts spontaneity – 'Hawthorne effect'	Less distorting effect of observer presence, but must select role carefully	Difficult to avoid involvement in 'dubious activities' – how and where to draw the line

3	No risk of cover being blown as no cover required	Researcher entry may be prohibited by some groups	May be only method of entry to some groups	Risk of cover being blown
4	Less chance of 'going native'	More distance between observer and world of observed	Gets closer to seeing world through eyes of participants through similar experiences	More chance of 'going native
5	Can interview to find out specific information without arousing suspicion	Imposes a degree of structure on research	Less structured	'Interviewing' must be disguised as natural conversation
6	Can record information openly	Open recording of information further restricts spontaneity	Can follow more spontaneous flow	Difficulty of covert recording – time, place, equipment

The main criticism of participant observation is likely to be that of its questionable reliability. The question of reliability could be put as follows: could other researchers precisely reproduce the research and have confidence that the method provides a sound basis for comparison of findings, uncontaminated by the vagaries of the method or the actions and interpretations of the researchers? How can studies be replicated and meaningful comparisons between them made when: 1) different sociologists may select different features from their observations which are important specifically to them or 2) differ in terms of their memory recall of events and 3) another researcher may have elicited different behaviour from the same group or interpreted the same behaviour differently?

These weaknesses in reliability tend to be inherent in the subjective nature of participant observation, but supporters of the method argue that they are a worthwhile trade off to achieve a close and valid representation of the world as experienced and understood by individuals and communities. Moreover, these criticisms can be answered to a limited extent in the following ways. Firstly, a number of observers of a group may be employed, as in the above mentioned research conducted by Riecken et al. Their findings can be compared to help produce a balanced and comprehensive overview of events. In the case of a mixed sex group, it may be particularly valuable to include both male and female researchers where possible as a female observer may pick up on the meaning of a female's actions in a way that may be overlooked by a male observer, and vice versa. Secondly, observers can be prepared so as to work within a common framework through using standardised observation manuals. Thirdly, as the focus of the research develops, it may be possible to use 'structured protocol sheets', which concretely define those activities and situational features to be documented in every case (Flick, 2011, p.227). Fourthly, detailed exposition of the processes involved in the research should be documented in the writeup to allow other researchers to evaluate and follow or modify them in their own research.

To uncover a detailed and accurate picture of life as it is, participant observation is a very time consuming method. Research employing this method is often of longitudinal duration, but is not usually recognised as longitudinal because involvement of the researcher with the group is a relatively continuous process rather than periodic. But when conducted alongside the utilisation of personal and public documents, in-depth interviewing and oral and life history methods, participant observation becomes part of a broader approach referred to as ethnographic (documenting life experiences) research, an approach which was pioneered by early twentieth century anthropologists who found it necessary to live with primitive groups to attune themselves to an understanding of their culture, rituals, beliefs and ways of life. The approach was then extensively applied in sociology in the community studies of the American Chicago School from the 1920s.

Research conducted by Roseneil sheds further light on the versatility of participant observation and ethnographic research. Her research was into life at the Greenham Common peace camp during the early 1980s. What is unusual about this research, and perhaps contentious, is that Roseneil only decided to conduct her research years after her involvement in the peace camp. In other words, information that she gained as a layperson participant, she later reviewed as a researcher. Backed up by open-ended interviewing of other participants at this later time and the retention of various personal and public documents from the past, Roseneil refers to her approach as 'retrospective auto-ethnography' (Devine & Heath, 1999, pp.180-187).

The **focus group** method can be viewed as a from of social survey. However, it is included in this section because it invariably applies a higher observational element than is the case with standard interviewing techniques. This method brings together small groups of participants who respond to issues within a framework clearly set by the researcher. In comparison to group interviewing, in which the aim is to obtain information from individuals within group settings (for example, in Willis's (1977) interviewing of lads), in the focus group, the focus is usually provided by the exposure of all members to a standardised form of communication, such as a film clip. The approach has been frequently used by political parties with the aim of obtaining a more in-depth understanding of the responses to political messages within social settings, studying how messages are picked up and attitudes influenced. Thus, whilst groups might be brought together to answer questions, the aim of the researcher is usually more to observe and record group dynamics and the issues that emerge in a reflective situation of group communication, information which would be absent in most standard forms of survey interviewing. So whilst, for example, attitudes toward immigration may be measured through a social survey, a focus group may prove to be a superior method to study communication and group dynamics behind such attitude formation. Of course, generalisation to the dynamics of natural everyday settings may be hazardous given the artificiality of the focus group setting.

A quite different approach to observation than that of participant observation is used in the **experimental laboratory** method (although in some applications the observational element is limited or even non-existent). In its most rigorous form, this approach, more often used by psychologists but in areas of topic interest to sociologists, claims scientific credentials through the setting up of a social equivalent to controlled scientific laboratory conditions. The method is therefore strongly positivistic.

The logic of the scientific laboratory can be summed up simply as follows. Controlled conditions are created whereby a cause, referred to as an independent variable (for example the application of heat) can be introduced and its effects measured on the dependent variable (for example, the application of a measured amount of heat to an iron bar and the measured effect of its expansion). Following the hypothesis (theorised prediction) that iron expands by a certain amount when heated to a certain degree, the above test situation can be designed whereby the dependent variable (the iron bar) is measured before and after the application of the independent variable (heat). The difference in the measurements is deduced to be the effect of the application of heat onto the iron bar and provided evidence by which the hypothesis can be tested.

There are various ways in which controlled measurements have been devised to attempt to follow a similar logic when applied in social settings. As a simple example, if one wanted to measure the amount of learning that had taken place by students attending classes on an elementary mathematics course, the following experiment could be set up. A test paper could be given before the course to measure the knowledge that each of the class members started out with. A test paper could then be set at the end of the course in which each of the questions on the first test paper could be matched with different questions measuring the same areas of mathematical performance and with equal degrees of difficulty. The difference between the two scores would measure the amount of learning (the dependant variable) that had taken place in between by each individual and for the group as a whole as a direct result attending classes (the independent variable).

Or would it? There are at least two problems here. Firstly, however unlikely it may be, it cannot be logically ruled out by this experiment alone that mathematical ability may not have naturally improved over the course of this time period. To allow for or eliminate this possibility, a comparison would need to be made with the measured performance of a matched group who did not attend classes at the same time intervals. Secondly, since people do not live their entire lives in laboratories (in this case the classroom) we cannot be sure that some students will not have benefited from receiving access to external tuition rather than or as well as classroom teaching.

The reader is now referred back to the example in the previous section and the comment that the panel survey is 'a type of incomplete experimental laboratory approach'. The problem with the pre-test, intervention and post-test design in the social sciences is that it cannot necessarily be deduced that the independent variable is the single cause of the differences measured at the two points. As de Vaus points out (1999, p.38) in the example of a measured decline in religious beliefs amongst students after studying at university compared to when starting, unless measurements are made at the same time interval for a matched sample not attending university and a decline in religious belief is not found, we cannot have confidence that the experience of university life alone is the cause of such a decline in belief amongst students.

To apply the logic of the experimental laboratory in the social sciences in its simplest form therefore usually requires the use of two groups. Prior to the experiment run, the composition of these two groups is matched as closely as possible regarding the size of the groups and their internal makeup in terms of gender distribution, age range, ethnic composition and social class spread etc. The purpose of matching the groups is to make the experiment as watertight as possible. It is an attempt to isolate the effect of the independent variable by screening out the effects that any of these other characteristics may have on the outcome of the research if the groups were not matched. The separate environment that each of the groups is placed in is also closely controlled and matched. Just one factor (the independent variable), the influence of which is to be measured, is then introduced into the environment of one of the groups. This group is referred to as the experiment group. The other group, the control group, is not exposed to this influence. Before, sometimes during, and after the experiment, the behaviour, attitudes or knowledge etc. of members of the two groups is measured. Any measurable differences which are detected between the groups are deduced to be attributable to the influence of the independent variable that was introduced into the experiment group but not into the matched control group. By such means, the precise influence of a number of individual factors can be measured by introducing new independent variables each time.

In one example of such a tightly controlled artificial laboratory experiment, Eysenck and Nias (1978) demonstrated that, compared to control groups that weren't exposed to television violence, experiment groups that were showed signs of aggression. From these findings, the researchers deduced that similar effects may be taking place when people viewed television violence in the broader setting of their everyday lives – a dubious conclusion but one that could provide fuel for groups in favour of the censorship of sexual and violent content in the media.

Although experimental laboratory research should be easily replicable and the findings of replicated studies directly comparable, the artificiality of the situation invariably means that the research is conducted overtly and participants' knowledge of their own participation in the research is likely to affect their behaviour in ways that it is difficult to know about or allow for. They may look for clues as to what they think that the researchers deem to be preferred or acceptable behaviour – a phenomena referred to as 'demand characteristics'. This artificiality also usually limits the potential for generalisation of the findings – it is questionable how far they can be applied to natural settings where there is no similar consciousness of being observed, however carefully the laboratory research is conducted. Furthermore, under experimental laboratory conditions the time span over which influences are assessed is often limited to a stimulus and response framework which may reveal little about the effect of exposure to long term influences in the natural setting. The information obtained from such studies also sometimes takes the form of quantified physiological data (for example a monitored change in heart rate, or level of perspiration) which gives the appearance of science. However, it is difficult to translate this data unambiguously into the meaning behind it. Heightened rates in an experiment group who were exposed to images of violence could denote feelings of aggression but could alternatively relate to excitement.

The degree of artificiality involved in laboratory experiments can introduce other uncertainties regarding the effect which knowledge of being observed can have on the behaviour of the participants. This contaminant is referred to as the 'Hawthorne effect', the name origin of which will shortly be explained. Some laboratory research attempts to get around this problem by use of unobtrusive observation. For example, attempts have been made to measure the impact of exposure to violence in the mass media under controlled laboratory conditions with the researchers observing behaviour through two-way mirrors.

In a more complicated version of the experimental laboratory approach, the psychologist A. Bandura, (1965), studied levels of imitative aggression acted out by children who had been exposed to film of adult aggression toward a bobo doll. The control group were just shown this film, whereas one experiment group was also shown the adult being rewarded for the aggression and another group shown the adult being punished for it. Afterwards, the behaviour of each child toward toys including a bobo doll was observed and levels of aggressive behaviour recorded.

An alternative approach to the experimental laboratory has been to introduce controlled intervention into more natural settings. This variation is referred to as the **field experiment.** The logic of this approach remains the same but the intention is to overcome the criticism of lack of generalizability from the laboratory to natural settings. For example, the classroom may provide an example of a natural field setting. We previously introduced the idea of pre-testing and post-testing a single group of students to measure the amount of learning that had taken place on a course. Let us suppose that this course had been delivered by traditional lecturing methods and one wanted to measure the comparative effectiveness to learning of a student centred approach which involved more student participation. As suggested before, pre-testing and post-testing by matching the test questions could be used to measure learning. Students would need to be allocated to classes in such a way that matched control and experiment groups could be set up. The lecturing method would be continued with control group but, following the same syllabus, more participatory teaching methods would be used in the experiment group. The comparative effectiveness of the two teaching approaches to the learning outcomes could be measured by the pre-testing and post-testing performance differences, and if researchers were present explanations could be supplemented by observational material.

There would of course be weaknesses in and limitations to the use of such a method. One weakness would be that although one is attempting to isolate the comparative effectiveness in promoting measurable learning by changing one variable in the experiment group – introducing a different teaching method - one cannot exclude the possible contaminating effect of different teacher personalities on the outcome of the experiment. And given the emphasis that is placed on numerical measurement in the use of this method, it may be easier to quantify progress in a subject such as mathematics than in a more discursive subject like English literature.

A pioneering piece of research which adopted the field method was conducted in the USA at the Hawthorne plant of the Western Electrical Company between 1924 to the early 1930s. The study attempted to measure the impact of changes in the work environment on the output levels of production line workers. By using an experiment and a control group, efficiency experts started by comparing the effect on the productivity of the experiment group of improving the level of illumination in their environment whilst leaving that of the control group as it was. Elton Mayo was then brought in to test the effect on productivity of other changes imposed on the experiment group such as changes to heating and humidity levels, changing the rest periods, the introduction of company lunches and shorter working weeks, etc.

It should be noted that only the effects of one independent variable at a time can be measured. Thus, if testing the effect of introducing a shorter working week on productivity level were to follow the testing of different illumination levels, the illumination level of the experiment group would first need to be returned to the same as that of the control group to ensure that what was being measured in its effect on productivity levels was the shorter working week alone. This procedure would be followed with the testing of each single successive independent variable.

Surprisingly for the researchers, during the research the productivity levels of workers in both control and experiment groups increased. Indeed, even when changes were introduced into the environment of the experiment group which were anticipated to reduce productivity levels, such as a reduction of illumination to just the equivalent of full moonlight, output increased! The researchers realised that by knowing that they were being studied, the workers' behaviour was being affected by their desire to please the researchers, as well as their improved sense of self-worth as a result of their regular consultation. This phenomenon confounded the original aims of the research since the independent variable of overriding effect on productivity levels was the workers' awareness of their involvement in the research itself. It made the measurement of the variables that the researchers were attempting to isolate impossible. The effect of such awareness by participants on their behaviour has subsequently become referred to as the Hawthorne effect.

To more fully utilise the benefits of the field experiment, some researchers have hidden or misrepresented the nature of their research to participants. For example, D. J. Smith (1977) set up a field experiment to measure the extent of racial discrimination in the labour market. Actors of different ethnic backgrounds but with otherwise matched CVs were used to apply for jobs; ethnicity was isolated as an independent variable whose effects on potential employers' decisions were to be measured. Measurements were taken of the written responses by employers and where interviews were obtained covert recording took place. Clear evidence emerged that employers were discriminating against ethnic minority applicants.

Overall, there tends to be a trade off between the different uses of experimentation in the social sciences. Using the experimental laboratory method, the investigator is able to apply tight but artificial controls. Although logically the effects of variables can be isolated and precisely measured, there are likely to be major doubts about the effect of the artificial environment on participants' behaviour and thus the validity of the findings, as well as the possibility for their generalisation to natural settings; the external validity of the findings is questionable. By contrast, in attempting to overcome these difficulties and enhance the validity of the findings, the more naturalistic the field experiment becomes, the more difficult it may be to impose tight experimental controls and the reliability of the research becomes more questionable.

A different approach to experiments is unique to ethnomethodologists and is referred to as **breaching experiments.** The theory behind this research method has been touched on in the chapter on sociological perspectives and will be explained in more detail in a further section of this chapter. Essentially, the purpose of breaching experiments is to illustrate that everyday life is dependent on shared understandings between participants in situations which are so routine that participants lose awareness of this structured understanding upon which ordered interaction takes place. Breaching experiments are set up to break rules and cause disorder. By doing so, the nature of the taken for granted rules and understanding becomes highlighted and attempts by participants to reconstruct meaning can be observed. In one such experiment, Harold Garfinkle (1984, pp.47-49) prepared some students to act like paying lodgers for a short period of time on their return home at vacation and to record the responses they received. The aim of the research was to lay bare the taken for granted rules concerning appropriate interaction between family members and to document the way in which attempts were made by puzzled members of the family to re-establish a sense of meaning and order into the situation.

3. Primarily through utilising documents

Various types of document are available to sociologists, usually but not exclusively in the form of secondary research material – material which already exists independently of the research and will not have been originally compiled according to the needs of the researcher. A distinction can be made between sources in the form of personal 'life documents' and **official documents** which emanate from a variety of private and public organisations. Official documents may be held in archives to which there will be a greater or lesser degree of public accessibility, as can be seen in comparing newspaper articles and medical records respectively.

Official documents have been extensively used in pioneering sociological research. For example, Frederick Engels, in his study of working class life in England in 1844 entitled 'The Condition of the Working Class in England', relied heavily on the reports of Royal Commissions and newspaper reports.

When, in the mid nineteenth century, Tocqueville studied the origins of the French Revolution of 1789, he relied quite heavily on gaining access, through having been a member of the French Chamber of Deputies, to official government archives. Although overstating his case, Tocqueville maintained that:

> 'in a country where a strong central administration has gained control of all the national archives there are few trends of thought, desires or grievances, few interests or propensities that do not sooner or later make themselves known to it, and in studying its records we can get a good idea not only of the way in which it functioned but of the mental climate of the country as a whole' (Tocqueville, 1966, pp. 24-25).

Research into social history may be reliant on accessing dated historical records. In this case, parish and census records may be useful. For example, Peter Laslett (1972) utilised information gleaned from parish records in his study of family life before the Industrial Revolution.

Official documentation is stored by a broad range of public and private organisations, but access is usually denied to information held in the form of personal details and that which is deemed to relate to national security. Where information is accessible, the advantages of cheapness and immediacy of access may be available, especially through use of the internet. However, the introduction of computer technology has also meant that documents can be lost through being overwritten when updated.

Sociologists are usually cautious in their use of official documents. They will need to consider which organisation produced the documentation, how it produced it and what the purposes behind its production were. Such sources are often the product of a process of sanitization from the point of view of practitioners and organisations, for example to cover up mistakes that have been made in a professional capacity, to put a particular political slant on events or to present information to generate a favourable public image and maximise sales and income. Official minutes of meetings will not contain off the record comments, the availability of which may have been very revealing. There may also be a substantial difference between official records and action, as for example in comparing course syllabuses and lesson plans with what transpires in classrooms. In this case, a more valid approach would be to supplement the study of official records with observation.

Life documents relate to people's lives in a more personal and intimate way than official sources usually do. These documents may include personal diaries, letters, e mails, photographs, videos, and even autobiographies. As such, they will tend to supply detailed qualitative information and lend themselves to small-scale in-depth research or case studies (see later in this section). These documents, along with oral histories, may form part of a broader life history approach in which family photograph albums as well as household objects may be referred to during in-depth interviews to spur the recollections of the interviewee. Plummer (cited in Seale (ed.) 2004 pp. 282-290) even refers to a search through the attic as a potential source of rich documentary and interview material. In historical research, documents may also be the only source of information available if the person concerned and their friends and relatives are no longer alive.

Some life documents in particular need to be reviewed with a degree of caution. A key factor here is whether the information was originally recorded on a strictly private basis, as in most personal diaries, or written with an audience in mind, as in the case of letters. In the latter form of document, the writer may well have chosen to put a particular angle on events to influence the recipient. The researcher may therefore be keen to investigate the understanding of the communication by the recipient and their response. Moreover, the letters and diaries of public figures may have originally been carefully written with the expectation of future publication to a broader audience in mind. Autobiographies that select and sanitise this information therefore introduce at least two levels of distortion into the material and may consequently be of doubtful validity. And it may not just be the small scale of the research and the availability and selection of documents through which we may question the representativeness of these materials, but also the fact that they disproportionately focus on the lives of the more powerful, literate or articulate.

In an electronic age, records of e mails sent and received and activity on social media are likely to be replacing letters as a source of more ephemeral personal document.

Not all research that uses life documents is dependent on documents that already exist. A form of primary research documentation is used to provide sociologists with **time budgeting** material. This method requires the participants to keep a detailed diary of activities or events for use as research material. A good example of the time budgeting method was employed in Young and Willmott's (1973) study of family life where participants were asked to keep a detailed record of the domestic activities and tasks that they engaged in. A further example of the application of this method is provided within research conducted by Oscar Lewis (Seale, 2004, p.283) into the lives of a small number of Mexican families. Compared to personal diaries, the key difference in this type of material is that to some extent its collection is structured by the requirements of the researcher and the way that the informant behaves and records the information may be influenced through their consciousness of its future use.

Often applied to the study mass media output, broadly speaking a **content analysis** approach studies the use of words and phrases in a communication by applying a classificatory system to group those that come within a similar meaning range into appropriate categories. This method therefore largely lends itself to a form of quantitative analysis of a document or communication. In its simplest form, the analysis of a message may be based on a count of words or phrases deemed to be of key significance or the incidence of coverage of particular news items. Political parties may also scrutinise the output of television channels. In the case of the BBC, content analysis may be used to check that they have fulfilled their statutory requirements of engaging in overall balanced and objective political coverage.

Within social surveys, sociologists will either formally or informally apply content analysis to categorise the answers provided by respondents to open ended questions into a limited number of types for post coding. This structuring of responses assists quantitative analysis. The method has also been applied to the study of personal documents for the purpose of gaining insight into a person's frame of mind or their attempt to influence others.

The effectiveness of content analysis is dependent on a number of factors. One is that the coding system applied needs to be reliable. This would mean that a number of coders of some particular material should make the same classificatory decisions. Another relates to the coder. A person coding scripts may over time through growing familiarity with the system gradually change the way that they classify content. To avoid such changes or variation between coders, computers can be used. However, computers will not have the human capacity to extract the precise contextual meaning of words with multiple meanings.

A more subtle approach to content analysis might look at the positioning of articles and / or pictures in relation to each other and attempt to decode underlying messages and identify intended reader manipulation. Such analysis might reveal, for example, the intentions behind newspaper articles on unemployment and immigration that are placed in close proximity, leaving the reader to make the desired connection - an insight that is unlikely to develop through simple content analysis. This approach borders into **semiotics** (the study of signs and codes) which analyses communication with the purpose of revealing underlying or hidden meaning. For example, semiotics has been used to reveal techniques involving the transference of symbolic meaning into products in advertising by connecting them with an appropriate image of a well-known celebrity which draws in the potential purchaser through connecting the purchase of the product to their aspirational lifestyle (Leiss, et al, cited in Seale (ed.), 2004, pp.341-344).

Semiotics was applied in a broad range of research conducted by the Glasgow Media Group, including television coverage of strikes in the 1970s and more recent research into the Arab and Israeli conflict. In the former case, although equal coverage may have been given to both sides in disputes, it was argued that the symbolic context of interviews - smartly dressed management in offices, perhaps stocked with authoritative texts, compared to workers standing near a burning brazier on a picket line – was likely to convey a message of legitimate authority and worthiness of respect toward management from many viewers. It is therefore clear that semiotics moves the analysis of communication in a more qualitative direction.

A method which ranks amongst the largest in scale and grandest in sociology is that of **comparative and historical research.** It utilises information from historical events and therefore relies heavily on various sources of historical documentation. The method adopts a form of experimentation, but unlike the field experiment social causes are not revealed through the manipulation of the situation. Instead, the deduction of causes is made by process of controlled comparisons. Through making systematic comparisons between societies or social groups within societies, this method aims to tease out key causal influences on social change by identifying factors that are prominent in some societies or groups and not in others.

For example, sociologists who are interested in explaining the different educational performance levels of different ethnic minority groups might engage in a comparative study of social, economic and cultural differences between the ethnic groups as well as treatment of different ethnic minorities within educational establishments. By painstaking comparisons, it may be possible to tease out the impact of specific influences on the varied performance of different ethnic minority groups.

The comparative and historical method was comprehensively adopted by the founding theorists in sociology. For example, Durkheim used this method very effectively in his 1897 study of the social causes of suicide (Durkheim, 1970) by applying painstaking comparative analysis of official statistics on suicide rates between and within European societies going back many decades.

Max Weber, during 1904 – 1905 (Weber, 1978), also applied the comparative and historical method to reveal key influences contributing toward England being the first country to experience the transition to modern capitalism. Clearly, a study of English modernisation alone would have been insufficient to identify influences which were present there and assisted the process but were relatively absent in countries that made the transition to capitalism later. Only careful historical comparison would bring these influences into clear relief.

In a more recent piece of research, T. Skocpol (1979) engaged in a comparative analysis of the French, Russian and Chinese Revolutions in an attempt to develop a general theory of the origins of revolutions. This makes an interesting comparison with Tocqueville's research. However insightful, the latter was only based on the study of events leading up to the French Revolution. It was effectively a large-scale case study (see below) and therefore, as it stood, Tocqueville's theory could only legitimately be applied to the French case. By engaging in comparative analysis, Skocpol could claim greater universality for her theory than Tocqueville.

A further example of the application of the comparative and historical method is evident in the research of Barrington Moore (1969). Moore compared the role of the peasantry and the upper landed orders across a number of societies to explain the circumstances through which agrarian societies modernised either into representative democracies or fascist or communist dictatorships.

The application of the comparative and historical method has been used during times when nations were viewed as relatively enclosed societies. One may speculate that the extent to which processes of globalisation are cutting across national boundaries may at least complicate the way in which this method can now be used.

As noted above, a key source of information in Durkheim's study 'Suicide' was **official statistics.** In Britain, statistical information is accessible from a variety of official bodies, such as the Office For National Statistics. It is readily available to the public in such publications as Social Trends and can be used by sociologists for statistical analysis of social phenomena. Official statistics are available on a broad range of phenomena including health, crime rates, strike activity, the distribution of wealth and income, student examination performance, church attendance rates, unemployment levels, births, deaths, marriages, and divorce rates. This information will have originally been compiled through a variety of methods. Some organisations must record certain information. For example, schools are obliged to provide information on the educational attainment of their pupils so that league tables can be compiled to show the relative performance of different institutions and assist parents and children in their choice of schools. All births, deaths and marriages have to be officially registered. Government surveys, in particular the national census which it is a legal requirement to complete, provide detailed demographic information.

Although convenient to use by sociologists as this type of information has already been gathered by others and is cheap and easily accessible, it nevertheless has well recognised limits. Reliability may be an issue. Sociologists would be vigilant to detect whether there have been changes over time in the categories used to compile the statistics. If this is found to be so, questions of comparability in the data arise, as in the case of unemployment figures and crime statistics. Sociologists using these figures will have to somehow factor in these changes and adjust the data to be able realistically study trends over time.

The validity of official statistics may also be questioned; do they really measure what they claim to measure? On this dimension, the validity of government unemployment statistics as a measure of all people who are not employed or are underemployed and seeking work is open to doubt since it is based on eligibility to claim benefit to which some who are seeking work may not qualify, whilst some who claim may not be actively seeking work.

There may be powerful influences on the organisation providing the information, such as performance targets, sometimes related to funding, which distort the statistics provided. Educational institutions and the police service are organisations which have each found ways to work the system in the statistics that they provide. In the latter case, in the interests of improving clear up rates, police forces have commonly adopted the process of not vigorously pursuing certain reported crimes and subsequently reclassifying them as 'no crime' in those cases such as alleged rape and domestic violence where there is a high incidence of victims later withdrawing charges.

It is also well known by comparing official statistics to information gained from surveys that statistics in many areas underestimate the extent of the phenomena measured. This uncertain degree of underestimation is referred to as a 'dark figure', in which the official statistics are likened to that part of an iceberg which is visible above the surface of the water and the dark figure that which is submerged. Since the extent of the dark figure is uncertain, there may be doubt as to whether an increase or decrease in measurements through official statistics represents a real change in the incidence of the phenomena or, by analogy, the visible proportion of the iceberg increasing or decreasing. For example, a 177% increase in the recorded incidents of rape in England and Wales between 1980 and 1990 would need to be interpreted against the backdrop of Home Office recommendations to police forces in 1986 to restrict their 'no crime' practice and a likely increased willingness of victims to come forward given a more victim centred approach by the police (Edwards, cited in Stephens & Becker (ed.), 1994, pp.134-139).

Another problem is that there may not be official statistics readily available in the form in which or from areas that the sociologist is interested in. Such areas of interest may include unofficial work stoppages, membership of new religious movements, marriages in a state of separation, people working in the black market and undetected and unreported crime.

A criticism specific to ethnomethodologists is that the factual appearance of data in the form of official statistics masks the fact that it rests on official interpretations and classifications of behaviour in the first place. Thus, it has been suggested that figures showing a high incidence of working class juvenile delinquency are to some extent the consequence of stereotypical judgements made by officials, especially but not exclusively police officers, who may view and classify similar behaviour by middle class participants more leniently. Number crunching sociology based on such data is therefore seen from this perspective as a spurious science. This point will be followed up in more detail later in the chapter.

Despite their many weaknesses and limitations, of all the methods so far mentioned, the use of official statistics offers one key advantage over others such as interviewing and most observational methods – the sociologist is unobtrusive, thus avoiding the influence of demand characteristics and the Hawthorne effect on the data.

Under this section can also be included an approach which could be referred to as **library based research.** This approach can utilise various forms of document for research purposes. The documents and information accessed may be in the form of physical copies or they may be electronically generated. The information might be of raw secondary nature, such as official documents or statistics, or research and theories which form the body of academic sociology. What can distinguish this type of research is the tendency to utilise academic sources for further theoretical analysis. As such, it may rely on one searching through the findings of research based on any of the methods mentioned above. Researchers who adopt this approach are sometimes referred to disparagingly as 'armchair theoreticians', but some of the greatest contributions to sociology, such as Durkheim's 1912 study of religion (Durkheim, 1976), have relied heavily on the study of other academic sources.

As people increasingly communicate in cyberspace, so the methods of study used by sociologists must be capable of adaptation. For example, via **online research**, ethnographic studies may include cyber observation or participant observation of chat room communication to which ethical guidelines similar to those traditionally applied to participant observation have been developed.

Given the opportunities for sociological research that new technology offers, it is likely that ethical guidelines will need to evolve. This can be briefly illustrated through the issues raised by online research conducted at Harvard University. To study how friendships emerge, sociologists at the University in 2006 accessed 1,700 Facebook profiles. However, access had taken place without students' knowledge. Moreover, as research assistants were used to download the data, even when privacy settings limited access to friends, if the research assistant was a friend that access could be gained. Having arguably breached ethical guidelines of student privacy at the research stage and released part of the information in 2008, Michael Zimmer (Parry, 2011) has argued that a) given the uniquely titled courses referred to, the data can be seen to refer to Harvard undergraduates and b) it would be possible in some instances to establish the identities of particular students.

The **case study** approach often combines a range of methods from this and the two previous sections of this chapter, thus defying simple classification. A case study is the study of a 'bounded system' (Stake, 1995, p.2) – a single unit of working parts with its own identity and sense of boundary. The unit of the research could be, for example, a person, a group, a neighbourhood, an institution or even a country. The case study approach often entails detailed and protracted study providing depth of insight into the subtle complexities that make up the subject area. The use of multiple methods enables multiple viewpoints and contradictory information to emerge. Advocates of the case study argue that rather than being problematic, this reflects the complexity of social life which may be viewed differently from the vantage point of different participants. Thus, within a college, one should not be surprised to find different vantage points on reality experienced by students, lecturers and managers.

The case study method can be used to follow and document social change in detail as it takes place. A community about to undergo urban development or a school about to go through an inspection may provide fertile ground for the case study approach. In the study of any institution, background information can be trawled, for example on the internet, before contact and, hopefully, entry is made. This information, of course, is likely to be highly partial. Early contacts that engage informants in a conversational style of interviewing will be useful for getting a feel for issues that concern them and provide a starting point from which the researcher can pick up on leads and move on to other people. Observations can provide another source of information, as would gaining access to institutional documents. Later, the use of semi-structured interviewing and even survey questionnaires may help to provide more information on areas that are coming into focus as the research progresses. Using such a broad range of methods, the end product is likely to be a highly complex and multi-faceted account of institutional life.

A number of ethnographic studies are in effect case studies. The same could be said about most participant observation studies, although these may tend to lack the rich combination of methods that characterise the use of the case study method at its best. Again, Tocqueville's (1966) study of the causes of the French Revolution was a case study, but a rather one dimensional one through its heavy reliance on the use of official documents.

Although generalisation of case study findings is not sustainable beyond the individual case, their findings may be tested on a broader scale. For example, insights derived from Tocqueville's study of the causes of the French Revolution were more recently broadened into a theory of the social psychological causes of revolutions by J. Davies (1962) and T. Gurr (1980). Furthermore, it only takes the findings of one case study to disprove a hypothesis and undermine the theory from which it is derived. Thus, Goldthorpe and Lockwood's (1969) study of affluent workers primarily working at the Vauxhall Motors car plant in Luton, previously referred to as employing the social survey method, provided case study evidence which was taken to disprove the broad theory that affluent manual workers throughout society were becoming middle class.

Researchers may also bring together a range of case studies carried out by other researchers to develop a broader understanding of social phenomena. In his work 'Communities in Britain', Frankenberg (1973) drew on a variety of case studies of community life from which he was able to distil the key features necessary to construct a rural and urban classificatory scale.

Some case study work adopts a retrospective approach. If the focus of a retrospective case study is on the individual, it may take the form of a **life history** approach which often combines the use of life documents and oral history. In such studies, the interviewee is gently guided by the researcher to provide biographical details of their life, often with the purpose of identifying the formative experiences that have influenced the type of person that they have become. Oral reflections are often supplemented by personal and public documents - which can themselves be used as prompts - and interviews with family, friends and acquaintances can provide a check on the reliability of the interviewee's memory and the validity of the information. Life history information is likely to be of a highly personal, descriptive and qualitative nature, which for positivist minded sociologists makes it too subjective and unrepresentative to be of much worth.

An example of the life history case study focussing on the individual is Clifford Shaw's 'The Jack Roller' which documented the life of a delinquent boy, 'Stanley', in 1920s Chicago. Through the use of autobiographical material, diary entries and interviewing, Shaw was able to offer, much through Stanley's own words, a case study of the circumstances which led to the development of his delinquent behaviour.

It is argued by advocates of the life history approach that micro case study research can provide a very rich source of information from which can emerge a detailed understanding of the experiences of such groups as immigrants and delinquents which would otherwise not emerge through the use of more pre-structured methods such as the social survey. The life history case study may therefore provide very fruitful leads for further research.

Life history research may also form the basis of a larger scale case study of a neighbourhood or community. Amongst the most comprehensive of such examples is Thomas and Znaniecki's extensively cited 1919 study of 'The Polish Peasant in Europe and America'. This work looked at the culture of Polish immigrants and their integration into American society during the early twentieth century. The documentary evidence utilised by Thomas and Znaniecki comprised 750 letters provided by members of the Polish community.

In reality, much research conducted by sociologists applies a number of methods to obtain information and the case study approach potentially carries this to the extreme. Ethnographic approaches may for example employ participant observation, unstructured interviewing and the study of official and life documents. In this type of research, the methods which complement each other are mainly of a qualitative type. Sometimes research combines quantitative and qualitative methods in an attempt to maximise both the reliability and validity of the findings. To add to the different viewpoints which different participants may bring to an understanding of a situation, the information derived from different methods may not match well or can even appear to be contradictory. At the end of the day, much will rely on researchers applying what C. Wright Mills termed 'intellectual craftsmanship' in their struggle to best represent the complexity of social reality through their research.

Box 3 provides a breakdown of the main research methods covered in this chapter in terms of their classification through the three main categories employed and their approximate positioning on the positivist and interpretivist scale.

Box 3	**Classificatory scale of research methods**	
Positivist Methods Methods which deal with quantitative data to establish cause and effect relationships	**Interpretive Methods** Methods which use qualitative data to study the meanings behind actions	
Primarily Asking Questions	Social Survey *Closed Open ended > ended questions questions* Longitudinal Surveys	Interviews *Semi-structured Unstructured Conversational Oral history* Longitudinal In-Depth
Primarily Observing Behaviour	Experimental Field Laboratory Experiment	Participant Observation *Complete Complete observation participation* Breaching Experiments Focus Groups
Primarily Utilising Documents	Official Documents Content Analysis Comparative and Historical Official Statistics	Life Documents Time Budgeting Semiotics

Research methodology and founding perspectives

As has been illustrated in the previous sections, 'research methods' comprise the tools or practical means by which sociologists acquire information. The term 'methodology', whilst constituting research methods, has a broader meaning. It refers to theories, based ultimately on philosophies regarding the most appropriate ways to approach the truth (epistemologies), which provide different guidelines for research processes and use of methods. There has been much dispute in sociology during the twentieth century about the most suitable methodological approach to effectively study society. Such disputes have often related to philosophies about the very nature of social phenomena and the appropriate approach to social 'science'. The following sections build on the distinction already made between positivist and interpretive approaches.

Positivist methodology – social facts and hypotheses testing

The philosophical position behind positivist methodology is essentially that the means by which the social realm can be understood are not too dissimilar to those by which the physical sciences reveal the processes involved in the physical world. The application of science to the physical world has shown that its workings can be understood in terms of causes and effects. Positivist methodology is therefore based on the view that causes and effects operate in their own way in the social world. The social world is therefore also amenable to understanding in cause and effect terms and the methods of science are the means by which this understanding can be revealed.

Positivism originated in the work of the pioneering French social thinkers St.Simon and Comte. We have previously seen (in Chapter 2) that Comte explained the advance of science through his law of the three stages and the hierarchy of the sciences. According to Comte, the absence so far of the effective application of science to the study of society was not to do with its inapplicability to this area of study but because of the unique complexity of social phenomena. The causes and effects by which he claimed society operated and the methods of research necessary to study them provided the greatest challenge to science. However, he argued that once this was achieved, social science would come to eclipse religion and philosophy and provide the rational means for both analysing society and organising intervention to improve its condition.

A clear link exists between positivist methodology and the functionalist perspective. Durkheim, a functionalist in the positivist tradition, emphasised that social processes exist in a realm that is external to individuals, constrain their actions and work in a cause and effect type way. For Durkheim, society is viewed as an entity which imposes patterns of regularity on individuals in the form of laws, roles, institutions, moral pressures and customs. Durkheim referred to these external social forces as 'social facts' (1964b, Ch1) which he maintained could not be changed by the action of individuals. It would therefore be inappropriate to view society as an aggregate of freely acting individuals. Instead, it was a realm in itself, the influence of which on individuals could be measured through statistical data. Durkheim applied this methodology in his study of suicide in which he used official statistics on suicide rates to evidence the effects of the condition of the social environment on individual behaviour.

Against this background, a tradition in sociology developed which used methods to acquire data to test speculated patterns of social cause and effect. This emphasised a structured approach to sociological research in the form of establishing the truth through theory testing. To test a theory, it must be formulated in such a way as to generate 'hypotheses' which are smaller theoretical offshoots of a theory. Hypotheses enable social predictions to be made based on speculated causes and their effects. The data of science must be that of observable and measurable facts. When hypotheses are 'operationalized', they are converted from theoretical level statements to concrete statements which enable predicted facts and observations to be made based on the provisional assumption that the theory is correct. Measured facts and observations enable these predictions to be tested and the outcome to be fed back to the originating theory.

For example, as a general theoretical perspective, functionalism views society as like an integrated organism which changes in the nature and extent of its integration. From this perspective, Durkheim (1970) speculated that a decline in community integration is a social malady with damaging effects on individual well-being. It could be hypothesised that a particular damaging effect of declining social integration would be an increase in suicide levels. To convert this hypothesis to a directly testable form, it may be predicted that suicide rates will be higher within the anonymous environment of urban life than within small integrated communities. It may also be higher within countries or regions where the predominant religion allowed believers relatively free enquiry and individual autonomy (Protestantism) compared to those where religion required individual commitment to a church community and unquestioning acceptance of imposed beliefs and rituals (Catholicism). The broad functionalist theory of the damaging effect of decline in community integration could therefore be tested through using suicide statistics to test the prediction that rates would be higher within anonymous urban environments and Protestant communities than within integrated and Catholic communities.

To recap, in positivist research, the ideal is that the researcher adopts the stance of a clinical analyst who objectively measures social phenomena. Theories take the form of causal relationships which are speculated to exist in society. Theory and research work in a complementary way. Theoretical speculation guides and structures the research process, since without theory there would be no focus for research. From theories are generated hypotheses in the form of statements making predictions of what is expected to be true and which, when converted to the level of concrete predictions, can be precisely tested through quantifiable measurement in research findings.

Despite what would seem to be a very mechanical approach to sociological research, creativity and insight are required to speculate on theoretical issues, to convert theories into hypotheses and to design research programs. However, to provide a rigorous test of a theory, highly pre-structured procedures are likely to be followed. Social phenomena must be reducible to hard data which can be precisely measured. Appropriate methods are chosen to provide the required quantifiable data and procedures for their application are precisely specified. Regarding research methods, those which provide data which can be quantified and statistically analysed to demonstrate levels of correlation (association) or, ideally, causality at work within society are strongly preferred. In the attempt to apply the rigorous of scientific laboratory conditions to the study of human behaviour, the experimental laboratory approach rests well within positivist methodology. However, this method is essentially restricted to micro level research. Positivists prefer to use methods which enable causality to be studied in society at a macro level. Such methods would include highly structured social surveys, the use of official statistics, and comparative and historical method. For example, if a social survey is used, a questionnaire will be predesigned to elicit the precise information required, a sample of respondents will be selected according to statistical sampling techniques and interviewers will be prepared to interview in a uniform and non-directive way. The quantified data will then be analysed to establish whether the anticipated cause and effect relationship is present.

From a positivist viewpoint, sociological knowledge advances through the interplay between theory and observation. Any sociologist making observations or selecting data will be doing so at least implicitly against a background of theoretical knowledge. There is a creative interplay between theory and observation in which theory makes certain observations relevant and observations assist in further construction and refinement of a theory.

Viewed broadly, from a positivist perspective, the progress of social science takes place through endless cycles of research, a process sometimes referred to as the hypothetico-deductive model (Worsley, 1970, pp. 69-71). Research findings fed back to theories help theories to become more finely tuned and finely tuned theories more precisely steer the research process. If analysis of the research information proves the hypothesis to be incorrect, both theory and hypothesis must be modified to take on board the refuting evidence and new research set up to test it again. If analysis of the new information leads to confirmation of the hypothesis, the theory is substantiated, but only ever until further notice.

Through making predictions, gathering data, and taking measurements, knowledge is able to progress in scientific fashion as hypotheses and the theories from which they derive become increasingly attuned to the world of facts. These procedures enable positivist researchers to claim that their methods are highly reliable. They follow set procedures which can be replicated and the findings checked or compared with other research that follows these procedures.

In summary, the methodological basis of positivism is the belief that through impartial application of research methods, a social scientific approach can achieve truth about an objective reality.

Social action theory – an interpretive social science

The following sections signal a progressive move away from positivist methodology. The methodological position of social action theory, as developed by Weber, is arguably a complex one and is quite open regarding research strategy. It challenges the view that social action can be adequately understood through the application of cause and effect analysis to the broader social structure. This does not mean that the quest for ethical neutrality and academic rigor has to be abandoned. It does mean that as the sociologist has to take account of micro and macro contexts of action, of individual free will as well as social constraints and the influence of cultural meaning within a broad social context as well as the subjective meaning held by individuals when they engage in social action, a different approach to 'science' will be necessary for studying society than that advocated by positivists.

A fundamental distinction in social action theory is made between behaviour and action. Strictly speaking, behaviour refers to pre-programmed or stimulus response activity, whereas action is activity which is mediated by meaning and conscious individual decision making based on choice. Human action within society is not predetermined in the way that behaviour is in the animal world. Neither is social action simply the outcome of imposed social constraints. It is meaning directed and meaning ultimately rests in the consciousness of individuals. Weber thus rejects all approaches which view society as an entity with a law like direction of change of its own, carrying along relatively passive individuals. Society is not such an entity in its own right and the idea of such irresistible social laws is sterile, shallow and offers an incomplete understanding of social action as it ignores the input of meaningful and wilful active agency resulting from subjective interpretation of individual actors. The challenge for Weber was to reconcile individual subjective meaning behind social action with the possibility of developing a scientific sociology.

Viewing society at the macro level, the details of social life throughout history present the sociologist with a virtual infinity of phenomena. To assist in making sense of this extraordinary amount of detail, sociologists have to develop concepts and 'ideal types', which are theoretical devices for selectively identifying social patterns through the template of prefect logical constructs. These ideal types can never replicate the detail of the real world but should be seen as orientation devices for sociologists to help them to grapple with a much greater complexity. Those developed by Weber for this purpose include traditional and rational-legal types used to help frame an understanding of the transition to modern capitalism. By constructing such ideal types, different cultural meaning contexts can be identified which can help the sociologist to understand the cultural influences behind individual subjectivity and action as well as broader social change.

Action is nevertheless the consequence of conscious choices which are ultimately made by free agents. If we are to establish the 'causes' behind action, we must look to the meanings, motives, means and ends envisaged by individuals. This is only possible through the process of 'verstehen' whereby through the observer's own capacity for meaningful action they can attempt to empathise themselves into the subjective world of the observed to uncover the meanings and motives which are at work behind that action. Understanding social action must thus take account of the complex interplay between the influence of broader cultural values and the micro level context of everyday action which is ultimately determined by the conscious decision making of the participating actors which itself feeds back into the broader social and cultural domain.

The implications of Weber's position for research methodology are vast and just how to combine the micro and macro in research is left open by Weber. The range of potential methods is all embracing. At the micro level, participant observation and the study of personal documents will be important methods to get to personal meanings. At the other extreme, Weber himself utilised comparative and historical studies to help tease out key 'influences', terminology which is about as close as can be approximated to 'causes', behind broad social change.

Weber was also aware that since sociologists are also laypersons, it is inevitable that what they study and the way that they study it will be influenced by their personal values. However, in conducting their research, he insists that they must strive to adopt a value free approach – a matter of fact intellectual predisposition of ethical neutrality. They must be clear in their use of methods and avoid biasing their findings toward how they would want the world to be – taken to be a condemnation of what was seen as the politically biased approach taken by Marxists.

In summary, social action theory rejects positivist approaches to social science but still claims that a science of a sort appropriate to the study of society is possible. Realistically, one should remain cautious about the findings of social science. For one thing, there will always remain uncertainty as to whether an observer of action has accurately interpreted the motives in the mind of the actor. For another, even if something as strong as causality can be accurately attributed to action which has taken place, one can only talk in terms of probability in predicting future action.

As sociology developed in the twentieth century, the early positivist emphasis was retained in functionalist and Marxist perspectives, if a little less naively. Other developments concentrated more exclusively on the micro and subjective dimension also emphasised by Weber. These interpretive approaches include symbolic interactionism, phenomenology, and ethnomethodology.

Micro approaches – interpretive methodology:

Interpretive approaches developed after Weber's social action theory tended to focus more exclusively on micro contexts of social interaction at the expense of an interest in the broader social structure. Some took a key extra step away from positivist methodology in abandoning the search for a causal understanding of the social realm altogether. This was because the phenomena of the physical world and social phenomena were seen to be so fundamentally different that to explain regularities in each required fundamentally different approaches.

The nature of this break was highlighted in the work of Peter Winch (Cuff et al, 2001, pp.116-120). For Winch, the search for causal and law like regularity in the physical world is appropriate there as laws demonstrate that the regularities which exist are impelled regularities. An example can be used in the fact that the movement of planets is absolutely impelled by forces and can be explained in terms of gravitational laws. By contrast, regularities in the social world are a consequence of following rules and conventions and are underpinned by symbolic meaning to which analysis in terms of causality is not appropriate.

To illustrate this distinction, Cuff et al provide the example of rules of the road. When stopping at a red traffic light, it is not the colour red that has a direct physical effect of invariably making traffic stop. Instead, stopping at a red light is a consequence of a shared cultural understanding of what the red light symbolises within the context of rules of the road. It is the meaning attributed to the red light which induces regularity of behaviour. To apply a physical science approach to explaining this type of regularity would be blind to the fact that it was based on meanings and rules which could be broken by mistakes or circumvention by the purposeful action of individuals – for example by jumping the lights.

The important point is that there is nothing intrinsic to red which means stop. A different colour could have been used to symbolise the rule 'stop'. It is the common interpretation which brings about the regularity of behaviour. If we broaden out this example, since different cultures provide different meaning contexts for behaviour, to understand the regularities of behaviour in an unfamiliar cultural environment, one would need to live in that environment and by observation and questioning learn the symbolic meanings behind the behaviour.

Symbolic interactionism – a humanistic methodology

Symbolic interactionism was pioneered as a social philosophy by a number of American theorists writing in the early decades of the twentieth century, a key figure amongst whom was G. H. Mead. From these more philosophical foundations was developed a theoretical perspective which viewed society as largely built on interaction between individuals in small group situations. The underpinning of this interaction is the exchange of meaning through shared understanding of the meaning of cultural symbols (speech, written language and body language in particular) which act as a medium of communication. Social situations are viewed as fluid encounters in which images are created, manipulated and imposed and identities and meanings are negotiated. For symbolic interactionists, the extent to which society is structured and ordered (the acknowledgement of which varies between different theorists) is largely the emergent outcome of these fluid micro level meaning sharing and negotiated processes.

Whilst social interaction can be observed, there may be various different possible meanings and definitions exchanged between the participants. The actual exchange of meanings between the actors in such encounters can only be revealed through painstaking study. It is therefore the task of the researcher to prioritise understanding the participants' meanings and this can only be achieved through an open minded quest to gain intimate familiarity with their reading of the situation in question. By so doing, an insider's view can be achieved which will reveal some of the subtleties of the interaction process which would be missed if one were to adopt the more distant and clinical methods of positivist methodology which are only likely to touch the surface and achieve a distorted outsider's view of the situation.

Symbolic interactionism formed the main theoretical backdrop to much small-scale ethnographic (studies of everyday life) work carried out by the Chicago school of sociology in the United States during the 1920s and 1930s, and much micro research since. For example, Goffman (1968) was able to discover through largely covert participant observation the operation of unofficial practices within an asylum which would probably not have been revealed by adopting a more overt and pre-structured positivist approach to the research. And although this research took the form of a case study, it was suggestive of such practices in other institutions awaiting to be revealed by the use of similar methods of research.

There are differences of position between symbolic interactionists on the question of the possibility of developing causal explanations of behaviour. Generally, this is the less radical of the main micro interpretive perspectives. However, interactionists commonly reject the theoretical focus and research strategies adopted by positivists. It is argued that positivists place an excessive emphasis on the impact of the broader social structure and constraints in determining individual behaviour. Likewise, interactionists criticise in positivist research the tendency to impose researcher definitions and highly structured procedures from the start of research programmes. These act as barriers to understanding the social interaction experienced by the participants. To avoid this, and achieve a close correspondence between the research findings and the world as viewed by the participants, and thus a high level of validity for the research, interactionists advocate the need for researchers to 'sensitise' themselves to the world of social actors. The favoured methods for achieving this include lengthy participant observation, in-depth and unstructured interviewing and also the study of personal written materials – all of which provide qualitative information. Interviews are much more likely to be collaborative than hierarchical and the interviewer is regarded as more the novice than the expert.

It is seen as advantageous that the focus of research may start out as vague. This can help to attune the open mindedness of the researcher to the world of the participants. In contrast to positivist approaches, in interactionist research hypotheses are often generated and fine-tuned during the research process from the information that emerges, rather than set beforehand for testing. The research process is therefore more creative, enabling theory to be naturally grounded in the everyday meaning of the participants and sociological knowledge to grow through the accumulated findings of very many micro studies.

A more radical criticism of positivist methodology was adopted with the emergence of the interpretive perspectives of phenomenology and ethnomethodology.

Phenomenological methodology – the study of subjective meaning

The perspective of phenomenology was pioneered by Alfred Schutz between the 1930s and 1950s and provided a philosophical backdrop for the approach to sociological research later taken up by ethnomethodologists (indeed, the positions of the two perspectives are so overlapping that the work of some theorists such as Aaron Cicourel has been variously classified within either approach). Taking Weber's emphasis on the importance of subjective meanings which reside behind social action as his starting point, Schutz (1974) attempted to develop a more systematic understanding of the subjective construction of meaning. Subsequently, sociologists working within this perspective have launched powerful attacks on positivist methodology, especially in positivists' use of official statistics as if they were objective facts and their overlooking of subjective meaning.

For Schutz, to engage in their practical everyday activities, people adopt a structured understanding of the world. Structured understanding is possible through the development of classifications which derive partly from past personal experiences and largely from socially shared meaning systems and taken for granted assumptions. This all provides a sense of social predictability and order which is required for engagement in daily routines. Schutz refers to the daily experience of order and routine as living in the 'natural attitude' in which assumptions of order and regularity are a necessary requirement for practical action. Although shared meaning is the active product of social interaction, when it is not disrupted by unexpected events, the sense of structure and order which it creates appears to exist independently as an objective reality in its own right.

We have seen that in their criticism of positivist methodology, symbolic interactionists focussed on the nature of the social world as one of shared symbolic meaning. Criticism from phenomenologists of positivist methodology is more radical. They deny the possibility of causal explanations of social phenomena and adopt a subjectivist approach in criticism of what positivists take for granted – the existence of an objective social reality external to, independent of and constraining the behaviour of individuals, and making causal explanations possible. Instead, what appears to be an objective and factual reality is subjectively constructed.

The methodological position of phenomenology is based on the view that the existence of external social structures is the product of the subjective imposition of classifications and definitions on reality and nothing more. Consequently, there are no independent and externally existing social facts that are awaiting scientific discovery. All that those who engage in the scientific study of 'factual' data are doing is to quantify the products of subjective judgements and give them a spurious status of objective social facts.

The subjective process by which people apply meaning systems to classify and interpret behaviour is a process engaged in equally by the person in the street and people in official capacities. All official statistics are therefore the consequence of official classifications based upon shared meanings applied by people in their official capacities. Phenomenologists are therefore particularly critical of the way in which positivists tend to take official statistics as if they are hard scientific facts. Research undertaken from a phenomenological perspective has questioned the factuality of such statistics as measurements of suicide (Atkinson) and the apparently high level of working class juvenile delinquency (Cicourel). In each case, researchers have demonstrated that official statistics are the outcome of decisions made by officials in the classification of behaviour and are subjectively based on the application of stereotypes and common sense judgements. Those who use this data as if it were hard fact are thus basing their analysis, which has the appearance of objectivity, on data which is itself the product of subjective constructs.

For phenomenologists, since there is no stand-alone objective reality to society, the aim of sociology must be restricted to the study the subjective processes involved whereby people classify behaviour to provide a sense of structure and order. Thus, rather than adopt a stance of detachment from phenomena to analyse it as is possible when dealing with material objects in the physical sciences, phenomenology requires the researcher to be subjectively engaged with subjects in order to document the processes by which they order the world. The methods employed are therefore highly likely to be of a qualitative type. Indeed, in his study of the work of officials in the classification of deaths as suicides or otherwise, Atkinson engaged in observations at inquests and within the workplace of a coroner's office, discussions with coroners and the study of a coroner's record. Atkinson's writeup is a description of the processes involved in arriving at decisions on the cause of death, and thus the creation of statistics, in contrast to Durkheim's study which deals with official statistics on suicide as if they are simply objective facts.

Ethnomethodology – facts are provisional; just the means by which they are constructed should be studied

Out of the more philosophical origins developed by phenomenology, the closely linked sociological perspective of ethnomethodology developed during the 1960s and 1970s. The radicalism of this perspective takes the form of the questioning of any certainty in sociological knowledge. This puts it at loggerheads with positivist methodology and reflects the spirit of times when the authority and certainties of the 1950s came under great challenge in society. Although not itself a contemporary perspective, the attack launched by ethnomethodologists on the scientific orthodoxy of positivism with its claim to superior and reliable knowledge about society indicates some general similarities with the more contemporary perspective of postmodernism.

For ethnomethodologists, knowledge and behaviour is understandable relative to its meaning context. The aim of sociology is to research into small-scale everyday social encounters to understand how people make sense of each other's actions. The methods applicable are therefore likely to include participant observation and in-depth interviewing.

Contrary to a more positivist approach which looks at small-scale situations as structured by broader social constraints, ethnomethodologists view such situations as social encounters which people navigate their way through, sometimés in an improvised way, based on and leading to the emergence of a level of mutual understanding which is actively constructed by participants. For ethnomethodologists, the focus of sociology should be exclusively on identifying the methods that people use to achieve the sense of shared meaning necessary to everyday life for ordered and purposeful action to take place.

A key research method pioneered by Garfinkle to study the process of the construction of shared meaning is the breaching experiment. This method relies on the setting up of small-scale experimental situations where, through the disruptive actions of a prepared participant in the research, the background behavioural expectations of the other participants are violated. The aim of the research is to study the methods used by the participants to re-establish a shared sense of meaning and social order. An example from Garfinkle's research employing a breaching experiment is referred to earlier in this chapter. In this piece of research (Garfinkle, 1984, pp.47-49) on returning home, a number of students acted like lodgers in their own home for a short period of time and reported back the responses of family members. The extent of members' reliance on shared understanding of behaviour between family members was demonstrated by the confused and even hostile responses to the lodger type behaviour and attempts by members of the family to shore up their shared expectations of family interaction by searching for reasons by which they could rationalise the odd behaviour where the taken for granted rules were broken. For example, it was reasoned that perhaps the student was feeling unwell or had been overworking.

Another breaching experiment (Garfinkle, 1984, pp.79-94) involved one to one counselling sessions where undergraduates were told that they should prepare their questions to counsellors in such a way that advice could be given in the form of just 'yes' or 'no' answers. What the subjects did not know was that the 'counsellor' was in fact an experimenter who was reading off answers to each question asked from a pre-prepared randomised list of 'yes' or 'no' answers. Garfinkle found that students tended to report after the interview that their questions had been answered and useful advice given. They had constructed their own sense of meaning out of randomised disorder.

Ultimately, through detailed analyses of numerous such processes, ethnomethodologists believe that it is possible to extract general rules on the methods that people use in social situations to develop a shared structured understanding. Identifying the rules of the construction, negotiation and imposition of meaning should be the goal of sociology, nothing more.

As conversation is a key means of communication, conversational analysis has been an important research method for ethnomethodologists. Conversations are viewed as improvised activities of reciprocal sense making and are accomplishments of the participants. For ethnomethodologists, conversational analysis requires detailed study of not just words but inflections, pauses, breathing sounds and non-verbal communication etc. Detailed analysis of conversations has led ethnomethodologists to identify how fit takes place as conversation progresses and to show that participants tend to share an understanding of conversational rules and structures, such as appropriate introductions and terminations of conversation. Ethnomethodologists study these communicative exchanges to show how shared taken for granted understanding of conversational rules and processes is demonstrated in a variety of settings such as job interviews (Button, 1987), telephone conversations (Schegloff, 1979) and political speeches (Heritage and Greatbatch, 1986). They also study processes of breaching repair, should a participant stray from the rules.

What is so important about this seemingly trivial enterprise? The following points are worthy of mention. Firstly, ethnomethodology breaks down the barriers raised between the sociologist and the layperson that are erected in more positivist research. The traditional status and expertise of the specialist sociologist over the layperson is undermined as ethnomethodologists recognise that the sociologist is encapsulated in the world of everyday meanings which he / she is trying to understand just as much as the people whose interactions are the object of study. Even the activities of sociologists, engaged in research or otherwise, can be studied in the same way as other everyday social encounters. Sociology is thus 'disprivileged.'

Secondly, the perspective recognises that practical sociology is conducted all the time in the everyday encounters of ordinary people as they interpret meanings and rules.

Thirdly, the sociologist takes the lead from those being observed, rather than vice versa as is the case in more positivist approaches.

Fourthly, all social encounters are of equal worth for study – establishing the relative truth of different groups' views is not the purpose of research, but simply the processes involved in the emergence of shared meaning.

Ethnomethodologists have pointed out fundamental weaknesses in the tendency of positivists to base causal explanations on the analysis of supposedly hard scientific data such as official statistics or that derived from survey interviews. For ethnomethodologists, official statistics are themselves the outcome of judgements, interpretations, definitions, stereotypes, etc. made by officials. The task of sociology should therefore be to analyse the encounters and judgements through which interpretations of the behaviour of others by officials are made. This would show that the resulting social statistics are highly provisional. When positivists base their research of the uncritical acceptance of official statistics which are viewed as if they are hard facts, the causal theories that they build on them are likely to distort social reality to that which reflects official viewpoints.

This perspective was applied by Cicourel in his 1976 study of juvenile delinquency in two American cities. Cicourel found that judgements made by officials – police and probation officers – were key to decisions over whether or not a person had officially engaged in delinquent behaviour. If a youngster who had engaged in anti-social behaviour exhibited those characteristics which officials stereotyped as associated with juvenile delinquency – for example were black, or working class, or from run down areas – they were more likely to be viewed as delinquent than others from white middle class backgrounds who had engaged in similar behaviour. The different rates of juvenile delinquency which the figures show are not objective facts but the product of subjective judgements influenced by the application of common stereotypes. Theories of delinquency which are based on treating the resulting official figures as facts are therefore reducing the study of reality to an uncritical reflection of stereotypes used to interpret behaviour by officials. From an ethnomethodological perspective, studies of delinquency should be examining the different capacities which different groups have for imposing definitions and negotiating justice.

Likewise, in the case of social survey interviews, rather than trying to understand society in terms of the apparently hard data provided, the object of study should be the interview process itself and an examination of how this particular encounter is based on shared or constructed assumptions about how the process is conducted (for an overview, see Box 4).

Box 4

<u>**Positivism and Ethnomethodology**</u>

Positivism

The study of 'facts' treated as hard data.

Upon such 'facts', causal theories are tested and developed.

'Facts' –

e.g. official statistics, survey data..

Ethnomethodology

Research must simply look at the social processes behind the creation of 'facts'.

It stops at the point where positivist approaches start and shows that 'facts' are highly provisional as they are based on judgements and interpretations of behaviour which are themselves provisional.

More contemporary approaches to sociological research:

Despite disputes between positivists and social action theorists over the question of subjectivity, methodology, and the actual research methods preferred, there tended to be agreement that a basis for truth could be established, that explanations in terms of causality should be aimed for, and that it was the role of the researcher to be a neutral analyst. What distinguishes some contemporary from these more established approaches is the calling into question the fundamental canons of science. A major departure from positivism has already been signalled in the approaches of phenomenology and ethnomethodology. In this section, approaches will be introduced which radically challenge the assumptions of positivist sociology and may even question the possibility of achieving objective knowledge.

Critical theory – neo-Marxist methodology and consciousness raising

Critical theory is based on insights derived from Marxism, but revised to accommodate the circumstances of the twentieth and twenty first centuries. Marx had developed a critical theory of capitalism which aimed to enlighten working people as to their plight and enhance the potential for political liberation through enlightened collective action. From this perspective, it is argued that all research takes place within power structures and so, even from a position of supposed methodological 'neutrality', the views of the powerless are unlikely to come through. Regarding the alliance between positivist methodology and functionalism, scientific social research, often funded and framed by governments, is seen to be used as a tool for government intervention in support of capitalism. As such, value freedom and scientific neutrality are used as a cloak whereby the interests of the powerful can be supported, but covertly.

For Lee Harvey (1990), it is more appropriate to refer to 'oppressed groups' rather than 'the working class'. Given the inequalities of power and influence, truth from the point of view of oppressed groups tends to be suppressed. To counter this, the role of critical sociology is through research to articulate truth from their perspective(s). The aim of critical methodology is to promote social improvement for oppressed groups by using research to reveal how they are oppressed in terms of broader social structures and through their adoption of dominant social values. Sociological theory and research can be used to encourage such groups to acquire new insights through which they may be able to improve their lives. Critical theorists usually agree with more established methodological traditions that research can uncover truth. However, they argue that truth can be selective and partial and serve the interests of different social groups. Moreover, they oppose established approaches by maintaining that the role of the researcher is not just that of revealing the truth but crucially also that of using research findings to encourage action amongst oppressed groups to improve their lives.

To a limited extent, critical methodology has affinities with interpretive approaches. It opposes the hierarchical nature of positivist research procedures and engages the subjects of the research in discussions of findings to assist validity. Research may often be small-scale, study the life of the underdog, and prefer to use qualitative methods. However, in the critical approach, the importance of the broader picture remains paramount as findings and insights are aimed at developing a critical awareness of the repressive nature of the social structure and dominant values of capitalism. This emphasis has been fundamental to the neo-Marxist Frankfurt School of social theorists. Theorists such as Habermas and Adorno have worked loosely within a Marxist tradition which was developed to generate new radical insights appropriate to contemporary capitalism. From this perspective:

1) Science and technology provide capitalism with efficient means of production and administration but the ends to which they are put are not seriously questioned. The culture of consumerism has had a dulling effect on critical awareness with the masses manipulated into a sterile contentment of low culture mass entertainment and technological gadgetry as an end in itself. The advance of the mass media has thus made ideological control all the more pervasive.

2) Positivist methodology claims that values of what 'should be' are not applicable to scientific procedures and that by applying these procedures to the social world it is adhering to principles of scientific neutrality. However, from the point of view of critical theorists this neutrality is deceptive. In fact, it accepts that what is should be and is therefore inherently conservative – it assists the perpetuation of existing arrangements of power distribution and social inequality.

3) As when Marx was writing, there is a need to enlighten oppressed groups through the insights of social theory and social research, but theory needs to be revised to accommodate advanced capitalism which

now includes a diversity of oppressed groups. The role of social theory and research is to empower people through enhancing their critical awareness in the face of the pacifying influence of the mass media and the mentality of consumerism.

Feminist methodology and consciousness raising

Feminist approaches to research can also be viewed as a form of critical methodology. Up to the post-war period, the experiences of women or even women themselves have figured little in sociological theory or research. For example, in studies of social mobility, the social class position of the household was invariably measured by the occupation of the male head of the household. This meant that females' social class was read off from that of males and reflected the subordinate position of women in society at the time. Such 'subordinate' activities as housework were also given little attention in sociology.

A rising consciousness amongst many women to challenge male domination throughout society accompanied the feminist movement of the late 1960s. This movement was also reflected in sociology through a growing interest in issues of gender inequality and identity. Whilst feminist sociologists focus on gender as the key category of social oppression and provide an alternative standpoint from which society can be viewed to that of 'malestream', they have also become increasingly aware of the extent to which such factors as social class, ethnicity, age, disability and sexuality comprise differences between women. But in particular, they have aimed to bring to the fore the once neglected voices of females and investigate areas of concern to women from their standpoint including housework, mothering, sexism, sexual harassment, violence against women, divorce, infertility and sweat shop labour.

Feminist sociologists tend to associate the structured and hierarchical positivist approaches to sociological research with male dominance in society and in the subject of sociology. In sociology, positivist approaches emphasise the importance of maintaining a detached and clinical relationship between researcher as expert and the passive subjects of the research who are treated like objects. For example, the formality and objectivity aspired to in traditional survey research reduces the respondent to the position of being just an object of data provision. For Ann Oakley, the supposed intellectual superiority of clinical rationality, objectivity, detachment and hierarchy in research closely corresponds to the values of traditional male culture (Oakley, cited in Lincoln and Denzin, 2003, p.251). This approach is justified by positivists in terms of the protection of the findings against the intrusion of subjective bias into research and in the interests of standardisation and replication. Viewed from the positivist and traditional male paradigm, 'getting involved with the people you interview is doubly bad: it jeopardises the hard-won status of sociology as a science and is indicative of a form of personal degeneracy' (Oakley, cited in Lincoln and Denzin, 2003, p.252).

Feminists have been strong to challenge this outlook. For example, Oakley emphasises that the application of positivist methodology in sociology disempowers the subject and overrides opportunities for the feedback of insightful information and personal experiences which a more collaborative relationship in research would reveal. The use of interpretive methods, such as unstructured and in-depth interviewing, can improve the validity of information by establishing closeness and empathy between interviewer and interviewee, especially in the case of female interviewers interviewing female interviewees on topics of particular interest to female standpoints.

But this is not just a matter of male preference for positivist methods and feminist preference to use qualitative and ethnographic approaches, which itself is a vast oversimplification anyway. It is more to do with the way that methods are used. Feminists have developed their own approaches to using methods and conducting research and tend to argue that feminist methodology needs to go well beyond traditional methodological parameters. For Oakley, even the establishment of rapport with interviewees is traditionally shaped and imposed by the interviewer. She argues that for research to not be exploitative, it is legitimate for the researcher to offer help, advice and friendship to participants to enhance a relationship of greater equality. This degree of give and take may help to overcome inhibitions and distortions to feedback introduced through more hierarchical approaches and participants can be consulted over the interpretation of the data. Extending this process, a relationship of co-authorship may even be established whereby the validity of an interviewer's interpretations can be checked by revisiting their accounts and allowing the interviewee to revise them as appropriate.

Moreover, feminists often feel it legitimate to go beyond the stance of value neutrality and detachment expected in most traditional approaches to research. Although research is about participants, feminists are usually keen to emphasise that the purpose of research is that it should be primarily for them. Participants are not just objects who are unchanged by the interview process. Since all interaction influences the consciousness of participants, it can be seen as valid that participants in the research are encouraged through participation, along with readers of the findings, in their intellectual liberation – a feature in common with critical sociology. With reference to her own research, Oakley puts it this way:

> 'I regarded sociological research as an essential way of giving the subjective situation of women greater visibility not only in sociology, but, more importantly, in society, than it has traditionally had. Interviewing women was, then, a strategy for documenting women's own accounts of their lives. What was important was not taken-for-granted sociological assumptions about the role of the interviewer but a new awareness of the interviewer as an instrument for promoting a sociology for women - that is, as a tool for making possible the articulated and recorded commentary of women on the very personal business of being female in a patriarchal capitalist society' (Oakley, cited in Lincoln and Denzin, 2003, p.253).

A good example of feminist methodology in practice is provided in the research of Roseneil into the life of women at Greenham Common who opposed the siting of cruise missiles at the air force base. The research methods employed included participant observation, in-depth interviewing and the analysis of documents, and much of it was retrospective. Roseneil was keen to document her feelings and experiences as a protester along with the other women. Identifying closely with the cause of the women, Roseneil argued that she should express her own values within the research against which the reader could judge her findings. She was keen to portray the women as active and from this micro research show connections with the issues of the broader women's movement. (Devine & Heath, 1999, Ch9).

Feminist sociologists have frequently argued the merits of a uniquely feminine approach to research by which females can: 1) provide a view of reality from their own standpoint, interests and insights as an oppressed group which, in providing one truth amongst many, is as valid as that of any other group, 2) reveal feeling and intimacy in a more subjective approach to research which itself should be highly valued, and 3) raise the consciousness of women as an oppressed group for purposes of promoting social change.

Interestingly, some of the comments above refer to the existence of different gender related qualities which parallel common stereotyping. However, it is central to sociology that gender identity is largely socially formed and inequality is socially structured. Whilst not denying that different qualities and unique experiences exist based on sex and gender differences and that gender inequalities have shown themselves to be remarkably resilient, there is also evidence of a narrowing of gender identity differences and inequality. This would suggest the prospect of a growing area of common ground in the approaches of men and women in the study of society.

Postmodernist methodology – the end of social science

Many postmodernists claim that contemporary societies have so fundamentally changed compared to those of the modern era that conventional criteria and methods for establishing truth should now be rejected. They claim that established ideas of a knowable social structure and methods for gaining certain knowledge of it were part of the pattern of discourse of the modern 'metanarrative' (an all-embracing story of how society operates). In the modern era, characterised by the emergence of science and industry, conventional sociological research took place within the premise that methods and procedures can be applied to provide information by which certain knowledge about how society works can be gained. The social policy dimension of this approach is that such knowledge can then be applied to improve society.

Postmodernists emphasise that this view is part of an Enlightenment metanarrative which accompanied the period of industrial and scientific modernisation. This metanarrative placed faith in the capacity of science to promote social progress and emancipate humankind from slavery to old religious dogmas and superstitions. Sociology emerged within the modernisation process and its accompanying metanarrative. It is in this context that sociological positivism formed. In the positivist tradition, the idea of social engineering was related to the belief that scientific method would provide a reliable basis for establishing the truth through research and enable social intervention to remedy social ills such as poverty, misery and conflict. For postmodernists, the modern era has disappointed. Naïve faith in science and progress has been shattered by the events of the twentieth century.

Different writers that could loosely be called postmodern emphasise different key aspects of the postmodern condition. This variety includes an emphasis on post-industrialism, information society, post capitalism, postmodern capitalism, global media dominance, post-bureaucratic organisations and political revolutions ending communism etc. A common thread to them is that the postmodern environment exhibits, compared to modern society, a decline in social and moral unity and uniformity and a breakdown of rigid social structures. To claim that postmodern society is here or is emerging is to claim that a radically new social environment is unfolding. This environment is dominated by an electronic world of fleeting and diverse but all embracing media images which break down uniform identities of, for example, family life, social class and gender which were once prevalent in modern society. A radical postmodern position adopted by Baudrillard suggests that this media saturated world produces a 'hyperreality' in which media symbols, images and language are referenced by other media signs, symbols and language. These representations of reality thus become disconnected from the real world, the truth or underlying reality of which cannot now be known.

Given this environment, postmodernists are highly critical of conventional sociological research methods and claims to truth. They see conventional research as part of the old metanarrative of modernism which claims superiority for professional scientific knowledge. In postmodern societies, the modern matanarrative of truth based on rational thinking and scientific method collapses. As truthful knowledge of social reality can no longer be achieved, it is no longer possible for sociological research to claim validity. Sociological research therefore loses its privileged status in claiming a superior understanding of society to that of any other explanation. Social science becomes just one of a number of competing narratives for understanding society and there is no way that it can rightfully claim privilege to a singular truth. Society is diverse, its condition is ephemeral and all knowledge is both tentative and relative. There is no longer any overriding criteria by which superiority for knowledge based on empirical research can be claimed.

Where then does this leave sociological research? Postmodernists often focus on the way that language is used to create the appearance of order and truth. They therefore argue that postmodern analysis should take the form of the scrutiny of texts written by others so that the techniques used to create the appearance of truth can be brought out into the open. In other words, research should take the form of textual analysis to reveal the justifications used for claims of truth by the author. This technique is referred to as the deconstruction of texts. Thus, when writers of sociological research claim validity for their findings, this is just one of a number of ways in which writers of texts claim legitimacy for their story.

A telling criticism of this activity is raised by Mats Alvesson (2002) who regards it as both negative and parasitic, pointing out that if all social theorists were to engage in such a venture, the study of the social realm would degenerate into little more than a type of sociological literary criticism. Furthermore, Devine points out that this would lead to the need to deconstruct the texts produced by those deconstructing texts and so on endlessly. One could argue that there are surely more important and constructive concerns facing sociologists, such as attempting to understand the causes of war or poverty (which for postmodernists such as Baudrillard we apparently cannot be sure even exist) which can make the above preoccupation seem morally offensive.

In conclusion, there may well be validity to the claim that societies have entered a new era of social diversity and rapid change, but it should not be beyond the ingenuity of sociologists to respond with new techniques and approaches which would provide informed understanding of the social world as the basis for enlightened social intervention. This is the position adopted by Anthony Giddens who views the contemporary world as having reached a high modern as opposed to postmodern state.

4 // Sociology of Families and Households

Abstract

This chapter introduces the reader to some of the difficulties involved in attempting to achieve a relatively impartial stance when adopting a sociological approach to the study of family life. At the outset, the reader is alerted to the importance of reflecting on and examining personal experiences and values regarding 'the family' to enhance awareness of any personal bias and encourage a broad overview of family diversity. It is emphasised that this overview needs to be guided by theoretical awareness and research findings. It should also be noted that with regard to founding theoretical perspectives and research of the post-war decades the author feels it appropriate to use the term 'the family' whereas reference is made to 'family life' to represent the greater diversity of lifestyles in more contemporary times.

Following the introduction of some founding concepts, the founding sociological perspectives of functionalism and Marxism are utilised to provide general theoretical starting points and contrasting interpretations of the role of the nuclear family in society. A sketch of the broader social and historical context to changes in the family is also provided. Some well-established sociological research into the extended and the nuclear family is then reviewed and provided as a benchmark against which more contemporary patterns of family life can be later compared. Reference is made to feminist responses which highlight the disadvantages to women of traditional family structures.

The reader is encouraged to appreciate that evidence can be assembled and looked at in different ways to provide different messages and some guidance on the interpretation of information is given.

Although also a founding perspective, it is suggested that symbolic interactionism offers greater flexibility and accommodation of analysis to more contemporary trends of growing diversity in family life than functionalism or Marxism can. Evidence of such growing diversity is then introduced in relation to the question of whether it can be best interpreted in terms of decline or change in family life.

Political and social policy preferences and interventions in response to changes in family life are referred to with reference to new right, New Labour and coalition government policy.

More contemporary sociological approaches emphasise that society has been undergoing fundamental changes which render the founding perspectives of functionalism and Marxism increasingly redundant for the purpose of explaining the contemporary pattern of family life diversity. These approaches include postmodernist and high modernist perspectives which raise issues of freedom, tolerance, and lifestyle and identity choice in the context of a rapidly changing society that is increasingly devoid of past structures and constraints. Within this context, it is argued that viewing life in terms of life course rather than life cycle or family cycle has become more appropriate.

It is emphasised that personal identity related to different stages in life should be regarded as a social construction rather than a direct consequence of biological aging and that rather than universal it has been variable throughout history and between societies.

It is also shown that a recent emphasis in researching family life has been to refocus on the definitions and perceptions of participants.

The sociological challenge

What guidance can be picked up from the previous chapters to prepare us to adopt a sociological approach to the study of households and families?

Firstly, it is important to pause and reflect on our personal experiences within our own family and be vigilant regarding any personal bias that these experiences may predispose us toward. Given the highly personalised nature of family life, there may be emotive issues that we need to stand back from if we are to review this area as impartially as possible.

Secondly, one needs to be on one's guard against the bias of nostalgic reflection regarding family life, as for example may be encouraged by certain historical television documentaries. More generally, the view that there was once a more distant golden age of family life that has been lost tends to overlook evidence which points to the severity of life for the majority of people in previous generations and centuries.

Thirdly, one should also be aware that personal experiences of life within our own family may not be very representative of the experiences of others. Personal experiences can provide helpful insights, but will constitute a far too narrow and subjective basis from which to generalise about family life for sociological purposes. There exists a wealth of research findings on families which one should be prepared to delve into.

Fourthly, as sociologists, we should be cautious of explanations that rely heavily on human instincts or human nature to justify particular forms of family organisation as natural or superior. If the precise form of the family were determined by a narrow and fixed human nature and instincts, we would expect to find 1) a high level of uniformity in family life throughout the world and 2) little scope for change. In fact, anthropologists have pointed to the diversity of family forms which have existed across the world and are embedded in different cultural belief systems and customs. Additionally, even in such a brief period of history as the last sixty years in Britain there is evidence of both substantial change and growing diversity in family life. Whilst the very being of society is dependant on instincts to procreate and provide care for the vulnerable young from a significant proportion of the population, there is great potential diversity of arrangements through which this is possible.

This leads to a fifth point. The very diversity of family life which now exists within contemporary western societies requires great care in the formulation of definitions of family life. The nuclear family may have once provided a powerful reference point as a social norm and majority institution. However, sociological concepts have adapted to reflect the trend of recent decades toward increasing diversity of lifestyle options. Consequently, sociologists are now more likely to use less restrictive terms such as 'families and households' or even 'primary groups' rather than 'the family' with its value laden overtones.

As a sixth point, whilst life within families may be experienced as very personal, direct and private, it is also situated within the broader social setting. As we have seen, C Wright Mills has argued that one needs to be able to apply the sociological imagination to think about the connection between the micro and the macro, in this case to enhance our understanding of changes in family life.

Having raised the point of the need for caution, how can we become armed with a more analytical approach to the study families? For a start, we can utilise and build on the sociological perspectives raised in chapter two to see what light they shed on family life. Furthermore, we can use more concrete information obtained from research. Theory and research findings will provide access to a broader range of insight and information on family life than that which could be derived from our personal experiences. However, it is important to remember that perspectives are touchstones and that theory must remain open to critical evaluation.

It is particularly instructive in the study of family life to be aware that the moral values that provided a compass bearing for past generations may have been experienced as prejudices by those who deviated from them and, for example, had children out of wedlock in that generation. These prejudices have become more broadly recognised as such in generations since as society has changed. It is important, but perhaps more difficult, to appreciate the likelihood that outlooks and ways regarding family life that are taken for granted today will be looked back on likewise as based on prejudices by future generations. Developing this awareness can help us step back to recognise and question any taken for granted assumptions that we may have about family life.

Definition of main concepts

Sociologists need to be clear about the definitions that they use and the measurements they take. A range of sociological concepts regarding families will therefore be introduced and defined, beginning with those relating to more traditional family life.

The term **monogamy** refers to the exclusivity of marriage of a person to one partner, traditionally of the opposite sex, at any point in time. This pattern, reinforced by cultural, religious and social values and legal constraints, has been the traditional form of family life in western societies. Changes in social and cultural values have been paralleled by legislative changes which have allowed single sex monogamous marriage in a number of countries and civil ceremonies in some others. However, monogamy itself is not a universal family form. Within some non-western cultures, various forms of **polygamous** (marriage to more than one spouse simultaneously) familial arrangements are endorsed as perfectly natural to members of these societies.

The sociology of family life has changed along with changes in the family itself. In modern western societies, theory and research in the 1950s took place within the social context of a widespread standard family institution referred to as the **nuclear family**. This family type, strongly sanctified by religions and traditionally sanctioned within churches, comprised married parents of opposing sexes and their children, living together under the same roof. There would sometimes exist a clear sense of boundary in relation to the outside world and a recipe for separate but mutual responsibilities between husbands and wives.

There is evidence of relatively high levels of conformity toward this family type at the time. For example, in 1961, 38% of households in Britain conformed to the above definition. An immediate reaction may be that this is not a particularly high figure for the date in question. It needs to be born in mind, however, that once children had left home, the unit was, within this definition, no longer a nuclear family. Additionally, if the numbers of people living within nuclear family units were counted, the percentage for 1961 would be significantly higher than that of households since on balance other household units were smaller than nuclear family ones. Most children were therefore raised within a nuclear family setting. Stigma acted as a powerful force to control deviations from this norm. For example, the pejorative term 'illegitimate' (and worse) was commonly applied to children born outside of marriage and strong moral pressures for a 'shotgun wedding' would often be applied on the partners in the case of pregnancy outside of marriage.

Research evidence has suggested that a spread of growing prosperity from the late 1950s was accompanied by a growing tendency of the family to establish a clear boundary between life within and the broader community. The term **privatised nuclear family** was used to refer to this phenomenon.

Roles are the patterned activities that people engage in which involve them in relationships with others. They are usually based on broadly recognised social guidelines but can also sometimes leave scope for negotiation between participants. Role relationships generate reciprocal expectations regarding appropriate contributions by family members. Post-war sociological research tended to take the nuclear family as given and focussed on studying, via social surveys, changing role relationships within this family form. The term **conjugal roles** was used to refer to role relationships and the division of labour between partners within marriage and a distinction was be made between two different types of marital role relationship. **Segregated conjugal roles** were relationships in which a clear distinction was made between the activities of husband and wife. The required roles followed traditional gender expectations: the husband was the sole or major wage earner, with the wife being responsible for the daily running of the household and the raising of the children. This is referred to as the breadwinner and homemaker model. These role distinctions were often themselves passed down the generations through socialisation and strongly maintained by social and moral pressures. However, related to various broader social changes and, the evidence suggested, initially more commonly within middle class households, **joint conjugal role relationships** were emerging as alternative arrangements between couples. Such a role relationship took the form of a greater involvement of the husband in household chores and childcare and a degree of merging of domestic activities between husband and wife, with the wife more likely to be in employment. The concept of the **symmetrical family** is very similar to, but can be distinguished from, that of joint conjugal roles. As applied by Young and Willmott, the term 'symmetrical' places a lesser emphasis on the merging of roles. Although traditional assumptions loosely remained regarding the primary role responsibilities of husbands and wives, symmetry refers to greater role flexibility and a more equal participation in household chores.

The term **role swap families** has been used in situations where conjugal roles remain largely segregated but where the wife becomes the main breadwinner and the husband's primary role involves domestic chores and childcare. Such arrangements are often related to situations where the career opportunities and earning capacity of the wife are superior to those of the husband.

Extended families, whilst including the nuclear family unit, also encompassed a more extensive community of relations (established through marriage or blood relatives). Comprising a higher tier of generations and a broader span of relatives, extended families would potentially include members over three generations as well as uncles, aunts, nephews, nieces, and cousins. Extended family members would not necessarily all live in the same abode but traditionally resided in close proximity to allow ease of face-to-face contact and mutual help. Reciprocity was therefore an important expectation with different members exchanging different types of support. There is evidence that extended family life was once abundant in many stable working class communities, especially prior to the development of the welfare state. However, it is important to recognise that extended families have taken various forms. For example, they have been very important means of shoring up power amongst royalty and the aristocracy, whereas in contemporary Britain extended family life and powerful parental pressures on choice of partner may remain important within Asian communities.

Although the term **kinship** has sometimes been applied to relationships within the extended family, it more strictly refers to people who feel related due to some real or imagined common descent traceable from an identified person. More traditional cultures were sometimes organised along kinship lines, with Scottish clans providing an example of this form of identity.

Reconstituted families are family units which come together following the break-up of previous family units. These family types have become an increasingly familiar part of the family landscape with the increase in divorce rates and relationship breakups followed by the establishment of new partnerships. They include children from at least one of the previous marriages to whom new parents may become step-parents.

The term **beanpole family** has been used to describe a family structure which is high generationally but narrow in breadth across each generation. This structure reflects relatively recent demographic changes. These changes relate to a combination of increased longevity leading to the possibility of four generation family relationships and smaller family units due to declining fertility rates, single parent families and higher divorce rates. In this family structure, the vertical generational relationships of reciprocal help between members may become more important and those across the generations become narrower and less important.

Families may reside within **households**. However, as a household comprises people living within a common residential unit and sharing facilities, these people do not necessarily constitute a family and, dependant on how families are perceived or defined, not all family types necessarily share residency.

Founding sociological perspectives on the family

Two contrasting theoretical perspectives on the family, functionalism and Marxism, will now be introduced. Both perspectives took the nuclear family encompassing segregated conjugal roles as the standard family type. This is understandable given the social and historical context of the development of these perspectives. However, the reader may feel them to be very dated. It should be considered whether these theories can be adapted to adequately explain family life in the context of contemporary society and whether there are insights that can be salvaged from them.

Functionalism – the functional fit of the nuclear family

American functionalism, represented in particular by the towering influence of Talcott Parsons, was a highly influential perspective within sociology during the 1950s. Parsons identified the nuclear family, comprising a segregated conjugal role relationship between married a male and female, and their children, as a key institution which fitted perfectly with the functional needs of modern industrial societies. How did it do so? According to Parsons, this family unit 1) synchronised perfectly with the efficiency needs of modern capitalist society, 2) provided an upbringing of children as well moulded future citizens, and 3) provided the psychological benefit of an emotional haven and outlet for the parents.

Applied to any social institution, the term 'functions' refers to the positive contributions that it makes toward the well-being of society and consequently the lives of members of society. The family is a key social institution for functionalists because it is seen as transmitting quite uniformly society's core norms and values through successive generations, thereby promoting both social consensus and continuity. To explain how this process operates, Parsons (1951) places a heavy emphasis on primary socialisation which he argues is an essential function of family life. He maintains that at birth the mind of the baby starts as a relatively blank slate. The child's mind gradually awakens to society's values, rules and norms through experiences within the nuclear family. These values, rules and norms become transmitted by the parents and internalised into the child's personality structure, and as they are relatively uniform across society, this process is functional because it equips the young to fit into society and provides the basis for social harmony and stability.

For functionalists, it is a necessary prerequisite for a normal and healthy state of social stability that society only changes relatively gradually. This requires a high level of social reproduction (the continuation of social structures and values) from one generation to the next and for Parsons the family plays a vital role in this process. Thus, parents have been socialised within their families of origin into society's dominant values. As parents, they socialise their children likewise. This forms the cyclical basis for social and cultural continuity and on-going social order and stability. But how, then, does society and the family change at all? This issue will be addressed at the end of this section.

The family unit benefits from role specialisation. Parsons argues that in an increasingly competitive and impersonal social world external to the privatised family, the male is best suited for the breadwinner role through which the family is financially supported, and the female is better equipped for childrearing and domestic responsibilities. Interestingly, despite Parson's emphasis on the impact of environmental influences and primary socialisation on the personality structure of the child, natural predispositions of the different sexes also enter the analysis. Parsons backs up this complementary role specialisation by an emphasis on the apparently natural and inbuilt differences between the sexes in the form of male capacity for instrumental and rational thinking, naturally suiting him for the world of work, and female affective, expressive and emotional qualities, which are suited to a domestic and child rearing role and providing emotional support for the working husband.

Parsons attempts to locate changes in the family within the context of long-term and broader social changes. Here it is important to recall that from the functionalist perspective, the family is viewed as a social institution whose changes synchronise with changes in the broader social structure. In terms of this social structure, pre-industrial society tended to be a relatively closed social hierarchy, offering few opportunities for social mobility – ie. little movement up or down the social hierarchy between the generations. People's status within the social structure was relatively ascribed, or fixed, at birth. There was also little geographical mobility or industrial dynamism. Life tended to follow established traditions and agricultural routines. Little health, welfare or educational provision was available to the vast majority outside of the family which had to take on much of these functions as best it could.

Within this social context, it is argued that the extended family is a logical adaptation. Ascribed status within the family, usually determined by age and gender, was compatible with ascribed status within society. Nepotism – using one's position to place relatives in employment – was common and not dysfunctional (damaging to society) since it shored up the closed social hierarchy. Any boundaries between family life and the outside world were often quite permeable as communities were usually small scale, integrated and intrusive. People knew their place.

For Parsons, the transition from pre-industrial to modern industrial society involved a fundamental change in the nature of the social hierarchy from one governed largely by inherited social status to a society in which social position had to be achieved on merit. In modern society, there are more opportunities for geographical and social mobility as an efficient social and economic system needs to more effectively utilise its range of human resources. It does so by offering high levels of economic reward to those who have demonstrated their individual ability and drive by competing successfully with others in a relatively open social structure. By such 'meritocratic' means, people become impartially allocated to different occupational levels within the system.

What, according to Parsons, are the implications of these changes for the family? One is that the privatised or isolated nuclear family is a necessary adaptation to the needs of modern industrial societies. It is argued that if the extended family were to persist, there would be a growing inconsistency between ascribed positions within the family and achieved occupational status, possibly leading to disharmony within family structures. Nepotism would also be dysfunctional in a society where occupational standing needs to be allocated on individual merit rather than family connections. Also, by becoming more privatised, the nuclear family, in shearing its emotional and supportive bonds with the broader network of the extended family, is able to acquire the necessary geographical and social mobility that dynamic modern society requires of its workforce.

In addition to socialising children into such core social values as the need to compete, to be enterprising and to respect private property, for Parsons a further key function of the privatised nuclear family is that it is ideally suited to provide for adult members – especially the male breadwinner – the possibility of retreat from the competitive demands and formality of the workplace, so as to provide replenishment within a haven of emotional security. Moreover, it caters for the therapeutic needs of adults to act out childish residues – affective, childlike behaviour which would not be acceptable in the outside adult world but which nevertheless need release.

Functionalists argue that as society modernises, new institutions emerge to take on increasingly specialised functions. Functional specialisation accompanies 'structural differentiation' – the growing complexity of social structures. Through these changes, more efficient specialist institutions are producing goods and services and engaging in exchange relationships in a functionally integrated society. For Parsons, the family loses some of its functions from the pre-industrial world in this process. In modern industrial societies, it is no longer a significant unit of economic production or provider of education or welfare as specialist institutions external to the family have largely taken over these functions. In so doing, they enable the individual to unlock his or her fortunes from what their family can provide for them and strive to achieve a place in society on merit. But, Parsons argues, this does not mean that as a consequence the nuclear family is a less important institution. It has adjusted to the needs of modern society through developing male and female conjugal role specialisation, providing a privatised protective environment, and focussing on the key functions of the primary socialisation of children and the stabilisation of adult personalities.

Other writers in the functionalist tradition include George Murdock and Ronald Fletcher. Whilst Parsons focussed essentially on the contemporary American family, Murdock studied the family across 250 societies and concluded that it was a universal institution because it catered for a number of essential social needs and functions. Thus, societies must reproduce their populations to survive, but the functionality of reproduction within families is that this institution is necessary for social order and stability by providing a shared understanding of rules of sexual access and responsibility for the upbringing of children. Along with Parsons, Murdock emphasises the functional importance for social harmony of socialisation within the family (which he tends to refer to as the education function). And Murdock also identifies the economic function of the family in terms of complementary gender role specialisation, again similar to that proposed by Parsons.

Fletcher acknowledges that with the advent of modern capitalism, external institutions are catering for many of the functions, such as health, welfare and education, which in pre-industrial times were left largely to the family to cater for. However, it is argued that this has not weakened but assisted the family in the specialist support that these institutions provide. Furthermore, although the family has also largely lost its pre-industrial function of being the main unit of economic production, its economic function has been transferred to that of consumption and is thus the main target of consumer advertising.

It is likely that the reader will have already identified some problem areas in the functionalist approach to the family. Amongst the more obvious is the fact that it portrays an over simplified, over uniform and idealistic view of family life to support a theory of social harmony which justifies patriarchal power and largely ignores the darker side of family life, such as domestic violence and sexual abuse.

The charge of excessive uniformity in the functionalist portrayal of the family would appear to be a strong one given the extent of diversity in family life (see later in the chapter) that can be witnessed early in the twenty first century. However, up to a point, some defence can be made of the functionalist position. This uniformity was arguably a more realistic snap shot of family life in the 1950s America that Parson's theory was applied to. Arguably, the greater diversity of family life that has since developed can be accommodated within the functionalist approach. We have already seen that at a general level this approach emphasises that changes in the broader social structure affect various institutions, including the family, all of which need to adapt and synchronise with each other. The problem is that the Parsonian model does not easily explain how these broader social changes come about in the first place. Through the emphasis placed on the pervasive effect of socialisation and its key role in social reproduction, one can understand from this perspective the continuity of dominant and shared social values (if they are that shared) over time. What is less clear is what drives social change, especially rapid change, in both family life and society.

Parson's answer is that the natural state of society is one of equilibrium – society gravitates toward a state of balance. However, it only takes change in one area to disrupt this balance and other institutions have to adapt for a new state of equilibrium to be established. Thus, economic innovation which led to the Industrial Revolution had to be paralleled by changes in social values and institutions, including the family, for a new social balance to emerge.

The issue of the extent of diversity in family life in contemporary times is, however, a difficult one to resolve within the functionalist framework which emphasises so much the importance of shared values and family uniformity. David Popenoe (Steel et al, 2012, pp.40-41) adopting a neo-functionalist perspective, argues that such diversity is problematic in that it is disruptive of social stability and that alternative arrangements to the nuclear family, especially those that marginalise the father, disadvantage children during their upbringing. He argues that a new standard family model needs to emerge that is appropriate for the contemporary age.

Marxism – the nuclear family as a support mechanism for capitalism

Classical Marxist theory also adopts a very traditional view of the family as headed by the male breadwinner and as a key institution of socialisation, social reproduction and support for the social system. However, this perspective fundamentally challenges functionalism on the nature of the system. From a Marxist perspective, a society of achievement through individual merit – a meritocracy – which functionalists claim capitalist industrial societies to closely approximate, is incompatible with capitalism. In reality, there remains within capitalism a relatively closed class structure. This closed structure is one of economic inequality which is perpetuated by the inheritance of private property and the family is regarded as the main transmission belt of this form of social reproduction.

Arguing from a Marxist perspective, for his colleague Engels, the institution of the monogamous nuclear family derives historically from the economic conditions that promoted the production of sufficient private property to enable its unequal distribution. This became the early basis for social class inequality. When private property became concentrated in the hands of males, its protection down the male line required, particularly amongst the more wealthy, the means by which legitimate inheritance by sons could be assured. According to Engels, the patriarchal monogamous nuclear family, which controlled women's sexual behaviour, emerged in response to this economic necessity. The social reproduction emphasised by Marxists is therefore that of the social and economic inequalities of the class structure, the perpetuation of which down the generations the family is regarded as the key safeguarding institution. This analysis leads to the conclusion that the patriarchal nuclear family will remain a dominant institution as long as the capitalist system remains.

Why then is the nuclear family also a necessary feature of the life of the majority of the largely propertyless working class in this analysis? In the context of modern capitalism, the inheritance of very little property places working people in a situation of being perpetually dependent on the need to supply their labour to earn an income. The owners of business constitute a capitalist class who rely on the supply of exploitable and disciplined labour to enhance their profits. The profits of one class are dependent on the exploitation of the labour of another class who need to work. The worker cannot escape exploitation within this system; with the pressing needs of subsistence and family responsibilities he becomes tied to the workplace. The domestic support provided within the family by the housewife is essential for the maintenance of the productive worker. For this, the worker must provide economic support. However, the employer only pays the worker (in part) for the work directly provided. Therefore, from the position of the employer, the female support role for the worker's labour is a free one.

Marxists argue that the patriarchal family supports capitalism in other ways. As an instrument of his employer's profit, the worker is treated as a commodity and is controlled as an efficient object in the productive process. The consequent experience for the worker is one of alienation – a feeling of powerlessness and meaninglessness in carrying out work. The worker is depersonalised and dominated for the purpose of maximising the production of value and level of exploitation which the provision of labour makes possible. Within this context, the family is seen as acting as a safety valve against potential class conflict between employers and workers as other members of the family absorb aggression from the breadwinner which has been generated through negative experiences within the workplace.

Additionally, Marxists focus on the role of the family in terms of bringing up the next generation of exploitable labour, again at maintenance cost to the worker. Within the home, the young are socialised into submission to the authority of the father figure. This relationship works as a form of preparation for acceptance of the authority of future employers over workers, thus assisting in the social reproduction of class relationships. As a fall-back position, women constitute what Marxists refer to as a 'reserve army of labour' which can be taken up when beneficial to employers, for example during economic booms when workers might feel themselves to be in a stronger bargaining position, and more readily disposed of back to the family, for example during economic recessions.

Marx was confident that the stresses between classes that were built into capitalism could not be soaked up indefinitely and that this system would eventually self-destruct in class revolution. However, as capitalism has endured, other schools of Marxist thought have emerged which are less sure of this outcome. For example, neo-Marxist (modern revisionist) writers of the Frankfurt school, such as Herbert Marcuse, retain the basic Marxist analysis of class exploitation under capitalism, but recognise the growth in the seductive influence of the mass media. Marcuse argues mass media advertising is often aimed at the family and encourages an appetite for domestic consumption by associating the acquisition of technological appliances with the image of freedom. The housewife is thus portrayed as free from heavy domestic drudgery if she has the latest domestic gadgetry. Acquiring a new fast car is also associated with the image of freedom. This enhances the demand for goods to help keep capitalism buoyant. But, more than this, it locks workers further into un-free, repressive and exploitative relations within the workplace to be able to afford these goods or keep up payments. From this neo-Marxist perspective, the attractions of consumerism distract workers from recognising the need for genuine freedom which can only be achieved through replacing capitalism with a social system in which the means of production are commonly owned and labour is not exploited for private profit. The view of 'freedom' often associated with conspicuous consumption is therefore viewed from this perspective a 'false consciousness' that in fact binds workers more to capitalism and the workplace whilst enhancing its economic buoyancy.

A major criticism of the classical Marxist model is the economic determinism built into the theory – the view that the economic forces of capitalism are the key determinant of the form of all social institutions. Regarding the family, this leads to the view that only the monogamous and patriarchal nuclear family can adequately serve the needs of capitalism, despite evidence of substantial diversity of family life between cultures and increasingly within societies that are capitalist.

Feminists such as Abbott and Wallace (1997, p.45) have been particularly critical of the fact that in focussing exclusively on class exploitation of male labour provided in the workplace, the classical Marxist position has not sufficiently recognised the value of domestic labour provided in the housewife role and only attributed secondary importance to patriarchal domination and gender exploitation.

Clearly, functionalist and Marxist perspectives on the family are diametrically opposed. The former idealises the family as a haven of sanctuary within a competitive society of achievement, whilst the latter views it as a prop for an exploitative class system which offers the majority few opportunities. However, they both strongly emphasise the powerful constraining force of social structures and forces of socialisation working in uniform ways to mould individuals to society.

This issue of the growing diversity of family life will later be reviewed, along with the question of the decline of the family, and alternative theoretical perspectives will be considered. Firstly, a brief review will be made of changes in the family from a social and historical context. This will be followed by an identification of areas of interest established in traditional sociological research into the family, again providing a backdrop against which contemporary family life can be compared.

Family change from a broad social historical context

The theories that have just been reviewed place the family within historical frameworks. Research by social historians has attempted to piece together evidence and identify patterns of change in family life. Ideally, this would provide the means by which the theories can be evaluated. However, there is some uncertainty regarding family life and how it has changed over the centuries, as the further one goes back, written details tend to provide some information on the lives of the literate and educated minority who were more likely to be found in the upper ranks of society but little about the majority. The patterns that have emerged from research suggest a degree of consensus on the general findings but also point to a complex picture of change in the family and likely regional variability.

Life in medieval societies was for most experienced in a rural and agrarian setting. In Britain, most people lived out much of their lives within local communities which were well established social hierarchies in which there was little opportunity for social mobility. Research, for example by Shorter, has suggested that romantic attraction or expectations thereof played little part in choice of marriage partner or married life itself. Instead, for the wealthy, marriage was a means of consolidating wealth and power. In poorer households, it brought together members into an economic unit of production as the home was often also the workplace.

Here, family members engaged in agricultural or handicraft activities with a degree of gendered work differentiation whilst young children were usually allocated the housework. In some cases, boys were apprenticed into other families to learn a trade and became part of that household. For landless agricultural workers (serfs), life was often brutal and harsh, limiting the possibility of the cultivation of romantic feeling. Moreover, they were bonded to their landlord who effectively owned them and had legitimate control over most aspects of their lives, including a final say on whom they may marry. Affection between partners may at best grow over time. For most, therefore, both modern conceptions of romantic attraction as the basis for marriage and the separation of home and work would have made little sense.

To what extent does historical research square with the functionalist model which suggests that the extended family was prevalent in pre-industrial society and then declined to fit the needs of more dynamic industrial capitalism?

Lawrence Stone adopted what Michael Anderson has referred to as a 'sentiments' approach to the study of family life in Britain during the period of about 1500 to 1800 (Sclater, 2005, pp.38-40). This approach is reliant of qualitative information such as that obtained from diaries, literature and family artefacts. According to Stone, 1) at the beginning of this period, the smaller family unit often tended to be integrated into broader community and kinship ties, was hierarchical and male dominated, and was a unit of shared economic interest. It was thus unlikely to be a source of affectionate relationships between partners. However, 2) from about the 1550s, whilst remaining a patriarchal institution, there were signs of a growing separation of the nuclear family from more extended family and community ties and the emergence of more affectionate relationships within. From 3) about the mid seventeenth century, changing cultural values were emphasising a growing importance of individual autonomy and privacy, and with this evidence of a further isolation of the nuclear family and romantic attachment and emotional warmth between partners, referred to by Stone as the emergence of 'affective individualism'.

According to Stone, there was also a social stratification element to these changes. During this period, choice of marriage partner and family life experience was initially shaped by economic and hierarchical factors. In the early phase, the experience of romantic liaison tended to be limited to extra marital relationships between members of the upper social orders. By the middle phase, marriage through romantic attachment and family life within a more isolated nuclear family environment were becoming more common amongst the better off. By the end of the period in question, the experience of romantic choice of partners and a relatively closed nuclear family had percolated down the social hierarchy and become more characteristic of family life amongst the working class.

Historical research into family life in England between 1564 and 1821 conducted by Peter Laslett (Sclater, 2005, pp.36-37) adopted a more demographic approach. This means that the focus was more on the data profiles of populations. Information from early periods relied heavily of parish records and census information was only available to cover the period from 1801. Laslett's findings also suggested that extended family life was not particularly common in the pre-industrial period, with only about 10% of families including kin beyond the nuclear and household sizes averaging about 4.75 persons. Given the time period of Laslett's research, which stretches from pre-industrial into industrial society, he concludes that the relative rarity of the extended family and commonality of the nuclear family in the pre-industrial period suggests much greater historical continuity in the form of family life with that of early industrial society than was once thought.

However, Anderson (Sclater, 2005, pp.40-42) found that in the industrial textile town of Preston in 1851, 23% of households contained kin other than nuclear. Adopting a household economics approach which involved studying documents relating to people's economic circumstances, (for example records regarding employment, property ownership and family budgeting) Anderson argued that living as part of an extended family had become more of a pragmatic strategy for survival by this period than necessarily being a preferred way of life. David Starkey supported the drift of both Laslett's and Anderson's findings by arguing that the view of the prevalence of the extended family in pre-industrial society is a sentimental myth without historical substance and that the only time when it may have been more commonplace was during the very difficult times that many people experienced during early industrialisation.

Sociological research on the family in post-war Britain has suggested that the extended family has undergone significant decline. When put together, all of this evidence seems to support a three stage model of the extended family rather than the two stages suggested by functionalist theory. In general outline, this would suggest the prevalence of the nuclear family, slowly withdrawing from absorption into the local community, during pre-industrial times. The extended family (including within it the nuclear family) emerged mainly as a response to the hardships of life experienced by poorer sections of the population during the early phase of capitalism and remained a common feature within such populations well into the industrial period. It was giving way to the privatised nuclear family by around the middle of the twentieth century.

What accounts for the above findings? Firstly, in pre-industrial society, life expectancy was relatively short, so it is likely that any three generational families would also be relatively short lived. Secondly, the common practice of primogeniture (the maintenance of property intact through its inheritance by the eldest son) meant that non inheriting family members would have to make their own way in the world. In line with these findings, both the nuclear family and the work ethic could be argued to precede and assist industrialisation rather than adaptively emerge from or with it as the functionalist theory suggests.

What changes did industrialisation involve? Advances in science and technology, culminating in England in the late eighteenth century, brought about a revolution in the productive process. Workshops and factories were able to utilise powered machinery which could produce standardised goods more cheaply and efficiently than cottage industry workers in a domestic setting who largely relied on hand powered machinery were able to. Unable to compete, there was increasing pressure on cottage workers to seek employment in factories, bringing about massive population movements from the countryside to the towns.

Some of the important changes that industrialisation promoted regarding the family can be summarised as follows: 1) a redefinition of work as something external to the family where labour was sold to an employer in exchange for wages, 2) an increase in extended family living as a coping mechanism, and 3) the development of new segregated conjugal roles with the male becoming the chief breadwinner and the female taking on domestic chores. Taking each of these in turn:

1) The emergence of the factory system meant that labour had to be increasingly offered outside of the domestic setting to an employer who owned the new productive technology which required the concentration of waged workers in factories to maximise productivity. Seccombe (Sclater, 2005, pp.36-37) adds that as fewer families had any means of production to pass down the generations, this assisted the change from viewing marriage in property terms toward the importance of romantic attachment.

2) When workers moved to the towns, their accommodation would invariably be rented. Sometimes one family member, usually the father, would make the first move and acquire employment and accommodation. Employers often relied on workers to put in a word for other family members (nepotism). These members would then follow and employers would come to take on whole families. This process allowed the intensive occupation of meagre accommodation and the greater dividing up of the cost of rent. In such circumstances, extended family life offered some safeguard of mutual support to cover for situations of adversity such as ill health and unemployment at a time when little welfare provision was otherwise available.

3) From the 1830s, the consequence of the passage of the Factory Acts, restricting the employment of children in the harsh conditions of factory employment, was that young children and women tended to withdraw to the home, a location which was now viewed as a non-work environment. If women did work outside their own family, it was often as domestic workers, thus reinforcing their association with the domestic sphere.

To sum up, despite the complexity of the phenomena, the evidence from historical research suggests that the view that extended family life was more common in pre-industrial society is a myth. Functionalist theory which sees a transition from extended family to nuclear family as an adaptive adjustment to the transition from pre-industrial society to industrial society, is not supported by historical evidence however neat the argument may be in theoretical terms. The nuclear family was more widespread in pre-industrial times than the theory suggested and the greater mobility that it allowed, along with the emerging cultural values of individualism and respect for privacy, may have actually provided an environment that was conducive to industrialisation. And following the Industrial Revolution in England, there is evidence that at least for a period of time in the nineteenth century, the extended family became a more, not less, common feature of the landscape, especially amongst the poor urban working class.

There are a number of reasons for a degree of caution over the evidence though. Care needs to be taken regarding the units of analysis that researchers use. For example, Laslett used evidence of household sizes averaging about 4.75 persons to indicate the relative rarity of the extended family in pre-industrial and early industrial England. However, it may be questioned whether 'household' is the most appropriate unit of measurement in this case. Post-war studies such as Young and Willmott's (1974) mid 1950s research have revealed substantial evidence of extended family life when 'living in close proximity' was an alternative measure. Of course, there are also likely to be social class and regional variations in family life, as well as the fact that the findings regarding pre-industrial England may not apply to other pre-industrial countries. For example, evidence suggests that extended family life was more prevalent in some pre-industrial eastern European countries, thus possibly inhibiting their industrialisation.

Traditional sociological research:

1. The extended family

The extended family proved to be a durable arrangement in some working class communities well into the twentieth century. Whilst employment opportunities were stable and populations remained settled, work placement through nepotism was able to continue. Men often put in a word at work to find employment for their sons and other male relatives as, for example, in the case of dock work. Meanwhile, a key role for women was to provide the daily contacts of mutual support which comprised the extended family networks in the domestic setting and local community. Indeed, Young and Willmott still found such life to be quite common in working class communities of Bethnal Green in the mid 1950s, where local ties were further enhanced through the common practice of mothers ensuring that their daughters' names were put on local housing lists. However, broader forces of change were beginning to undermine the cohesion of the extended family in this and other localities. What were these changes?

One factor was the development of post-war welfare state provision. This enabled people to fall back more on the impersonal help of the benefit and welfare system during times of need rather than feeling bound by the reciprocal obligations associated with extended family help.

Another change related to housing in the context of post-war reconstruction. From the 1950s, families were being re-housed as new towns and new housing estates were built further out from slum areas such as in parts of the East End which were demolished. Such re-housing usually led to the departure of the young nuclear family unit, attracted, as many interviewees in research conducted by Young and Willmott stated, by the prospects of a better environment for their children.

Industrial change, for example in the form of a decline in the availability of dock work in the East End, meant that younger family members could place less reliance on nepotism for finding work locally. Consequently, they sometimes needed to work or even move outside the area in which they had been brought up. And soon, the expansion of service sector employment and changing social attitudes toward female employment enabled more women to find work outside of the home, thus diluting their role at the hub of the extended family.

So, to what extent did the extended family continue to decline and family life retreat into the world of the isolated nuclear family? The evidence appears to be a little mixed. For example, Young and Willmott found that when young nuclear families were re-housed further out from the East End, wives' direct contact with extended family members declined significantly and they often experienced loneliness and isolation. However, in some cases, husbands retained employment in the locality of the original extended family and through their visiting of relatives whilst working in the area were able, to some extent, to perform the role of a link person in a continuing extended family.

More recent and general research conducted by the British Social Attitudes Survey (1995) has indicated that, when measured in terms of seeing a specified relative outside of the nuclear family at least once a week, the extended family remained more a feature of working class than middle class life, that women were still the main participants in maintaining contact, and that contact was more likely if there was a dependent child. Thus, in working class families with dependent children, 65% of mothers had 'regular' contact with a relative whereas only 33% of males in non-manual occupations and without children retained equivalent levels of contact.

Increased access to private transport has enhanced the opportunities for regular face-to-face contact with relatives over greater geographical distances. Thus, Rosser and Harris (1965) found in their study of working class family life in Swansea that although extended family membership was more disbursed and day-to-day practical help more difficult to maintain, there remained strong affective bonds between members. Interestingly, a more recent large scale survey conducted in Swansea by Charles et al (2008) found the number of single person and small household units to have increased and households of three generations to have only remained within the Bangladeshi community.

Part of the reason for lower levels of face-to-face contact between middle class extended family relatives may have been related to greater dispersal as their occupations and careers tended to require higher levels of geographical mobility. Despite this, research evidence from Colin Bell (1968) in Swansea and Young and Willmott in the 1980s from a North London suburb suggests that there existed similar levels of positive concern within middle class families to maintain contact, even though it may be by such means as telephone and letter. Bell found that practical help by parents was often substantial when their sons and daughters were starting up new homes and families.

During the 1970s, the American researcher Litwak discovered that affective ties between extended family members remained strong despite sometimes substantial geographical separation, over which contact was often maintained through private transport, telephone and by letters. The family in this form he referred to as the 'modified extended family'. More recently, the growth of the internet and new technological communication devices are surely enhancing opportunities for maintaining instant contact with relatives over vast distances. Assessing the survival of the extended family into the present day may therefore require taking into account the extent to which these new technological forms of communication are comparable with or an effective substitute for the help and support which once came from face–to–face contact with relatives living locally.

We are now in a position to call further into question the functionalist account of the extended family. Historical evidence suggests that it was not a common part of the fabric of pre-industrial life, but became more prevalent during the early phase of industrialisation. And sociological research into post-war society has shown that the extended family, along with the practice of nepotism, remained relatively vibrant in some communities. Even in contemporary society, it has shown some resilience, even if, as suggested above, in transformed form. The functionalist argument that the extended family is at odds with the needs of a modern dynamic economy should therefore alert us to the fact that if theoretical perspectives are to illuminate our understanding of society, we must apply them cautiously. We should not be blinded to alternative evidence just because it contradicts the self-contained logical consistency of a theory.

2. The nuclear family

As in post-war functionalist theory, so in post-war sociological research, the nuclear family was taken as the standard family form. The main focus of attention in research was initially on role relationships between husbands and wives and the designation of domestic tasks within the nuclear family. The research of Elizabeth Bott and Young and Willmott illustrates this well.

Bott's pioneering small scale study of families in London – 'The Family and Social Network', (1957) – generated some early insights into the social influences behind whether husbands and wives engaged in segregated or joint conjugal role relationships. She found that a connection existed between type role relationship that existed between couples and the type of friendship network that they were connected to outside of the family. Her evidence suggested that segregated conjugal roles, in which clear demarcation existed between men's work and women's work, were more likely to be found in situations where each partner had established a closely knit friendship network outside of marriage; one in which many of the members knew each other. This friendship and conjugal role pattern also tended to be more common in working class families. Joint conjugal roles, where there was more role overlap and common participation in domestic tasks, were more characteristic of middle class partners who had established dispersed friendship networks outside of the family, in which few members knew each other.

How could this relationship between type of friendship network and conjugal role relationships be explained? Bott argued that marriages tended to be super-imposed onto pre-existing friendships. She speculated that the continuation of a pre-existing close knit friendship network after marriage draws partners into friendship activities outside the family and provides shared gender norms that reinforce gender stereotypes, emotional support and help. Loosely knit networks, by contrast, provided a less cohesive body of norms and degree of control over individuals and fewer opportunities for providing mutual assistance and emotional support amongst members. In this situation, couples had to turn to each other more for emotional fulfilment and achievement of tasks.

Young and Willmott's larger scale research entitled 'The Symmetrical Family' (1973) came to some similar conclusions to that of Bott's regarding middle class and traditional working class family roles. In their research, the term 'symmetrical' was a similar concept to that of joint conjugal roles. Although role symmetry referred to a blurring of once more firmly segregated conjugal role boundaries, it did not equate to an equal allocation of the same tasks between husbands and wives, but rather different and more equal contributions and responsibilities as well as a less patriarchal and more 'companionate' relationship. Compared to segregated conjugal role relationships, symmetrical relationships were regarded by Young and Willmott as a sign of social progress. This later study of working class nuclear families found evidence that contrasted to their previous documentation of traditional segregated conjugal roles within the context of extended family communities. It showed that the development of symmetrical role relationships was associated with growing working class affluence and home centred consumerism. Husbands were spending more time on DIY household chores and more wives were taking on paid work. It was argued that a convergence toward the pattern of role relationships that had been more typical within middle class families was related to sections of the working class gaining access to middle class levels of affluence. There was, nevertheless, little evidence of anything approaching an equal sharing of participation in child rearing or domestic chores.

Again, evidence of trends toward joint conjugal role or symmetrical relationships is a departure from the family of the Parsonian functionalist model. However, such changes are not necessarily inconsistent with the functionalist perspective per se as they could be argued to represent an adaptation of nuclear family roles to broader social changes. Thus, as pressures of consumerism and changes toward a service orientated economy brought enhanced work opportunities to and put more pressures on women to gain employment, a change toward more egalitarian role relationships within the family can be interpreted as a necessary adaptation.

This view of change in role relationships is sometimes referred to by the optimistic term 'the march of progress'. However, a contrary position has been adopted by those who refer to disadvantages, some new and increasing, experienced by women in terms of 'dual burden' 'double exploitation' and 'triple shift'. These terms will be briefly defined. The concept of dual burden relates to the growing tendency for women to work outside the family, sometimes in a full-time capacity, yet be expected to retain many of their traditional domestic responsibilities. For Rapoport and Rapoport (1982), double exploitation refers to the continuing pressure that women are under to provide 'free' domestic labour whilst also pursuing work in which both career opportunities and pay are limited. And the term triple shift adds to the features of the dual burden the view that the management of the further emotional pressure that is placed on relationships under these circumstances falls disproportionately on the shoulders of women.

What did further research evidence reveal regarding these optimistic and pessimistic positions?

One area considered was that of the perception of equality or inequality of contribution to tasks within the household by partners themselves. A British Social Attitudes Survey of 1987 suggested that there were differences in perception between men and women on the practice of gender equality in household task allocation within the family. 16% of men believed that household tasks were shared equally, but only 9% on women thought so. These different gender perceptions may well relate to different starting points and expectations.

Sociologists themselves sometimes disagree on the interpretation of research evidence. This can relate to their sociological perspectives with regard to gender. Whilst Young and Willmott were confident that their research findings indicated the emergence of more equal role relationships within families, the feminist Ann Oakley was much more cautious about their findings. She suggested that their optimism was undue since their starting point for purpose of comparison was that of segregated conjugal roles and that measurements were taken in such a way that even modest evidence of husbands' involvement in household tasks was taken as a sign of growing symmetry of contributions. Young and Willmott were therefore accused of over interpreting their data. By contrast, Oakley's (1974) study of housework, conducted through in-depth interviewing of partners in 40 families in London, found more symmetry in the role relations of middle class parents than that of working class, but that even in the former symmetry was found to be minimal.

Oakley's research may, however, have had its own inbuilt bias. R. Pahl's (1984) research found that conjugal role relationships can be effected by the stage reached in what was then regarded as the typical family life cycle. Greater symmetry or joint conjugal roles may be a more workable option for couples without children. However, if couples have children, it was found that the wife was more likely to give up employment when they were young. More segregated conjugal roles were likely to be associated with this phase in the family cycle. Later, as parenting responsibilities declined, the wife may re-enter the workplace and domestic roles and responsibilities would tend to become more equally allocated again. The important point here is that Oakley's research may have been predisposed against finding evidence of equality of contribution between husbands and wives, since all of the housewives in the sample had young families.

Research by J. Gershuny (1983) found that even when they engaged in paid employment, women still tended to spend more time on housework than men. However, from other research that detailed time allocation, Gershuny (1992) showed that husbands committed more time to domestic work as wives increased their involvement in paid work. Moreover, between 1974 and 1987, husbands of wives in full-time employment doubled their involvement in cooking and cleaning activities. Wives, nevertheless, still tended to retain primary responsibility for housework. Gershuny concluded that such findings demonstrated that a process of 'lagged adaptation' was taking place. This meant that there was a delay in the adjustment of old ways and cultural values to the new economic situation of women increasing their participation in the workforce. It could also be argued, of course, that these changes could be burdensome on husbands who may be caught between the pressures of traditional cultural values that emphasised sole breadwinner responsibility for the family and those by which he was expected to contribute far more to household tasks and childrearing. Such changes take time to resolve themselves and reveal new temporary adjustments.

From Sullivan's research (2000), it was found that as men worked fewer hours, their contribution to household work increased. However, it appears that there can be exceptions to this pattern since research findings by Morris (1990) showed that men who became unemployed but whose wives worked contributed little more to household chores than when they had worked. It appeared that in this case, both the experience of becoming unemployed and any participation in domestic work were regarded as a threat to their perceived masculinity.

Focussing on conjugal roles and task allocation alone within the family may tend to overlook other areas of potential gender inequality. Such areas can include decision making and control of family finances. These dimensions are more to do with the use of power as viewed in a sociological sense – that is, the ability that some have to exert control over others. Research conducted by Stephen Edgell (1980) found that although there was evidence of more participation by husbands in child rearing, males tended to predominate in making decisions which were defined by the couples as major and important, whilst females had responsibility for more routine and less important decisions. Interestingly, research carried out by Jan Pahl (1993) discovered that although a variety of decision making arrangements existed between couples, husbands still tended to have more control over family finances and that both partners experienced highest levels of marital unhappiness in situations where husband's control was strong. However, research by Laurie and Gershuny (2000) which compared survey evidence from 1995 with that of 1991, did find a decline in the practice of husbands providing a housekeeping allowance to wives and greater equality in the making of major financial decisions.

Another area which has been researched covers a rather more subjective dimension – that of emotional input into relationships. Evidence from Duncombe and Marsden (1995) found that male partners were less likely to recognise the necessary extent of emotional input required to keep a relationship together and that women put in most of the work in this area and also took much of the strain.

In summary, this section of the chapter has concentrated on quite dated research that has tended to take the nuclear family as given and found that there has been some evidence of a modest growth in gender equality. Within this institution, both the evidence and its evaluation can vary significantly. Those who take a position of segregated conjugal roles as their starting point may find it easier to argue that substantial change has taken place, whereas many feminists have maintained that the changes are modest and token and that new burdens have fallen on women. There is a broad range of research evidence which suggests the need for some caution regarding the extent and inevitability of nuclear family life adaptation to modern society's apparent requirement for far greater gender equality. However, we will shortly consider evidence of a growing diversity of family types which makes research based exclusively on the nuclear family itself look very dated and today a more narrow area of concern.

Feminist viewpoints on family life

A number of the issues discussed above have clearly been of concern to feminists. This next section will consider viewpoints adopted from a general feminist perspective of women's experiences within the family.

The family is regarded as of crucial importance to feminists as it is here where definitions of women's role and the use of patriarchal power are so pronounced. But how did we get to this position? Across much of society the economic unit of production in pre-industrial society was often the family itself in which various work roles were allocated. Although the male often had important powers and decision making, the output was usually recognised as the product of the work of all family members and women and the young had important roles to play.

We have seen that the Industrial Revolution brought about changes in the location of work, its definition and who were recognised as engaged in work. A fundamental consequence of the Industrial Revolution was to provide work in factories owned by others in places separated from the home. Whilst initially whole families were often taken on, legislative restrictions became placed on factory owners regarding the employment of women and children who became a less attractive employment proposition. This was the beginning of the retreat of women and children to the domestic environment. According to Abbott and Wallace (1997, p.142), these changes were already becoming well established in middle class households during the early nineteenth century and by the 1850s were being rapidly followed in working class family life. Whatever the contributions made by women there, the home was becoming redefined as a non-work environment and a unit of consumption rather than production.

This separation of male 'work' and female domestic responsibilities in the nuclear family headed by the male breadwinner led to male workers, supported by trade unions, pressing for a wage level that was sufficient to support a family. Women were not in a position to make such claims. It was not they who 'worked' to support families. Women's withdrawal from participation in the workplace became supplemented by the view that this was the natural order of things. As in recent decades women have entered paid employment in almost equal numbers to men, they have had to battle against male vested interests for the principle, though doubtfully fully realised yet in practice, of equality of access and promotion opportunities and equal pay for equal work.

Feminists have long challenged the patriarchal nuclear family as an ideological construct which attempts to make male power and female dependence appear as part of the natural order and limits not just the possibilities for women of gaining economic independence but also their self-actualisation. It has been argued that powerful moral and institutional pressures are placed on women to marry and devote much of their lives to domestic responsibilities and child rearing. Beechey (1982) has pointed out that these pressures are backed up by the ideological view that the nuclear family and segregated conjugal roles are both universal and desirable arrangements. We can recall that a similar stance was adopted by many functionalist writers, and in the work of Parsons justified by the view that females naturally have affective and males instrumental qualities.

Of course, anthropological studies which point to evidence of substantial diversity of family life throughout the different cultures of the world show the universality argument to be unfounded. Moreover, there has been a significant growth in the diversity of family life in contemporary industrial societies. However, the key point about the ideological effect of the traditional nuclear family was that this institution protected the interests of a dominant group (males for feminists, capitalists for Marxist feminists) whilst providing the appearance of operating in the interests of the subordinate group (here women). After all it was surely the true vocation of all women to be economically supported in the realisation of their natural and fulfilling role as child bearers and carers and providers of domestic and emotional support for husbands within the protective confines of the family.

The approach of feminists not only opposes the traditionalism and ideological bias inherent in functionalism, but in contrast to the structural approaches of both functionalism and Marxism argues that one has to get inside family life to understand how it is experienced by housewives and mothers. For example, Young and Willmott (1973) claimed that within the nuclear family more egalitarian and companionate relationships were emerging between husbands and wives. This claim has been strongly challenged by feminists. As early as 1966, through using unstructured interviews, Hannah Gavron had found that against enhanced expectations of greater freedom in married life compared to that of their parent's generation, the experience for many young married women was one of feeling trapped in an existence of domestic chores, often experiencing negative psychological consequences. Oakley's research in 1974 discovered that for many of the housewives that she interviewed, compared to the ideology of domestic bliss, housework and domestic life were found to be as unsatisfying and alienating an experience as that which is often found in industrial labour. Such research findings, highlighting experiences of isolation and alienation experienced by women in traditional domestic roles, emphasise the point that experiences of family life are likely to be quite different for women than for men.

It could be countered that there has been a massive shift in the direction of diversity regarding family life (which will shortly be documented) and that present day feminists are fighting battles of the past. There is some need for caution regarding this assertion though. Firstly, social surveys tend to show that public attitudes and values remain quite strongly in favour of the nuclear family, if less so amongst younger people. Secondly, the main political parties have shown a clear preference for this institution. The political responses from the main parties of government will be sketched later. At present, it will be emphasised that support for the nuclear family came powerfully from the Conservative new right governments of the 1980s and early 1990s. During this period, single parent families faced political stigmatisation and the Party came to launch a 'back to basics' campaign which provided strong moral sanction for the nuclear family. New Labour governments from 1997 to 2010 continued to view the nuclear family as fundamental to the promotion of social order but placed greater emphasis on the support role of state agencies and came to recognise that growing family diversity was a reality that they had to live with. The Conservative led coalition government have attempted a delicate balancing act of supporting the traditional family institution whilst distancing themselves from past Conservative attacks on single parenthood and legislated to allow marriage between same sex couples. Thirdly, what appear to be quire radical alternatives to the traditional nuclear family are not necessarily quite so much so. For example, although the numbers of couples cohabiting has substantially increased, these are now often stable relationships between couples whose roles may still sometimes closely correspond to those of the male breadwinner and female child carer in more traditional family units.

Symbolic interactionism – family as defined by participants

Positivist research tended to view 'the family' as conventionally defined and utilise official statistics and large scale surveys as the preferred method for obtaining information about it. Although it could be recognised as one of the founding sociological perspectives, interactionism may better equip the sociologist to approach the diversity and fluidity of contemporary family life than positivism and its associated perspective of functionalism. Interactionists emphasise that individuals participate in social situations where roles are chosen, negotiated, constructed and redefined by the participants' purposeful actions. Rather than functioning as a structured imposition on people's lives, for interactionists broader society, as the product of their wilful action, can be dynamic and diverse.

Interactionism also emphasises the importance of sociological researchers seeing society as through the eyes of social participants. Interactionists studying the family would therefore attempt to gain an understanding of any family life viewed as such by people themselves rather than working from preset definitions of what counts as a family. This approach enables the sociologist to adopt a neutral attitude toward family diversity. It emphasises, in contrast to positivist approaches, that sociologists should not base their knowledge entirely on the convenience of using social statistics on the family derived from official definitions of what it is. Such number crunching loses sight of a broad diversity of relationships which are meaningful as families to participants. By adopting a micro approach, interactionists might certainly look at the experiences encountered by married couples as they negotiate married life and experience divorce (with marriage and divorce being the milestones provided in official data). However, they would also study those in other relationships which the participants define as a family and which may not form the basis of official statistics on the family, but which are equally worthy of study. In other words, sociologists should be guided in their research to try and understand all social life in ways meaningful to individuals or groups rather than the blinding convenience of easy to acquire social statistics based on conventional definitions. The sociologist who limits him or herself to the latter task risks the bias of making themselves an instrument of convention.

Symbolic interactionists are particularly interested in understanding the processes involved by which a family may identify insiders (members) and outsiders (non-members) and how processes on mutual adjustment between members take place over time. Of special interest may be the study of life in the early stages of partnerships or in newer family forms such as reconstituted families and same sex partnerships where participants have to navigate their way forward without necessarily having such clear role scripts provided for them as in the case of the conventional nuclear family. To understand the subtleties of symbolic communication, interactionists are likely to resort to the study of personal documents such as diaries and letters, time budgeting records and use unstructured and in-depth interviewing to obtain qualitative information.

Studies adopting a broadly interpretive approach have provided fertile ground for developing new ways of looking at family life in a contemporary setting and there is some attraction of interactionist type approaches to feminist researchers. For example, Finch (2007) utilises the concept of 'display' to explain that members of families engage in actions to constantly define and redefine their relationships within families and denote to others that the group that they are in is regarded as a family by them. Roseneil and Budgeon (2004) claim that what constitutes 'the family' is now far more contested and that friendship relationships are often becoming viewed more as family like, especially given the growing numbers of people living without partners.

The family – decline or change?

1. Divorce

Increase in divorce

One area frequently associated with the question of the decline of the family is that of rising divorce rates. Official statistics are available on petitions filed and divorces granted which make it clear that throughout the twentieth century there has been a substantial rise in divorce. Depending on how one measures divorce, it could be argued that divorces peaked in England and Wales in 1993 and have fallen somewhat since then, or it could be argued that divorce has reached a plateau from 1991. This is because divorce can be looked at either in terms of simple aggregate totals or rates. Aggregates simply express the total number of divorces granted during a particular year. By contrast, divorce rates refer to the number of divorces per 1,000 of the married population per annum. Aggregate numbers are useful if interest is primarily in measuring the total magnitude of divorce. Figures from Social Trends,1993, show, for example, that there were about 25,000 divorces granted in England and Wales in 1961 and that by 1986, the figure had reached approximately 154,000. If these figures were expressed in terms of rates, they would be 2.1 and 12.9 respectively – showing a greater than six-fold increase, which is roughly in line with the proportionate increase in the aggregate totals indicated above for this time period.

However, there is a sense in which rates may offer a more revealing measure when interest is in change over time. As they relate to a standard gauge of divorces per 1,000 of the married population, changes in rates may not always exactly mirror aggregate changes in divorces. For example, compared to the 1993 peak in the total of divorces of 165,018 when the rate was 13.8, the 1994 total fell to 158,175, yet the rate increased to 14.2. How is this possible? It is because the rate per 1,000 relates to the total number of people married. If there are fewer people married, then the ratio of divorces to the numbers married can increase even if the total number of divorces declines (and of course the opposite is also true).

There has been a general decline in recent decades of both the proportion and numbers of people getting married. For example, in 1971, over two thirds of the adult population were married. The figure has since fallen to about 50%. In addition to this trend, a peak in the number of divorces can also leave fewer married couples from which the rate for the successive year will be calculated, thus leading, other things being equal, to an increase in the rate.

As well as enabling comparable measures of divorce over time, divorce rates can be used to provide a comparative measure of proportions divorcing in different sections of society. For example, comparisons can be made between the rates for different ethnic groups, social class categories and age groups. Regarding the latter, it is interesting to observe that divorce rates amongst the over 60s have recently been increasing despite evidence to show that overall rates have been decreasing. Between 1991 and 2011, the rate for men over 60 has increased from 1.6 to 2.3 and for women from 1.2 to 1.6. A number of reasons have been put forward to explain this opposite trend. One is that this time period will have included a greater proportion of women who have worked for substantial periods of their life and accumulated access to improved pensions. By acquiring greater financial independence, more women may feel that they can free themselves from unhappy marriages. Another is that as people are living longer, they have a potentially longer period of unhappy marriage which they may not be prepared to endure.

Understanding statistics

Attempting to understand statistics in sociology can be quite baffling. The author suggests that one way of making the task easier is to invent a situation where the figures are much smaller and rounded. For example, imagine a small town in which there are 2,000 married people. If in a given year there were 22 divorces, the rate would be 11 per 1,000 married people. However, if in another year there were only 1,000 married people, then the same aggregate of 22 divorces would represent a leap in the rate to 22. The same logic can be applied to the much larger figures outlined further above, and, of course, this type of exercise is worth inventing to assist the understanding of statistical information in other areas of sociological study.

Why an increase in divorce?

How can the relatively high divorce rates of recent decades be understood sociologically? To do so, one needs to look at various aspects of the social context. One reason is that changes in divorce laws over the last 160 years have gradually made divorce more accessible. Such reforms are referred to as 'enabling legislation'. The statistics show that as well as a general upward curve in the divorce rate, there is usually a jump in the figures following enabling legislation. This jump would include a number of divorces which would have been more difficult to actualise under the conditions of previous legislation.

However, enablement alone is insufficient to explain the very substantial increase in decisions to divorce over much of this period. As the law changes, it usually reflects society's changing moral values which it codifies. Therefore, more liberal divorce legislation has accompanied a decline in social stigma against divorce. But it is not necessarily the case that there is a clear cause and effect relationship whereby changing moral values bring about corresponding legal changes. It could also be argued that the greater frequency of divorce which the legislation makes possible will have an impact on moral values by reducing the stigma against divorce which is becoming increasingly common, thus opening up possibilities when previously taboo. Changes in moral values and legislation can thus feed off each other.

This arguably still does not explain why more people decide to divorce. One explanation requires the application of historical understanding of the practical choices available to people, their expectations associated with marriage and the nature of marital bonds. Edward Shorter (1977) argued that in much of pre-industrial society, the family was a relatively uncaring environment, organised around the perpetuation of property or the domestic work unit. The economic necessity of the marriage remaining intact was often of prime importance. By contrast, following industrialisation, the workplace moving outside of the family reduced the extent to which ties were based on economic necessity. Of further importance was a cultural change. As marriage became accompanied by high expectations of romantic attachment and emotional fulfilment, these have become the more shaky mainstays of modern marriages. Such high expectations can be easily thwarted, often leaving little else to hold the marriage together.

Secularisation is a further dimension of social change which may be relevant to the long term rise in divorce rates. Secularisation is the assertion that the significance of religion in people's lives declines with the process of modernisation. This assertion will be reviewed in greater detail in a later chapter – we cannot assume that it is a simple proven fact. However, from the point of view of this topic area, it can be argued that religion and the church may play a diminishing role in people's lives, when measured by the increase in marriages in registry offices and other licensed premises compared to church weddings. The implications for divorce are that the sanctity of the church and the belief that a sacred promise has been made before an all seeing god (given at least the probability that overall a greater proportion of people who marry in church hold religious views) are more powerful sanctions making for a marriage to endure. Moreover, those who elect to have a church marriage may include a greater proportion of people with traditionalist attitudes toward married life in the first place. One would need to know more about the reasons why people marry in church or choose a secular setting and whether the choice has been freely available to them. For example, as divorce has increased and is frequently followed by remarriage, if any church retains a traditional attitude of not marrying divorcees, then more people may be pushed toward secular remarriage options.

Other social factors which coincide with the steep increase in divorce rates since the early 1960s include, as well as higher marital expectations, a greater assertiveness of women which accompanied the women's liberation movement from the late 60s. Feminists in particular have highlighted the issue of domestic violence, suffered mainly by women at the hands of men, and raised the profile of behaviour which should be no longer tolerated. From about this time, women also gained more opportunities to become economically self-supporting through improved female employment opportunities accompanying the expansion of the service sector. As we have seen, despite increasing expectations of personal fulfilment in marriage, these work 'opportunities' have involved some women in the stress of a dual burden if husbands' involvement in domestic chores remains minimal. Putting all this together, it should not be surprising to find that divorces filed by women rose to become a significant majority.

Despite historically high divorce rates, a majority of those who divorce will remarry and statistics show that their future marriage will also be more prone to divorce. Indeed, over a third of marriages are now a remarriage for at least one of the partners. Although people are living longer, the period of time over which marriages endure is decreasing. For example, figures for 1951, show that 10% of marriages ended in divorce within 25 years. By 1981, 10% were divorced within 5 years (Sclater, 2005, p.74).

In 1970, the American writer Alvin Toffler argued that a trend was emerging in contemporary societies toward an accelerating pace of change and increasing human longevity in which the odds were increasingly stacked against couples developing and remaining together for life. He argued that a change in family life toward 'serial monogamy' – an emerging pattern of sequences of temporary marriages - was already under way. Toffler predicted that the traditional expectation of lifelong marriage would give way to the anticipation of relatively short lived marriage and further declining stigma against divorce. Couples would be increasingly confronted with key decisions when their paths diverged on whether to go their separate ways and find a more parallel path with another partner. Such issues will be touched on again later in this chapter.

Why a decrease in divorce?

Figures from the Office For National Statistics (11/2/2014) show that since the turn of the millennium, there is some evidence of a decline in both totals and rates of divorce in England and Wales. In this period, the total peaked at 153,065 in 2003 and the rate peaked at 14 in 2004.

There was subsequently a steady year by year decrease in both totals and rates through to 2009 when the figures stood at 113,949 and 10.5 respectively. This total was the lowest since 1974 and the rate the lowest since 1977, and although both totals and rate increased again in 2010, there were further decreases in 2011 and an increase in 2012. What possible explanations could there be for this more recent reversal of the longer term upward trend in the divorce rate?

At this stage, the explanations are somewhat speculative. Until recently, there has been a long term decline in the numbers of people marrying. A reversal of this decline was evident in 2010 and figures showed a further increase in 2011. Time will tell whether the start of a new trend is emerging. However, at present, it can be argued that those who marry are now a smaller but harder core of those committed to marriage.

The average age for first marriages now for both men and women is seven years later than in 1971 and may sometimes follow a protracted period of cohabitation. With the growing acceptability of cohabitation, only those committed to marriage may feel it necessary to take that step. On the other hand, there is also evidence to suggest that prior cohabitation is associated with the increased chance of divorce!

A further influence on the downward figures for divorce may relate to high immigration figures during the early twenty first century. Many immigrants that enter Britain hold traditional cultural values regarding family loyalty and commitments.

An association between economic recession and an increase in divorce has been identified as sometimes holding (for example in the early 1980s and 1990s) and the phenomena were arguably linked by the extra stresses placed on partnerships during difficult times. However, this argument is probably too simplistic. Firstly, explanations are not likely to be reducible to the single causal effect of economic influences. Secondly, even if the state of the economy is an important factor in the explanation, it can equally be counter argued that during economic recession it is more difficult economically for people to divorce. This argument may tentatively tally with the declining divorce rates following the long recession after 2008.

2. Growing family and household diversity

This section will look at evidence of the growing diversity of family life in Britain. Although reference is made to general trends and the bigger picture through the use of official statistics, we will later see that recent sociological approaches to the study of family life are focussing more on understanding the meaning of its different forms from the points of view of the participants, indicating a more interpretive emphasis.

As those who divorce often remarry or form new cohabiting partnerships, the result can be an increasing number of 'reconstituted' families. Such families bring together children from different marriages into a single home and can vary considerably in the extent to which they follow a traditional nuclear family pattern or not. A major problem, though, is likely to be that of mutual adjustment between family members. For example, children may feel that a stepparent is treating them unfairly compared to the way that they treat their own biological children. These 'binuclear' or stepfamilies may also pose the problem of the relative authority over children of step parents within the family unit and biological parents outside who continue to exert an influence. The issue of access also requires past partners to work at establishing arrangements that work, although there is evidence of a tendency for biological fathers outside of the new unit to drift out of involvement.

When families break up and reconstituted families are formed, there has been much dispute over the type of post-divorce arrangements that work in the best interests of children. Thery summarises two opposing positions (Cheal, 2002, p.64): the 'substitution model' and the 'durability model'. Substitution emphasises that the best way forward is in a clear break between ex-partners and the establishment of a new nuclear family unit as a stable environment for children in which the new spouse takes over full parental responsibilities from the biological parent. By contrast, the durability model emphasises the importance of continuity in that the biological parent retains regular contact with their children in the new family unit. As a result, step and biological parental roles become differentiated. It is this latter approach which policy makers have generally come to prefer, in the belief, supported by some evidence, that continued contact from the biological parent (invariably father) will improve the support for and development of the child.

Statistics indicate that there has been a fall in the number of marriages in England and Wales in recent decades from an annual average of almost 400,000 between 1965 and 1975 to under 300,000 by the mid 1990s and, despite increases in the early years of the twenty first century, a fall again to 244,710 in 2005. The figure of 243,808 marriages in 2010 represents approximately a 5% increase on the 2009 figure and the provisional Office for National Statistics (11/2/2014) figures for 2011 show a further small aggregate increase. Even so, in the context of population increases, the rate of marriage has recently remained static and the general trend remains that of a gradual fall, with civil wedding ceremonies comprising an increasing proportion of the total (70% in 2011, from just over 50% in 1992). If further allowance is made for the increasing divorce rates throughout the twentieth century, the tendency for divorcees to remarry, and the fact that the above marriage figures include an increasing number of second marriages or beyond, there is evidence to suggest that the population has been dividing into a declining proportion of people who are marrying, more of whom are divorcing and many remarrying, and a significantly increasing proportion who are not marrying. So what is the evidence of alternatives to marriage that are emerging?

There is clear evidence in recent history of increased rates of cohabitation. However, it is misleading to see cohabitation as just a relatively recent phenomena. From a longer historical perspective, pre-marital sex, cohabitation and transient relationships were not uncommon features of life amongst poorer sections of the working class in the eighteenth and nineteenth centuries.

From research conducted in the United Kingdom in the 1950s, approximately 5% of married women said that they had cohabited with their husband prior to marriage. Although not in strictly comparable form, the findings from General Household Surveys indicated that the percentage of women cohabiting doubled between 1981 and 1996 to 25% and that the average time period of cohabitation was significantly increasing. The figures also showed different cohabitation rates for different age groups and different rates for males and females within the same age group. The highest rate was for males in the age range of 30-34 where the figures exceeded 40%. It is, of course, possible that an element of this increase, especially when compared to the early figure, may be due to people feeling freer to volunteer this type of information than in the past when such arrangements were more heavily stigmatised. Also, just because the rate of marriage has tended to decline and the figures for cohabitation have increased, the extent to which cohabitation is forming an alternative to marriage may be a little more questionable than the statistics suggest. This is because many cohabiting couples eventually marry and high rates of divorce mean that more new couples need to await the completion of a divorce before they are able to remarry and may cohabit during this time.

Cohabitation itself subsumes a diversity of arrangements. These may range from short term relationships with little commitment to longer term commitments and the raising of children. Overall, though, a range of snapshot surveys for 2007 – the General Household Survey, the Labour Force Survey and the Annual Population Survey – together provide consistent evidence that approximately 2.25 million opposite sex couples are in cohabiting relationships in England and Wales and that the proportion of never married amongst these is increasing. Although future projections should always be treated with caution, most predictions suggest that the number of cohabiting couples will increase significantly in the coming decades. For example, according to Population Trends research, the figure is expected to rise to about 3.8 million couples by 2031.

Changing attitudes appear to correlate with these trends. A British Social Attitudes Survey of 2001 found that long term cohabitation was becoming accepted as relatively normal and that only just over 50% of those interviewed believed that people should marry before having a family, compared to almost 75% in 1989. Few, however, dismissed marriage which remained viewed as a viable lifestyle choice.

There is, of course, reason for some doubt over the precise accuracy of official figures on cohabitation. The issues can be raised of how officials on the one hand or the parties themselves on the other define a relationship, and the extent to which there may be incentives, such as claiming benefit, which are likely to encourage some people to hide cohabiting relationships from prying officials and others.

According to official statistics, single parent (usually female headed) households in the United Kingdom have increased from 8% of all families with children in 1972 to 15% in 1989-1990 and 26% by 2012. This latter figure represents approximately two million single parent households, 91% of which are headed by females. Although revealing a massive increase in single parenthood, there is much that these statistics alone also hide. Firstly, they are just a snapshot measurement. Many single parents and their children will have lived in or come to live in married or cohabiting households for part of their lives. Secondly, in reality the distinction between married or cohabiting and single parent households may not always be quite as clear cut as definitions suggest. In some married households, the requirements of certain occupations such as travelling salespersons or some that are involved in the holiday business, can necessitate that a partner be frequently absent. In other cases, the partners may be separated or a partner might be in prison, whereas some single parent households have frequent contact with or support from a partner. Thirdly, the category of single parenthood is of diverse composition made up of changing proportions including a declining fraction of widowed and increasing proportions of divorced and never married single parents. Situations may also vary significantly in terms of opportunities to work, support from other family members and friends and financial security available, but generally the never married single parents are more likely to struggle on low income.

Providing a succinct historical overview, Robertson Elliot (1996, p.22) has extracted information from Social Trends to show that in 1960 about one birth out of every twenty was outside of marriage, whereas by the early 1990s the proportion had reached almost one in three. Of these, approximately a half were born into cohabiting relationships and a half born to single mothers.

The figures for those living alone (referred to as singletons) have shown a significant increase in recent decades. For example, in 1998, 12% of people lived in single person households compared to 3.9% in 1961. These comprised 12% of households in 1961 and 28% of households in 1998, since by definition they comprise the smallest household units. By 2008, singletons made up 30% of households, a figure that remained about the same by 2012. However, pausing here for a moment may alert us to some of the complexities behind these apparently straightforward figures. The routes to living alone are diverse and many who live alone do not do so through a positive decision of their own. This can particularly be the case for elderly people through the death of a partner. The singleton figures for those under retirement age may therefore be more indicative of positive choice. These comprised 4% of all households in 1961 and 12% in 1996-1997.

An increase in the proportions of singleton households may be related to an increase in divorce rates and a tendency for people to marry later in life than they used to but it is also likely to both reflect and further promote the view that living alone is now more socially acceptable. Young people are less likely now to go straight from their family of origin to family of destination but may instead leave home to set up their own home. However, as a word of caution, at the time of writing (2014), increases in university debt, rises in house prices and the difficulty of obtaining a mortgage appear to be associated with a rise in the proportion of young people aged 20 to 34 living at home with their parents. These figures have now reached record levels of over 1 in 4 or 3.3 million in total.

But how exactly are single person households defined? Take the example of a house divided into three separate flats, each let out to a student. Each flat may count as a single person household, but is this quite the same as people living alone in separate dwellings? What if each student in each flat shared common kitchen facilities and a television room? Do they still live alone and constitute single person households? Whether for definitional purposes they do or do not, presumably, qualitatively, their domestic lives would be quite different from those living in isolated and self-contained flats or separate dwellings. Furthermore, statistics only take a snapshot view of the domestic situation. Presumably, many of these students would return to families during vacation times, so to what extent have they 'left home'? Longer-term profiles would therefore more realistically show the varying domestic situations experienced than any snapshot measurement could.

Another aspect of family diversity relates to the ethnic diversity of British society. The cultural identity and ways of different ethnic groups are acquired through socialisation into cultural traditions. These traditions may persist or change in the cultural environment of the host population.

When ethnic minorities migrated to Britain, their own cultural values and family structures were sometimes accentuated as a form of defence against the racism that they suffered from the host population. However, a substantial proportion of the ethnic minority population is now second or third generation. A key question at this point is whether life in British society is narrowing the differences in family life between different ethnic minorities and white British people or whether ethnic traditions are more resistant to change and thus contribute to another dimension of family diversity.

The complexity of differences both between and within ethnic groups regarding family life cannot be tackled here, only emphasised. As two quite contrasting examples, South Asian and Afro Caribbean family life will be briefly commented on. Generally, South Asian families have retained the highest marriage rates and low divorce rates, they tend to partake in extended family life where possible (including contacts with and visits to relatives in their country of descent), sometimes still exert pressure towards arranged marriage, and tend to place a strong emphasis on traditional segregated conjugal roles and patriarchal power. One important difference between Pakistani and Indian families, though, is that in the former, the influence of Islamic strictures is more likely to require a wife to remain within the household or family business to minimise contact with non-family males. Although single parenthood in both Indian and Pakistani families has significantly increased, this is from a very low base, and reaching about 5% remains well below that of the white British population.

By contrast, single parent families are much more common within West Indian communities, marriage rates are relatively low, divorce rates high and cohabitation, at a rate of about 10%, is not uncommon. However, research has also shown there to exist a diversity of Afro Caribbean family life in both country of decsent and in Britain. This is partly economic based. Economically successful West Indians are more likely to follow a model of family life similar to the conventional British nuclear family. By contrast, common law families are more likely amongst the less economically successful. A third pattern identified is the female headed households in which males play only a peripheral role and the mother, usually working, relies on the help of female relatives or neighbours to run the family.

The question of whether cultural influences or situational circumstances of a more economic nature best explain family patterns of ethnic minority groups has been of much debate. If within the same ethnic minority culture, family structures vary according to economic factors and give rise to families similar to those of other ethnic groups in similar economic circumstances, it could be argued that situational circumstances such as social class may have at least as strong an influence on the way that people live as do ethnic cultures.

Whether the structure of family life of ethnic minorities is converging with that of family life of the host culture is a very complex matter and is likely to vary both between and within ethnic minority groups. However, it begs the question of convergence to what given the diversity of family life that exists. On the one hand second and third generation youngsters may have to delicately manoeuvre their behaviour between a family life in which parents hold traditional cultural values and the more permissive liberal ways of broader society, whilst parents may be keen for their part on safeguarding their cultural traditions from what they feel is a corrosive environment of 'anything goes'. Overall, the data from surveys and more in-depth research suggests both quite high levels of continuity in the different ethnic traditions and some diversity of family life within each of the ethnic minority groups. This would tend to add to the overall diversity of family life in Britain.

Although people can now be more open about gay and lesbian relationships, it is difficult to obtain any accurate measure of the changing extent of these relationships in society due to powerful past taboos. The greater moral uniformity of the post-war decades placed very strong pressure on people with homosexual inclinations to either repress these tendencies, engage in clandestine relationships or face the risk of criminalisation or 'corrective therapy'. Only from 1969 did homosexual acts between consenting adults over the age of 21 cease to be a criminal offence.

One feature of gay and lesbian relationships is that they are relatively free from the imposition of conventional male and female gender stereotypes. Hence, there is more scope for negotiation of roles which tend to be more egalitarian than in heterosexual relationships. This was indeed found to be the case in Gillian Dunne's (1999) study of lesbian households and Weeks et al (2004) add that there tends to be a more equal sharing of emotional work within same sex partnerships.

In a growing number of countries, people in same sex relationships have been able to acquire legal recognition of their relationship. In some of these countries, a distinction is made between same sex partnerships and heterosexual marriage, with the former restricted to the status of 'civil partnerships'. This is essentially a distinction of legal terminology and status based on religious sensitivities, although the exact legal differences vary somewhat from society to society. Same sex civil partnerships were pioneered in Denmark in 1989, to be followed by Norway and Sweden in 1993 and 1994 respectively (countries which also showed early evidence of increased cohabitation rates), France in 2000, Germany in 2001, and Britain from December 2005. Other countries and some states or localities in countries with federal political systems such as Argentina and Australia have followed since.

In Britain, the established position of the Church of England is that the purpose of marriage is to fulfil god's purpose by promoting a committed and faithful relationship between a man and woman for the procreation of children. The term 'marriage' holds a degree of religious connotation and the state recognised this by initially limiting single sex partnerships to civil status, officiated by a registrar at approved premises. However, in Britain the status of civil partnership does confer on partners legal equalities to that of married couples, for example in terms of taxes and benefits, protection against domestic violence and rules regarding migration and nationality. The Conservative led coalition government has since legislated to allow same sex partners access to full married status, with weddings made available through religious organisations that are willing to 'opt in' and conduct ceremonies. The Quakers are one such organisation that have decided to 'opt in'. However, due to strong opposition from the Churches of England and Wales, the legislation provides a ban on conducting same sex marriages within these institutions.

At the time of the legalisation of civil partnerships, it was estimated that in Britain approximately 4,500 would be granted in the first year. This figure was actually exceeded by over 10,000, demonstrating a surge effect of enabling legislation, and has settled in recent years at an annual figure of above 6,000. As not legally defined as marriage, breakups of these relationships are not referred to as divorce, but as 'dissolution'. However, the procedure follows a similar one to that of divorce whereby the partnership must have endured for at least a year and face irretrievable breakdown. It is quite early to refer meaningfully to yearly dissolution rates, but by the end of 2010, 1.6% of male civil partnerships had been dissolved and for female partnerships the figure was 3.3%.

On the one hand, such reforms can be seen as the government's response to demands for gay rights and an advance in social tolerance. However, it has also been suggested by Jennie Bristow (11/2/2014) that following decades of decline in marriage rates and substantial increases in numbers of cohabiting couples set to continue, this is more of a 'top down' initiative by a government which is worried when people live their lives 'beneath the radar of the state'. Civil partnerships and same sex marriage allow these relationships to become opened up to official recognition. To take the point a little further, legal recognition may be presented as a liberal reform but provides the government with greater powers of surveillance over its population and may be seen by governments to be beneficial to social stability by extending legal ties.

Holland (April 2001) was the first country to completely eliminate the distinction between same sex and heterosexual marriage, followed by Belgium in 2002. In Holland, 2,400 same sex marriages were officiated in the nine months of 2001, whilst for the twelve months of 2003 the number had fallen to 1,500.

The Papacy, as the custodian of Catholic traditionalism, remains strongly opposed to same sex partnerships, and Pope Benedict XVI referred to homosexuality as an "intrinsic moral evil". More surprisingly, therefore, the third country to pass legislation enabling same sex marriage was Spain in 2005, a country where a substantial majority of the population still see themselves as Catholic. The Roman Catholic Church and many conservatives bitterly opposed the reforms of a socialist government, which also passed legislation to speed up the process by which couples could divorce.

Both Canada and South Africa have since passed legislation allowing same sex marriage. However, the situation in the United States is complicated as laws apply on a state-by-state basis. Whilst California has recognised same sex civil partnerships and Massachusetts marriage, a broader debate has emerged in which attempts have been made to pass a constitutional amendment prohibiting legal recognition of such partnerships.

In late 2006, opposition between religious traditionalism and state reform on issues of sexuality and discrimination surfaced in Britain regarding the issue of adoption. It became possible for same sex couples to adopt in 2005. The Catholic Church, which runs a small number of adoption agencies in England and Wales, opposed the placement of children for adoption through its own agencies with same sex couples in civil partnerships which, in reference to religious scriptures, it did not recognise as equivalent to marriages which had to be a union of man and woman. The timing of this statement of opposition related to the then forthcoming 2007 Equalities Act (Sexual Orientation Regulations) which made it illegal to discriminate against anybody on the grounds of sexuality, including cases of adoption by same sex couples. In its response, the Catholic Church threatened to close its adoption agencies if it were forced to comply. Losing an appeal in 2010 for exclusion from the terms of the legislation, agencies now face the prospect of loss of charitable status should they not comply.

The above section illustrates the diverse forms which family and household life now takes in contemporary Britain. The reader is reminded that even within each of the family types referred to above there will also be found diversity. This pattern of change is generally typical of family life in western cultures. A broader question still, in the context of globalisation and economic modernisation, is the extent to which cultural and family life in those eastern countries which have traditions of community orientation and loyalty to more extended family structures will converge with the western pattern and through growing affluence and the process of individualisation develop greater family diversity and smaller family units. Analysing this question is beyond the scope of this chapter.

Responses to changes in family life – sociology, politics and social policy

There have been a variety sociological interpretations and political and social policy responses to changes in family life. For example, one position adopted has been that despite evidence of lifestyle diversity, the nuclear family still remains the standard family form in contemporary British society. An alternative view sees the diversity of modern family life and evidence of high divorce rates as alarming indicators of the breakdown of the family and a sign of a broader social malaise. For yet others, evidence of growing diversity of lifestyle should be viewed positively as indicative of the emergence of a more pluralistic and tolerant society. These positions can be briefly elaborated as follows.

The first position was strongly argued by Robert Chester in the mid-1980s. Much of his argument is based on the way that statistics on family life are viewed. On the issue of spiralling divorce rates, Chester argued that the contemporary disruptive effect was not too dissimilar to that resulting from marriage breakups through much higher mortality rates during the nineteenth century (Robertson Elliot, 1996, p.34). Increased cohabitation and declining marriage rates amongst the young during the 1980s were interpreted by Chester as a period of adjustment as the young were delaying the age at which they married. Cohabitation in the 1970s and 1980s tended to comprise more short term relationships which were often child free rather than a full alternative to or rejection of marriage. Moreover, although the number of single parent families was rising, it was argued that single parenthood was often either preceded or superseded by nuclear family life. Whilst in 1981, households with married parents and their children comprised only 32% of all households, being on average larger units, they included 49% of people. Additionally, since these figures were only a snapshot of family life, they did not show the fact that a majority of people lived in a nuclear family at some time in their life, even if this institution had changed somewhat with more women entering the workforce. For Chester, the nuclear family, or neo-nuclear with wives in employment, was thus still a popular majority institution. However, since his writings, figures have shown a significant decline in the nuclear family whilst the numbers of those opting for an alternative, often long term, to the traditional nuclear family have continued to increase. Chester's argument therefore now appears to look rather dated.

The second position has been adopted by functionalists and the political ideology and social policy of new right Conservatism of 1980s and 1990s governments. We have seen in a previous section that from a traditional functionalist position, the widespread nature of the traditional nuclear family was regarded as proof of its functional appropriateness to the needs of modern industrial society. As well as serving the economy, the nuclear family was part of a society unified around a dominant moral culture which promoted social stability and order. From this perspective, moral and family diversity tend to be viewed as dysfunctional and disruptive of social order.

In a similar vein, new right Conservatives, whilst liberals and supporters of free market policy in economics, felt that moral values were becoming too liberal in terms of tolerance of alternatives to the nuclear family. Singled out for particular concern was the increase during the 1980s in the number of never married single parents. It vexed the new right that what was viewed as irresponsible behaviour engaged in by a growing number of people often required state support and therefore the placing of additional tax burden on others, including those who already supported conventional families. These views found an ally in the writings of the American Charles Murray who associated the social problem of what he referred to as a growing 'underclass' with a high reliance of welfare. For Murray, single parent families were prominent within this underclass. He argued that their dependency on welfare and the absence of a working male parent to instil respect for authority and a work ethic, encouraged in their children a similar culture of dependency. The costs to society were a deterioration in social discipline and the penalty of higher taxation on working heads of households.

New right social policy, which intended to encourage traditional family roles and responsibilities, included the introduction of new child support arrangements and care in the community. Set up in 1993 to pursue absent parents, the Child Support Agency (later replaced under the New Labour Government in 2006 by the Child Maintenance Enforcement Agency) operated to assert traditional family responsibilities of the male provider for the female child carer by imposing financial contributions on absent parents. In so doing, it aimed to combine the purpose of enforcing moral responsibility with saving treasury expenditure, but could be a difficult arrangement for women who wanted to sever links with a previous partner.

De-institutionalisation and the promotion of care in the community had the effect of placing an enhanced burden of care, especially for the aged, on the shoulders of female relatives. For example, research by Nissel and Bonnerjea (1982) into care for the handicapped elderly found that, on important care activities, for each one minute contributed by husbands, nineteen minutes was provided by wives.

Running through the reforms of the 1990s was John Major's moral message of 'back to basics', particularly regarding the traditions of family life. However, this became a hostage to fortune with publicity of the private lives of a number of Conservative MPs which fell short of this model and helped set the tone for the defeat of the Conservatives in the 1997 general election.

When New Labour came to power, the government continued to emphasise the importance of stable traditional nuclear family life to the maintenance of social order and the upbringing of responsible citizens. However, the reality of growing family diversity was also becoming acknowledged. New Labour's 'third way politics' (explained in the politics chapter) emphasised a new type of arrangement between state agencies and families in which it was the responsibility of families to provide for their own independence and state agencies to play a supporting but not controlling role in enabling them to do so. This included early intervention through the extension of pre-school education and the passing of legislation to provide possible parental leave for fathers to be with their families. Legislation allowing single sex civil partnerships was introduced, and whilst avoiding stigmatising single parents, the government were looking at ways to encourage them to return to work when their youngest child was twelve years of age rather than sixteen.

During their period in opposition, debates within the British Conservative Party regarding policy on the family ranged between those of traditionalists to modernisers. Traditionalists advocated strong support for marriage between heterosexual couples as the superior institution for the raising of children, if being somewhat more cautious in their condemnation of alternatives to this model. Those who saw themselves as modernisers opposed what they saw as the excesses of the new right and adopted a more tolerant stance toward the diversity of family life that had emerged.

The leadership of David Cameron broadly accepted the position of the modernisers and in opposition he had supported New Labour legislation on single sex civil partnerships. When the Conservatives returned to power as the senior partner with the Liberal Democrats in the 2010 coalition government, Cameron as Prime Minister was keen on cultivating his own nuclear family image and signifying a preference for the nuclear family institution, whilst signalling a break from past new right ideological hostility against single parents.

The 2010 Conservative Party manifesto aimed to provide financial incentives and reduce financial disincentives for traditional family life. However, the reality of coalition government and the austerity programme that they have pursued have had other more marked impacts on family life. Opposition has come from many of their own natural supporters to the withdrawal of child benefit to higher rate tax payers. Moreover, the imposition of a three year freeze on child benefit and cuts to child tax credits, whilst not having a beneficial effect for married couples, was anticipated would result in a substantial increase in child poverty experienced in households that were reliant on benefit. Evidence in 2013 of children going to school hungry and an increase in the number of people reliant on food handouts seems to support this prediction.

On their reformist agenda, the government has legislated, to some consternation within the Conservative Party, to allow single sex marriage to be officiated within religious denominations that are forthcoming, whilst providing an exclusion to the Church of England. There therefore appears to be a degree of convergence between the main political parties in the acceptance of family diversity without either fully embracing it.

Finally, Rhona Rapoport is representative of the third position identified above. This stance commends the diversity of family and lifestyle types which have come to characterise contemporary life in democratic societies. For Rapoport, tolerance of such diversity is seen as enhancing people's human rights to choose to live as they wish.

Pause and reflection

Sociological theorists and the theories that they develop are arguably to a large extent prisoners of their times and social contexts. Thus, although both Marxist and functionalist perspectives may have revealed much about the family during past eras, they tend to be locked into a dated analysis of society and the family in which the traditional form of the family fits into a theory of the broader structure of the time. For example, Marxism traditionally saw segregated gender roles within the family as a vital prop to capitalism by providing both outlets and support for productive male workers and the disciplining of future generations of productive labour. Women formed a reserve and expendable army of cheap labour from within the working class. Capitalism has however adapted and thrived despite evidence of a breakdown in segregated conjugal roles, a substantial advance in the diversity in family life and the integration of women into the workforce.

The emphasis placed by functionalism on the nuclear family tended to claim the superiority of a model of family life for which there was much greater social consensus at the height of the influence of this perspective in the 1950s. This indicates an inherent conservative predisposition in the functionalist perspective – it takes what is, argues that it therefore serves social needs, and makes supporting justifications. Although the perspective should be able to anticipate and explain changes in the family as part of the mutual adjustment of institutions as society changes, functionalism has tended to remain associated with the 1950s model of the family. Furthermore, it is questionable whether it is possible to go far enough within this framework to explain the extent of change in family life and relationships in the contemporary context of globalisation and, arguably, new emergent conditions of postmodernism or high modernism.

Ultimately, it is up to sociologists, through the scrutiny of theories and evidence, to come to their own decisions on the extent to which such theories can be accommodated to or retain applicability in the understanding of family life in contemporary times.

Symbolic interactionism was argued to be a more flexible perspective through which to understand the diversity of contemporary family life. However, as a micro perspective, it has far less to say about the broad social and historical changes which have accompanied this diversity. Some more contemporary approaches have attempted to explain diversity within this broader perspective.

Developments in sociological approaches to family life

A number of theorists are in broad agreement that society has in recent decades been changing fundamentally and that modernist explanations and concepts such as those utilised within Marxism and functionalism and post-war research are no longer adequate for explaining contemporary society and family life. Two theoretical approaches take the form of postmodernism and high modernism, although the distinction between these general perspectives is not always clear cut.

Postmodernism – almost anything goes

For postmodernists, advanced societies have been undergoing a major transition from the modern to postmodern social condition. Emerging in the latter decades of the twentieth century, a key feature of the postmodern environment is that the moral uniformities, social structures and social controls which were characteristic of the modern era have broken down in the face of accelerated and directionless social change. This change has led to a greater diversity in social and family life, allowing a massive scope of choice in terms of the way that people may decide to define and construct their own lifestyles and familial relationships. Such changes are usually viewed positively as liberating, against the backdrop of the modernist era when the nuclear family was the dominant institution of social and moral conformity in western societies in the post-war era. According to postmodernists, certain assumptions were built into the modernist view, the key ones being:

1. That absolute truth based on scientific certainty could be established and that as a result, social progress could be assisted as rational analysis would enable informed social intervention and planned social improvement. Regarding the family, this meant that social policy interventions could be orientated toward supporting the nuclear family.

2. That being the most technologically advanced, western societies held an image of the future for less developed societies. This view tended to assume that progress is unilinear – ie as less developed societies develop, they converge with the ways of more advanced societies. Thus, the tendency toward the universality of the nuclear family could be argued.

Considering the first point, it is argued that a postmodern era has emerged in which there has been a breakdown of faith in the scientific certainties and uniform moral standards that were more typical of modern industrial societies. Postmodernists argue that the diversity of family life has become so advanced that there is no single moral consensus about a preferred family type and that policy interventions cannot and should not favour any particular family form. Moreover, the capacity for effective social intervention by the state has been overtaken by the speed of social change and the collapse of a sense of change in a progressive direction. Thus, governments have, perhaps reluctantly, had to accept that social policy has lost its grip in moulding family life toward a single preferred type. Lifestyle can be increasingly based on individual choice, so long as it does not transgress the like rights of others. A new level of tolerance has accompanied a massive increase in the diversity of types of family life and lifestyle variations.

Regarding the second point on convergence, it is clear that as well as an explosion of diversity within postmodern societies, there remains diversity between societies regarding family life which relate to cultural differences. And further challenging the first point raised above, through bringing into contact different cultures and belief systems, globalisation may be enhancing the process of family diversity within societies.

For writers such as Baudrillard, postmodern society is a world of fast communication and media images in which people are free to choose from an array of lifestyles and identities as they search for successful formulas for their lives in an ever changing social world. This is a world of high consumerism in which no single family form is able to establish a moral monopoly and no particular way of life or family form is universally recognised as superior to others.

Judith Stacey's research (Haralambos, 2013, pp.571-573) in the United States adopts a postmodernist stance in which she argues that high technology and globalisation have brought about rapid change and the need for flexibility in people's work lives which brings forth the need for adaptive changes in their personal and family lives. Her small scale stydy was conducted in the 1980s, and focussed on participants in the post-industrial economy of Silicon Valley, which, because of its technological advance, was argued to provide an image of family life in more developed postmodern conditions. Stacey discovered that participants were finding innovative ways of developing familial relationships to contend with uncertainty and change in their lives. She suggested that these practical responses were particularly embraced by those in working class occupations, thus questioning the march of progress assumption of 'stratified diffusion'; that the middle classes invariably set the trend of change which the working class follows.

In other research, Stacey found that gay and lesbian families were amongst the more reflective and creative in defining their own families which were less restricted to blood ties and more likely to include friends – a finding which has been supported by other research, such as that of Roseneil and Bubgeon (2004).

Postmodernists argue that bewildering choice and relativism in terms of truth and lifestyle are here to stay. There is no likelihood of a return to the predominance of the nuclear family or the emergence of a new single family form generally agreed to be the model to conform to and there is no detectable direction of change other than that of growing diversity of family and lifestyle.

Variations of high modernism

There can be a very fine dividing line between views of the social condition adopted by more moderate postmodernists and sociologists who adopt a high modernist perspective. As in the case of postmodernists, those viewing the family from a high modern position emphasise that society has entered a new phase which is characterised by far greater social fluidity, diversity and individual choice compared to the relatively structured and stable world of post-war modernism and the constraints of nuclear family life. However, unlike those who adopt a more extreme postmodernist position (eg. Baudrillard), high modernist writers do not maintain that modern society has been eclipsed by the transition to a postmodern world saturated by media images, dominated by fashion and experiencing a complete breakdown of past social structures and moral unity to the extent that it is beyond rational understanding and control. Instead, it is argued that modern society has entered a new and advanced phase. This phase is one of advanced modernism in which rational analysis of social change is possible if sociology develops new and sufficiently sophisticated theories and concepts. This means that, more difficult as it may be, it is possible to fashion social policy interventions to support family life in its diversity, but a further problem is the pressures that the state is up against in terms of financial constraints within an environment of competitive globalised capitalism.

Ulrich Beck distinguishes between 'first modernity' (capitalist industrial society up to the 1960s) and contemporary 'second modernity', the latter being referred to as 'risk society'. Beck adopts a similar position to that of Giddens regarding the emergence of new risks in the context of social change and uncertainty. He relates a decline in traditional social constraints particularly to the advance of individualisation which accompanied first modernity and has reached a new level in second modernity. By the advance of individualisation, Beck means that the scope of choices facing individuals in their daily lives has massively increased. The thinning out of constraining social structures and identities of social class and gender stratification and the decline in traditional family life and communities means that people have had to take on the burden of navigating their own way in life whilst experiencing uncertainly and lack of control in doing so. Their intimate relationships therefore become more important in an increasingly impersonal and insecure world in which people seek such relationships as a form of refuge. However, with the breakdown of a once more singular system of norms and a standard model of family life, the guidelines for these relationships must now also be fashioned more by the partners themselves. The advance of educational and career opportunities for women as part of this openness means that trying to make a relationship work can increasingly become a source of conflict based on new and differing expectations between partners. Beck's rather bleak outlook is that with the advance of individual freedom and opportunity, it becomes more difficult to establish a common ground of satisfaction and fulfilment in intimate relationships, which, in the search for security in a risk society, themselves become increasingly precarious.

In a similar vein, Zygmunt Bauman views contemporary societies as having reached a heightened level of social fluidity and individualisation which leads to the experience of a heightened interplay between the inescapable advance of individual freedom and the search to establish a degree of security. Life has become uprooted from past traditions and structures and modern technology opens up broader networks of acquaintances but fewer lasting relationships. Bauman refers to this advanced stage of modernity as 'liquid modernity' in which intimate relationships are likely to be more transient.

Anthony Giddens conceptualises contemporary society to have advanced to a 'high modernist' stage of development. This stage is characterised by a change in the nature of people's commitment to intimate relationships which reflects a breakdown of social structures and personal commitments and ties that were more typical of modern society. From modern society has emerged a more fluid social condition in which individuals must ongoingly engage in a process of interpreting a rapidly changing environment (referred to as 'reflexivity') to make sense of the world and navigate their course in life.

In 'The Transformation of Intimacy' (1992) and 'Runaway World' (2002), Giddens put forward a broad ranging model to explain changes in the nature of intimate relationships. According to this model, in pre-modern (traditional) societies, families were built around the economic imperative of property consolidation or operated as working units of economic production. For most, the severe conditions of life were not conducive to the development of romantic intimacy as the mainstay for attachment. High infant mortality rates meant that the social tradition of marriage for procreation was embedded in traditional culture and worked in harmony with the needs of nature.

A key feature of the modern industrial era was the application of reason to the aim of improvement, which promoted social change. Thus the hallmark of the modern period, compared to life in traditional society, was the emergence of a degree of 'reflexivity' – the need to weigh up and monitor traditions and institutions with the prospect of redesigning them to improve their effectiveness. This period, from the late eighteenth century, saw the appearance in the higher social orders, supported by the culture of the romantic novel, of romantic love as the basis for attraction and the binding of individuals in marriage. Increasingly, romantic attraction, the acceptance of the rituals of marriage and family bonds formed the basis of family tradition and social stability in the modern era.

In contemporary or high modern societies, through scientific intervention and improved social conditions, populations have become self-sustaining at low reproduction rates. Consequently, these societies contrast to those of the past in that sex can become free from the need for and cultural emphasis on procreation, and advances in contraception have enabled people to acquire more choice on whether or not to have children. In this sense, for Giddens, intimate relationships exist at 'the end of nature'. The separation of sex from the imperative of reproduction enables key modernist and traditional assumptions on family life to undergo fundamental change.

Firstly, Giddens argues that relationships tend to become contingent. Rather than being constrained by the finality of having chosen the right person and pressures to remain together come what may, partners strive to achieve purer relationships in which the continuance of each is contingent on the emotional rewards and satisfactions derived. This marks a step change in reflexivity which reaches new levels as partners continually reflect on the purity of the relationship and whether or not to continue within it. Giddens refers to this as type of conditional relationship as 'confluent love'.

Secondly, a growing diversity of relationship types emerge. This diversity allows individuals greater choice in the construction of their self-identity and their search for genuine self-fulfilment with opportunities to experiment and shape their own lives. Many new forms of family require on-going reflexivity by partners as they are relatively free from the constraints of long established norms and can construct relationships that work for them. As part of this diversity, the greater tolerance of same sex relationships is not just associated with more liberal attitudes and the breakdown of traditional family values but is a further logical consequence of the separation of sex and sexuality from reproduction which the conditions of contemporary society enables.

Thirdly, in terms of the development of sociological concepts, sociologically it is now more appropriate to refer to 'coupling' and 'uncoupling' than to marriage and divorce. There are now higher levels of cohabitation and although the institution of marriage retains some popularity, Giddens views it as a 'shell institution' whose contents have changed, since decisions on whether to remain together are now more often based on individual choice in seeking a pure relationship. Marriage remains a possible ritual commitment and tradition which can help to stabilise a relationship, but this is now more a matter of free choice for couples. Although often still a traumatic experience, divorce or uncoupling now holds far less stigma than divorce used to and it is recognised as a relatively high possibility for those who enter into relationships. Marriage or coupling now introduces new risks into people's lives at a very personal level as many of these relationships will break up.

Fourthly, Giddens optimistically suggests that the advance of tolerance, freedom and individual agency promotes a greater equality in sexual relationships which mirrors political advances that are taking place in society and globally. There is a parallel between the advance of democratic political freedoms and personal relationships based on equality and mutual respect. The ways of democracy undermine the confines of tradition and embrace global cosmopolitanism – the contact of a diversity of cultural traditions in a climate of tolerance. There has been an increase in the number of cosmopolitan families as globalisation brings together people from different social and ethnic backgrounds. By contrast, fundamentalism is a reaction to increased social openness and an attempt to re-impose traditional certainties and constraints regarding gender inequalities. For Giddens, issues of gay rights, marriage and gender equality are at the centre of the battle between the democratic forces of cosmopolitan tolerance and the often religious based authoritarianism of fundamentalism which seeks refuge in moral certainty amidst global complexity and relativism.

In criticism of high modern views of the destructive effect of individualism on family life, Bottero (2005, pp. 122-124) identifies the argument that new forms of relationship have come to reflect changing wage level patterns in which a distinction between 'full wage' and 'contingent wage' employment needs to be made. The latter wage level would not enable the earner independent living, whereas through a full wage support of a family would be possible. Clearly, the traditional employment pattern would concentrate women in contingent wage and men in full wage employment, with women being dependent on the income of a male breadwinner. Although women have largely remained employed at contingent wage level, their greater access to the labour market has undermined the full wage (family wage) argument of males – a process further exacerbated for manual workers by economic reforms from the 1980s that have enhanced wage inequality and pushed more of these workers into a contingent wage status. In more such households, there is a new interdependence based on the necessity of both partners having to work for contingent wages which would not enable independent support for each.

From life cycle to life course and beyond

Life in traditional societies held much to ceremonies which took the form of 'rites of passage' that marked the transition to new stages in life which encompassed new responsibilities. These would often have been fixed by age, marking down the course of the future with a high level of predictability. Given the absence of dynamic change in such societies, old age often carried high social status and respect associated with acquired wisdom.

With transition to modern western industrial society, we have seen the emergence of more finely graded age groupings. In the post-war decades, family life was strongly typified by the nuclear family and a standard family 'life cycle' seemed to be applicable as a realistic sequencing of life for many. Protected from work and provided with education, childhood within the nuclear family was a period of being cared for and controlled by parents. The emergence of youth culture amongst the later age group of adolescents during the 1950s and 1960s often resisted parental and social convention and with greater spending power led to youngsters acquiring more independence in both economic and identity terms. However, formal expectations of marriage and family life remained strong and given the relatively early age of marriage, the transition from nuclear family of origin to family of destination with work and family responsibilities of adulthood was often very rapid. The concept of the 'life cycle' was related to the prevalence of the nuclear family and the view that nuclear family life goes through predictable cycles. Thus, after the child rearing stage, late middle age often provided financial respite when children left home and retirement was associated with old age, declining income and purchasing power and increasing infirmity.

The concept of the life cycle was a product of the period of modernism when the lives of individuals were encapsulated within social institutions and structures which prescribed expected pathways and stages in their lives. This was shown in research conducted by Neugarten et al (1965) who found a high level of agreement throughout American society as to the best age for women to marry (19-24) and men to have established a career (24-26) (Hunt, 2005, p.20). By the 1960s, sociologists had developed life cycle models of increasing sophistication.

However, it has been shown that the social uniformity upon which such models were based has given way to greater diversity in family life. Given the transition to the social conditions referred to by high modernist and postmodernist writers, it became highly questionable whether the concept of life cycle could any longer be meaningfully utilised. Instead, the concept of 'life course' has tended to replace the life cycle model in sociology. Although society still shapes our experiences, these experiences are that the community constraints and confining structures associated with the modern period have largely collapsed. Individuals are left with the burden of planning their course in life and identity choice with far greater freedom and with few obligatory rites of passage to steer them. The concept of life course offers a more flexible, open and subtle alternative to conceptualise directions taken in life through the agency of enhanced individual choice.

If postmodernists are correct, there is some optimism in the fact that even stages in the life course are becoming deconstructed, and thus even the concept of the life course, which suggests a number of possible life trajectories as opposed to a once common view of a universal cycle of stages, is losing its usefulness. Individuals are increasingly able to fashion their own identity. People are living longer, may retire earlier or later, are in better health and are more active than the elderly of previous generations. As society is rapidly changing, older people tend to become out of touch and dependent as opposed to economically productive. Social status once associated with the wisdom of age has declined in the face of youth culture. On the other hand, pressure groups have emerged to represent the interests of older people and this age group are increasingly being targeted as consumers and voters. The traditional stereotypes of the elderly are thus being challenged and there is more freedom and variation in the construction of lifestyle and image for the elderly, whilst reproductive technologies have offered new possibilities of parenthood to infertile and gay and lesbian couples.

The social construction of age groups

This section will introduce some issues regarding cultural variability in the definition of age groups and identity. The stages in life which we tend to take for granted – infancy, childhood, adolescence, adulthood, elderliness and old age – are by no recognised as universal or fixed categories with the same meanings. Different divisions and meanings have existed in different cultures and periods of history and are still in a process of change.

An important starting point is to distinguish between the biological and the cultural. Clearly, human life is a biological process of growth from conception and birth through to maturity, followed by deterioration and eventually death. However, viewed sociologically, one can recognise the impact of environment on biology in at least two important ways. Firstly, the social conditions of living, working and access to medical care impact on our biological condition. This impact can be measured in terms of infant mortality rates, health and longevity and shows significant variation between and within societies and throughout history. Secondly, sociologists show how biological aging and sex differences are not just expressed directly but are strongly mediated through an environment of social and cultural meaning which provides socially constructed identities and self-perceptions. Although these identities vary historically and between different cultures, they are often justified as biologically determined and viewed as if they are natural and universal. To illustrate this point, feminists have been at the forefront of emphasising the ideological aspect of the apparent fixity of social roles justified in biological terms of sex differences. They thus point to the biological basis that Parsons claimed for segregated conjugal roles in the traditional nuclear family as an ideological construction using biological differences to justify the perpetuation of socially organised male privilege.

An area of growing interest in sociology has been the study of childhood as a socially defined, socially variable and historically relative concept. For example, research conducted by Aries (1973) showed that the contemporary western distinction between childhood and the stages leading up to adulthood, with the former distinguished as a time of vulnerability and absence of adult responsibility necessitating protection in the family, was alien to medieval society where from the age of about seven years 'youngsters' were seen as small adults, not children, and treated as such. Aries' research pointed to the fact that the notion of childhood was a European development from the eighteenth century within the middle classes and later in the nineteenth century within the working class with the advance of protective legislation in the workplace and the development of state education.

Nevertheless, the harsh realities of life for the young amongst the poorer sections of many developing countries often require them to work as cheap labour to help support their families. Even within Britain, an estimate based on the 2001 Census suggested that 175,000 youngsters of school age face the reality of caring for parents (Steel, 2012, p.181). These youngsters often provide this support in a low profile capacity to avoid the risk of being taken into care themselves.

Functionalists such as Parsons viewed childhood as a formative process in which children are made into the stuff of future good citizens within the cocoon of a nurturing family unit. There is an absence within this perspective of seeing childhood from the perspectives of children themselves – they are just being shaped by social forces. Furthermore, Foucault's perspective on this protective and shaping process emphasises the negative aspects of surveillance and social control.

In recent years, sociologists have become more interested in understanding childhood as perceived from point of view of children rather than through parentally and socially imposed viewpoints and definitions. Research has tended to use ethnographic methods in attempts to view families through the eyes of children. The findings point to the fact that children are often very active in the way that they construct their viewpoints of family life rather than being just the passive recipients of adult views and can come to define their family in ways that differ from that of adults. They may thus make their own subtle judgements and distinctions between members in reconstituted families and have often been found to perceive their pets as part of the family.

Viewed sociologically, adolescence, although often commonly regarded as a biologically and psychologically situated stage in the maturation process, and thus assumed to be universal, is also a product of the cultural environment. In fact, adolescence is historically a relatively recent development of post-war times during which adolescent identity emerged with the extension of education and growing affluence. As youngsters acquired more purchasing power and leisure time, advertisers and the media recognised a new source of profitability in music culture and fashion. This assisted the formation of adolescent subcultures with their own symbols, identity, norms and values.

Research into adolescent subculture has often focussed on deviance from and conflict with mainstream culture of the mature adult world, and thus, along with coverage in sections of the mass media, perhaps provided an exaggerated perception of these aspects of adolescence. Interestingly, from a feminist viewpoint, Abbott and Wallace (1997, p.124) cite McRobbie and Garber's comments that adolescent subcultures have been studied as a largely working class and virtually exclusively male phenomena. Feminists have emphasised that through the greater parental control and surveillance of adolescent girls and traditionally the magazine promotion of romanticism, female adolescent culture has found an important outlet and location in bedroom pinups and the adoration of pop star heroes.

The expansion of higher education in the 1970s, growing diversity of alternatives to the nuclear family and later marriage, has led to a more protracted period of adolescent lifestyle experimentation. However, Postman (1994) has argued that early exposure to the adult world of sex and violence through modern technology and the more common experience of sex at a young age has led to the 'death of childhood' in the form of a loss of innocence.

The phenomenon of parenthood has been complicated by substantial changes in family life. One such change is the growth of single parent families where the role of child rearing and provision of economic support may need to be provided by the single parent (usually female), sometimes assisted by persons external to that unit such as parents and ex-partners. Another change is an increase in divorce or relationship breakups. In this case, children invariably again remain with the mother, either within a single parent family or a reconstituted family unit. An interesting point is made by Kathryn Beckett (Sclater, 2005, p.89) regarding fatherhood in this situation. She argues that commonly within the mother and father family unit, the mother mediates the relationship between the father and children. After the breakup of the family unit, the father will often be faced with the difficult task of trying to construct a new relationship with his children without the mediation of the mother. This could at least partly explain the tendency for fathers to slip out of involvement in their children's lives.

The aging process is often seen as a biological aspect of the life course in which people pass through socially recognised life stages. Feminists point out that these stages are often quite prescriptively applied to women in terms of their biology, and that although biologically rooted definitions could be applied to the aging process of males, this tends to be less the case. Since reproduction and certain images of beauty are viewed as central to the lives of females in contemporary western culture, older age holds particularly negative connotations for them. Since for males the productive process is viewed more as an economic one, their productivity can continue well beyond women's reproductive capability – although medical advances have again shown that this phase can be extended. In old age, women, who tend to live longer than men, often find themselves alone, lonely and undervalued and having to subsist on lower incomes due to at best limited occupational pensions to supplement their income from the state.

However, according to postmodernists, retirement is less automatically associated with the onset of poverty, declining health and the feeling of being cast onto the social scrap heap. Through improved health and longevity, there is more opportunity for elderly people to live active lives. Greater diversity and choice of lifestyle is available. New cosmetic appliances and technology, for example, are now able to assist older people to retain a more youthful appearance and combat the effects of biological ageing, thus enhancing control of their image and conceptions of self.

A subjective refocusing of personal relationships

Recent developments in sociology which focus on personal and intimate relationships have been taken up mainly by a number of sociologists who adopt a type of feminist interactionist approach to the study of family life. From this perspective, Carol Smart opposes the high modernist view that individuals are cut adrift to navigate their own way through life. Instead, they are now freer to construct their own emotional relationships. Placing the personal and intimate at the centre of studies challenges the conventional view of bounded family life and recognises that in contemporary society people construct 'families of choice' which can include friends with whom they share emotions and common memories. Further, as personal life is the focus of attention, the complexity of relationships and situations is recognised from the point of view of the different perspectives, experiences and interpretations of the various participants.

Likewise, for Jacqui Gabb, approaches to the study of family life which focus on relationships in terms of the structuring of obligations and responsibilities are not a good lens for appreciating the intimate relational world of family life. For this to be possible, Gabb (8/6/14, Abstract) argues the need to 'reframe the analytical lens'. This refocussing needs to put emotions and intimacy at the centre of family life. Emotions and intimacy constitute the very glue of family life but are a dimension which has traditionally tended to be sanitized out of sociology as a too subjective area to be worthy of academic rigor.

For Gabb, small scale and qualitative research which includes autobiographical and anecdotal information and starts with feelings assists entry into this world of intimate reciprocity, allowing a 'dramatically different framework of thinking' (Gabb, 8/6/14, 3.7) to that which uses hard data to provide a patterned and structured picture of family life. This refocussing requires that 'we need to think more imaginatively if we are to capture the feelings and relational practices of intimacy that are in evidence all around us' (Gabb, 8/6/14, 8.3).

Gabb argues that we need to start with the everyday life of feelings and emotions that are part of the intimacy of family life. She therefore argues in favour of the use of sociological methods which enable a qualitative insight into family life as experienced by the various participants. Information may be gleaned from conversation, observation and personal written documents etc.

Viewing family life in terms of the intimate experiences of family members takes us into dimensions of everyday experience that are usually screened out in more conventional analysis of family life, one of which is the importance of cross species connections as part of the world of emotional experiences of family members. Taking a lead particularly from the viewpoint of children, pets are often seen as a part of the family, nurturing love and affection of family members. Family routines take pets into account and grief is experienced at their loss or death.

Parent and child relationships provide tactile pleasure at play times. Shared intimacy enables family relations to cut across broader cultural boundaries of generational and sexual distance and power relationships.

Even human relationships to objects play a role in family life. For example keepsake objects have personal and emotional meaning. Relating to such artefacts can provide a reawakening of past experiences and the sharing of stories, feelings and emotions between family members.

This re-focussing is clearly anti-positivist. But Gabb's approach also runs counter to the macro high modernist approaches adopted by Beck, Bauman and Giddens that emphasise the advance of risk and individualisation in contemporary life. For Gabb, initiating research at the micro level of intimate relations leads to a recognition of reciprocity between significant others rather than a society in which numerous individuals find themselves at the centre of life but cut adrift.

5 // Social Stratification

Abstract

Social stratification is defined as the hierarchical layering of society into different levels. Developing personal awareness of one's position in a social hierarchy and a range of associated experiences and opportunities may be a starting point for understanding social stratification. However, the reader is alerted to the fact that this would not be an appropriate point from which to make generalisations as a sociologist about the nature of stratification in society. This chapter will show that approaching the area sociologically requires a more detached and systematic approach. To assist in the preparation for this process, a number of key concepts are introduced.

It is important to gain a broad social and historical perspective on stratification in contemporary western societies or Britain more specifically as part of a considered assessment of the degree of openness of the social structure. For this purpose, examples of the basic features of more closed stratification systems are introduced through reference to slavery, caste society, feudalism and apartheid.

Established theoretical approaches of functionalism, Marxism and Weber are introduced to help the reader develop an understanding of some of the founding concepts used and explanations of stratification dynamics. At this point, the reader is encouraged to ponder a number of questions raised on the viability of these perspectives.

Social class is a well established feature of stratification and the question of why and issues of how sociologists measure it and some of the problems that this entails are raised. This leads on to a consideration of some of the findings of social mobility studies. Logical scrutiny of the degree to which contemporary societies can be regarded as truly meritocratic – enabling position in the social hierarchy to be achieved through individual effort and ability – is undertaken.

Theories of change in the class structure comprise another section in this chapter and the theories of embourgeoisement, proletarianisation and decomposition are introduced. However, there are other dimensions to stratification in contemporary society than social class. In this chapter, gender, ethnicity and status are also considered, indicating the complex nature of social stratification.

In approaching this subject, the reader is encouraged to recognise connections across different topic areas since, unlike the topic areas of sociology, the social world does not exist in clear cut compartments. Links are made from themes raised in this chapter to those in other chapters. For example, understanding gender stratification can be related to the impact on the family of industrialisation and more recently the expansion of the service sector. Evaluating the extent to which contemporary British society is meritocratic requires an understanding of issues of meritocracy in education.

Finally, more contemporary approaches to stratification are introduced in the form of postmodernism, high modernism and globalisation. These perspectives raise the key issue of the high state of fluidity of contemporary society and raise fundamental questions regarding the continuing viability or otherwise of the more structured approaches of the founding theorists that were earlier introduced.

The sociological challenge

Social stratification presupposes the existence of a social hierarchy which is divided into layers, each comprising a distinct level. In a general sense, these layers or strata (stratum in the singular) are structured in terms of inequality in the social distribution of resources deemed within a society to be important. Such resources typically include wealth, income, knowledge, culture and lifestyle. Access to these resources will be socially structured, for example by legal title of property ownership, rules of inheritance, and strategies that some groups adopt to exclude access to valued resources by others. The typical shape of stratification systems is characterised as a pyramid structure, emphasising that as one ascends this structure greater concentrations of valued resources, usually accompanied by concentrations of political power, reside in the hands of fewer people.

If social stratification simply referred to social layering in terms of the unequal distribution of resources, a fundamental problem for the sociologist would be that of identifying the key points at which the boundaries between such layers take place. Two main criteria have often been emphasised. Firstly, the existence of a degree of shared values and common outlook amongst people which distinguish them from others can be a good guide to identifying stratification levels. Secondly, there would usually be far more upward and downward social mobility within these groups than between them.

Social stratification, though, is a very complex matter as: 1) it includes various dimensions such as social class, social status, gender and ethnicity, 2) there are complexities in measuring social stratification on any one of these dimensions which, 3) interact with each other within the context of, 4) society undergoing constant change.

The study of social stratification poses a number of problems. The most obvious one is the fact that the everyday usage the term social class can be vague and pejorative, often implying judgements of quality. Issues of judgement in everyday definition also relate to gender and ethnicity.

Another problem may be the tendency to deride other societies and cultures from the viewpoint of the society to which we are accustomed. As analysts, it is important to guard against the block that this ethnocentricity puts on understanding and be prepared to ask, for example, how position in society tends to be justified to women in Islamic culture.

Furthermore, we may take for granted a certain view of the way that our own society is stratified. This may include the belief that equal opportunity for success is available to each individual by virtue of merit. As sociologists, we need to be prepared to give careful consideration to evidence by which we can evaluate such taken for granted assumptions. It may be a sobering thought to appreciate that in the future, others may look back with incredulity at what we take for granted regarding the stratification of our society (especially given the sociological knowledge that we have) in a similar way to the way that we may view with amazement what was taken for granted in past societies.

At a personal level, we must always remain aware that our experiences from our own position within the stratification system may bias the way that we view social stratification. Although personal experiences may be revealing to a limited extent, it is important to psychologically stand back and review theories and evidence regarding stratification from the more objective viewpoint of an analyst.

In Britain, sociologists have traditionally viewed social class as the major dimension of stratification. However, in recent decades they have been grappling to understand the changing and complex impact of the relationship between class and other dimensions of stratification such as status, gender and ethnicity.

More recently, some sociologists have come to question whether even viewing society in terms of structural components is any longer valid. They argue that rapid social change and complexity are so advanced that society should be viewed as in a state of constant fluidity. At best, this would mean that new sociological concepts need to be developed to grasp this reality. And it may be that society is now beyond the grasp of structured analysis?

Definition of main concepts

In sociology, the term **social class** refers to a social category of people in terms of economic factors. Marx argued that ownership or non-ownership of the means of production was the key economic determinant of class divisions, separating a capitalist class of employers from a class of workers. He also distinguished further gradations at the bottom of each of these categories, referred to respectively as the petit bourgeoisie (small capitalist) and the lumpenproletariat (with some similarity to more recent references to an 'underclass'). More contemporary approaches, tending to derive from the tradition of Max Weber, measure social class by reference to occupational levels and categories of occupation distinguished in part by limited rates of social mobility between them. **Social mobility** refers to the extent of upward and downward movement experienced by individuals in the occupational hierarchy throughout society. It is usually measured in **intergenerational** terms, comparing the occupational level achieved by members of one generation with that of their parents. When one's position is **ascribed**, social mobility will be extremely low (in theory non-existent) since position in the social hierarchy is restricted to correspond to that of parents. By contrast, when social position is open to individual **achievement**, we expect to find relatively high levels of social mobility. However, even within quite open social structures, some groups may attempt to enhance **social closure.** This refers to strategies adopted to preserve exclusive access to valued resources, such as privileged education or professional organisations, by denying access to others. Examples of social closure are most apparent amongst the 'establishment' who, evidence shows, tend to utilise the top public schools and the 'old boy network' to enhance their children's access to elite professions.

Distinguishing **social status** from social class can be difficult. Indeed, the two concepts are often very closely connected. At this point, it will be emphasised that social status refers to the judgements made within a society regarding the prestige of a social group and its members. Social status is culturally defined by social values given to different ways of life, knowledge and possessions, and carries with it views of superiority or inferiority of different groups. Thus, although social class refers to the economic dimension of occupational and income differences, occupations may also carry with them status connotations which relate to associated types and levels of education and skill and degrees of exclusiveness. As in the case of social class, if status is ascribed, the social structure fixes people into the stratum of their birth for life. Such a stratification system is referred to as **closed**. Examples of relatively closed societies include slavery, feudalism, caste society and apartheid, all of which will be reviewed shortly in this chapter. By contrast, **achieved class and status** is associated with a more **open stratification** system which enables individuals to occupy positions in the social structure derived from personal characteristics, primarily effort and ability, whatever the status or class of their family background. Most modern industrial societies are recognised as relatively open stratification systems, although sociologists disagree over the exact extent to which they are so and the varied importance of social class, social status as well as other features of stratification that may provide barriers to individual achievement.

These other dimensions of stratification include those of gender and ethnicity. **Patriarchy** is a term used to emphasise gender based stratification in which men have power over women. This may exhibit itself in the form of gender related concentrations of people in different occupational spheres (horizontal segregation) and hierarchical levels (vertical stratification), inheritance practices and domestic responsibilities. Values supporting such gender inequalities, often with reference to different presumed innate male and female qualities and capacities, are referred to as **sexist**, and to the extent to which they are viewed as distorting reality to justify male privilege would be referred to as **sexist ideology**.

Discriminatory practices against ethnic minorities are an important aspect of ethnic stratification. Such discrimination may be partly responsible for the concentration particular ethnic groups in certain occupational spheres and levels as well as in residential in areas. Attitudes which justify discrimination in terms of racially based notions of superiority and inferiority are referred to as **racist,** and, in a similar way to sexist views, can take the form of **racist ideology**.

The sociological concept of **life chances** refers to ways in which opportunities of access to quality of life and standard of living may be open or restricted according to the openness of the social structure and a person's position within it. Life chances can include access to and in turn derive from different levels of education and healthcare. There is a close correlation between life chances and the distribution of wealth and income in society. However, inequalities in life chances may be more or less determined by family background in more or less closed stratification systems respectively. Thus, in comparing different societies or societies at different times in history a key question to ask is, to what extent are people constrained by inherited life chances of the position that they are born into to remain there or to what degree can they rise above them and create their own life chances? Ultimately, the effect of life chances can be measured by such indices as socially patterned differences in health, life expectancy and infant mortality rates.

The concept of a **meritocracy** has often been applied to modern industrial societies. According to this term, these societies are viewed as open stratification systems, enabling social mobility, both upward and downward, to reflect individual merit. It is therefore a useful concept against which to measure such stratification systems.

A glimpse at closed stratification systems

History offers many examples of relatively closed systems of stratification in which life for the majority was often brutal and oppressive. However, even in the most oppressive societies, social hierarchies were supported by justifying ideas and values as well as by coercion. Viewed at a social and historical distance and with the knowledge that we now have, the ideological nature of these values may often seem clear. The following models extract the essential features of four different types of closed stratification system.

Slavery is a system of stratification most commonly associated with the early civilisations of the Greeks, Egyptians and Romans. Although in detail slavery exhibited different features between these societies in terms of its severity and responsibilities to the slave population, a characteristic common to them all was that there existed legally recognised and enforced social inequality through which slaves were owned as the property of others. Often taken through conquests, slaves would be put to a variety of tasks from heavy labour in mines or the building of monuments to teaching or even running estates. The main curb on the treatment of slaves by their owners might be their continuing effectiveness as productive labour. Control could include coercion in the form of the threat of physical punishment or inducement of fear of offending the gods. There were usually hierarchical grades within the slave stratum and in some cases control may take the form of inducement through the possibility of slaves working to obtain freedom from slave status. Acquiring freedom (manumission) might be possible for slaves in the Roman empire who through hard work and personal loyalty could be freed in the will of their owners. Others, when paid, could save up and purchase their freedom.

A more recent example of slavery is found in American history. During the slave trade, Africans were transported to the southern states and put to work on plantations. Their lives were highly regulated by their white masters. Slave status was reinforced by beliefs in black racial inferiority and the encouragement of the slave population to adopt Christian values of the virtue of humility. The institution of slavery was only formally abolished by constitutional amendment in 1865 following the defeat of the south in the American Civil War. However, it took a further century and the emergence of the Civil Rights Movement by the early 1960s for a fundamental challenge to remaining racial segregation and disadvantage to become effective.

Less dated examples of slavery can also be provided. One is the use by the Nazi regime of the forced labour of subjugated peoples and minorities during the Second World War. Another is the hidden pockets of slave labour which have been found to exist in contemporary societies such as Britain and France in the form of sex trafficking and debt bondage.

Caste stratification in its classic form was peculiar to traditional Indian society. In this society, a rigid form of stratification was sanctioned by the religious beliefs of Hinduism. The strata (varna) of this society were closed by rules limiting association with other varna and prescribing appropriate behaviour and rituals. Brahmin priests, as men of learning – and often also significant owners of land - formed the upper varna. Central to the Hindu teachings which the piesthood conveyed were the ideas of reincarnation and the relative purity of the different varna. The priestly caste were required to live the purest life, conduct religious ceremonies and administer the law. In descending order of purity followed the warrior, trader and labouring strata. Below them were placed the outcastes who engaged in the most degrading occupations. This hierarchy of prestige required the retention of caste purity through social separation to avoid contamination from inferiors, and thus comprised a closed status hierarchy.

Acceptance of this closed hierarchy was perpetuated by the belief in reincarnation – a concept referring to a continuing cycle of rebirth after the death of the physical body. Prospects for future life (dharma) were tied to conformity in the present life. To defy the codes of one's caste would lead to rebirth into a lower caste, whilst conformity could lead to rebirth into a higher caste. Fatalism in the here and now, conformity, and merit were all therefore intertwined and a closed stratification system was supported by the prospect of social mobility through reincarnation. Likewise, one's current position could be justified by one's supposed behaviour in a previous life (karma).

In **feudal** societies, life was essentially agrarian and lived out in local communities. Feudal life was typified by European societies during the Middle Ages, but examples could be found further afield in, for example, Japan and China. In England, the key to power was land ownership, and this was concentrated in the hands of the two upper strata (estates), the nobility and the church. The third estate, or commoners, comprised mainly small landowning peasants, craft workers and landless serfs. The latter worked the land of the nobility and the church. They were required to give both produce and labour to their landowners, and lived under inferior legal rights. Opportunities for social mobility were very limited as this section of the population were kept in perpetual servitude and legally recognised as bonded labour.

In this social system, deference (looking up and deferring to the superiority of those above) was expected by the upper orders to be shown from the lower estates. By tracing their lineage back through many generations, the landed nobility were able to justify their superior status through claiming the inheritance of leadership qualities by appealing to the notion of superior 'social breeding' – a concept which harmonised well with the practice of animal breeding that was familiar in an agrarian society. In some cases, acquired wealth could be used to purchase social title (as it still can!) but in this case the key feature of family lineage would be absent.

The social forces which would disturb this balance in the rural hierarchy would later emanate from a section of the population who resided more on the margins of the defining agrarian relationship – the more urban based traders, merchants and early industrialists.

Apartheid is sometimes viewed as a form of caste stratification. It refers specifically to a system instituted in South Africa shortly after the Second World War and which lasted until 1992. Under this system, a white minority dominated non-white groups defined, in descending order, as mixed race or coloured, Asian, and black. Under this system, racial segregation was enforced in public places and black South Africans were forced to live in separate shantytown homelands. Given these segregated regions, members of a racial group would take care to avoid straying into a territory closed to them. Blacks who worked as domestics for whites would have to show an ID pass and often work at night. Even when working in the same occupations as white workers, the wages and conditions of employment of black workers were inferior. Infant mortality was far higher within the black than the white population. Political gatherings were banned and discontent ruthlessly put down by police or military force.

This system which kept blacks down was justified by reference to theories of racial types which had grown to prominence during the period of colonial expansion of the nineteenth century. Such theories maintained that different races contained different genetically inbuilt characteristics and that the white race had demonstrated its superiority of intelligence and determination over the blacks. In the hands of an apartheid regime, this reasoning could be used to justify the need for maintaining racial purity and making racial intermarriage taboo. The life chances of blacks could be kept vastly inferior to that of whites and this in turn could provide 'evidence' of black inferiority.

Although racial stratification was the defining feature of apartheid, other elements of stratification were discernable. For example, the white stratum mainly comprised groups of British, German and Dutch extraction, with the former at the top of society tending to control the economy, and the other groups often owning land. Whilst Indians and Asians were often less poverty stricken than blacks, race would remain a barrier to social mobility which application and the acquisition of money could not overcome. Within the black stratum, social divisions would take the form of tribal groupings, with Zulus tending to comprise the dominant group. Throughout all strata, patriarchal relationships tended to prevail with girls brought up to be good wives and domestic servants.

Founding sociological perspectives on social stratification

The coming section will review three major founding perspectives on stratification – functionalist, Marxist, and Weberian. Each are macro perspectives, ie. they adopt a broad view of social structures. As traditional perspectives, they all analyse stratification in terms of social class, although not all do so exclusively.

Functionalism – the realisation of an open social structure

It is often useful to consider the social and historical context in which social theory emerges to more fully appreciate its leaning. Functionalism is traceable back to the French social philosopher Auguste Comte who was developing his system of thinking in a period of French history following the Revolution of 1789. Comte regarded European societies at the height of feudalism, around the twelfth century, as stable and well established social hierarchies whose social order was sanctified by shared dogma in the religion of Catholicism. Following a long period of decline, the Revolution finally swept away feudal society in France. The problem diagnosed by Comte in the post Revolution period was that of protracted social instability. The once socially integrating belief system of Catholicism had come under attack and the old social order had been overthrown but a new and stable order had not yet emerged. The social ill of instability needed to be remedied.

Through Comte, functionalism emerged as a reaction to the socially destabilising effects of the French Revolution within a social climate of the desire to re-establish social order and stability. As such, the perspective emphasises the normality of stable social hierarchy. To underpin social stability, modern societies, just as much as traditional societies, need their own supporting value systems which members of society share and adhere to. Functionalism, as it has developed since the works of Comte, has remained true to this heritage.

Comte's ideas were built on by the French sociologist Emile Durkheim. For Durkheim, modern industrial societies are like organisms which grow in size and complexity (1964a). Technological advances extend the division of labour and promote an increasingly complex occupational structure. State education plays key functions in maintaining the social structure.

It promotes the shared values necessary to build social consensus as well as the need for obedience to authority and conformity to rules. Education also helps to select and train people in the skills necessary for appropriate occupational roles and positions in the social hierarchy. People's acceptance of their position in this hierarchy has to be justified according to shared values appropriate to modern industrial society. This society requires the efficient utilisation of human talent. Both the process of educational and occupational selection and the prevailing social values that match these requirements are therefore those of a meritocracy – a society in which social position is achieved according to effort and ability and would be accepted as such.

The distinction between the feudal social order and that natural to modern industrial societies is clearly established in the writings of the American functionalist Talcott Parsons. For Parsons, social hierarchies are a prerequisite (pre-requirement) of all stable societies but the basis upon which people acquire positions within social hierarchies varies with the type of society in question. Value systems must reflect this process by which people are positioned within the stratification system – values and processes of allocation must synchronise if order and stability are to be maintained. So what were the main features of feudal society? Life was local centred, agrarian and custom and tradition predominated. Religious thinking prevailed. The social hierarchy was a relatively closed one. People married within their own stratum and the chance of movement out of the stratum of birth was for most highly unlikely. In this society of inherited privilege, social superiors expected shows of deference from those of lower social rank. The minimal social mobility that existed was likely to derive from sponsorship by a known patron. Parsons refers to this type of social relationship as 'particularistic' – opportunities for advancement were dependent on particular personal relationships in which favour may be bestowed by social superiors toward the less fortunate.

By contrast, modern industrial capitalist societies are large, impersonal, complex, integrated and interdependent social structures with a high division of labour. They are noted for their dynamism and efficiency. The materialistic motive force of the quest for maximising profit and waged income enhances competition between individuals. However, given this complex interdependence, conflict in any area of society can cause widespread disruption. It is therefore important that as well as striving for individual success and income maximisation, people accept their position within the stratification system as justly arrived at. For Parsons, American capitalism best typifies the appropriate value system around which social consensus can be based in modern capitalist societies. These values include enterprise, competition, individual opportunity and achievement, self-support and materialistic aspiration.

The occupational hierarchy will need to be a highly differentiated hierarchy of income reward. This is because in modern complex societies the highest occupations place great demands on those who carry out these roles and who must have acquired sophisticated planning, managerial and organisational skills. Social efficiency requires that, at this and other levels of the occupational hierarchy, there is a close match between the ability and training of those who occupy roles and the demands of the occupational role. Consequently, there is maximum utilisation of human resources and the resultant productivity levels enable materialistic values and goals to be realised.

To effectively utilise the pool of talent in society, the social structure of modern industrial societies must be a highly open one. High levels of upward and downward social mobility will be likely as members of society are sifted for occupational roles which match their individual ability, training and effort. Compared to the allocation of social position by birthright or favour in traditional societies, occupational position must be acquired through individual competition according to impersonal and universally applicable performance criteria. Parsons refers to social relationships within this context as 'universalistic'. The shared values which correspond to this type of society are those of a meritocracy – a hierarchy of social inequalities in terms of social status, economic reward and power, which is justified by the widespread belief that whatever position an individual attains closely reflects their own abilities and efforts.

In the post-war years, the American functionalists Davis and Moore focussed on the nature of this occupational structure by referring to it as a 'ladder of opportunity'. They argued that stratification is a feature of all societies, as it is a 'functional prerequisite' for the stability of societies to place people in different hierarchical roles. The form that this process of allocation takes in modern industrial society is that in an open and competitive social structure, society benefits from talented people moving up into demanding occupations in which they are more highly rewarded for conscientious application of their special abilities. For Davis and Moore, high income differentials within the occupational structure provide the motivating factor which enhances competition. They offer due return to talents in scarce supply in society and compensatory reward for the sacrifices made by individuals in extending their education and training (Crompton, 2008, p.13). Substantial income differentials in the context of an open stratification system are viewed as functional. Such stratification systems and their accompanying value systems, functionalists argue, are not consciously devised and constructed. They are the naturally evolving outcome of the quest for efficiency maximisation between competing capitalist industrial societies.

The functionalist view of these American theorists can be summarised as follows. The functional importance of substantial inequality of monetary reward in modern capitalist societies is dependent on 1) a broad consensus existing on the relative social importance of different occupational functions and that 2) this provides the basis for a matching consensus on the different levels of reward that are appropriate for different occupational positions, 3) the allocation of people to which is justified through belief in the working of an impartial selection process that matches talent to occupational position on the basis of equality of opportunity.

At this point, it may be beneficial to raise a number of questions that are critical of the functionalist perspective. The reader is recommended to pause and think through these questions and search for evidence that may support or undermine these criticisms. 1) Does not the emphasis on social consensus, order and hierarchy tend to underplay the existence of conflict that exists between people within different social strata? 2) To what extent is the belief that society operates as a meritocracy shared throughout society or, alternatively, the wishful thinking or self-congratulatory justification of a minority who may or may not owe their success entirely to individual merit? 3) Even if society is meritocratic, what degree of income differential is necessary between upper and lower level occupational levels to motivate individual competition? 4) How has this income differential been changing over recent decades? If there is increasing stretch between the top and bottom of the social hierarchy, might this lead to a breakdown of consensus in the legitimacy of such an extent of inequality, leading to possible social instability?

For functionalists, the social system is viewed as naturally and beneficially self-adjusting. It is claimed that the functional importance of an occupation to society and the degree of scarcity of skills required carry out the tasks now corresponds to the position of the occupation in the occupational structure and the level of economic reward attached. However 5), it could be asked to what extent there is a naturally adjusting free market system of labour which determines income differentials between different occupations or, alternatively, the extent to which these differentials are partly the result of strategies of professional self-interest and the use of power that different groups are able to adopt? 6) How can the relative functional importance to society of different occupations be assessed objectively? If there is no way of doing so, does not the concept of functional importance just collapse into a justification of the prevailing inequalities in the occupational hierarchy and reward structure? 7) It may be that meritocratic values are broadly shared, but this may be on guarantee that rewards will match public perceptions of fairness. For example, the public may express strong criticism of massive severance payments given to certain public figures to terminate their employment as a result of poor performance or incompetence. 8) It is argued that within the context of a meritocracy, substantial income differentials provide the incentive for the application of talent as a means for the talented to achieve social mobility. In terms of enterprise values, claims of openness of the stratification system and the extent of income differentials, America is one of the highest placed capitalist industrialised societies. Yet research has shown (Markus et al, 2006) that compared to the Nordic countries of Denmark, Finland, Norway and Sweden, where income differentials are less stretched, America, followed by Britain, have shown the lowest levels of earnings mobility between the generations. It would appear that there is great disparity between values and perceptions of opportunity, if these are broadly shared, and reality in these societies where income differences are more stretched.

The reader may be able to add further questions to this list to reflect on. One further question to be raised at present is a very fundamental one which will figure elsewhere in this chapter and in the chapter on education. 9) Meritocracy refers to having equal opportunity to compete for unequal monetary reward, status and power in a stratified occupational hierarchy. How can the very stratification system that is meant to separate out talent, motivate individuals and create a level playing field of competition work as envisaged when inequalities the produced in one generation become unequal life chances which impact right from the start of life on the opportunities of next generation?

Marxism – capitalism remains a class stratified social structure

Marxist theorists strongly dispute the meritocratic nature of modern capitalist societies. For Marxists, capitalist societies are highly stratified in terms of class division. Moreover, this division is one of class opposition, which Marx believed would eventually become open conflict that would destroy capitalism.

Marx applied the term class more broadly than most sociologists. He maintained that class stratification, shaped by economic factors, has existed throughout much of human history. Once early societies had settled and developed rudimentary means of production, they were able to produce more wealth than was necessary for the basic subsistence of the community. The surplus above subsistence enabled inequalities of wealth to emerge. These inequalities became institutionalised and transmitted down the generations through the recognition of private property rights, laws of inheritance and private ownership of the means of production. Through their consolidation of wealth, those who owned the means of production acquired the power of a ruling class and were able to exploit the labour of others who were kept in a state of subsistence. However, throughout history, the means of production have developed, accompanied by the emergence of new classes who own them. Conflicts in which aspiring ruling classes owning modernised means of production challenge established ruling classes have been the motive force of social change. Successful challenges result in new ruling classes replacing old ones as societies move by revolution through a series of different social and stratification systems.

Marx, then, developed a theory which attempted to explain dynamic social change driven by class conflict throughout history. It placed ownership of the means of production at the centre of an analysis of class conflict and social change. The key social relationship in stratified societies is between those who own the means of production and those who own only their labour power. Just to subsist, the latter are compelled to supply their labour to the service of the former. For Marx, political power, broadly defined as the ability of some to impose their will over others, derives from economic power. The owners of the means of production therefore constitute the ruling class and those whose labour they utilise comprise the subject class. The power of the ruling class enables them to engage in an unequal exchange relationship with the subject class in which the latter do not receive full remuneration for the labour that they contribute to the creation of value in the productive process. Marx refers to this shortfall as class exploitation. The extraction of this value excess from the labour of others is the means by which resources become further accumulated in the hands of a minority and the means of production expanded and advanced. It is also the basis of class conflict between the ruling and subject class.

How can this broad sweeping theory be applied to the stratification of modern capitalist societies and how did the latter emerge? Marxism offers an explanation of how capitalist societies grew out of medieval feudal societies. In feudal societies, the main means of production were land, animals, agricultural buildings, machinery powered by natural forces and hand implements. Most production derived from the land and the greatest concentrations of wealth took the form of concentrations of land ownership. Serfs were agricultural workers who toiled the land but did not own it. The key class relationship was thus between major landowners (the various ranks of the nobility and the church) and the serfs who worked the land and lived in a state of perpetual subsistence, bonded to landowners who extracted economic surpluses from their labour.

Although landowner and serf was the defining class relationship of feudalism, many other gradations and occupation existed. Some peasants were small landholders who worked their own land. Craft workers made goods for the market. Others were occupied in trade, commerce and rudimentary forms of industry. It was amongst these latter groups, involved in forms of enterprise and risk taking that moneyed wealth was gradually accumulating.

This increasing wealth accumulated by the owners of early industrial means of production was assisted by the competitive drive to apply advances in science and technology to make the productive process more efficient. Capital assets put into economic activity to enhance the creation of value provided, in part, income for workers, but also income to early capitalists, the owners of capital, and, by reinvesting in the business, the opportunity for the further growth of capital. In time, the development of powered machinery and the factory system massively increased production and drew a rapid influx of workers from rural and agricultural pursuits into industrial employment in expanding towns. The consequent expansion of industrial wealth by employers provided them with the political power to challenge the social dominance of the old landed elite, enabled the transfer of class power to a new entrepreneurial (risk taking and private business owning) elite, and marked the transition from the remnants of feudalism to capitalism. This was a revolutionary break from the past (for example in the form of the Industrial Revolution in Britain) which replaced a feudal ruling and subject class with a capitalist ruling and subject class. In this system, new relations of production emerged between the new social classes. Contractual relations of employment between business owning employers (forming a capitalist class) and waged employees (forming a working class) replaced a relationship of labour bonded to landowner. These relationships structured new divisions of conflicting class interest.

For Marx, although all class societies by definition contain opposing class interests, open class conflict is often averted. To understand how this is possible, the superstructure and infrastructure need to be defined and their relationship explained.

In Marxist theory, dominant social institutions and ideas are referred to as the superstructure, whilst the economy and the class divisions and stresses that it generates are referred to as the economic infrastructure. The function of the superstructure is to contain and dissipate class conflict which is generated by exploitation that takes place within the infrastructure. For example, the police and the courts and at times even the military can control outward expressions of social discontent. However, that discontent can often itself be averted if the subject class are not consciously aware of their true plight. For this to be possible requires an ideological distortion of reality. Ideology refers to a plausible and systematically distorted image of society. The ruling class are in a powerful position to project this image – under capitalism by justifying social arrangements in terms of freedom of contract and a fair wage – onto the subject class. The purpose of such ideological distortion is to encourage the acceptance, conformity, and application of the subject class and hide the reality of their exploitation. Internalisation of an ideologically distorted view of society leads to a 'false consciousness' in the subject class. For example, the institution of private property is upheld by dominant social values and enforced by the law of the land, protecting rightful owners of property from theft. There is widespread public awareness that theft is a criminal offence and detailed statistics are available on such crimes. However, from a Marxist perspective there is one form of crime which is continuous but hidden by dominant values – class based theft by employers of a proportion of the value created by workers. Ideological distortion hides this reality of exploitation through the concept of rightful profit to the employer.

From the viewpoint of the Marxist perspective, the economy provides the objective reality of structured class opposition of interests, but conflict of class interests will not lead to class conflict if the situation is not apprehended as such by the subject class as a consequence of the distorting effect of ruling class ideology.

Marx believed that he had demonstrated the objective forces that would lead to class conflict and ultimately revolution, but such an outcome was dependent on a leap in the consciousness of the subject class. Marx argued that there are powerful tendencies within free enterprise capitalism which would bring this about. Capitalists must compete with each other to sell their goods and services in the market to make a profit and ultimately to survive. They therefore have to constantly innovate to increase efficiency of production through introducing new technology and reducing their labour costs. Those who are successful will have instituted efficient procedures and kept wages low. Thus, although workers under capitalism are better off than serfs under feudalism, the wealth of their employers has increased even more through combining the labour of workers with highly efficient means of production. Through this tendency for wealth to polarise, the rift between the classes can become more evident. However, the low purchasing power of depressed wages leads to decreased demand in relation to increased productivity, periodic economic depression and mass unemployment, further pushing wages down. Marx argued that it is at such times of inevitable economic malfunction that ruling class ideology becomes vulnerable. It is more likely to be seen through by workers whom capitalism has concentrated in large numbers in factories and urban communities. Under these conditions, a common class consciousness is likely to emerge between workers. Should this transpire, the objective reality of conflict of class interests built into capitalism becomes subjectively evident to the working class. False consciousness transforms into class consciousness. Exploitation becomes recognised. The solution of class revolution can become clear. The majority class may then rise up against the minority class and take the means of production into common ownership. By such means, according to Marx, a communist society would replace capitalism. Since the means of production would now be taken into common ownership, this society would by definition be a classless society.

It is clear that within this perspective, social classes are not just descriptions of different levels of socially structured economic inequality. They are explained within a theory that views them (dependent on the readings of Marxist theory) as potential or inevitable categories of organised social action that provide a motive force for social transformation.

A number of questions can be raised with regard to Marx's theory and the reader is recommended to pause and reflect upon those raised here and others.

1) One issue is the charge of reductionism. This term refers to the simplification of something which in reality is far more complex by reducing it to basic categories of analysis. In the case of Marxism, social stratification and conflict becomes reduced to that between classes and social class becomes reduced to people's relationship to the means of production. As a consequence, both Marx's view of classes and of social conflict may be criticised as being too simplistic. This criticism will become more evident when Max Weber's approach to social stratification is introduced.

2) Another matter relates to the question of the potential or inevitability of revolutionary social transformation. Even if Marx was correct about the economic forces at work within capitalism, is it possible to predict with certainty that economic inequalities will inevitably trigger a mass revolutionary response? If so, at what point does this take place? Marx was a little ambiguous on these points and this has led to different readings of and schools of Marxism. Capitalist societies have weathered numerous recessions and depressions since Marx developed his theory, but the

advanced societies have not succumbed to proletarian revolution. Indeed, capitalism may be more entrenched at the beginning of the twenty first century than ever before. Can the absence of the predicted revolution be answered within Marxist theory or does it require a rejection of the theory?

3) Marx developed his analysis of capitalism against the backdrop of a free enterprise system which emerged in England by the mid-nineteenth century. This raises certain questions regarding the contemporary relevance of Marxist theory. For example, at the time that Marx was writing, under entrepreneurial capitalism, private enterprises were often owned and run by individuals, partnerships or families who made the key decisions and took the profits or faced the losses. There was arguably a clearly defined capitalist class who owned the means of production outright. But is this now the main form that capitalism takes? The expansion of corporate enterprises in the twentieth century into very large and complex organisations has required highly trained managerial employees and professionals to take charge of much of the decision making process. Control has thus arguably been wrested from owners (now usually shareholders) and, as proposed by those who believe that there has been a managerial revolution, managers may not be driven by the same ruthless profit maximising motives as the entrepreneurs of earlier capitalism. Moreover, as controllers of workers but nevertheless employees of the organisation, people in these managerial occupations may experience a contradictory class position. Class is further complicated by a massive expansion of lower ranking white collar employees and middle ranking professionals, all of whom Marx would classify as working class but who may adopt a more middle class consciousness.

4) A further important issue relates to the question of just who now owns the means of production? The development of joint stock companies over the last century and a half has enabled millions of people to become shareholders. As such, whilst most of these people need to work for a living, they would also be, according to the Marxist model, through their share investments, part owners of the means of production and therefore have a foot in each of the opposing classes as defined by Marx. They would occupy a dual class position.

Is it not the case that these various changes in capitalism, combined with the development of welfare state security and improved standards of living, would suggest, contrary to Marx's predictions of radicalised workers and class revolution, the emergence of a new form of capitalism; one with which a large middling stratum of de-radicalised workers will tend to identify as at least tolerable or even working in their interests?

What other weaknesses in the Marxist stratification model can the reader identify and analyse?

Weber – the importance of social status

Like Marx, Weber provided a conflict theory of stratification. He agreed with Marx that social class derives from economic factors. However, by contrast, Weber maintained that stratification is not exclusively reducible to social class, but includes status and party dimensions. Whilst recognising that Marx's conceptualisation of class may be applicable in certain social and historical conditions, Weber argued that Marx was wrong to 1) relate social class formation exclusively to the means of production 2) view class conflict as the primary driving force of social change and 3) not recognise the significance of other forms of stratification such as social status. Weber was critical of the strong tendency in Marxist theory toward economic determinism; the view that the nature of social relationships, the state of consciousness and action are determined by forces originating in the economy. For Weber, the relationship between the economic structure, consciousness and action is more open and contingent.

Weber related social class to occupations in the competitive labour market which require different skills and qualities from workers. In return, workers receive different levels of remuneration, security, work conditions and perks. A person's marketability in the employment market will effect, amongst other things, their income level and the goods and services that they have access to. Social classes are formed and can be analysed through the clustering of occupations that are alike in the skills required and rewards offered which makes them distinguishable from other occupational groups. Within particular social classes, people will experience similar life chances and opportunities.

Social groups do not necessarily relate to a competitive labour market passively but often actively struggle to maximise their returns. They may adopt strategies and use power in an attempt to control the labour market. Sometimes, the threat of or actual use of collective action can be the strategy applied in the attempt to maximise rewards or improve terms and conditions of employment. Another strategy can be that of restricting entry into an occupation compared to demand for services, thus creating a degree of labour scarcity as a means to bolstering rewards. Workers are therefore not necessarily as powerless under capitalism as the Marxist model suggests, and neither do they act within a perfectly free market. For Weber, opportunities and rewards can be partly influenced by purposeful action.

Weber identified the growth of large bureaucratic organisations as a key feature of modernisation. This process gives rise to an expansion of white collar occupations and classes around the middle of the stratification system. He therefore disputed the Marxist analysis of tendencies toward social polarisation into two opposing social classes. By contrast, the class system was fracturing into a more complex hierarchy. This, along with the subjective independent mindedness of actors, reduced the likelihood of the emergence of a mass working class consciousness and the prospects of the destruction of capitalism through mass class based revolution.

Weber also analysed stratification in terms of social status. Social status is analytically distinguishable from class but both conceptually and in the real world there is often a complex symbiotic interrelationship between them. Before tackling this complex area, social status can be simply defined in the following way. Weber distinguished status stratification from the economic dimension of occupational class by defining it in terms of cultural judgements of social prestige. Essentially, status judgements relate to lifestyle which includes types of leisure activity, patterns of consumption and the symbolic meaning of goods acquired, and involvement in community activities. A status group comprises people who share a similar type of lifestyle which is viewed by themselves and to varying degrees others in terms of superior or inferior levels of prestige. At a personal level, status may be associated with one's social standing and reputation.

Building on Weber's analysis, what are some of the stratification complexities that can be derived from the studying the interplay of class and status?

1) The status of a person or group may derive directly or indirectly from their occupation, hence the possible overlap between cultural status and economic class. This is because occupations themselves may be perceived in status terms. Thus, a person working as a hospital consultant is likely to be perceived in superior status terms to a hospital cleaner. These perceptions are likely to relate to differences in educational background, skill level and income associated with the occupations. Furthermore, the range of lifestyles available to people in these occupations is itself likely to be strongly influenced by different income levels as well as social contacts and tastes.

2) On the other hand, status stratification may impact on class stratification through influencing access to occupations in various ways and to varying degrees. Its impact has been particularly prevalent in traditional and closed stratification systems. For example, in the traditional Indian caste system, impenetrable social status barriers were also barriers which restricted social access to a limited range of occupations. In feudal societies, the contrasting status positions of nobleman and serf were well established in the value system of social breeding. And the ascribed social status of racial inferiority consigned black South Africans in the apartheid era to lowly occupations with poor pay and conditions of employment. In such closed stratification systems, social status can be seen as strongly and consistently impacting on class by restricting the occupational opportunities of people within designated status groups. However, even within the relatively open stratification systems of most contemporary societies, status ascription, for example in terms of stereotypes regarding a person's gender or ethnicity, may influence opportunities for access to occupations.

3) In more open stratification systems, status mobility may be acquired through the use of economic assets derived from class mobility, but it may take time. Culture, in the form of taste and manners, is an important dimension of status judgements. People who have become well off financially but are seen to lack etiquette may be judged as brash in status terms by others, even if the latter are less well-off economically. Thus, during the nineteenth century, some who claimed high status by virtue of the more aristocratic notion of established wealth and cultured upbringing, looked down in status terms on the upwardly mobile who had achieved new wealth through business enterprise and viewed them as

'Philistines' who lacked cultural refinement. The response of the moneyed businessman was sometimes to use their new made wealth to enhance the status of their children by sending them to public school to gain the appropriate cultural attributes that would enhance their social status.

4) A person's position in social status terms may be quite separate from their social class position. This is likely to be a feature of relatively open stratification systems. For example, status can be derived from living in a particular residential area. Although a residential area may tend to attract residents from similar occupational groups and levels of income – ie classes in Weber's terms – there is unlikely to be a hard and fast correlation of status area with occupational class. Such a residential based status group can therefore include people from different social classes. Alternatively, within the same occupational category (social class), status distinctions may be made between people with different types of educational background and cultural tastes. Viewed either way, when this autonomy of class and status leads to people occupying substantially different positions on each of the scales, the term 'class and status dissonance' is used.

5) Irrespective of class, social status itself can be a complex phenomena in which individuals may project an image of status inconsistency. For example, a person living in a poor housing area and driving a top of the range expensive car may convey a confused image of status ambiguity in the minds of others.

6) In contemporary societies, social relationships, especially in large towns and cities, are likely to be of a more impersonal nature than in small traditional communities. The quicker pace of life is likely to lead to people engaging in quite fleeting acquaintances. In the more open social structure which contemporary urbanised societies arguably exhibit, a person's social status may be judged by the external show of possessions in the form of status symbols that hold stereotypical meaning rather than others' close personal knowledge of the individual. There may therefore be more room for personal manipulation of status by the acquisition of widely recognised symbols of prestige, even if acquired through means of the availability of credit and indebtedness.

7) Even in relatively open stratification systems, social status can play a part in gaining or restricting access to key institutions. The universities in

Britain tend to be status ranked with the traditional institutions of Oxford and Cambridge at the top of both the league table and the university status hierarchy. But how does one gain entry to the higher status universities? Clearly, ability is a prerequisite but statistics suggest that prior access to independent sector education, which normally requires the advantages of parental capacity to pay fees, also appears to be a significant factor. There is hence arguably a degree of social closure in access to the elite universities and consequently some of the higher occupations which recruit from them.

8) Although attributes of social status may be broadly recognised across society, worthiness of status is sometimes contested. For example, opposed generational interpretations may be made of the status of celebrity culture, and within schools, the status of a youngster within a subculture is likely be quite different from their status within the school culture which they may deride.

9) Challenges may also emerge to the derivation of status from class and authority in the work place. For example, within a college or university, managerial positions may earn a higher income and hold more decision making power than those of lecturers. In occupational terms, managers are likely to rank higher, but what about social status? Whilst lecturers have to accept managerial authority within the organisational structure, they may try to enhance their own sense of relative status through emphasising the symbolic worth of their academic qualifications and even judging managers as non-academic or failed academic mercenaries.

'Party' was a further dimension of power and stratification for Weber, which yet further complicates the picture. As used by Weber, party brings together people with shared interests and aims and can therefore include common identification with mass political parties or pressure groups. Party identification may or may not correlate closely with people's social class or status. For example, in the case of a trade union which is fighting for the interests of a particular section of workers, party identification and class stratification are likely to be closely associated. However, party can also bring together people from different class and status groups who intend to pursue shared aims, even if the aims are pursued for different reasons. Opposition groups to new road building schemes can illustrate this point. Such groups have been known to bring together major local landowners and other local residents, concerned primarily with issues of quality of life and property prices, and geographically mobile members of new environmental pressure groups that advocate direct action. These people are likely to be highly distinguishable in terms of class and status differences. They may often have little time for each other. Yet, in terms of their shared aim of halting road building, there have been examples of local residents providing meals and washing facilities for direct action environmental protesters.

In conclusion, Weber's approach to stratification suggests weaknesses in both functionalist and Marxist stratification models. For example, the remuneration of groups within the occupational structure might not simply reflect the functional importance of an occupation or the workings of the free market as functionalists maintain. Instead, in the struggle over access to resources, it may derive from strategies pursued by occupational groups, such as control of entry into a profession, to enhance the market position and income of their members. And as well as the effect of economic inequalities on the life chances of people, status distinctions may also provide barriers to equality of opportunity for individuals to arrive at merited positions on the occupational ladder.

Weber's analysis leads to the view that stratification is a highly complex and multidimensional phenomena. There are many possible combinations of position in class, status and party terms that people occupy as well as making decisions to form shifting alliances with others as they engage in the pursuit of their common interests. For Weber, attempts by Marxists to reduce an analysis of stratification to that of class and of class to the means of production, both lacks subtlety and distorts reality.

Social stratification – traditional sociological issues:

1. How to measure social class

As we have seen, when analysing stratification in industrial societies, theorists within the sociological tradition have focussed primarily on social class and status. Measuring social class requires the translation of theoretical concepts into key measurable indicators of the concept and the one that is overwhelmingly selected is occupation. Social classes are then viewed in terms of occupational categories, a procedure referred to as the 'employment aggregate approach' (Crompton, 2008, p.50). However, there is much dispute over how such measuring devices can best be constructed and applied.

Most social survey research will attempt to measure respondents' social class. This is because class has been shown to be an important influence across a broad range of social phenomena and thus an explanatory factor in research. A major area of interest in studies of stratification in modern industrial societies has been the measurement of social mobility – the amount and range of movement of people throughout society up and down the social hierarchy. If the extent of social mobility could be quantified, evidence would be provided of the degree of openness of modern social structures as potential meritocracies. But how can social mobility be reliably measured? The conventional means has been for sociologists or government officials to construct occupational scales which bracket occupations into a hierarchy of categories, usually referred to as social classes. Such scales can be used in research as standardised measuring devices by which can be quantified the frequency and range of movement up and down the social structure, usually by comparing the occupational levels achieved by one generation with those of their parents.

Traditionally when occupational scales were used, only the occupations of males were recognised in the measurement. Thus, within a household, all members were deemed to be of the same occupational class as the male breadwinner. If married females or daughters still living at home were questioned in social mobility research, which they often were not, their social class position was read off from their husband's or father's occupation. This practice was strongly criticised by feminists as typical of patriarchal society and occupational scales now tend measure the occupational position of women as important in its own right.

Constructing occupational scales poses a number of problems. For example, what criteria should be used for grouping occupations into categories and deciding on the number and cut off points of class divisions? Should the organising criteria be based primarily on level of income, work skill, social prestige, power in the workplace, etc. associated with an occupation or a combination of these? If the latter, what is an appropriate formula for that combination? These matters remain open to dispute. And whichever emphasis if given, there remains the problem of locating all occupations in a society into their appropriate groupings. It is not surprising, then, that a number of different occupational scales have been devised.

In the construction of a social class scale, it is debatable whether judgements of the social prestige of occupations should form part of the organising criteria since prestige is the key criteria of social status. However, it could be argued that this is an academic distinction and that in the real world these concepts may overlap. Scales which conflate the two concepts should therefore more realistically be referred to as 'socio economic scales'.

Further, although occupational scales are intended to be used as standardised measuring devices, there may be a shift over time in the underlying criteria for organising the scale, leading to a change in the way that occupations are classified. This may reflect attempts to realign the scale with changes in the occupational structure, but it is likely to undermine the capacity of the scale for making standardised comparisons in measurements over time.

The first occupational scale to be applied in Britain, the Registrar General's scale, was devised by a social statistician for the government's statistical department in 1913 and used from 1921. It originally comprised five occupational categories – two of which contained predominantly white collar occupations (upper and lower professional occupations) and three predominantly blue collar (skilled manual, semi-skilled manual and unskilled manual occupations). To reflect a subsequent expansion in white collar clerical occupations, the scale was reconstructed in 1971 as a six class scale by the addition of a further white collar division below the other two white collar categories. When applying the terms with sociological precision, although occupation was used as a basis for social class classification, the organising principle of occupations on the scale up to this time was the rather subjective and status based criteria of 'standing within the community'. It is therefore a socio-economic scale and could even be regarded more as a social status scale. From 1981, the scale reorganised occupational categories in terms of skill differentials between occupations, but understandably has been criticised by sociologists for its conceptual confusion and lack of theoretical underpinning. Its use has now been superseded by other scales.

A rather different approach to measuring stratification is adopted in the form of geodemographics (Crompton, 2008, p.54). Used mainly by commercial companies for marketing purposes, this type of scale combines measures of economic class and social and cultural status in identifying different types of neighbourhood through the use of postal codes. Clearly, such scales would need to be regularly updated to accommodate housing developments and changes in fashion regarding areas of residence.

We have seen that the Registrar General's occupational scale was originally constructed by a government social statistician. This begs the question of whether there may be a more organic way of tying in a scale to the phenomena which it is intended to measure. A key approach to achieving this has been to conduct social surveys which ask respondents to rank occupations in accordance to specified criteria and basing a scale on their responses. Using this method of scale construction, Hope and Goldthorpe (1974) were able to devise a scale which ranked occupations in terms of their 'perceived social desirability' and North and Hatt in the United States (1947), constructed a scale which positioned occupations via their 'social standing' (Crompton, 2008, p.55).

For many sociologists, there remain two main problems with the scales that have been identified above. One is that whilst referring to the categories as social classes, they organise occupations in terms of status related frameworks. The question may therefore be asked to what extent they are measuring social class or social status or a rather confused and subjective mixture of both. The other point is that they are largely descriptive – they lack a foundation in sociological theory to their formulation of social classes and the relationships between them.

Approaches to scale construction which take their lead from sociological theory have rested mainly on Weberian or Marxist foundations of how social classes are formed. Scales that are linked closely to Weberian theory of social class formation will emphasise that the construction of class categories should reflect the life chances and marketable skills associated with the occupation. An early Weberian based approach by Goldthorpe (1972) also included the criteria of authority in the workplace. Thus, occupations would be classified in terms of 1) levels of pay and other material rewards, job security and career prospects, and associated life chances and 2) degree of power and authority and control and autonomy experienced by the worker in the workplace. These combined criteria would be applied to guide decisions in the construction of the scale with regard to the number of class categories in society and the positioning of cut off points between the classes could be guided by evidence from previous research which showed social mobility pinch points.

Goldthorpe's original scale, utilised in the Oxford Mobility Studies, comprised seven occupational categories. These were bracketed into three main social classes. The term 'service class' was used to apply to the two occupational categories of higher and lower professions respectively. Higher professional occupations included managers in large companies and amongst lower professionals were included high grade technicians. An 'intermediate class' comprised the three occupational categories: routine clerical work, small business proprietors and self-employed, and lower grade technicians and supervisors. Finally, a 'working class' consisted of two occupational categories – skilled manual work, and semi and unskilled manual work.

From this starting point, Goldthorpe's scale has gone through a number of revisions but remained essentially loyal to Weberian theory. A more recent adaptation of this scale has changed the organising criteria to that of 'employment relations' and developed eight occupational categories through the subdivision of routine non-manual occupations into higher and lower grade categories. This clearly recognises the expansion of lower grade routine office work and takes on board criticisms by feminists that when such work is undertaken by females it is often in the form of a dead end job rather than more typically for males as part of a career structure. In this case, routine clerical work needed to be reallocated a position on the scale below that of skilled manual occupations but above semi-skilled and unskilled occupations. Now recognising the gendered aspect of occupational stratification, female routine office workers would be placed in this new category seven on the eight category scale.

Strongly influenced by Goldthorpe's revised scale, the Office of National Statistics developed the National Statistics Socio Economic Scale in 1998. On this scale the traditional distinction between white and blue collar occupational categories which invariably placed the former largely above the latter, has been discarded and replaced by positioning in terms of degrees of work routinization. A category 'never worked and long term unemployed' has also been introduced at the bottom of the scale. Furthermore, the positioning of the household on the scale is now identified through the occupational position of the highest earner, irrespective of whether they are male or female.

Marxists dispute the theoretical basis upon which neo-Weberian scales are constructed. For example, Braverman emphasised that, despite the various divisions of occupational categories that such scales divide the population into, in capitalist societies there remains a single majority working class, defined by the necessity to sell its labour, and a capitalist employing class. Braverman acknowledged that the development of capitalism in the twentieth century has given rise to an intermediate class who are marginal to the other two. This class comprises upper managerial positions, the occupants of which, despite their reliance on a salary, are well paid to do the bidding of their employers with whom they largely see eye to eye. However, Marxists generally maintain that conventional scales misleadingly construct separate class categories within the working class, wrongly base these divisions on labour market criteria and are largely unable to pay recognition to the existence of a small but powerful capitalist class.

Erik Olin Wright has adopted a Marxist framework, but eventually developed a more elaborate scale of twelve finely graded occupational categories (Crompton, 2008, pp.56-59). Exploitation is the key organising feature of the scale. The primary division is therefore between owners of the means of production and employees. Further divisions are then made in terms of the number of employees businesses employ, and amongst employees scarcity of skills and relation to authority. The scale ultimately divides owners of the means of production into three categories and employees into nine. From this, a dilemma faced by Marxists is apparent. The traditional two class distinction is likely to appear over simplistic and outmoded in relation to contemporary complex occupational structures. On the other hand, in its complexity, Wright's scale has been criticised by Marxists for its departure from the classic Marxist model and has further proved difficult to operationalise (apply in research).

Occupational scales may be useful tools in the hands of positivist inclined researchers as when used in social surveys they provide a mass of quantifiable data. This would be particularly so for measuring the frequency of social mobility, a topic area which occupies the next section of this text. However, as valid measuring devices for social class (can we be sure that they are measuring what they claim to measure), these scales do have certain weaknesses.

Firstly, these scales tend to neglect a key dimension of social class - a perception of class community amongst its members. Constructing categories of like occupations is no guarantee that a sense of class community exists amongst people within those grouped occupations or that any subjective experience of class corresponds to the categories on the scale.

Secondly, although occupational scales correspond quite closely to a hierarchy of income, the wealth held by people who work at similar occupational levels (for example share and property ownership) is not taken into account and differences can be substantial.

Thirdly, preoccupation with social class and status has led sociologists to traditionally overlook the importance of gender and ethnicity to stratification. Only in more recent years have attempts been made to develop scales which reveal more about gendered and ethnic aspects of stratification.

Fourthly, there are many theories about the way that the class structure is fundamentally changing in contemporary society. Are we all becoming middle class? Is the class structure completely breaking down? In response to the latter question, the construction of continuous occupational scales without division into class categories has been proposed. To construct such scales and to enhance their validity, surveys are carried out in which people are requested to locate occupations against one another.

Fifthly, whether occupational stratification even remains a significant aspect of life in contemporary society is an issue which will be addressed in more detail toward the end of the chapter with reference to postmodernism.

2. Measuring social mobility

Before reviewing some research findings and issues regarding social mobility, the reader may find it beneficial to consider the meaning of social mobility at an individual level. We have seen that occupational level is regarded as the single best rough and ready measure of a person's social class. The question to ask regarding 'intergenerational' social mobility is how does an individual's occupational level compare to that of their parent's (traditionally male's to father's)? If measured on an occupational scale, has there been upward or downward mobility and to what extent, or has the position remained about the same? This must, of course, only be a starting point to help envisage the meaning of intergenerational social mobility throughout society. Individual perceptions of the openness or closed nature of the social structure may reflect one's personal experiences, but such perceptions do not provide evidence of broader social patterns. Sociologists attempt to reliably measure patterns of social mobility across society. This is achieved through the statistical analysis of measurements taken from a sample of the population. Using the measuring device of occupational scales, the openness or fluidity of a social structure can be calculated in terms of movement between social classes. Such a measure is of 'absolute' social mobility levels.

Since the Second World War, a number of social mobility studies have been conducted in Britain and other countries. Some studies have made comparisons of mobility rates between societies. Comparisons can also be made over time to measure whether levels and patterns of social mobility are changing. These comparisons between place or over time are referred to as measures of 'relative' social mobility. Traditionally, studies took the family unit to be headed by a male breadwinner. Consequently, the occupational category of all dependent household members would derive from the location on the scale of the male breadwinner's occupation. These studies focussed on measuring the social mobility of males by comparing occupational levels achieved by sons with that of their fathers.

The use of occupational scales to measure large samples from populations is intended to provide objective statistical data on levels of social mobility. This statistical information can be conveniently summarised in table form. Tables, as illustrated below, comprise a grid of data on which a statistical comparison of father's and son's (the horizontal and vertical dimensions respectively) occupational level is summarised.

The following table summarises the findings of the Goldthorpe research into occupational mobility in England and Wales in 1972 (Abercrombie & Warde, 2006, p.135). The information is here compiled in the form of an 'outflow' table. This means that the table takes as its base or starting point the father's occupational level and from this is measured the percentage of sons from each of the father's occupational backgrounds who end up in each of the various occupational categories themselves.

David Goldthorpe, Oxford Mobility Study, England and Wales Outflow Table

Father's occupational category	Son's Occupational Category, 1972							Fathers in sample	
	1	2	3	4	5	6	7	No.	%
1	**45.2**	18.9	11.5	7.7	4.8	5.4	6.5	688	7.3
2	29.1	**23.1**	11.9	7.0	9.6	10.6	8.7	554	5.9
3	18.4	15.7	**12.8**	7.8	12.8	15.6	16.9	694	7.3
4	12.6	11.4	8.0	**24.8**	8.7	14.4	20.5	1329	14.1
5	14.2	13.6	10.1	7.7	**15.7**	21.2	17.6	1082	11.5
6	7.8	8.8	8.3	6.6	12.3	**30.4**	25.9	2594	27.5
7	6.5	7.8	8.2	6.6	12.5	23.5	**34.9**	2493	24.6

In Goldthorpe's research, an early version of the seven occupational category scale, as referred to in the previous section, has been used. In the table, the 1-7 category column on the left refers to the father's occupational background. The figures in each box running across each row indicate the percentages of their sons who ended up in each of the seven column headed occupational categories. Toward the end of each row is given the total number of fathers in the sample in each occupational category and these figures are converted into percentages to indicate the relative size of each category in the father's generation.

How does one read the table? Look at the figure of 11.5% in column three of the top row. This means that 11.5% of sons from occupational category one background (their father's occupation) were working in category three occupations. The 6.5% figure at the bottom of the first column shows that 6.5% of sons from occupational background seven were upwardly mobile into the occupational group one category. The same approach can be applied to any figure on the table and it is worth pausing to work through a number of the figures to familiarise oneself with reading such tables.

To interpret the table requires a broader view and an element of judgement. We will start with some simplified observations which will later need to be qualified. One approach would be to assess how far the pattern of evidence suggested that society was removed from a completely closed stratification system. If the stratification system were completely closed, the bold figures in the diagonal from top left toward bottom right would all read 100% and all other cells would contain 0%, showing that all sons worked at the same occupational level as their fathers. This is clearly not the case – some intergenerational social mobility is clearly evident. However, the highest figures do fall on or near to the diagonal. These figures further indicate that the highest levels of self recruitment come from category one and category seven occupational backgrounds and that those from group three backgrounds are the most occupationally mobile. Overall, there is therefore evidence of relative closure at the top and bottom of the occupational structure, more openness around the middle, and only limited long range social mobility.

Another approach would be to compare the research evidence with the expected distribution of figures within a completely open social structure. In such an open structure, the figures would be more evenly spread across the rows and certainly much higher toward the corners opposite the diagonal, indicating higher levels of long range social mobility. Significant impediments to total openness can be judged from the research figures which show that whilst 45.2% of males from category one backgrounds are found in category one occupations, only 6.5% appear in category seven employment (which is also a much larger occupational category) and 34.9% from level seven backgrounds are in level seven occupations whilst only 6.5% achieve level one occupations (a smaller category though).

On the other hand, compared to the findings of a study previously conducted by Glass et al in 1949, there is some evidence of relatively higher levels of long range social mobility. Although the findings are not strictly comparable as different occupational scales were used (Glass used the Hall – Jones scale), the earlier research, based on a smaller sample, showed that only 1.5% of males from category one backgrounds were found in category seven occupations and 0% from category seven backgrounds achieved level one occupational status.

Other studies of relative social mobility have attempted to make international comparisons. Pioneering work in this area has been conducted by Lipset and Bednix (1959) and somewhat more recent research has been carried out by Erikson and Goldthorpe (1993). Whilst recognising the problem of standardisation of data in such research (differences in occupational structures make the use of standardised occupational scales for direct comparison impossible), these studies provided comparisons of nine and twelve industrial countries respectively. They found that a very similar profile of moderate social mobility pertained to all of the societies. The one main exception for Lipset and Bendix was the limited upward social mobility from lower occupational backgrounds in Italy which related at the time to a less developed economy and a larger agricultural sector.

Although social mobility studies were not available at the time, perceptive observers of mid nineteenth century America such as Alexis de Tocqueville were impressed by the apparent degree of openness of the social structure and the opportunities available for social mobility. In this regard, America was viewed as exceptional. If this observation was valid, more recent research has questioned whether it remains so. Although Blau and Duncan (1967) characterised the United States as a society of high social mobility, they evidenced a high degree of self-recruitment into some of the upper occupational categories. More recent research by Jantti et al (2006), in comparing occupational mobility between the United States, the United Kingdom and four Nordic countries (Denmark, Finland, Norway and Sweden) has found that, as in the case of previously reported findings, there is a generally higher level of intergenerational social mobility in the Nordic countries than in the United States (the UK often appears in an intermediate position). The research indicates that in the country (USA) with the most stretched occupational hierarchy in terms of income differentiation, the sons of the lowest earning groups are relatively more likely to remain in the lowest earning category and the sons from the highest earning occupational backgrounds are relatively less likely to experience long distance downward mobility. This would appear to raise questions regarding the justification of high income differentials as an incentive for the competition that is necessary for a meritocratic society – as proposed in functionalist theory and the politics of the political right.

3. Analysing society in terms of meritocracy

There is a close link between an open social structure and a meritocracy. Since a meritocracy is a society that enables individuals to reach occupational positions entirely in terms of their own efforts and abilities, its existence presupposes an open social structure. But we will see that the two are not exactly the same thing. Research statistics on social mobility through the occupational structure suggest the existence of a partially open social structure in Britain. Interpreting this degree of openness, especially in terms of meritocratic opportunity, is fraught with difficulties.

It can be argued that a society that appears to exhibit a degree of social closure may still be highly meritocratic. How can this apparent contradiction be reconciled? It has been suggested that social mobility levels that on the surface fall short of the very high mobility levels that one would expect to accompany a meritocracy may be the consequence of social class related differences in levels of intelligence and (or) effort. In this case, it is argued that those of higher occupational background have inherited higher levels of innate intelligence and acquire more aspirational values and those of lower occupational background, lower levels of each. If this were the case, it could be claimed that society offers equal opportunities to all, but that social mobility levels short of those otherwise expected in a meritocracy can be explained in terms of these differences in levels of ability and effort related to class background.

A strong advocate of this explanation is Peter Saunders. His arguments derive from a Conservative new right perspective. This position offers a strong defence of the liberal democratic institutions and individual freedoms of capitalist societies. It is emphasised that the dynamism of such societies is enhanced by substantial inequalities of occupational income, which promotes individual competition. A highly differentiated occupational reward structure with large disparities between top and bottom is therefore the motivator for individual success. As the main criteria for success are effort and ability, success does not just benefit individuals exhibiting these qualities, but by appropriately placing people in suitable occupations it enhances living standards for all through the efficient utilisation of human resources. A highly differentiated income structure can thus be legitimised, as can the accumulation of private wealth based on individual achievement.

Saunders argues that class linked differences in innate individual ability and also effort go a long way toward explaining the differences in occupational achievement of people from different social class backgrounds. And whilst he acknowledges that modern Britain is not perfectly meritocratic, his research also indicates that ability is closely associated with occupational destination. Where differences in ability alone cannot sufficiently explain variations in level of occupational achievement, then differences in individual motivation, related so social background, also have an important impact.

In considering these arguments, there are reasons to be cautions or critical of Saunders' position. Firstly, the proposition that there are inherited ability differences that derive from social class background requires examination. The importance of educational opportunity and achievement to meritocracy is established in the chapter on education. In that chapter, it is argued that evidence of class related differences in inherited ability are not compelling. Any ability differences will therefore have very limited effect on explaining levels of closure in social stratification from one generation to the next. Instead, it is argued that the way that intelligence and educational performance are assessed reflect class related differences to the advantage of the middle classes. The educational system is further bent toward the middle classes through the extra help that parents are often able to make available to their children to enhance their prospects of academic success. Such a class based distortion built into education will have consequences for both educational and occupational achievement to the extent that occupation is related to educational achievement.

Furthermore, if levels of motivation and individual effort are related to social class, the argument can be taken in different directions. If those of manual working class background tend to be more fatalistic in terms of their occupational destination, on the one hand it can be argued, as did Hyman, that it is these negative values which act as self imposed barriers to success whilst nevertheless society is basically meritocratic. The fault lies in the adoption of negative values, not in inequalities in the social structure. On the other hand, from his research of a group of working class lads, Willis suggested the explanation that in their lesser effort to succeed at school and aspire to higher level occupations than their fathers, they made a realistic assessment of the limited opportunities available to them within a society which was far from meritocratic. In other words, the lack of aspiration is more a consequence of the realization that society is not meritocratic.

A number of other reasons to be cautious in claiming British society to be highly meritocratic can be made. One of these is to do with changes that take place within the occupational structure. The size and makeup of occupational classes changes over time. For example, during the post-war decades there was a period of rapid expansion in professional occupations. However, the fertility rate of the middle class was lower than that of the working class. During this period, it was difficult for expanding professional occupations to sufficiently recruit from the young of the middle classes alone to fill all posts. Under these conditions, even in a relatively closed social structure there would need to be some social mobility as the numbers of children born in the different social classes is not mirroring the needs of a changing occupational structure to have positions filled. Goldthorpe's research covering this period indicated greater levels of upward than downward mobility and more long range social mobility compared to the previous findings of the Glass research. This particular pattern of social mobility enabled more people of manual working class background to gain access to middle class occupations without threatening to displace many from middle class backgrounds. It is therefore doubtful whether such opportunities for upward mobility should be equated with a meritocracy. They are likely to be highly contingent on the conditions identified which did not threaten the advantage of middle class occupational self-recruitment. A measure of social fluidity which more closely represents that of meritocratic mobility would therefore need to extract changing social class sizes and different fertility rates from the calculations.

The expansion of the 'middle classes' during the latter part of twentieth century has been more toward the bottom end in the form of relatively low paid and low skilled office work. As the more professional levels have gone through their period of expansion, pressures for upward mobility to that of the professional middle classes are now likely to meet their resistance. As the structure above the middle classes narrows and is arguably more closed, there is little opportunity for their upward mobility. Upward mobility from below would therefore spell displacement of more children of the professional middle classes downward. Consequently, the concept of a meritocracy is likely to be less appealing to the middle class who will want to defend their position against the threat of downward mobility through such means as providing access to educational privilege and utilising social contacts for their children. Unsurprisingly, more recent studies have indicated a decline in upward mobility.

A further problem for the meritocracy thesis is that whilst a totally open social structure is a prerequisite for a meritocracy, a high level of social mobility is not in itself sufficient proof of mobility through meritocratic means – that of fair and legitimate competition based on individual effort and ability. Levels of social mobility derived from marriage into wealth or through criminal activity would hardly equate with the normally accepted means of meritocratic success.

Another issue regarding a weakness of general occupational scales is that they lack the precision to measure social mobility levels at the very pinnacle of society. For example, in Goldthorpe's sample, the top occupational category on the scale comprised 7.3% of fathers' occupations and by implication the size of that category in the population during the father's generation. This class had grown to 13.6% of the son's generation. However, a researcher's focus of interest may be in measuring social mobility into the 'elite'. In occupational terms, this category will include such professions as ambassadors, senior judges, high ranking officers in the armed forces, members of parliament (especially the Cabinet), high ranking civil servants, and directors of major industrial, banking and insurance companies. This group borders onto a propertied upper class and in total comprises only about 0.1 – 0.2% of the adult population. Occupational scales which do not have a separate social stratum to reflect this will not be sensitive enough to measure social mobility across this point. Moreover, in general social mobility studies, only about 1 or 2 participants from this category per 1,000 in a representative sample of the population are likely to be included. There will therefore also be insufficient participants for statistical purposes to measure levels of social mobility around elite occupations.

An alternative approach could be to select a sample of people comprising entirely those in elite occupations. Such groups, however, tend to be wary of the enquiries of prying sociologists. The study of this stratum needs to be approached from another angle. One way of going about this is to obtain a measure of the percentages of people in elite professions who have attended the most exclusive public schools and compare these figures with those of people in other occupations or for the rest of the population. Massive disparities in favour of the elite occupations do in fact exist, which offers strong evidence of non-meritocratic elite self-recruitment.

According to Peter Saunders, 'a meritocracy is like a race where everybody lines up together at the start' (Saunders, 1990, p.44). Assuming that this is a close account of the basis of opportunity in society appears to be a remarkably superficial view. Even if competition for occupation and income level is largely determined by ability and effort, this does not explain how the resulting accumulation of wealth and its inheritance squares with a meritocratic society. The distribution of wealth is even more unequal than that of income. Saunders defends the legitimacy to pass on legally acquired wealth to others. However, the problem here is that even if wealth in one generation is entirely achieved by merit, through right of disposal to descendants, it, and the advantages that it provides, would then not remain acquired by meritocratic means to that and to subsequent generations.

Another way of approaching these issues is to imagine the creation of a meritocracy from a social blank slate. For the first generation, all would start, as Saunders suggests, on an equal footing to compete for occupations in terms of ability and effort. Assuming the motivation for competition to be a substantial inequality of income associated with different levels of occupation and assuming the existence of a system of private property and inheritance, it is quite obvious that the meritocracy would be undermined in the following generation through the inheritance of different life chance starting points based purely on accident of birth, offering some the advantages deriving from their parent's achievements and others the disadvantages of their parent's lack of achievement. These advantages and disadvantages can include different study conditions and educational privileges, and differences in nutrition, health and access to levels of healthcare. Such factors are often interrelated.

It is well documented that the physical and health condition of those of manual working class background is generally inferior to those of middle class background. Individual competition for academic achievement and occupational status will not be taking place on a level playing field.

The above reservations have related primarily to social class. In terms of class stratification, although modern Britain (and like western democracies) is a relatively meritocratic society by very broad historical comparisons, evidence and arguments show it to be substantially short of being a pure meritocracy. However, there is also an ideological dimension which may colour assessment of this area. Functionalists and supporters of the political right find meritocracy to be compatible with capitalism. In fact, they tend to utilise the concept of meritocracy to justify massive inequality of income as a motivator for competition and the achievement of social mobility. However, it has already been demonstrated that when international comparisons of occupational mobility rates have been made, there is evidence that the society which ranks amongst the highest in income differentials demonstrates relatively low levels of long range social mobility and relatively high levels of occupational closure at the top and the bottom. The values and justifications of meritocracy are therefore not born out by evidence of its existence. Critics from the political left tend to question the need for vast income differentials and are likely to be more cautious of the extent to which modern capitalist societies are meritocratic. Moreover, as suggested earlier, it could be argued that there is a logical contradiction between the institutions of capitalism itself and meritocracy.

Assessing the extent to which contemporary society shapes up as meritocratic can only be more comprehensively evaluated when other dimensions of stratification such as gender and ethnicity are also considered and questions raised regarding the continuing existence of institutions of privilege and status that perpetuate birthright. Our political leaders are often keen to appeal to the concept of Britain as a meritocratic society but less keen on engaging in or encouraging others to engage in joined up thinking in this area. Pursuing this logical analysis too far may raise awkward questions which point to the incompatibility of some of our social institutions, from which many of them and their children have been beneficiaries, with the realisation of a meritocracy. Indeed, following such an analysis, the reader, at a personal level, may have come to feel more or less comfortable with the idea of meritocracy in principle or practice. However, as a sociologist, the aim should be to enlighten, not obscure. An attempt must be made to step outside of society and assess it in terms of a comparison with the logical outcome of the application of such concepts as meritocracy.

Class stratification – changing but how?

Linked to the areas of dispute between the founding theoretical perspectives on stratification (functionalist, Marxist and Weberian) are a number of interpretations of how the class structure in the second half of the twentieth century has been changing. One such interpretation was the 'embourgeoisement' (becoming middle class) thesis. This thesis was rooted in the experience of full employment and growing affluence of the late 1950s and early 1960s and was associated with such writers as Jessie Bernard and Ferdinand Zweig. Zweig's research, for example, suggested that within this context more affluent manual workers were looking to maximise their income within the system rather than to change it. Viewed broadly, as a consequence of economic modernisation, traditional working class occupations, such as dock work, mining and agricultural work, were undergoing long-term decline. However, a new type of blue-collar employment on modern production lines was expanding and enabling workers to earn incomes increasingly comparable to those of the white collar middle classes. In the resultant mass consumer society, affluent blue collar workers were gaining unprecedented access to consumer goods and holidays and as a consequence were apparently adopting an attitude to their work, a lifestyle, status and even political views which were regarded as more typical of those in middle class occupations. The traditional working class was therefore argued to be in decline both in terms of size and class consciousness, whilst the middle class, now comprising a growing proportion of affluent blue collar workers, was expanding.

There are clear theoretical implications of this interpretation of change. One is that Marx's analysis of the essence of class conflict to capitalism and his predictions of class polarisation, enhanced working class consciousness and political radicalism, were fundamentally mistaken. According to proponents of embourgeoisement, Marxist analysis looked increasingly dated and redundant as capitalism became able to transcend class conflict and evolve toward a largely single middle class society. This emphasis on 'middleclassness' as a basis for shared values and social integration would certainly align embourgeoisement with the consensus theory of functionalism.

It has been well established that the embourgeoisement interpretation was undermined by research conducted by Goldthorpe and Lockwood during the early to mid 1960s. Their research focussed on a sample of affluent blue-collar workers in the Luton area and found that they were neither traditional working class nor had they become middle class. This conclusion can be viewed on various dimensions. For example, the research found that although their work provided access to income levels more characteristic of workers in white collar occupations, they did not expect nor experience a degree of job satisfaction or close identity with the firm that was more typical of white collar workers. Instead, the affluent workers held a practical and instrumental attitude toward their work as a means to an end of good pay. They were relatively isolated from one another through working from fixed production line work stations which allowed little opportunity for the development of a workplace collective community. Any collectivism therefore tended to be of an instrumental nature, through commonly emphasising the importance of trade unions to bargain for higher wages rather than to change society.

The affluent workers' view of the social structure did not tend to follow a more traditional industrial working class ideological class conflict model characterised in the imagery of 'us versus them'. Nor did it take the form of an attitude of deference toward social superiors within a rightful hierarchy which had been traditionally more common amongst agricultural workers. However, neither did it regard the social structure through the more typically middle class image of a ladder of career opportunity and a prestige hierarchy. Instead, they viewed the social hierarchy in terms of economic class divisions.

In their lifestyle outside of work, the affluent workers tended to adopt a consumerist and privatised, home centred life. They were frequently owner occupiers. This and the spread of their neighbourhoods did not facilitate the type of working class community relationships that were more typical of tightly packed terraced housing layouts. However, privatisation also extended to them not seeking to befriend white collar workers.

The affluent workers were not deserting the Labour Party for the Conservatives, the party of the middle class, as the embourgeoisement thesis would suggest. In line with their orientation toward trade unions, the attitude of the affluent workers toward political parties was one of practical or instrumental as opposed to ideological commitment. At the time, their support for Labour was numerically high but was based on the calculation of a Labour government being of practical benefit to them rather than out of any deeply held working class convictions.

In conclusion, it was found that the affluent manual workers experienced a more privatised life than traditional industrial workers both in the workplace and in their neighbourhoods and the collectivism that they experienced towards trade unions and voting Labour was more instrumental than ideological. They were seen to be a modernising section of the working class. Such findings point to a more differentiated stratification system implied in Weber's perspective.

A rival interpretation, from a Marxist perspective, suggested that very different dynamics of change were taking place in the class structure. This explanation highlighted the process of 'proletarianisation'. Marx had argued that the logic of capitalism drove businesses, in the struggle to survive and maximize profits, to innovate and introduce new technology, expand in size and cheapen labour. As a result, social polarisation would take place between a small number of increasingly wealthy surviving capitalists and a mass of impoverished workers, resulting in a potential for growing consciousness of their position by both camps.

Working within this theoretical perspective, Harry Braverman (1974) maintained that despite absolute improvements in standard of living and the expansion of white-collar occupations, a mass working class still existed. Technological advance by no means guaranteed an upgrading of work skills. By contrast, it was argued that through the advance of mechanisation in the workplace, many blue-collar occupations had undergone a process of 'deskilling'.

From the early decades of the twentieth century, small workshops employing highly skilled craft workers were being replaced by larger businesses introducing repetitive production line work systems, employing low skilled workers following narrowly designed job specifications in large factories turning out mass produced standardised goods. Workplaces became increasingly organised around 'scientific management' techniques developed by the efficiency expert Frederick Taylor. Taylor argued that it was the responsibility of management to design systems of production in which the most efficient mechanical job procedures could be combined to maximise the productivity of shop floor workers. This meant imposing highly repetitive work processes in which jobs were drained of skill content, easy to learn and enabled employees to reach maximum efficiency very quickly. If management 'equipped' workers with these 'skills', workforce motivation and efficiency could be manipulated through piece rate payments that were related to productivity levels. Under such conditions, Braverman argued, production line workers, such as those working on car assembly lines, commonly experienced, compared to their predecessors, a loss of personal autonomy and heightened alienation in the workplace. As a contemporary example, one might consider the design of work systems in fast food outlets as archetypical of the efficiency of scientific management systems.

Of particular importance to Braverman, was the view that deskilling of work and workers was becoming an increasingly common feature of white collar employment. During the mid-nineteenth century, office clerks comprised less than 1% of the labour force. They usually worked in very small offices, had much contact with their employer, were significantly better paid than most manual workers, required a high level of education for their time, experienced relative job security and high status and did not join trade unions. However, the development of larger businesses led to the growth of white collar employment in increasingly large and mechanised offices. The twentieth century witnessed the expansion of white-collar employment increasingly in the form of highly supervised and low skilled office work which offered workers little autonomy and responsibility and few promotion prospects. Call centres may be taken as a contemporary example of such a trend in white collar work.

The proletarianisation thesis maintained that under modern capitalism there exists a mass working class which is identified by a common experience in the workplace. That experience is one of declining skill levels, autonomy and responsibility, increasing supervision and a heightened experience of alienation - processes common to a mass of relatively lowly paid blue-collar and white-collar workers, all with poor promotion prospects. Consequently, from a Marxist perspective, it is a false consciousness for this growing body of deskilled white-collar workers to distinguish themselves as middle class and separate from working class blue-collar workers just because they work in a white collar capacity, and occupational scales which make this distinction are themselves faulty measuring devices.

Research evidence regarding this theory is mixed. In the 1950s, Lockwood claimed that much white collar work had retained employment privileges and status superiority over blue collar work and in 1980 Stewart et al pointed to the retention of superior promotion prospects for many white collar workers. However, research by Crompton and Jones (1984) did find, in the automated offices that they studied, evidence of enhanced supervision and experience of alienation as well as restricted promotion prospects. Perhaps the uptake of trade union membership by white collar workers can be taken as an index of their deskilled employment situation.

Of the various criticisms of Marxist interpretations of the class structure, one of the most challenging has been the 'decomposition' thesis which was associated with Ralf Dahrendorf (1959). Dahrendorf argued that rather than the class structure of modern capitalist societies crystallising into two clearly opposed class camps as Marx had predicted, it was in fact breaking down or decomposing throughout.

During the early phase of capitalism in the first half of the nineteenth century, most businesses were privately owned and run by individuals, partnerships or families. In this form of capitalism, power, authority, ownership and decision making were typically consolidated in the hands of a social class of entrepreneurs, who were personally accountable for profits or losses made. This stratum comprised Marx's capitalist class. However, from the later nineteenth century, the predominant type of private enterprise was shifting in the direction of the joint stock company. This was a development which enabled the size of businesses to grow through accessing capital from a large number of external share-holding investors. For Dahrendorf, the emergence of the joint stock company led to a fundamental change at the top of the stratification system.

The implications of this change were radical and Dahrendorf argued that the consequences had been inaccurately portrayed by James Burnham's account of a 'managerial revolution'. For Burnham, the managerial revolution was essentially a revolution from above. As businesses grew in size, power had passed wholesale from those who privately owned the means of production, the entrepreneurs, to expert managers who were now in control of the productive forces. In Burnham's analysis, this still left capitalism with two homogeneous and opposed social classes: now managers and workers.

By contrast, Dahrendorf emphasised that the separation of ownership from control that emerged with joint stock companies led to a duality at the top of society. Those providing the capital were now investors in stocks and shares. They were not directly involved in the internal running of the company and their main concern was in the performance of their investment. Those running the company were trained and salaried managers, highly skilled employees who did not own the company. This separation of ownership and control, functions which were once consolidated in the hands of the entrepreneur, into two groups with somewhat different interests, Dahrendorf equated to a process of decomposition from a once single class. As he put it 'The roles of owner and manager, originally combined in the position of the capitalist, have been separated and distributed over two positions, those of stockholder and executive' (Dahrendorf, 1959, p.44). Furthermore, referring to executives, Dahrendorf maintained that 'this new ruling group of industry bears little resemblance to the old "full capitalists"' (Dahrendorf, 1959, p.43).

We could add that from this perspective, through the privatisations of nationalised industries in Britain from the 1980s, the social base of share ownership had been broadened, enabling more of the working population to also become part investors in and legally part owners of private enterprise. Thus, a significant proportion of the public, as investors in private enterprise, were becoming, in Marxist terminology, technically part owners of the means of production. The problem posed for classical Marxist class analysis of capitalism is clear. For Marx, capitalist and proletarian classes were distinct, exclusive and homogeneous groups with opposed interests. However, most investors today would also be in paid employment and therefore, according to Marx, also usually proletarian. The class dividing line between capital and labour had arguably become very blurred.

Dahrendorf also argued that a decomposition of labour was taking place. Central to Marx's thesis was that capitalism brought about a growing commonality amongst manual workers through the spread of deskilling. Dahrendorf acknowledged that this was a valid analysis of the consequences of the extension of the division of labour during nineteenth century industrial modernization. However, the twentieth century had witnessed a growing differentiation amongst manual workers which equated to the decomposition of the working class. In a complex occupational structure, the blue-collar 'working class' was fragmenting into a number of occupational strata comprising a growing proportion of skilled, a relatively static proportion of semi-skilled and a declining proportion of unskilled workers, each with different interests to protect and different levels of social status. Dahrendorf documented this decomposition in the following way:

> 'we find a plurality of status and skill groups whose interests often diverge. Demands of the skilled for security may injure the semiskilled; wage claims of the semiskilled may raise objections by the skilled; and any interest on the part of the unskilled is bound to set their more highly skilled fellow workmen worrying about differentials' (Dahrendorf, 1959, p.51).

Since Dahrendorf first published his thesis, more blue-collar workers have become owner-occupiers of their homes and achieved comparative prosperity, arguably introducing further distinctions within 'the working class'. According to this analysis, the 'working class' have been breaking down as a discrete stratum and experiencing a decline in common class consciousness.

Regarding the 'middle classes' (notice the plural), Dahrendorf argued that they consist of an extremely disparate social category. They comprise, for example, clerical employees through to supervisors and executives in a broad range of occupations. Employment may be in the state or the private sector. Some of the middle classes are engaged in a self-employed capacity. The middle classes, which were 'born decomposed', have expanded throughout the twentieth century. Moreover, the top occupations within this category, such as politicians, shade into the elite whereas at the bottom end, there is little distinction between, for example, some engineers and skilled manual workers.

Dahrendorf's model suggests that, contrary to Marx's predictions, contemporary capitalism has progressed to a more open social structure, differentiated by finely graded occupational levels, status groups and interest distinctions. Class conflict between two opposing classes has given way to rivalry between numerous sectional interests and individual competition. A wider variety of people feel that they have a stake in the system as power has percolated down to shareholders, and socially and organizationally accountable managers have replaced entrepreneurs. Compared to its mid nineteenth century form, capitalism has thus become more socially accountable and tamed. Such features of twentieth century capitalism identified by Dahrendorf as challenging the contemporary relevance of the Marxist model were actively promoted by new right policies through which privatisation spread shareholding and home ownership in Britain to more people than ever before during the 1980s and early 90s and heralded the advance of 'popular capitalism'.

Gender stratification – continuity and change

The existence of a sexual division of labour in society is sometimes justified by reference to biological differences which are said to form the basis of differences in emotional and intellectual qualities between men and women suiting them for different social roles. This division of labour has often disadvantaged women in terms of access to income and wealth and occupational and life opportunities compared to men. Although linked to biological sex differences, the term gender refers to socially constructed and modifiable identity. Looked at sociologically, there is significant scope for gender identity and gender roles to change as society and its institutions, culture and values change. The justification of fixed gender roles can therefore be viewed as ideological support for the continuance of male privilege and power over females – referred to as the exercise of 'patriarchal power'.

The issue of gender stratification is fact a highly complex one. For example, socialisation into gender identity is unlikely to be a uniform process across contemporary democratic societies, but varies, for example, between different ethnic groups, social classes and age groups. Clearly, there also exist significant differences between the cultures and customs of different societies with regard to gender identity. Neither, in stratification terms, do males or females comprise undifferentiated groups. In reality, gender stratification is mixed with other stratification influences such as class, status, ethnicity and age. Analysing the impact of these interrelated dimensions is an extremely complicated matter and it has become clear that traditional stratification analysis which focused so heavily on social class stratification seems to be poorly equipped to manage this complexity. The writer will first outline some of the social changes which have brought us to this current state of analysis and raised the profile of gender stratification.

Employment and educational opportunity as well as family relationships are key dimensions of gender stratification. How these have changed can be viewed in historical terms and the following comments can be related to the relevant content of chapters in this text on the family and education.

In pre-industrial Britain, quite a high proportion of economic production took place in domestic settings, combining work and family relationships. Although productive domestic work was often divided along gender lines, later notions of male (working) breadwinner and female (non-working) housewife were little recognised. Housework was likely to have been allocated to children.

Gender role segregation took on a new and pronounced form following the Industrial Revolution. As the productive process moved outside of the home and into the factory, work was becoming redefined in terms of this external setting in which workers were employed in large numbers in the pay of an employer. The introduction of the Factory Acts from the 1830s offered some degree of protection in the workplace for women and especially children, making them less attractive labour for employers to take on. Consequently, by the middle of the nineteenth century, the numbers of women working in factories were declining and their lives becoming situated within the home. Here, they engaged in domestic activities and childcare in an environment which was no longer regarded as a place of work. This gender based reconfiguration and the redefinition of work is sometimes referred to as the rise of private or 'domestic patriarchy', supported by the ideology of domesticity in which the 'natural' caring and serving qualities of females suited them to domesticity and dependence on the male wage earner. For their part, male workers often exhibited opposition to the employment of women as a threat to their employment security and justification of the need for a 'family wage'.

Throughout the nineteenth century, entry to many professions was either closed to women or their employment restricted, as in teaching or health care, to low level roles. The main employment available for working class women was that which reflected their perceived natural role: that of domestic service. According to Charles Booth, as many as 400,000 people, 85% of whom were women, were employed in domestic service in London alone in the late nineteenth century.

During the first half of the twentieth century, patterns of employment for women fluctuated greatly. Two world wars required the mass mobilisation of women into the workforce, where they often engaged in heavy-duty work to support the war effort. However, at the end of each conflict it was expected that they would return to their domestic duties so that men, if they returned, could 'rightfully' reclaim the jobs that it was emphasised they had only temporarily vacated to women.

After the Second World War, larger numbers of women resisted pressures to leave their jobs, but were often faced with male hostility and powerful government propaganda to resume their portrayed primary domestic role. However, from the 1960s economic change in the form of the growth of service sector employment (including white collar support work and a range of customer service occupations), enabled more women to enter the workforce, which nevertheless remained heavily gender segregated and stratified, restricting both the scope of work available, levels of pay and promotion prospects.

Against this backdrop and following the success of the civil rights movement in combatting racial discrimination in the United States, emerged the challenge of the women's movement. By the early 1970s, some of its theoretical advocates took up a radical stance. Radical feminists, such as Firestone and Millett, viewed patriarchal power as endemic throughout society and universally prevalent. For Firestone, such prevalence related to biological sex differences by which women giving birth and during childrearing become dependent on men. Gender stratification was thus viewed as more fundamental than social class; it predated social class which only tends to emerge at the point of social development when societies become productive enough to generate significant inequalities in the distribution of wealth. This argument can be referred to as a form of biological reductionism (gender stratification can be ultimately reduced to biological differences) or biological determinism (gender stratification is determined by biological differences). From this vantage point, the technological advance of the pill, in allowing female control of contraception, was regarded as having liberating potential.

Nevertheless, for radical feminists, male dominance exhibits itself throughout society and in ways as varied as inequalities of power within workplace hierarchies to violence within the family. It is the latter institution which is seen as the main perpetrator of patriarchal power and radical feminists usually argue that it needs to be abolished if women are to be more fully liberated.

By contrast, liberal feminism achieved its main impact amongst middle class careerist women in the context of an invigorated enterprise culture which accompanied new right governments during the 1980s and 1990s. Liberal feminists adopted a more reformist approach to progress. They argued that equality of opportunity between the genders can be enhanced through piecemeal reforms. Following the impact of the women's movement, legislative reform through the democratic process assisted advances toward equal pay and opportunities from the early 1970s. The growth of the service sector had enabled more women to enter the workforce and gain a degree of financial independence and in conjunction with liberalisation of divorce law had made it possible for more women to escape unhappy marriages. Family roles were becoming more flexible, educational materials less sexist and educational opportunity for females was significantly advancing. Liberal feminists were therefore more confident that such gradual changes across a broad front were leading toward a society of equal opportunities for women.

However, of particular concern to feminists from this period has been the implications of care in the community policy which was promoted in Britain from the early 1990s. Research has shown that much of the caring takes place within family settings and that the burden falls excessively on females. The costs involved in taking on this burden can be substantial. For example, as well as loss of earnings, carers lose out on making extra pension contributions. They are also likely to have missed out on retraining and promotion prospects and may find it difficult to return to work or when they do, face demotion. On top of these career and economic penalties, carers risk suffering anxiety and isolation which can affect their health and well-being.

There is also evidence that growing economic and social polarisation during the 1980s and 1990s had a greater impact on females than males. Whilst, particularly from the 1980s, the number of single, usually female, parents living in poverty was increasing, a growing number of women, although remaining minorities, were entering higher professional and managerial positions, some in dual career professional households. This improvement may be set to continue as more females are entering higher education than males, although at present females often need to be better qualified than males to enter equivalent occupations.

By the turn of the twenty first century, the workforce in Britain (and other western societies) includes an almost equal proportion of women and men. When scrutinised more closely, there is both evidence of continuing gender inequality and change in terms of patterns of concentration and stratification.

Firstly, in Britain women remain more highly concentrated in routine clerical level occupations than men. As a result, they tend to experience a different pattern of social mobility to that of men. Marshall et al indicated in the 1988 Essex Mobility Study that women are both more upwardly and downwardly mobile from a variety of occupational backgrounds as they tend to converge in the routine clerical occupational stratum. Moreover, these jobs are more likely to remain dead end occupations for females than males, who tend to use routine clerical employment as a career stepping stone.

Much debate has taken place as to whether routine office work has become deskilled. If this is so and these jobs offer women few promotion prospects, then it is possible, as Stanworth has argued, that women have disproportionately experienced the effect of proletarianisation. In contrast to this interpretation, Marshall has provided evidence that routine clerical workers have retained greater autonomy in the workplace than manual workers (Marshall, 1993, p.120) and that women's rate of social mobility is generally similar to that of men (Marshall, 1993, p.106).

Secondly, more women than men work part-time (about 43% as opposed to 9% according to 2003 Equal Opportunities Commission figures) or under flexible work conditions which can include zero hours contracts. This may be of advantage of both employers and to women with domestic commitments, but such employment is usually in the 'secondary' sector of the labour market which is marked by relatively low wages, poor employment prospects and employee insecurity. By contrast, proportionately more males tend to be employed in the 'primary' labour market comprising relatively secure employment and good career prospects, although there are signs that this market has been hit somewhat during the period of austerity post 2008.

Thirdly, there remains a pattern of gendered horizontal segregation in employment. Horizontal segregation refers to separation into different occupational spheres. There remain marked concentrations of women working in catering, cleaning, selling, education, welfare and health, and men in construction, extractive industries, the armed forces, the police and security services, and science and technology, with the segregation supported by gendered occupational cultures. However, there has also been evidence of a thinning of these gendered cultures and some convergence in employment patterns as females have been entering more traditional male preserves, such as the police and armed forces, and, vice versa males entering such occupations as nursing.

Fourthly, despite a growing number of exceptions, evidence remains of significant gender differences in access to the higher occupational levels. Gender therefore remains a substantial element of vertical differentiation within the stratification hierarchy. As a general rule, there is a correlation between the higher levels of pay and status as one ascends occupational hierarchies and a declining proportion of women employed at these levels. Certain occupations in which women have not progressed far, despite evidence of occasional successes, include entry to the upper echelons of the legal profession and the police and entry to the board of directors of major companies. Even in those occupations where women are more concentrated, such as in teaching and social work, they are particularly predominant at the lower levels and participate in declining proportions at the higher managerial and professional levels. In occupations in which males are concentrated, women are usually quite a rarity at the higher levels, revealing the limited opportunities that are available as a result of the combined effect of horizontal concentration and vertical stratification.

Despite the passage of legislation through the British Parliament during the first half of the 1970s with the purpose of to combatting discrimination in the workplace and promoting equal pay, and the impact of more recent EU legislation, women are still paid lower hourly rates than men, work shorter hours, are more likely to be in part-time employment, obtain lower pay for equivalent qualifications, and are more likely to be employed in the insecure secondary labour market. Even when comparing the hourly rates of males and females working full-time, females still only earn about 80% of male levels of pay. Some clarification is required here however. This calculation includes overtime work, which is often paid at a higher rate than work during a flat working week. When paid overtime is taken out of the equation, women earn about 90% of male levels of pay since men tend to partake in more paid overtime work. The remaining 10% difference is partly the result of men tending to occupy more senior positions, but experts have not been able to calculate how much of this 10% may still be due to the illegal practice of paying females less than males for carrying out the same work.

Clear evidence remains of continuing employment inequality between the genders, but there have been substantial changes which have narrowed the gap in opportunities between males and females. Recent evidence points in the direction of convergence in the form of a growing similarity in spread of occupations and social mobility rates for men and women. Moreover, when women take time out of work to have children, they are now more likely to re-enter career streams, whereas more men are faced with career breaks due to redundancy and some are able to avail themselves of paternity leave.

Measuring gender stratification – a case for individual assignment?

We have seen that sociologists such as Goldthorpe originally measured the stratification position of the family unit in terms of the occupational position of the male head of the household. Powerful social expectations supporting the housewife role meant that if women did work, their opportunities were restricted, employment was often recognised as temporary and their earnings were seen more as a supplement to the family income. As the husband's commitment to employment, as breadwinner, was usually the greater, it could be argued that his employment position in the occupational structure should be taken as the benchmark for the social class of the family unit. At a time when gender stratification was marked but more accepted, this dimension of stratification tended to be overlooked by sociologists focussing primarily on class stratification deriving from male occupation.

Women have since entered the labour force in far greater numbers and with diverse effects. Whilst many rely on a 'component wage' which is hardly sufficient to support themselves independently, more are now self-supporting and independent through employment and others make significant or major contributions to a family income or are the sole supporters of a family. It is therefore often felt to be unrealistic to measure the position of women in the stratification system in terms of the occupation of males assumed to be heads of households. Recognising some validity to these criticisms, use of the Goldthorpe scale now enables a woman's occupation to determine the class of the household if her occupation is the highest.

However, women's progress in the occupational sphere has been mixed. Despite evidence of the liberation of women from domestic patriarchy, there remains evidence, despite advances here also, of significant vertical and horizontal segregation patterns in male and female employment, working to the detriment of the females. Consequently, measuring the social class position of females in terms of the occupation, where it is possible, of a male partner, would hide these differences and the degree of gender based occupational stratification that still exists – a point raised by Abbott and Wallace (1997).

Alternative approaches to the measurement of the social class position of females have been developed which either allocate position in terms of occupation on an individual basis (for example Michelle Stanworth and Arber et al) or, if the household remains the unit of classification, take female employment into account (for example Heath and Britten). However, various complications and difficulties arise. In the case of families or partnerships, if both partners work, they often hold similar level occupations. In such cases, there would appear to be little problem or difference in measuring social class whether assessed individually or jointly. But there may be a problem of comparability between families. Would it be realistic to accord the same stratification position to a partnership where only one partner works but at the same occupational level as another with both working? Furthermore, if within a partnership both partners work but hold employment at different occupational levels, is it appropriate to allocate each to a different social class or to refer to the unit as a cross-class unit or to take an average position? Alternatively, is it more viable, as in contemporary use of the Goldthorpe scale, to just take the highest occupational position in a partnership, whether that of the male or the female, and read the social class of the partnership off from that designation? As well as being important regarding gender and social class allocation, answers to such questions also have implications for the measurement of intergenerational social mobility, the findings of which will be skewed by the base point used for comparison between the generations.

Because social class is indexed by occupation, radical feminists are likely to maintain that measuring stratification by occupation, however approached, may indicate little more than that class and occupation are also gendered. This does not bring out other aspects which, they argue, make gender stratification primary to and more fundamental than class, in particular the oppression of females by males in a broad range of social relationships and the existence of sexist attitudes, etc.

Differentiating race and ethnicity

The view that the human race can be divided into racially distinct categories defined by physical characteristics, especially skin colour, denoting different biologically inbuilt characteristics and capacities, developed in European thinking as white Europeans colonised different parts of the world. During the nineteenth century, this notion of racial types was commonly linked to evolutionary theory, in which, compared to the dominant white race, other races were regarded as relatively backward. Racial theory gained further prominence and the kudos of science in the early twentieth century with the emergence of the eugenics movement. However, the scientific basis behind the view of innate and fixed racially distinctive characteristics has to a very large extent been subsequently discredited.

In place of race, sociologists apply the term ethnicity to different cultural groups. Ethnicity is explained in terms of environmental as opposed to biological differences. Distinctive ethnic identities are formed by the process of socialisation into distinctive cultural traditions, religions, languages, and perceptions of ancestry. Viewing people in terms of their ethnicity avoids misleadingly attributing fixed and inbuilt racial traits to categories of appearance difference and also emphasises cultural distinctions within crudely designated racial groups such as Irish or Italian whites or Indian or Pakistani Asians. And then, of course, one should be careful not to stereotype people in terms of their ethnic culture, but to cautiously use the latter as a backdrop to understanding people's views, behaviour and experiences.

However, viewed sociologically, the problem does not finish with the intellectual defeat of the concept of race. A key sociological question is why, despite the discrediting of the assumptions behind racial types, race, racism and ethnic intolerance still constitute a 'common sense' for some people within society? Explanations have varied in their emphasis between cultural and economic factors.

Post-war immigration

Although there have been population movements into Britain throughout history, mainly in the form of invasions or as a result of those escaping religious or racial persecution abroad, it was only after the Second World War that black ethnic minorities were entering the country in significant numbers. Post-war reconstruction created a situation of low unemployment and as some of the white population were experiencing upward mobility, labour shortages existed in areas of unskilled manual employment. Against this backdrop, the British Nationality Act of 1948 offered relatively open access and rights of permanent settlement for citizens of Commonwealth countries and recruitment drives were launched abroad. From the late 1940s to the early 1960s, the main flow of immigration came from the Caribbean. Employment of members of this ethnic group was particularly focussed in relatively poorly paid and unskilled work in public transport and also in the National Health Service.

By the 1960s, more immigrants were entering Britain from India, Pakistan and latterly Bangladesh. Again, employment was often taken up at an unskilled level but these ethnic groups were concentrated more in the textile work occupations and engineering. Very few ethnic minority workers acquired employment in managerial positions during these decades and so constituted a growing proportion of the working class.

Tensions, both cultural and economic, often arose between the indigenous and immigrant populations. As clearly identifiable groups, immigrant workers brought with them what were perceived by sections of the white British population as alien beliefs and ways of living. They were also often perceived as competing for and taking jobs from the white population. The response of the 'host' population was therefore often unwelcoming and resentment could surface in the form of racism and hostility, as in the case of the first race riots in Notting Hill in 1958.

Traditional models and theories of ethnic stratification

How could the stratification position of recently arrived immigrants be understood sociologically and what would the future hold? Different stratification models, especially with reference to black immigrants, were developed to attempt to explain the dynamics of this situation, two of which have been frequently cited: the immigrant – host model and the white racism model.

The immigrant – host model, also referred to as the assimilation model, was pioneered by the Chicago School sociologist Robert Park to explain the integration of European immigrants into American society in the early decades of the twentieth century (Bottero, 2005, p.93). The model holds many of the characteristics of functionalist theory. It is a position which has tended to find favour with the political right and contains at least the implicit ethnocentric assumption of the superiority of the host culture over that of immigrants.

It starts from the position that before the arrival of immigrants, the host society shares a common national identity, culture and consensus of values and that there exists a stable stratification hierarchy. New immigrants are initially perceived as strangers due to their cultural distinctiveness and are likely to be concentrated in occupations toward the bottom of the occupational structure. When the host population experiences an influx of people unfamiliar in their appearance and ways, the response is often one of ignorance, suspicion and hostility which can take the form of racism. At this stage, contact can lead to conflict and animosities are likely to have a destabilising effect on society. However, Park argues that in time, an accommodating truce will emerge as a prelude to the full assimilation of migrants into – ie adjustment toward and integration into - the culture of the host society. Consequently, hostility, racism and discrimination decline as the culture of minorities melts into the dominant culture. This cultural homogeneity forms the basis for a new social stability in which the once disadvantaged minorities who faced racism and discrimination become integrated across the social structure and can take up their social and occupational position more on merit.

In Britain, Sheila Patterson applied the assimilation model to the study of first generation post-war West Indian immigrant minorities. Although they shared class disadvantage with some of the white population, due to their cultural distinctiveness and perceived threat in the form of competition for jobs, they experienced hostility in the form of racism and discrimination which separated them from whites. For this first generation, Patterson found that conflict was giving way to accommodation but that the stage of assimilation had not been reached. According to this model, only resistance to full assimilation on the part of ethnic minorities through the retention of their cultural traditions and separateness would continue to make them subject to racial discrimination and stratification and for this the problem is seen to be largely of their own making.

This model suggests that racist hostility and racial discrimination are likely to be a short term malady and temporary deviation from a normal state of social consensus. However, given evidence of persisting levels of separation and disadvantage experienced by black ethnic minorities compared to that of white minorities, it does not seem to have good predictive value.

An alternative interpretation of the dynamics involved is that it is the persistence of racism (values) and racial discrimination (action) from the white population which keeps black ethnic minorities separate from white society in a largely disadvantaged position at the foot of society. This analysis is sometimes taken in the direction of a Marxist critique of capitalism which analyses ethnic stratification as class and economic based in its origin. Ethnic stratification, racism and discrimination, however major an experience, are a bi-product of economic class stratification. Ethnic and racial subordination are status distinctions which can introduce animosities and cleavages within social classes. In this respect, working class racism against working class ethnic minorities is regarded as a form of false consciousness which is divisive in its effects. Like sexism, it divides and weakens a common economic class. From this perspective, ethnic minorities often provide (as do women) a cheap and competitive supply of labour. Sections of the white working class are therefore vulnerable to media generated hostility toward immigrants who are scapegoated as the cause of their insecurity through competing for their jobs as cheaper labour and threatening their way of life. The policies of far right political parties can hold some appeal within these sections of the population. From a Marxist position, although many ethnic minority people are through their employment position part of a broad working class, it is the false consciousness of white racism which excludes them from the white working class and helps to keep them at the base of society. From the vantage point of this theory, because racism and racial discrimination are viewed as a consequence of the class structure under capitalism, its persistence can be expected and there is little room for optimism in effective assimilation of ethnic minorities under capitalism.

A more Weberian approach to understanding the stratification position of many ethnic minorities has been adopted by Rex and Tomlinson. This position is distinguished from the Marxist model in that racial disadvantage is not just regarded as a bi-product of class stratification, but in the struggle for access to resources, ethnic minorities are seen as often experiencing multiple disadvantages compared to whites. Occupationally, they are more likely to be concentrated in the secondary labour market of less skilled, more casualised and less secure employment than the white male population. They are often concentrated in deprived inner city areas where co-existence alongside the white working class can lead to fractious relationships. They suffer lower social status due to racist discrimination and resentment and are likely to search for status within their own groups, thus enhancing their social and political marginality. Through a combination of class, status and power disadvantage, it can be argued that a significant proportion of ethnic minorities, along with other minorities, take their own distinctive place within an 'underclass'.

The concept of an underclass came to prominence during the 1980s against the political backdrop of neo-liberal thinking in the United States and new right politics in Britain. In America, Charles Murray applied the term particularly to inner city black ghetto areas where it was argued that moral, cultural and intellectual deficiency were associated with high levels of dependency and lack of aspiration. Arguing that an aspirational and meritocratic society essentially existed, the focus of attention on the problem could be shifted from the effects of discrimination. Instead, it was argued that more generous welfare intervention intended to alleviate poverty had encouraged the formation of an underclass by enabling people to live in irresponsible dependency combined with other unofficial sources of income. For Murray, the key to tackling underclass lifestyle was to reduce welfare support. As a result, some would be liberated from a life of dependency and illegality to that of aspiration and self-support for their and society's benefit, whilst others should be allowed to rightfully fail.

Although with less specific focus on ethnicity, a similar line was taken in Britain by new right thinkers such as Peter Saunders, who again argued that a broadly meritocratic social structure existed but that some sections of the population wanted nothing of it. Comprising disproportionately high numbers of Afro-Caribbeans ethnic minorities and an increasing number of single parents, these groups were characterised by negative and fatalistic values associated with a culture of poverty and the lack of a desire to assimilate into mainstream society. This underclass was analysed in status terms as inferior as they did not adopt the aspirational values of the majority and would be looked down upon as a drain on the wealth created by others.

Of course, one could argue that such groups can find themselves excluded from mainstream society, in part at least, through stigmatisation from those who view them in underclass terms and by anti-meritocratic discriminatory practices. Moreover, it tended to be supporters of the free market policies (the new right in Britain and neo-liberals in the United States) which enhanced economic polarisation in these countries who were keen to blame the victims for their supposed deficiencies.

Ethnicity and occupational profile – diversity remains

Evidence on the occupational profiles of ethnic minority groups compared to the white population and with each other provides an important gauge of their stratification position. From the early 1960s, and particularly with economic slowdown during the 1970s and the recession of the early 1980s, legislation was passed in Britain which effectively placed increasing restriction on non-white immigration. These restrictions were followed by a tightening of asylum regulation as more people wanting to enter the country, including economic migrants, were pursuing this alternative channel. With a stemming of immigration, most of the black ethnic minority groups now comprise majorities of second or third generation British citizens.

Compared to their predecessors, what is the more contemporary pattern of ethnic minority participation in the occupational structure? Valuable information for the period 1998-2000 has been provided by the Labour Force Survey. It showed that when ethnic minorities are taken together, differences in the occupational profile compared to that of the white British were very small. The same applies regarding aggregate gender figures. However, when the information for individual ethnic groups is studied, the picture is a very complex one of distinctive profiles.

For males, evidence of concentration in occupational sectors has indicated some continuity with past patterns of employment. For example, Pakistanis have remained highly represented in manufacturing, Bangladeshis and Chinese in hotel and catering, Afro Caribbeans in transport and communications and Indians in transport and communications and manufacturing.

In terms of occupational level, Chinese and Indian males have entered professional, managerial and technical occupations in larger proportions than whites but the proportion of Bangladeshis employed at these levels has remained substantially lower than that of whites. In the largely manual, partly skilled and unskilled occupations, Indians are represented in about the same proportion as whites but the percentages for Bangladeshis and black Caribbean groups remain substantially higher. These profiles bear quite a close relationship to respective levels of educational achievement, although recent substantial improvements in the educational performance of Bangladeshis would suggest the likelihood of a filtration through to higher occupational achievement.

For females, compared to whites, the figures have shown that significantly larger proportions of Chinese are employed in professional, managerial and technical occupations, but that smaller proportions of Pakistanis and

Bangladeshis are employed in these groups. A smaller proportion of Chinese than white women work in the partly skilled and unskilled occupations, whereas a substantially higher proportion of black African women are employed at this level. The latter's participation rates are also high. Whilst relatively high proportions of Pakistani and Bangladeshi women are also employed in these occupations, Bangladeshi women have the lowest rate of participation in employment outside the family. This reflects traditional family life and the values of Islamic culture and is a reminder that the study of stratification should also look at different patterns of family life and the distribution of power and resources within families.

Across the range of ethnic groups, women tend to hold lower occupational positions than men. The biggest gender difference in professional, managerial and technical occupations is amongst Indians where 47% of males are employed and only 33% of females. However, some groups provide exceptions. For example, there are higher proportions of women than men from black Caribbean, other black and black mixed groups working in these occupational categories.

In partly skilled and unskilled occupations, figures for female participation are consistently higher than for males with the exception of black Caribbean workers with 27% of employed males and 24% of females employed in these categories. Clearly, a fuller understanding of these figures would necessitate more detail on the actual occupations that males and females worked in.

A degree of gender stratification is evident across white and a range of ethnic minority groups. Moreover, evidence suggests that ethnic minority females are generally less differentiated in terms of income and occupational level from white females than is the case in comparing ethnic minority and white males. For some feminists, despite variations between the ethnic groups, this is taken as evidence of the overriding significance of gender stratification. As women are generally more concentrated toward the lower end of the occupational structure than men, there is less room for differentiation between females in the different ethnic groups.

In terms comparative achievement levels, the general evidence is positive but in detail remains mixed. The occupational restructuring accompanying economic modernisation from the 1980s has drawn in ethnic minorities in such a way as to narrow the occupational profile differences between themselves and white British workers. Overall, their distribution across the occupational structure is converging with that of white workers, loosely suggesting that a degree of assimilation has occurred. However, there remain greater differences between specific ethnic minority groups than between ethnic minorities as a whole and the white population in terms of both stratification level and differentiation into different types of occupation.

However, figures of occupational distribution within general category levels only reveal part of the picture. For example, evidence of more ethnic minority men now employed at the professional, managerial and technical level tends to hide the fact that relatively high proportions of minorities work in more precarious positions of self-employment. Moreover, it does not reveal the disparity of earnings and expenditure that still exist between the different ethnic groups and the white population. For example, evidence provided in Social Trends (2002) shows that the average income of Bangladeshi men was approximately only half that of whites and that average household expenditure for Bangladeshis is less than half that of whites.

Account should also be taken of hours worked, conditions of employment and treatment in the workplace, job insecurity and risk of unemployment, on all of which there is some evidence of ethnic disadvantage. For example, ethnic minorities have traditionally been concentrated in less secure employment. Thus, during the recession of the 1980s which hit manufacturing very hard, Pakistanis, Bangladeshis and Afro Caribbeans became unemployed at about twice the rate of whites. However, when employment picked up, it was also at a quicker rate for these groups than for white workers. This pattern of effect on ethnic minorities has been referred to as 'hyper-cyclical'.

Racial discrimination – grounds for optimism?

What evidence is available on racial discrimination practiced by employers and to what extent is the situation changing? To measure behaviour in such an emotive and sensitive area, the use of covert (concealed) methods may be necessary. Such an approach was adopted in research conducted by D.J. Smith and published in 1977. In this research, applications were submitted from applicants of white and ethnic minority background with matched work histories and qualifications for a range of blue collar and white collar jobs. Employers' responses to blue collar applicants indicated a tenfold preference of whites to blacks, and in the case of applicants for white collar jobs, those with names indicating Asian or West Indian background were 30% less likely to be even offered an interview than white applicants.

To what extent are ethnic minorities still disadvantaged by racial discrimination? In small scale covert research employing hidden recording devices, journalists in a BBC documentary (Black and White) visited the Bristol area in an attempt to measure racial discrimination, especially by employers and landlords. Taped and filmed evidence of racial discrimination was evident in this area. When the journalists followed up advertisements for jobs and accommodation, that which was unavailable when the black applicant turned up sometimes became available when the white applicant appeared later.

Another approach to the question of racial discrimination has been to conduct self-report surveys. National surveys conducted by the Policy Studies Institute have asked ethnic minorities about their experiences of racial discrimination. There was evidence here of differences between ethnic groups in their perception of being victims of racial discrimination. Measurements taken in the 1980s and 1990s revealed a consistent pattern that about 25% of West Indians perceived that racial discrimination had led to them being refused a job. The figures for Asians were substantially lower. Of course, the problem with such research is that the findings are based on subjective judgements and can be difficult to interpret. Whilst complacency should be avoided, it is at least an ironic possibility that the high figures of discrimination experienced may be partly the product of more enlightened times in which a greater sensitivity to being the victims of discrimination is felt.

New anxieties

More recently, issues of ethnicity have again returned to the theme of immigration. New concerns and hostilities have been raised in the media regarding suspected bogus asylum seekers who are in fact economic migrants, and levels of illegal immigration. Furthermore, as the European Union expanded eastwards to include countries such as Poland, Czechoslovakia and Hungary in 2004 and Bulgaria and Romania in 2007, a shortage of skills in the building and construction trade in particular, but also the attraction of vacancies for unskilled labour in areas such as agriculture, has attracted workers from these countries, especially Poland, to Britain. Compared to patterns of previous Commonwealth migration, these migrants are more likely to be in Britain temporarily, referred to as 'pendulum migrants' who work to return home with savings. Nonetheless, as documented in the 2008 BBC 2 series 'White Season', the concentration of these workers in such towns as Peterborough has often been accompanied by hostility from locals. Within this cultural climate, the use of cheap overseas labour even sparked a rash of wildcat strikes in power stations and oil refineries in January and February of 2009 when an oil company owned by the French company Total employed, through an Italian firm, Italian and Portuguese workers to carry out maintenance work.

Contemporary sociological thinking on social stratification:

The decline of social class?

Social class has previously been defined as primarily based on economic differences. Class stratification therefore to a large extent reflects the distribution of wealth and income in society. In a class stratified society, stratification primarily takes the form of different occupationally grouped strata within each of which people experience similar levels of income, as well as life chances and experiences and a degree of consciousness or subjective awareness of their distinctiveness from people in other social classes.

Social stratification by economic class was a well established feature of modern societies and a predominant theme in the sociological tradition. Class societies, offering prospects of social mobility but also imposing barriers to it, represent a position in stratification terms somewhere in between the extremes of highly closed and highly open social hierarchies. However, much sociological debate has emerged over the continuing prevalence of social class in the way that contemporary societies are stratified. Doubts over the salience of class stratification have taken various forms. From the late 1960s, both gender and ethnic stratification have gained greater attention and sociologists have come to realise the complex and sometimes unpredictable ways in which class and gender and ethnic status interact.

Moreover, a pattern of evidence suggesting the declining significance of social class has been emerging. For example, we have seen that Dahrendorf argued that social classes were decomposing or breaking up and Crewe has indicated the declining importance of social class as an influence on voting behaviour.

The growing importance of social status?

Social status has been defined in terms of values and judgements regarding ways of life that people aspire to and the acquisition of possessions of symbolic status significance, all of which accord individuals and groups levels of social prestige. Although we have seen that occupations themselves can be viewed in status terms, the link between social status and economics may relate more to what people do with their money than the occupation by which they have earned it. How people attribute symbols of status to the objects of possession and how owners of these objects derive status from them can be illustrated by the experience of changes in treatment on the road by other drivers that a person may experience with a change in the type of car driven!

Some sociologists, particularly amongst postmodernists and high modernists, argue that, in affluent consumer societies, social status is replacing social class as the predominant form of social stratification. From a broad historical perspective, the social structures of contemporary societies are relatively open. The objects and lifestyles of status aspiration can change rapidly with fashion, thus giving status a high potential fluidity. In a more open society, people are likely to feel free to aspire to status symbols of success and reinvent their lifestyles and self-image rather than being resigned to accepting their inherited occupational class position or the traditional status ascriptions associated with gender or ethnicity. The importance of status awareness in a more open social structure may mean that it is eclipsing that of class consciousness in a class stratified society. In relatively open status societies, people tend to compare themselves to others and base their sense of self worth on the signs of status achievement that they can project. Thus, from a once more class based community in a more uniform local authority housing estate, one can sometimes witness the personalisation of homes that have been privately acquired as a statement of individuality and status. More generally, this heightened status awareness and comparison with others can lead to new psychological anxieties associated with what Alain de Botton refers to as 'status anxiety'.

Postmodernism – the demise of social class

Postmodernist writers tend to adopt the farthest position in claiming demise of social class. Their broad view of history distinguishes three phases: traditional, modern and postmodern. In traditional or pre-industrial society, a person's possessions, rights and appropriate behaviour were heavily prescribed by their inherited position in the stratification system. Indeed, attempting to take on the ways of those higher in the social structure risked the charge of 'personation' – the non-legitimate copying of social 'betters'. As the old structure broke down and modern industrial societies emerged, enhanced occupational mobility opportunities led to competition for objects as confirmation of new status by new moneyed classes. The social structure nevertheless remained heavily stratified, now by new class relations, as strongly emphasised in the works of Marx.

Now, postmodernists claim, a new type of society has emerged in which, in contrast to traditional and modern societies, heavy structural constraints on people's lives have broken down. Through the capacity of advanced societies to generate growing affluence, objects have become less desired in terms of subsistence need or purely functional use and more in terms of the status image of their owner that they convey. In the conquest of necessity, it is not economic relationships within the system of production which determines people's position in a social structure, but the freedom of acquisition of possessions as status symbols which enables the individual to have much greater control over the construction of their social identity. Image related to consumption increasingly governs perceived social status and liberates individuals from the constraints of old class stratification systems. People are viewed much less in terms of what they do and much more in terms of their lifestyle image. It is therefore the symbols associated with products and lifestyles that are desired by consumers and changing fashions fuel insatiable desire. The old class structure of the modern period becomes replaced by a more free floating, superficial and ephemeral world of fashions in relation to which individuals have a high degree of freedom available for 'self-assembly'.

Postmodernists tend to emphasise the positive aspect of these apparent changes. Such a position is adopted by Pakulski and Waters who argue that in postmodern society the structuring effect of and concern with social class has collapsed. This is because the productive capacity of a contemporary society of abundance has made the old social class battles driven by economic necessity redundant. The achievement of economic security has led to a society preoccupied with the acquisition of products and the leading of lifestyles more for the images that they convey in a highly consumerist and media saturated world. Economic security enables people to choose products and lifestyles more freely and independently of occupation. As a result, social status becomes increasingly decoupled from social class, and even for people with similar income levels, status based on lifestyle choice – cultural differences – distinguish them as they freely shape their lifestyles. In postmodern society, stratification boundaries rooted in social class have collapsed as abundance has enabled symbolic meaning to become independent from and ascendant over past economic constraints. Indeed, it is increasingly possible for those living on modest incomes to aspire to higher status than others better off by adopting prestigious lifestyle choices, especially with the easy availability of credit.

The values, lifestyles and fashions associated with social status are ever changing. Furthermore, individuals are much freer to change their personal lifestyle choices than they would have been to change their social class. Social stratification therefore enters a new level of fluidity in which, in contrast to old homogeneous class structures and gender and ethnic status stratification, status becomes more individualised as individuals partake in a variety of status groups. For Pakulski and Waters, social stratification in the postmodern world is a pick and mix 'status bazaar'.

The implications for stratification analysis of this position are profound. Society can no longer be understood in terms of socially structured economic inequality which once provided constraints that shaped identity and behaviour, enabling society to be amenable to causal analysis. Toward the end of the modern period, the social structure and its analysis was complicated by class decomposition and the mutually cross cutting effects of class, gender and ethnicity. At the postmodern phase, even this complex structure gives way to social fluidity. Culture and image increasingly prevail and because of the highly fluid form that they take and the enhanced capacity of individuals to create and recreate their own identity, society is not amenable to causal analysis. Postmodern society therefore renders the possibility of social scientific understanding redundant and with it social policy intervention to tackle economic inequality futile. And one could add that this fatalistic outlook provided a convenient accompaniment to the neo-liberal reforms which, from the 1980s, had a polarising effect on the distribution of wealth and income.

High modernism / late modernism – the individualisation of risk

Although the analysis of high modernists often highlights similar features of contemporary society to that of postmodernists and is sometimes difficult to distinguish, for high or late modernists, the new phase that advanced societies have entered represents the high point of the modernist era rather than an entirely new era of a postmodernist society. In claiming this, they challenge the postmodernist view that scientific understanding of contemporary society is impossible. Instead, they argue that the theory and concepts of classical sociology are becoming unfit for purpose in a rapidly changing world which is feeling as if it is out of control. To regain a grip on understanding society as the basis for enlightened intervention, sociology requires a new toolkit of theories and concepts that are relevant to the contemporary age.

In the works of writers such as Anthony Giddens and Ulrich Beck, the hallmark of high modern or late modern societies respectively is the emergence of new types and levels of risk. In modern society, the need to create wealth and conquer poverty were the key aims of science and technology. For Beck, in this context the unequal distribution of limited resources and risks in life prioritised social class in people's experience. By contrast, late modern society is characterised by the fact that material need has been largely met. Despite the fact that inequalities of class societies remain, new risks, which are the consequences of development, have emerged. These risks include nuclear hazards, environmental damage and possible global economic meltdown. The geographically widespread nature of such risks means that people right across societies are vulnerable to their effects, against which wealth can only offer limited protection. Exposure to risk therefore becomes more equalised. As they operate across and tend to dissolve both class and national boundaries, the way that risks are experienced becomes more individualised. For example, in the face of rapid technological change, people need to prepare for frequent retraining and career change. Innovation and the risk of unemployment no longer hit manual workers hardest but tend to spread their impact more equally across the lives of service sector workers in an increasingly service sector type society. In such a risk society, individuals are left equally free of career structures and class constraints to navigate their own way reflexively (always having to weigh up options and adapt) through life.

For Beck, class analysis is of very little relevance in understanding this new reality. Continuing to use such concepts equates to the application of 'zombie categories' which have remained more alive in sociology than useful in the study of a changed social world.

Zygmunt Bauman refers to the transition from solid modernity to liquid modernity. The phase of solid modernity was one in which the quest for security emphasised the importance of occupation and production in a class stratified society. This stage of modernism has given way to a consumerist society in which, through security of productive output, status is achieved through freedom of consumption. This status freedom places new burdens on individuals to constantly weave their own status patterns without workable traditional recipes to fall back on.

Bottero (2005, pp.246-247) has criticised of both postmodernist and high modernist positions with regard to the issue of the demise of social class. It is argued that individual freedom (for good or ill) to adopt a chosen lifestyle or construct a status image is not distributed equally to people across all levels of economic income. Indeed, it is suggested that writers from these perspectives emphasise lifestyle choice from the position of the middle classes which gives them more choice because of their class position – thus substantiating the view that social class remains an important feature of society.

Globalisation and liquid modernity – the polarisation of mobility, the domination of capital and the detachment of the individual

Theorists disagree on the impact of globalisation on social stratification. The most optimistic position is adopted in the neo-liberal approach of Ohmae who sees in globalisation evidence of movement toward a borderless global economy. For Ohmae, this is a world of mobile capital and free enterprise capitalism. Governments most go with the grain of change and work to promote such open global economies by which in the long run all will benefit as consumers in their choice of goods and services available.

Not all writers on globalisation are so optimistic or likely to downplay the importance of social divisions. For Zygmunt Bauman, despite his analysis of the burden of status freedom, globalisation accentuates differences in mobility chances which fall along class lines. This has led to increased social polarisation which works to the detriment of workers.

In modern societies (as explained in Marxist theory), in social and work hierarchies, employers and workers had relatively fixed positions and relationships. Social class and industrial relations included direct conflict and settlement, with both sides locked into mutual dependence. At this 'solid modernity' stage, the potential for disruption by organised workers introduced the threat of uncertainty which business managers and owners had to take account of.

Bauman argues that in contemporary conditions of global capitalism, wealth has polarised and has been accompanied by a polarisation of mobility chances. Given the greatly enhanced mobility of capital and information made possible through the cyberspace of contemporary global technology, 'liquid modernity' has enhanced the threat of disengagement of capital from local rooting and has become an uncertainty to workers who remain relatively geographically rooted. For Bauman, mobility, wealth and power polarisation now fundamentally disadvantages workers and 'frees' them from the possibility of effective collective response to the interests of capital due to the constant threat of the withdrawal of employment opportunities which highly mobile capital presents (Gane, 2004, pp.25-27).

In liquid modern societies, individuals thus become detached from collective action and forced into a freedom of taking responsibility for their self-determination in situations of transience and uncertainty. This environment leads to increasing social polarisation as geographically mobile global elites become disengaged from the masses who, dependent on providing their labour for income, are relatively tied to their localities and left to struggle with this new 'freedom'.

Postmodernism celebrated the emergence of positive individual freedom to choose identity and transcend class ties. For Bauman, given the economic inequalities of liquid modern societies, only elites really have this privilege. The freedom that workers now find themselves placed in is not the positive freedom of the old entrepreneurial middle class. For many, the experience is primarily of the negative aspect of freedom – the freedom of being cut adrift, like it or not, from the confines of a secure class structure. Individualisation in the contemporary context means de-identification and the perpetual burden of uncertainty and striving for identity (for many of the poor throughout the world, not even this negative freedom is available). This leads to new conflicts in the form of 'recognition wars' in which people attempt to impose both their own identity and force identities onto others. A key resource here is use of PRs, spin doctors and access to the mass media. Furthermore, growing insecurity can lead people to the search for culprits and popular government responses in the form of toughness on crime and immigration.

6 // Sociology of Education

Abstract

This chapter begins by alerting the reader to the fact that a sociological approach to education cannot be based on generalising from one's personal educational experiences. Some key concepts relevant to the sociology of education are then explained. To transcend the personal view, various theoretical perspectives are introduced – functionalist, Marxist, Weberian and interactionist, and at the end of the chapter postmodernist and high modernist – to offer a range of explanations of the relationship between education and broader society.

At a more empirical (evidential or factual) level, social, historical and political factors are reviewed to help provide a contextual understanding of the influences behind educational developments in England. This historical dimension is then carried forward into a review of post-war educational policy.

Issues of genetic inheritance versus social environment regarding intelligence and educational achievement are raised. These issues are firstly related to social class where the perennial issue of different levels of social class achievement is introduced. The validity of explanations in terms of inherited differences in intelligence levels related to social classes is strongly contested and a number of established sociological explanations which identify a range of environmental influences are provided.

Similarly, in the case of gender, the viewpoint of different inherited intellectual capacities, here based on biological sex differences, to explain different achievement rates between the genders, is challenged from an environmental viewpoint. In distinction to biological sex differences, it is emphasised that associated gender identity and opportunity is a product of the social environment. Changes in this environment are touched on regarding women's liberation. Later, evidence is provided which shows a remarkable advance in the educational performance of females.

Next, regarding ethnicity, geneticist arguments regarding the educational performance levels of different 'races' based on supposed inherited intelligence differences are strongly countered. The scientific validity of the concept of race to explain evidence of different levels of academic achievement is challenged. Instead, the environmental concept of the influence of different ethnic cultures is utilised. The reality of prejudice based on racist beliefs and the stereotyping of different ethnic groups are also part of an environment of influences on performance. As in the case with gender, evidence is provided that the educational performance of different ethnic minority groups is rapidly improving alongside social change, thus contesting the view of different fixed intellectual capacities being innate to different races.

Developments in education policy are sketched to explain a change from a post-war political consensus on the social democratic model and the social engineering of education to promote a more just society. It is shown that this change takes the general form of a greater emphasis on a market driven approach which has been followed by governments of the Conservative new right, New Labour and the Conservative led coalition.

Statistics on educational achievement and the associated issues of educational standards and the worth of qualifications are presented and discussed with reference to 'grade inflation' and 'credential inflation'.

As an exercise in applying the sociological imagination, the concept of meritocracy in society and education is explained. The reader is guided through some of the issues by which one may arrive at assessments of the degree to which the English education system is meritocratic.

The question of the complexity of our educational system and the issue of diversity and choice are finally related to theories of postmodernity and high modernity.

The sociological challenge

The British educational 'system' is complex and diverse with different regional and local patterns of provision, including national variation between England and Scotland. This issue of complexity and choice will be reviewed later. The challenge that first needs to be addressed is to recognise that our attitudes toward education generally, and different types of school and the process of selection more specifically, are likely to reflect our own educational experiences. These experiences and attitudes may run deep. Do we have a general loathing for grammar schools? Do we sympathise with the aims of comprehensive education? Do we admire the excellence of independent education? Whatever they are, our personal judgements and their implications in terms of our broader view of the educational system are likely to be influenced by our personal experience. This may make it difficult to engage in impartial analysis of the educational system. Yet, as sociologists, we must be vigilant against the bias of our personal experiences. How can we attempt to achieve this?

We need to raise our awareness of potential bias by stepping back and examining our own experiences and attitudes. By so doing, we can become prepared to study and evaluate sociological theories and explanations of education in a more open minded way. These theories offer frameworks to make sense of educational processes and experiences as well as encouraging us to look at educational systems within social and even global contexts. We can apply sociological concepts systematically and analyse to what conclusions they take us. We can also review research findings. As a result, our own views on education may be refined or even fundamentally changed. We should not fear this possibility, but recognise it as the reward of engaging in sociological thinking.

It would also be wise to step back and consider what the aims of education are, could be or should be. For example, to what extent should education tend to prioritise the acquisition of employment related skills or focus more on personal growth and development. How can educational resources be best allocated? To what extent should education have a role to play in delivering social justice and how could this best be delivered? These are more questions of value, the relevance of which the reader may relate to the issues raised throughout the chapter. At this point, central to the definition of concepts, several functions of education can be identified.

311

Definition of main concepts

One way to look at education sociologically is to identify a number of **functions** that it performs. The concept 'functions of education' refers to ways in which education provides various benefits for society or is functional for society. For functionalists, these functions tend to be viewed as universal requirements – in one form or another they are necessary for the well-being of all social systems.

Through the **economic function**, education imparts appropriate work related skills and knowledge and also behavioural guidelines and values which enable individuals to perform effectively in employment situations and support themselves and their families. The prosperity of businesses, economic productivity and ultimately society itself are dependent on the effective operation of this function.

The processes through which the system selects people for different types and levels of education are referred to as the **selective function**. This function is closely connected to the economic function since selection in education feeds through to employment roles and positions in the occupational and social structure. If in the education system pupils are selected through competition to achieve and progress academically entirely in terms of their own abilities and effort, sociologists refer to the existence of opportunities for **contest mobility**. In a society of such educational opportunity, functionalists emphasise that education would service an open occupational and social structure in which the allocation of all people to positions is based on individual merit. Such a society is referred to as a **meritocracy**.

Education is also an important vehicle for the **transmission of culture**. Culture used in this sense refers to society's traditions, values and identity which are communicated through language and symbols. Whilst society changes over time, functionalists emphasise that through the transmission of culture function education helps society to achieve both continuity and cohesion through conveying a shared cultural identity from one generation to the next.

Social order is promoted through the **social control function**. Through following rules and regulations and showing respect for authority within educational institutions, education lays the groundwork for a society of law-abiding citizens. For functionalists, this is vitally important because however effectively the other functions are preformed, society is likely to be damaged by high levels of disorder if there is no agency to adequately socialise the young into accepting a certain level of compliance.

The officially stated content of subjects is referred to as the **formal curriculum**. Teaching, learning and assessment are guided and constrained by course curriculum. However, **hidden curriculum** processes and influences may also be taking place alongside the formal curriculum. As an example of the impact of the hidden curriculum, an issue highlighted by feminists has been the effect of gender stereotyping. This can work in a variety of ways. School timetabling of subjects based on gender stereotyping can make it difficult for males or females to take certain subject combinations. Teachers may think in terms of gender stereotypes when advising students on choice of courses and careers. The content of academic materials can also affect pupil's choice of subjects and how they relate to them by conveying positive or negative gender messages. These processes can affect pupil's experiences, opportunities, self-perception and levels of achievement. Bringing them to view has initiated much educational reform.

Returning briefly to develop an overview of the functions of education, it should be emphasised that the above distinctions that have been made are somewhat artificial; the functions are divided up for academic purposes to help clarify processes and assist analysis. In the real world, these functions intermingle. For example, the impact of them all can be identified in the economic sphere. The economic function, viewed in a restricted sense, provides the economy with variously educated and skilled workers. But the way that the selective function works has an important bearing on the matching of individual abilities and skills to the requirements of occupational roles. The key question within the education system is the extent to which academic selection separates out individuals in terms of merit. Again, the cultural values conveyed may be more or less favourable to the formation of attitudes, such as commitment, application, competition and enterprise, that are conducive to the needs of the workplace. And social control, in nurturing certain levels of self-discipline as well as obedience to authority and the structuring of the school day according to timetables, can be viewed as preparation for individual responsibility and the acceptance of authority and structured routines by the individual within work institutions. Clearly, recognising the combined effect of functions in this way helps to identify the significance of the hidden curriculum in educational processes.

Viewing education as a system which is functionally connected to the social system enables one to analyse types of social policy interventions that may influence the functional effectiveness of education for the overall benefit of society. Ultimately, the implementation of education policy from this viewpoint is a political matter in balancing and prioritising particular educational functions.

Founding sociological perspectives on education

Functionalism and Marxism provide major founding perspectives on education. They are both macro theories – they locate an understanding of how education operates within their own analyses of the broader social system. However, these perspectives differ fundamentally in their view of the nature of that broader system and therefore the role of education in society. For functionalists, education, like the family, is a vital element of the social bedrock. It should contribute toward the maintenance of an efficient and stable society. To do so effectively, the way that it operates must synchronise with the needs and key characteristics of the broader social structure. Therefore, as society changes, so must the education system. Locating an understanding of education within this holistic approach of functionalism alerts us to the priority of firstly gaining an overview of the key features of society and how it changes. Only then can sense be made of the changing nature of educational provision.

Functionalism – education services a meritocratic society

When adopting a broad historical vantage point, functionalists point to the relatively closed structure of social hierarchies in pre-industrial or traditional societies (at their height under feudalism in the Middle Ages). This means that there were few opportunities for people to rise above their place of origin in the social order. Their social status was 'ascribed' and the position of the privileged supported by ideas of family lineage and birthright. The sons of the wealthy were the main beneficiaries of formal education through having virtually exclusive access to private tutors and elite higher educational institutions. Their formal studies included traditional subjects – for example theology, philosophy, law, and Latin – which, if they did not live off the inheritance of an estate, prepared them for entry into elite professions such as the church, the law or government office. Through their privileged access to education, they would also develop the etiquette, manners and leadership qualities appropriate to their social rank.

The commercial classes may have been able to purchase a different form of education for their sons. The type of education would very likely have been relevant to commerce, placing an emphasis on such practical areas of study as trade, commercial law, arithmetic and accountancy, thus providing preparation for commercially related activities.

For the vast majority of peasants and labourers, there was little or no provision of formal education. Instead, children assisted parents in their work from an early age. Whilst occasionally a wealthy benefactor may assist in enabling a child of lowly social background receive an education, such assistance was in the gift of the patron. It was a personal favour and certainly not an established right. This type of personal relationship is referred to by Talcott Parsons as 'particularistic' – it was particular to the personal inclinations of the benefactor.

To sum up, in traditional society, the way that the selective function of education worked closely synchronised with and helped to perpetuate a relatively closed social hierarchy. The position of parents within the social structure largely determined access or otherwise to and type of education received by their sons and largely denied to their daughters. Education, or lack of it, itself served to perpetuate privilege or disadvantage from generation to generation and access to education bore little relationship to individual talent.

Functionalists argue that, by contrast, modern industrial societies develop highly open social hierarchies and require a well educated and highly trained workforce. New technology necessitates that more people are prepared for higher levels of work skills. The development of new and more specialised occupations leads to highly differentiated occupational structures. To prosper in a dynamic and more integrated world of industrial competition, modern industrial societies need to utilise their human resources far more effectively than did traditional societies. Consequently, the allocation of people to occupations must take place according to their assessed ability rather than by birthright. Educational provision has to adapt to these broader social changes. To do this, it must become universally available in institutions external to the family and offer opportunities for achievement and success based on individual merit. In so doing, it can act as an intermediary between the family (a closed social hierarchy) and society (an open social hierarchy) and liberate successive generations from educational provision which once only reflected what family background could provide. By such means, education offers opportunities for occupational and social mobility. In modern industrial societies, the selective function in education adapts to synchronise with the needs of a more meritocratic society. This is particularly the emphasis of the American functionalist Parsons who refers to education provided as a matter of right and selection by individual competition within the context of impersonal and impartial standards as 'universalistic' – rules are applied impartially and formally to all.

Emile Durkhiem, writing around the turn of the twentieth century, was acutely aware that modern society has to balance merit and individual achievement with the need for the maintenance of order and stability. Compared to pre-industrial societies, where people were expected to know their fixed place in the social order, a more competitive and meritocratic system could increase individual discontent and social disharmony if an excessive focus on individual competition and achievement promoted a preoccupation with the self and unrealistically raised individual expectations. To rein in the socially damaging effects of excessive individualism, Durkheim emphasised that society needed also to impose realistic constraints on individual ambition and remind individuals that they also have obligations to society.

To this effect, functionalists emphasise that the school effectively works like society in miniature, moulding and preparing future citizens. For the benefit of society, as well as encouraging individual competition in pupils, Durkheim argued that education must impose order and a sense of obligation by the individual to the collectivity. Schooling should therefore nurture in the individual a sense of pride in and identification with its body of members and the school institution. It must expect obedience to rules and regulations and the acceptance of the school hierarchy. The school promotes social cohesion amongst its pupils through developing its own collective rituals (school assemblies and award ceremonies) and sense of respect for its symbols (the school uniform, badge and mottos). These rituals and symbols, in tying the individual to the collectivity, find their functional equivalent in society in the form of nationalistic sentiments and reverence for such powerful symbols as the national flag and anthem, all of which bind society together. As well as their formal curriculum content and the promotion of academic learning, the study of such subjects as history, literature and social studies would perform the important (hidden curriculum) function of developing a sense of shared national identity and teachers would provide a generational link in the transmission of national culture, identity and moral standards.

Talcott Parsons agreed with Durkheim regarding the importance of education in the promotion of shared values and a sense of national identity. We can see this within American education in the prominence given to allegiance to the Constitution and the national flag. However, in adapting functionalism to a more individualistic and competitive enterprise culture context, Parsons placed greater emphasis on education as promoting competition in a social system with an occupational hierarchy which is highly differentiated in levels of monetary reward. It was important that members of society shared meritocratic values and that society itself was seen to be meritocratic. Parsons maintained that although emphasising the individual, it is the shared nature of these values of enterprise and fair individual competition that would provide the bond which held society together as people accepted their position within the social order as the rightful outcome of this fair competition.

For both Durkheim and Parsons, the development of educational institutions in modern industrial societies enables individuals to separate their achievement and ultimately their social destination from that of their parents. Furthermore, schooling provides a bridging role between the personalised world and established hierarchy of family life and the formal requirements of adult society. The intermediate institution of the school performs the key function of moulding individuals to the needs of broader society from a young age and over a protracted period of time. These needs include the acquisition of skills and values of competitiveness required in the occupational sphere. They also include the need for a common moral education which imparts shared values, moral standards and the need for engagement in co-operative behaviour. The school is therefore also a crucial institution in the development of individual self-restraint through the use of authority and discipline.

It can be seen that adopting a functionalist perspective therefore leads to an almost exclusively top down approach which looks at education in systemic terms and individuals as being constrained by functional forces and the needs of society. In so doing, it tends to lose sight of the capacity that people have for making choices and takes little account of individual autonomy and self-fulfilment. The question of the intrinsic worth of education for the development of the individual becomes buried below a focus on the needs of society.

A more specific focus upon the link between economic incentives in the occupational structure and academic competition was drawn by Davis and Moore in 1945. They argued that society's occupational hierarchy represented an income differentiated ladder of opportunity, with educational achievement through merit providing an important key to occupational success. Education instilled the values of competition and achievement and provided a proving ground for future occupational success and financial reward by placing those of proven ability in the most demanding, functionally important and highly paid occupations, and others accordingly throughout the occupational structure.

How convincing is this metaphor that the education system provides one big ladder of opportunity for all to compete to climb by their individual efforts and abilities alone? To pursue the metaphor, perhaps a more realistic view is that overall education comprises various ladders which provide different barriers to overcome and opportunities for ascent. In access to and ascent up these different ladders, the effect of family background is not negligible. Furthermore, one who manages by effort and ability to ascend high up a ladder with many obstacles may find that at the top there are doors to certain occupations that are virtually closed which other ladders give enhanced access to.

Marxism – education perpetuates the appearance of a meritocratic society

Whilst functionalists emphasise the functional importance of equality of opportunity within education to a harmonious, integrated, efficient and meritocratic modern industrial society from which all to some extent ultimately benefit through enhanced performance, Marxists point to the negative aspects of the capitalist nature of modern societies. They view capitalist society as inevitably divided by economic and social class inequalities which are strongly perpetuated from one generation to the next. In this sense, Marxists maintain that, despite appearances to the contrary, capitalist societies are not as different from the relatively closed social structures of past societies as functionalist accounts propose. Marxists challenge the view that education under capitalism can ever select impartially to educate individuals according to assessed ability and then match them to appropriate occupations and rewards.

Various insights have been developed from this general perspective by neo (more contemporary) Marxists. One is that education primarily assists social control in the workplace. It achieves this through promoting the acceptance of authority within educational institutions and oversupplying the labour market in terms of the skills required to empower employers in their selection of workers in the first place. It has been argued from this perspective (for example by Braverman, 1974) that capitalism has, in fact, brought about deskilling in the workplace as advances in the division of labour narrow down more jobs to highly repetitive processes, make labour more easily controlled, and increasingly reduce it to the experience of a meaningless activity. From this Marxist slant, the real economic function of education is to ensure that workers are prepared to be able to operate in a disciplined and efficient manner in the workplace, accepting authority and boredom and acquiring sufficient skills to effectively enhance their own exploitation.

The impression of equal opportunity within education and throughout life, conveyed by reference to a statistically small number of high profile cases of rapid social ascent, helps to legitimise the inequalities that exist within capitalism. The importance of this appearance is that it encourages people to believe that education and society are fairly based on individual competition. This both encourages personal application and, for those who fail, the tendency to view their failure in terms of personal blame. Viewed in Mills' terms, the social issue of restricted opportunity for the many becomes hidden in the personal trouble of the perceived inadequacy of those with ability but without economic or cultural resources who fail to progress. From a Marxist perspective, the overwhelming reality of the selective function of education under capitalism is in fact that it cannot provide equality of opportunity. Instead, it reproduces through family background from one generation to the next social class differences in opportunity which substantially distort individual educational and occupational outcomes away from the pattern expected in a meritocracy.

From a classical Marxist position, class is determined by relationship to the means of production. Viewed this way, education primarily assists those who own the means of production and benefit from the labour of others. The real function of education is therefore to perpetuate class differences across the generations and to shape youngsters with appropriate skills and discipline to become efficiently exploitable labour. Along these lines, Bowles and Gintis (1976) developed their 'correspondence theory', arguing that there is a correspondence between the organisation and authority structure within the education system and the requirements of capitalism for adequately skilled and disciplined workers. Thus, the needs of capitalism shape the education system and the education shapes future workers.

Bowles and Gintis argue that whilst the formal curriculum emphasises that education is about the development of thinking capacity and the acquisition of knowledge, through the hidden curriculum pupils are required to follow rules and regulations in preparation for the authority relationships that await them in the workplace. Employment roles require differentiated skills and the education system differentiates pupils by largely policing those in the lower grades, providing an experience which corresponds with the discipline that they will be expected to work under in the workplace, and allowing more autonomy to the higher achievers who are likely to progress to employment roles which require more autonomous application.

Through their research on senior pupils in a New York high school, Bowles and Gintis (1976) claimed to further show that the process of educational and occupational differentiation also relates back to social class background. They found that pupils of average measured I.Q. showed great variation in their achievement of qualifications and levels of occupational success. Additionally, level of qualifications obtained did not correlate closely with occupational levels achieved. Those of high I.Q.

did tend to achieve higher qualifications than others, but the researchers argue that I.Q. could be developed with length of stay in education which itself was related more to enhanced educational opportunities deriving from more privileged social background.

Overall, Bowles and Gintis argued that differences in social class background had a substantial effect on time spent in education, the development of measured I.Q., qualifications gained and occupational success. Social class background therefore showed a higher correlation with educational and occupational achievement than did individual ability. They concluded that rather than education performing a meritocratic selective process for the allocation of future occupational roles, social stratification, in terms of the impact of student's family background, tends to impose a non-meritocratic and class based selective process on educational performance and occupational outcome. Education only appears to select according to individual ability through the example of a relatively small minority of those from working class backgrounds who against the odds excel educationally and occupationally. But for capitalism to benefit, it is crucially important for a sense of fairness and motivation that this appearance is maintained. In reality, the key function of education in capitalist society is to help perpetuate the false consciousness of meritocracy within education and society to justify massive economic inequality, whilst in reality social class privilege and disadvantage tend to be passed down the generations.

Pierre Bourdieu has offered a more cultural explanation of education under capitalism from a Marxist perspective. He argued that dominant social classes were able to impose their culture into the education system as the legitimate medium for success. The culture of the higher social classes tended to be more highbrow, whereas that of the working class more allied to pop culture. For Bourdieu, there is nothing academically superior in the former, but it reflects the yardstick for assessment which derives from class power.

Furthermore, culture is not just about academic criteria but also relates to such matters as appropriate behaviour, manners, etiquette, speech, dress sense and taste. The higher classes are able to impose their class culture as the medium for educational success. The cultural environment within educational institutions is referred to by Bourdieu as the 'habitus', meaning that it is an environmental habitat to which some pupils begin more adjusted than others. Since the formation of a person's cultural attributes is acquired during early socialisation within the family, children enter school with different class cultural advantages (cultural capital) or disadvantages (cultural deficit) in an educational system where the culture of the dominant social classes comprises the environment and the worthy measure of success. Cultural capital can be acquired through the extension of formal education. However, those entering education with cultural capital are more likely to extend this capital as comfort within the habitus of the school will more likely enhance the prospects of extending their stay, which their parents are often better placed with 'economic capital' to prolong. Parents may also be more able to provide tutoring themselves or pay for private tutors.

By contrast, those lacking cultural capital in the first place have to attempt to adjust to the cultural environment as well achieving academically if they are to be successful in education. The outcome is to minimise the chances of working class pupils' educational success and access to the higher occupations as they are more likely to underachieve in terms of poor academic performance and drop out of education earlier compared to their middle class counterparts. The purpose of exams from Bourdieu's perspective is to offer the appearance of fairness and merit, since all students who sit them know that they take the same exams at the same time and under the same examination conditions. However, given the effect of different class cultures on educational and exam performance, certification formally legitimises upper and middle class success and working class failure. From this viewpoint, the transmission of culture in education does not, as functionalists maintain, take the form of a neutral national cultural consensus for the objective and meritocratic assessment of performance. It is class based, and its real function resides in maintaining social class privilege and disadvantage across the generations.

Allied with cultural capital are the influences of 'economic capital' and 'social capital'. These often all come together and are to some extent transferrable. Thus, a social background comfortable in economic resources which lacks cultural capital, can use economic resources to gain access to more exclusive institutions such as independent schools to assist in the acquisition of cultural capital, whilst the success that it assists through the currency of academic qualifications may later become transferred through occupational success to economic capital. Social capital refers to the resource of having access to networks of social contacts and the ability, enhanced through cultural capital, to utilise these networks to advantage and the exclusion of others. For Bourdieu, the children of the working class are disadvantaged through their lack of access to all of these forms of capital.

Weber – education as an arena of struggle

For Weber, different social groups compete to shape and obtain access to institutions as valued resources. Education is no exception. At the extreme, powerful groups will attempt to maintain a degree of social closure and exclusivity by denying access to other groups to the most valued educational institutions. Within this context, it could be argued that despite the expansion of and reforms to the state education system, powerful elites have managed to retain the benefits of exclusive access to the top public schools in preparation for entry to the elite professions, whereas throughout much of the state system, there has been increasing pressure in the direction of narrowing the education of the majority toward occupational training by the power of business. When using the state system, the middle classes have managed to gain disproportionate access to the more academically competitive institutions such as the prestigious grant maintained schools when they existed and now the few remaining grammar schools.

Symbolic Interactionism – labelling and self-agency

The interactionist perspective opposes both Marxist and functionalist accounts of educational systems as being too deterministic. By this it is meant that these macro theories emphasise the determining effect of broader social structures and educational systems on educational outcomes and pay little attention to the micro level of classroom situations as environments that are more autonomous from these broader forces and highly important in their own right. Rather than focussing on social systems, symbolic interactionists explain pupil behaviour and performance at the level of processes that take place within the social settings of classrooms. They look at how pupil's self-concepts (self-images) are influenced in these situations and usually focus on the effect that this has on their performance.

As explained in Chapter 2, Mead, from a symbolic interactionist perspective, claimed that self-identity is not something which is biologically pre-determined but the result of interaction with others. The self is shaped through the ability to see oneself by taking the viewpoint adopted by others of oneself. This capacity for socially generated self-consciousness is referred to as a process of 'representation'. However, the construction of self-image is not just a passive social product. Learning how to convey a public image enables the individual to also work the social environment. The self is therefore socially shaped but not socially determined. There is therefore the potential from this perspective for explaining educational processes as exchanges in the form of fluid social encounters involving the negotiation of meaning and identity.

In educational research, interactionism has often focussed on the impact of labelling by teachers on student self-concept and performance. Imposing a label refers to making a judgement, often with either positive or negative connotations, and acting toward another on the basis of that judgement. Labelling may rest on stereotyping which enables a short cut to be taken in 'understanding' individual behaviour by placing it within pre-existing categories. When teachers make judgements of pupils and communicate these to them, they may be based on a range of criteria such the stream that the pupil is placed in, their appearance, use of language, manners, application, conformity and the teacher's past experience of siblings or assessment of parents etc. These criteria and judgements may have little bearing on the ability of the individual student. However, when held and communicated, even subconsciously and unintentionally, they can strongly affect the self-image of the pupil, positively or negatively, and may develop responses that confirm the correctness of original label by virtue of the effects of its application.

Studying the effect of labelling imposed by teachers has been the main area of interest in interactionist research. From this approach, research has often provided findings which have been critical of the selective process of the old tripartite system of academic selection based around the 11+ and streaming or setting in schools, all of which can dampen down aspiration and influence underachievement for a significant number of pupils. Moreover, although focussing primarily on classroom interaction, interactionist studies have often found a conspicuous relationship between academic streaming and social class, with those of working class background overrepresented in the lower streams and pupils of middle class background in higher streams. Such findings thus can be related back to the broader issue of social class background and equality of opportunity.

Given the emphasis on the impact of teacher labelling on student self-concept and performance, interactionism has sometimes not been able to avoid falling into its own determinism since pupil performance is often seen as socially determined by the judgements and actions of teachers. This is because the teacher – pupil relationship is not an equal one due to the authority that the teacher has over the pupil. However, as viewed from the interactionist perspective, pupils are not powerless and may develop a range of responses, individual or collective, to manipulate labelling or negate its possible consequences. In research conducted by Margaret Fuller (1984) for example, black girls in a London comprehensive school were found to have strongly resisted negative stereotyping which they were determined to prove wrong by their application to their studies. This resistance enhanced their educational success.

From an interactionist perspective, the impact of pupil membership of school cultures, conformist or counter culture, on behaviour and academic performance has been effectively studied. This perspective should also be able to fruitfully analyse the generation of self-image through student to student interaction and the ability of pupils to manipulate teacher's perceptions of them in the first place.

Schooling – change in social and historical context

In pre-industrial England, sons of the wealthy landed classes had access to an elitist and traditional style of education and daughters were sometimes tutored in social airs and graces. The sons of the commercial classes were likely to have been equipped with a more commercial and practical type education. The education of children of manual workers and agricultural labourers would largely comprise the direct acquisition of work based skills and worldly wisdom through assisting their parents in their occupations from an early age. Most females were denied access to education, save the possibility of involvement in religious orders.

A complex mixture of fortuitous factors lay behind the Industrial Revolution which was apace in England by the late eighteenth century. The development of practical and scientific education in dissenting academies during the eighteenth century, to which we will shortly return, was part of the complex picture of influences. However, throughout much of the nineteenth century, as industrialisation developed, educational provision showed only limited advance and on an ad hoc basis with minimal state involvement. Some continental countries that had industrialised later than England were introducing state organised educational systems before England. For example, by the mid nineteenth century, Germany and Holland were developing systems of elementary education. Given the apparent connection between industrial modernisation and the need for a more highly skilled workforce and the emergence of a more meritocratic society, why was state education in England relatively slow to develop?

To begin to answer this question requires going beyond education systems and looking at cultural values, religion and social class dynamics. A strong culture of laissez faire (self support through individual enterprise and hard work) prevailed in England through the middle decades of the nineteenth century. This was a value system which particularly appealed to the successful industrial middle classes. England was the first country to industrialise and the process had therefore not been state planned. The benefits of non-intervention had apparently proved themselves. The rising entrepreneurial (risk taking owners of private enterprise) classes thus associated freedom and prosperity with the values of individualism and private enterprise. Individual success and freedom was associated with freedom from state interference.

This view was also linked to the preservation of religious freedoms. The industrial middle classes had a long tradition of religious beliefs which dissented from the Church of England. Consequently, they sometimes sent their sons to dissenting academies of their own religious persuasion (for example Quaker) where they would gain a more scientific and practical education. Since they paid for their own children's education, many felt entitled to resist also paying for state education of working class children through higher taxation. Furthermore, many feared that state sponsored education would interfere with their freedom of religious persuasion through the imposition of the state religion of the Church of

England. Indeed, the Anti-State-Church Association was a nonconformist pressure group set up to resist the state funding of education for this reason. It was also feared by some employers that a more educated working class may push up their labour costs and further that, in their defence of a highly ordered society, these people may forget their social station.

There were therefore powerful forces of cultural, religious, economic and social class self-interest which help to explain why the introduction of state education was delayed in this country. How, then, can the advance of state education later in the nineteenth century be explained? A number of factors coincide quite closely with the timing of the introduction and extension of universal elementary education dating from Forster's Education Act of 1870.

1) To explain the first factor, an analytical distinction needs to be made between social class and social status. Social class is to do with social levels or strata identified in terms of a hierarchy of occupational bands and income levels, whereas status refers to social groupings who share a common culture in terms of taste, manners and lifestyle from which they derive a certain level of social prestige. The latter decades of the nineteenth century witnessed a decline in the values of laissez faire enterprise culture. The reasons for this are complicated, but one thesis (J.W. Wiener 1981) argues that an important factor in this decline was the greater use of public schools by the entrepreneurial classes. Viewed as uncultured Philistines by those of more traditional elite status groups, many sought a more gentlemanly status for their sons. This could be achieved by utilising their economic resources to send their sons to public schools. However, it was in this elitist environment of classical education that they became ingratiated into a culture of disdain for industry.

2) England's waning economic performance during the second half of the nineteenth century, partly explained by the above culture change, meant that other countries were closing the lead in economic modernisation that England had once established. These later developers appeared to have benefited from the provision of universal elementary education. The economic function of universal education in the context of international competition was therefore apparent to governments.

3) There also existed a fear that, by being left to their own devices and setting up discussion and reading groups, the working classes were beginning to educate themselves and in so doing often spreading politically subversive ideas. This situation could get out of control. To counteract it, the state could promote the social control function by imposing a form of education which provided the indoctrinating experience of rote learning and 'safe' god fearing religious messages for the masses.

Despite legislation in 1876 and 1880 to require compulsory full-time school attendance for children up to the age of 10, elementary education and a rote style of learning was all that was available to most pupils without parental means, whatever their abilities. And despite educational reforms early in the twentieth century which offered a proportion of free grammar school places to able children of working class background, access to secondary education at the age of 11 remained largely on a fee paying basis up to the end of the Second World War. This meant that even though the minimum school leaving age had been gradually raised to 14 by 1918, most pupils without parents of means had to remain in elementary school through to the end of their education.

Educational reforms followed both the First and Second World Wars. Each time, the low level of education of war recruits had been identified. Additionally, wartime promises of reform in a range of policy areas including education were made to either circumvent the risk of political radicalism (First World War) or to raise wartime morale (Second World War).

Post-war educational policy – the social democratic approach and social engineering

Social policy refers to government interventions which steer social change and provide a framework within which to influence behaviour. It is guided by political ideology which provides a set of values and an image of an ideal society as a compass bearing on an improved future from the viewpoint of that ideology (note the more restricted use of the term ideology in party politics and social policy compared to its use in the Marxist perspective).

Politics during the post Second World War period was dominated by Labour and Conservative governments. Generally speaking, Labour favoured more state control, interventionist and redistributive policies, whereas the Conservative looked more to the free market. Nevertheless, the policy reforms introduced by each party in government can be seen as based on a 'collectivist consensus' which emerged during the war and remained relatively intact for at least two decades afterwards. This consensus between the main political parties and across much of society favoured state intervention to protect the vulnerable whilst enhancing opportunities for the able irrespective of their social background. Such intervention aimed to engineer social justice from the education system to broader society and has been referred to as the social democratic approach.

Against the backdrop of this consensus, reforms to the state educational system in England contained in the Butler Act were implemented by the post-war Labour government in 1946. Resources for the state sector were to be provided through public funding and delivered through the local authorities. The reforms included both the extension of the minimum school leaving age to 15 and the transition from primary to some form of secondary schooling at the age of 11 for all children within the state system, along with the abolition of fees for access to state secondary education. With the barrier of parental inability to pay fees removed and the introduction of standardised intelligence testing in the form of the 11+ exam, it was expected that this system would enhance the selective function to channel pupils with different levels of ability into different types of state secondary school. The reforms were therefore expected to extend pupils' equality of opportunity to demonstrate their inequality of ability irrespective of social background, and then to educate them accordingly. These were therefore meritocratic principles (although the independent fee paying sector, which runs counter to this logic, remained in place) which when applied in the selective process of the 11+ test for entry into the new largely tripartite system of secondary moderns, technical schools and grammar schools, were expected to show significantly improved access for able working class children to the academically challenging grammar schools. It was further expected that the incentive to achieve educationally through selection for occupations on merit would promote social mobility and assist overall economic performance through more effective utilisation of talent.

Research from the 1950s indicated that there was, in fact, little improvement in the access of children from working class backgrounds to grammar schools, proportionate to those from middle class backgrounds.

One of the criticisms of the tripartite system was therefore that selection still led to a degree of social class segregation in the schools attended. Children of the middle classes were far more likely to attend the academically challenging grammar schools whereas those of working class background tended to enter secondary moderns which provided a more concrete education and restricted educational and occupational opportunities. Secondary moderns, attended by a majority of pupils, also came to be viewed as schools for those who had 'failed' the 11+ test, thus also arguably dampening aspirations.

The reforms of the Butler Act were premised on the view that individual differences in intellectual ability were innate, fixed and scientifically measurable. However, the precision and infallibility of intelligence testing to provide a once and for all measure of ability and allocate pupils to different schools accordingly has since been much questioned. Sociologists do not tend to deny the existence or importance of differences in innate abilities. For example, even with the greatest educational and social support only very few people could reach the academic level of a professorship. However, they emphasise that 1) environmental factors can substantially enhance or retard the development of intellectual capacities, and therefore 2) a once and for all test at the age of 11 overemphasises the fixity of innate abilities and 3) such testing does not provide a neutral and precise means of measuring intellectual ability. It is therefore not surprising that research in the 1950s by Yates and Pidgeon indicated that approximately 70,000 children a year were wrongly allocated to their schools at the secondary stage.

During the 1960s, political party divergence opened up with the Labour Party supporting comprehensivisation and the Conservatives more intent on retaining the tripartite selective system. For Labour, comprehensive schools, which would take in pupils across the entire ability range and from a diversity of occupational backgrounds within their catchment area, linked in with the idea of the promotion of a modern classless society. Labour governments required local authorities to draw up plans to introduce comprehensives and through the establishment of Educational Priority Areas extra resources were targeted to deprived localities.

Research, for example by Benn and Chitty (1996) and Glennester and Low (1980), has shown that in comparison to performance within the tripartite system, comprehensive schooling (which has various models) has tended to improve the exam performance of those assessed as of average ability and below without detrimental effect on the performance of the most able. Furthermore, McPherson and Willms found in the 1980s that in Scotland comprehensive schooling had reduced the differential effect of social class on educational attainment.

Yet even with the growth of comprehensive education, which invariably continued the process of academic streaming, social class differences in achievement levels tended to remain remarkably resistant. It was therefore the case that rather than engineering social justice through the education system, broader social inequalities had an invading effect into the education system.

Traditional sociological themes and research:

1. Social class – the seemingly impenetrable barrier to equal opportunity in educational achievement

Much post-war educational research focussed on the issue of working class access to grammar school and levels of academic achievement. Given the meritocratic reasoning behind the post-war reforms, research tended to focus on establishing whether pupils of working class background were the main beneficiaries as may have been anticipated. In fact, much evidence confirmed that class related differences in terms of access and achievement remained relatively unchanged. For example, research conducted by J.W.B. Douglas (The Home and the School, 1964) compared the GCE O level performance of students of similar high measured ability but different social class backgrounds and found that performance levels declined in correlation with descending social class background. A far greater proportion of able lower working class students were also leaving school at the minimum leaving age.

Later research carried out by Halsey, Heath and Ridge (1980) found that, in terms of school leaving age, qualifications obtained, and entrance to university, the performance of youngsters from all social class backgrounds had improved when pre-war and post-war cohorts were compared. However, in terms of their relative underperformance, the position of children of working class background remained largely unchanged. Their chances of entering grammar school were three times less than that of children from professional and managerial backgrounds – a proportion little different from pre-war figures.

What are the main approaches to explaining these persisting social class related differences in levels of educational success? At a general level, a distinction can be made between explanations that emphasise differences in natural or innate abilities and others which refer to the predominant influence of environmental factors. The first approach tends to be more prevalent within psychology. For those adopting this position, such as Herrnstein and Murray in the United States, the relationship between social class background and level of educational achievement is seen as largely the result of social class differences in inherited intelligence levels. As far as this genetic inheritance argument goes, the data may appear to fit the interpretation. It would also enable evidence of limited levels of social mobility to square with the view that society is nevertheless meritocratic, in that there exists equality of opportunity, but that working class children inherit lower levels of innate ability which tend to keep them in their class of origin.

There are a number of major problems with this interpretation. Firstly, it may be questioned whether it is possible to measure innate intelligence levels that have not already been influenced by environmental factors. Secondly, even if working class parents are less intelligent than middle class parents whose occupations may demand higher intellectual qualities, there is no evidence from laws of heredity that from this starting point these same intelligence levels will be directly inherited by the next generation. Laws of heredity suggest that differences in innate intelligence are more likely to be randomly distributed throughout the social structure. Thirdly, the inheritance argument tends to be further undermined by a large body of evidence showing different levels of educational performance related to social class background when comparing children of similar measured ability. Fourthly, it is highly questionable whether testing only measures intelligence levels. For example, practice can often improve test performance but access to the opportunities for practice is likely to be a socially constructed inequality.

Whilst not denying the existence of innate differences in intellectual ability (nature), sociological explanations attribute far more importance to environmental factors (nurture) in influencing the development of ability and opportunities for educational achievement. One broad category of explanations emphasises the impact of differences in social class cultural environments. Culture, in the sociological sense, refers to shared usage of language, values and understandings.

An early explanation of the persistence of social class differences in levels of educational achievement which comes under this category of explanation was developed by Basil Bernstein (from 1961). He identified the importance of different class related linguistic codes. Bernstein argued that speech codes developed in working class families tended to be of a 'restricted' type. By this, he meant that communication takes place in the form of descriptive vocabulary. Grammatical form is often incomplete because it assumes that others have a shared knowledge of the particular circumstances to which it relates. In correcting children, parents are more likely to issue imperatives along the lines of 'don't do that or else...' By contrast, middle class families tend to use relatively 'elaborated' speech codes. This form of communication is more grammatically rounded, it tends to use abstract concepts, and provides more detailed explanations. In correcting children, parents are more likely to explain 'you should not do that because...'

Before even attending school, children are socialised within the family environment into the linguistic code of their social class as a way of communicating. As the mode of communication used by teachers within schools tends to conform to the elaborated speech code, working class children are at a social class disadvantage in getting onto the frequency of communication and expressing themselves in a way deemed to be appropriate in that context. It could also be added that intelligence testing tends to rely on pupils showing that they can deal with abstract concepts, that more working class pupils tended to fail their 11+, and that secondary modern schools were designed as appropriate for children who thought in more concrete terms, thus being heavily populated by children of working class parents.

Bernstein also related achievement to pedagogy, the influence of which works in the same direction to that of linguistic codes. School pedagogy refers to the creation of curriculum and educational processes designed to enable the learner to learn. It includes rules of the educational and learning environment. Bernstein argued that within schools there is an explicit and implicit pedagogy. The explicit pedagogy, in the form of rules of the learning environment that are clearly communicated, tends to be visible to all pupils. By contrast, the implicit pedagogy rests on the assumption that pupils understand implied expectations of the learning environment and how they should conduct themselves. Bernstein argued that this dimension of the school pedagogy tends to be picked up on by pupils of middle class background as something familiar, but that it remains more hidden to those of working class background. Although this relates little to their abilities, it is the criteria by which they are judged and can significantly influence their performance.

As identified in a previous section, Pierre Bourdieu offered a cultural explanation of working class relative educational failure through lack of cultural (as well as economic and social) capital. The reader may have recognised some similarities between Bourdieu's ideas and those of Bernstein. However, Bourdieu's concept of cultural capital is broader than that of Bernstein's linguistic codes and pedagogy and he also adopts an explicitly neo-Marxist analysis in which the power of the dominant social classes to impose their culture as the means of assessment disadvantages the working class. From Bourdieu's position, it is unlikely that such educational disadvantage can be overcome, even with the best of intentions, whilst society remains divided into economically dominant and subordinate classes.

A quite different approach which emphasised a cultural dimension to educational achievement was adopted by Herbert Hyman (1967). In a study of a range of research findings in the United States, Hyman explained educational achievement differences mainly through the effect of different class cultural values. He argued that the cultural values of the lower social classes place less emphasis on personal achievement than those of the middle class. They also place less value on striving for upward occupational mobility and educational achievement. Their values are more fatalistic. Children from these backgrounds become socialised into these fatalistic cultural values which do not prepare them well for success in education.

Although Hyman acknowledged that these values are in part a realistic reflection of the lesser opportunity that society offers the poor and the working class, the greater emphasis in his analysis is that it is the negative value system of these groups which is the barrier to their success within a society of opportunity. The key to combating the problem is therefore instilling, through education, values of individual competitiveness into pupils from more deprived backgrounds at the youngest age possible to counteract the culture of negativity and help them to reach their potential.

Barry Sugarman's cultural explanation (1970) related educational achievement to time horizons associated with parental occupations. Working class and middle class occupations tended to promote different time perspectives. The career structure of middle class occupations meant that planning for the future and making sacrifices now – referred to as 'deferred gratification' – would be recognised to pay off in the long run. As working class occupations did not tend to have a long-term career structure, but instead a wage structure that peaked quite early in life, they tended to encourage more of a present time orientation or 'live for today' approach to life. These different outlooks could influence children's orientation to education, which for success required individual application and deferred gratification.

Other explanations of differential achievement place less emphasis on class cultural values. One such is Douglas' (1964) research, which has already been referred to. Douglas identified parental attention to children in the pre-school home environment and interest in their children's education at school as particularly important to children's educational achievement. It was claimed, through measuring parents' school visits, that the middle classes expressed a greater interest in their children's educational progress. This way of measuring parental interest has been a contentious. However, Douglas also related educational success to other class connected phenomena such as the child's health, the size of the family, study and living conditions, and the quality of the school, all of which can count against the working class child. There was therefore a mixture of cultural and material social class factors affecting pupil's achievement.

For Raymond Boudon (1974), position in the class structure is more important than aspects of class culture in explaining class differences in educational attainment. Given their different class background starting points, Boudon argued that it would be misleading to suggest that working class youngsters with horizons for working class occupations hold more fatalistic values than middle class youngsters aiming for middle class occupations. He emphasised that educational systems offer various potential educational pathways and exit points, and argued that pupils engage in a rational process of costs and benefits analysis, which is partly but not exclusively economic, in making their educational decisions. The different class backdrops to these decisions means that pupils of different social class backgrounds may well come to different but equally rational decisions regarding their educational options. For example, the transition from school or college to higher education is a potential exit point where decisions have to be made. The prospect for a pupil of working class background of embarking on a higher education course which could lead to a profession may entail a distancing, both geographically and socially, from family and friends and the need to adjust to a new cultural environment and social circles. Since such a decision may not carry much support from family and friends who may not share these horizons, potential costs may appear to outweigh benefits. By contrast, in considering pursuing the same pathway, the pupil from a middle class background may assess that the benefits outweigh the costs as their family expects and supports further study and friends make similar decisions. For Boudon, both decisions may be equally rational and made by individuals, but they take place against the backdrop of the class structure which they then feed back into.

Nell Keddie (1973) applied an interactionist approach to the study of streaming in a comprehensive school. Although the research was focussed at a micro level, it raised broader questions regarding stereotyping and the relationship between streaming and social class. Keddie found that, in a school that adopted streaming but also ran a course that was not meant to be taught in a differentiated way, teachers still gave pupils from different streams differential access to course knowledge. 'A' stream pupils were viewed as academically able and easy to work with and so were given access to abstract curriculum knowledge. 'C' stream pupils were regarded as less able and seen as more difficult to work with because they tended to think in a concrete way. They were likely to speak up if their concrete experiences contradicted the teacher's subject knowledge. When this happened, their contributions tended to be dismissed. Keddie thus found that schooling tended to reward the ability of the predominantly middle class 'A' stream students to conform to the requirements of the curriculum and penalise the more critical contributions of the predominantly working class 'C' stream students.

Research by Paul Willis (1977) is unusual in that it was conducted at a micro level within a broader Marxist framework of analysis. In so doing, he came to some rather different conclusions than many sociologists who work within the Marxist framework tend to. In his small scale study of 12 'lads' of working class background, he found that their response to a school environment, which they experienced as alienating, was to develop a counter culture in which they avoided school work, played up, and ridiculed others whom they viewed as conformist swats. Whilst the 'lads' valued the superiority of street wisdom and quick wit, they also knew how far to bend the rules. According to Willis, they realistically anticipated their working class occupational destinations and so did not value academic conformity and achievement. By so doing, they became confirmed in their expected occupations.

Willis also studied the 'lads' when they entered the workplace. He found that the school had not been successful in inducing conformity to rules and application to work. Nevertheless, their school counter culture had prepared them with a type of pre-vocational experience in preparation for a workplace in which quick wit and manipulation of the rules were part of the shop floor culture in coping with tedium. In this way, working class culture and restricted horizons were actively reproduced. The lads did not feel that they were either just down beaten failures at school or suppressed in the workplace.

The above explanations comprise just a limited selection from a body of well established sociological research and explanations of social class differences in educational achievement. Given the variety of influences identified, it is hardly surprising that substantial class related achievement differences have remained so persistent despite reforms of the education system which would seem to be designed to enhance equality of opportunity to succeed. At first glance, explanations in terms of the inheritance of social class differences in intelligence levels could appear to fit the facts of the connection between social class and educational achievement levels. However, sociologists focus more on the effect of the social distribution of influences and opportunities for personal development and achievement to explain the same facts.

The above explanations suggest, from a sociological viewpoint, that it is more the impact of different class based life chances on educational performance that is transmitted across the generations than genetic differences in levels of intelligence.

2. Gender – changing social and educational horizons

Sex differences between males and females are biological differences that have been imposed by nature. By distinction, the term 'gender' refers to socially constructed differences in identity related to sex differences rather than the view that such identity differences are biologically predetermined. Being socially constructed, they vary from society to society and can change over time. As in the study of social class, sociology adopts a mainly environmental or nurture emphasis in explaining differences in educational achievement in gender terms. Within the framework of a broad historical outlook, gender roles and opportunities for many women in the western world changed quite rapidly and dramatically following the women's liberation movement of the late 1960s and early 1970s. It is more than coincidence that in subsequent decades the performance of females in education has dramatically improved compared to that of males. This pace of change in social liberation and educational performance is far too great to be explained in terms of evolution in inbuilt intellectual capacity.

Educational research in England has long established that girls have tended to perform better than boys up to about the middle stage of secondary school. They then used to fall behind the performance of boys and were less likely to stay on at school. Such a turn around could be explained in terms of a combination of different socially constructed gender expectations and discriminatory practices.

During the post-war decades, the expectations for many girls were that a future housewife role required little consideration of occupational striving and the necessity for gaining educational qualifications. These social expectations were often reproduced across a range of educational and general reading materials, appearing most prescriptively in Housekeeping Monthly in 1955 which explained how a woman should run the home, serve her husband and know her place. Even in the early 1970s, Sue Sharpe found that the girls in her London based research saw their futures mainly in terms of marriage and domesticity and gave aiming for a career little consideration (however, as many of the girls were of working class background, the possible combined effect of class and gender on their outlook cannot be discounted).

Discriminatory practices up to this time included gender quotas operated by some local authorities. Given the superior performance of girls at the 11+ stage, a number of authorities would raise the pass mark for girls compared to that for boys so as to level out the proportions of males and females entering grammar schools. At the margins, therefore, boys with a slightly lower mark than girls may have obtained grammar school places that girls were denied.

Females had also experienced widespread prejudice and discrimination in the workplace. Women who took on 'men's jobs', despite evidence that women had capably performed such work as part of the war effort, often faced extreme hostility. More generally, they were often denied promotion, offered lower rates of pay to men, and in some occupations were even expected to give up their work if they married, on the assumption that they would be 'kept' by their husband.

Early feminist writers such as Betty Friedan (1965) were challenging the restriction on their self-fulfilment that the traditional housewife role was argued to impose on so many women. By 1970, the emergence of feminist consciousness in a number of western societies focussed on challenging female disadvantage in a broad range of social contexts. Studies within education were beginning to reflect this change by paying more critical attention to gender issues. One area of attention was that of traditional sexual stereotyping, which related to presumed fixed and innate differences in abilities and predispositions between females and males, casting females as natural carers and males as their providers. From at least one strand of feminist thinking (radical feminism), views which emphasised these immutable differences were in fact male ideology – the ideas supported social arrangements through which males exercised power over females throughout society.

Studies focussing on the impact of socialisation in the formation of gender identity held liberating potential, since, if its effect was shown to be substantial, reform of the social environment and socialisation could bring about reformed gender identity. Research conducted during the 1970s and 1980s paid greater attention to the impact of early gender socialisation within the family and playgroups through the different treatment of boys and girls and different toys they were given to play with. School reading and teaching materials also came under greater scrutiny. For example, content analysis of stories in school books by researchers such as Glenys Lobban (1974) often revealed that gender stereotypes of male adventurousness and female domesticity were present. Such practices and materials were now exposed to more critical scrutiny.

A further issue was that subjects themselves were often gender stereotyped along the lines of maths and sciences being natural male subjects, whilst humanities and domestic science were regarded as natural female subjects. Traditional gender related subject choices were then sometimes reinforced by stereotypical assumptions built into school timetabling and often supported by teacher guidance. Researchers were also studying ways in which some subject texts were written which assumed one gender or the other to be the natural audience. And observational studies found widespread evidence of male dominance in classroom participation.

Reflecting the climate of growing awareness and criticism of gender inequality, the Sex Discrimination Act was passed in 1975. One consequence of this legislation was that the practice of operating different 11+ pass levels for boys and girls became illegal. Other social changes would encourage significant improvements in the educational performance of females. One was the perception of enhanced employment opportunities for women. This was associated with the expansion of service sector employment and examples set by some highly successful female role models in business and politics. A social and political climate of enhanced enterprise culture values during the 1980s emphasised the individual striving of career women, a position with some common ground in liberal feminism as opposed to the earlier more collectivist feminist protests. At the same time, rapidly rising divorce rates arguably placed greater importance on females to recognise the need to be able to prepare for financial independence.

These changes may be seen as constituting the backdrop of both enhanced opportunities and motivations for the dramatic progress in female educational performance which will be outlined later. This remarkable improvement over a short historical time period provides a powerful argument against those who maintain that substantially different intellectual capacities are built into the nature of males and females which prescribe different opportunities and roles in life.

3. Ethnicity – early period educational performance levels and general explanations

The Swann Report (1985) identified, despite improvements over the preceding ten years, that Afro Caribbeans were the ethnic group with the poorest record of educational performance. By contrast, 'Asian' (the ethnic categories used more recently have become more refined) pupils' performance was comparable to that of whites, even though they were often from lower occupational background. Evidence provided by the Department of Education and Skills tended to substantiate the findings of the Swann Report. Figures for 1989 that measure achievement in terms of passing at least 5 GCESs at grade C and above showed a 30% achievement rate for whites, 29% for 'Asians' (no figures for separate national classifications were provided) and 18% for 'blacks' (including Afro Caribbeans, but gain there were no figures for separate national classifications). By 1992, data from the Youth Cohort Study of 16 year olds showed the achievement level of whites to have improved to 37%, of Asians to 33% and 'blacks' to 23%. It is interesting to note that within the Asian category, more detailed classification became available which showed Indian achievement at 38%, 'other Asian' (including Chinese) at 46% and Bangladeshis (a minority who tended to arrive in England later) at only 14%.

The aim of this section is to provide a brief overview of a range of explanations from this period that have been used to account for differences in the educational performance of ethnic minority groups in England (a distinction will shortly be made between the terms 'ethnicity' and 'race'). In a later section, we will review evidence of more contemporary levels of academic achievement by ethnic group, touching on some explanations of the progress since made.

What explanations have been provided to account for such a variation in achievement levels? One type of approach attempts to explain the differences as being due to variation in inherited intellectual capacity between different 'races' that were defined in terms of skin colour and other physical features. This type of explanation can be traced back to colonial days when the view of different racial characteristics was used to explain and justify the dominance of white Europeans over other races, as well as the practice of slavery. An early exponent of the racial approach was the nineteenth century French aristocrat Joseph Gobineau, who essentially argued that the different races of white, black and yellow skin colour had different genetically inbuilt attributes. He claimed that the capacity of the white race to establish civilisations was because of its superior qualities of intelligence and organizational capacity, and that intermixing with other races would lead to the degeneration of these qualities. Similar reasoning has been applied in the twentieth century to support the institution of South African apartheid, Nazi persecutions and discrimination against blacks in the American southern states.

More recent geneticist arguments have attempted to add a gloss of scientific respectability to this position by comparing the findings of IQ testing of different racial groups. For example, in America, Arthur Jensen (1969) pointed to evidence that IQ scores for black Americans were about 15 points below that of whites. Herrnstein and Murray (1994), based on a summary of a broad range of studies, provided similar findings and concluded that IQ test differences were substantially influenced by genetic inheritance. These writers, along with H. Eysenck, maintained that about 60% of the measured IQ difference was the result of genetic differences between the races.

Charles Murray, with particular reference to the United States, also related the view that certain groups are intellectually inferior to what he referred to as an underclass, containing a high proportion of ethnic minorities who were trapped in poverty. He provided partly social and partly genetic explanations to account for this, each of which provided support for social policy that would limit welfare expenditure. The social component of his explanation was that prolonged reliance on welfare benefit encouraged an attitude of fatalism and a 'dependency culture' system of values which, when passed on to the next generation, curbed their capacity for self-help. However, the perpetuation of poverty was also seen as deriving from the inheritance of lower levels of intelligence within this stratum. Thus, attempting to tackle poverty through enhanced spending on education and welfare would be at best a worthless investment and at worst counterproductive.

Analysed sociologically, the argument that there are fixed differences in the innate intellectual capacities of different races is highly contestable. Various reasons have been put forward to explain why the validity of IQ tests (their ability to test what they claim to test – innate intelligence) can be questioned. A key issue raised is that the tests were usually initially standardised on a white middle class population. They are therefore not a neutral measuring device but are culturally biased and as such arguably depress the performance of other ethnic cultural groups. Moreover, regarding the middle class bias built into the standardisation, it must be remembered that a greater proportion of members of most ethnic minority groups occupy lower social class positions. And why is that? To what extent is this due to a lack of ability or the practice of discrimination? There is evidence to suggest, certainly during the time period that we are looking at, that the latter has played a very significant part.

At this point, it needs to be emphasised that sociologists tend to strongly contest the very use of the term 'race' as a useful concept and make a similar distinction between race and ethnicity to that of sex and gender. Just as gender refers to the impact of socially constructed identities over biological differences between the sexes, so ethnicity refers to the social impact of different customs, histories, and traditions over differences of appearance referred to as race. By emphasising the influence of social factors rather than innate characteristics, it becomes apparent that improvement can come through changes in the environment – for example from social reform. Furthermore, such crude racial categories as 'Asian' can be avoided, and the more subtle concept of ethnicity can be applied to help understand the differences in the educational performance of, for example, Pakistani, Indian and Bangladeshi ethnic minorities in England.

If for a moment we accept the view that I.Q. testing provides a neutral and scientific measurement of innate ability, new problems arise for the geneticists. One problem is that I.Q scores appear to be improving by about 3% per decade. How is this possible? It would appear to be far too fast as a measure of evolutionary change. Moreover, in the United States, the I.Q scores of black Americans improved at a faster rate than that of whites during a time frame which follows the civil rights reforms. This would seem to suggest that what black Americans had previously 'inherited' and has at least since been partly lifted, was the overwhelming effect of racial discrimination and disadvantage on their 'ability' to do themselves justice. In the case of social class, we have previously explained differences in attainment levels in terms of a broad range of environmental influences. The same would appear to be the case regarding gender and ethnicity, with a degree of greater optimism with regard to progress that these groups have made.

More contemporary evidence with regard to gender and ethnicity will be presented later to show that in England massive educational improvements in terms of the achievement of qualifications have been made by females, who have come to outperform males in all ethnic groups, and that certain ethnic minorities (Indian and Chinese) are significantly outperforming whites. Those ethnic groups who started well behind (for example Bangladeshis) have either substantially closed the performance gap with or even overtaken the performance of white pupils.

Given the number of ethnic minority groups and the variations in level of educational performance, a thorough understanding of the social influences on educational performance would require an extremely complex comparative analysis to tease out the relevant influential factors in each case. This is further complicated by the fact that even though evidence is available for more specifically identified ethnic cultures, each of these can be internally diverse and can change. Indeed, dismissing race and emphasising the influence of ethnic culture, McKenzie (2001, p.157) rightly warns that one needs to be cautious to avoid substituting a simplistic approach of ethnic absolutism for that of the discredited racial absolutism to explain differences in levels of educational achievement. Here, there is only room for the less ambitious task of sketching some general explanations.

Ethnic minorities have tended to face disadvantaged material circumstances compared to whites. However, the groups vary in the extent of these disadvantages and their capacity to resist the impact on educational performance. For example, Bangladeshis remain amongst the most economically disadvantaged of the ethnic groups, yet the performance of their children has improved remarkably over the last twenty years, suggesting major adaptation of second and third generation of this minority to the host culture. When family poverty is measured in terms of eligibility for free school meals, its negative effect tends to be less dramatic on the performance of any of the ethnic minority groups than on whites. Of course, the proportions of families where children are entitled to free school meals will vary between the ethnic groups, yet for Bangladeshis where we would expect eligibility to be high, those within this group who are eligible for free school meals perform almost as well as those who are not. Such evidence suggests the remarkable resilience in performance of this group to economic deprivation.

Although essentially dismissing 'race' as a valid approach to understanding educational performance differences, sociologists have to deal with the reality that racial prejudice and discrimination still exist, if now more covertly, and have consequences. Evidence of racial discrimination is provided elsewhere in this text. At present, it is reasonable to argue that its effect has been to over represent some ethnic minority groups (Afro Caribbean in particular and Indian less so) in poorly paid manual occupations and high levels of deprivation with little chance of improvement. The poorer educational performance of Afro Caribbeans could therefore be partly explained by their disproportionate concentration in poverty and working class occupations. Indeed, the Swan Report referred to the impact of deprivation, resulting from discrimination in both employment and housing, on educational performance, research conducted by Eggleston found that the fathers of 87% of Afro Caribbean children were employed in manual occupations (1986), and Smith and Tomlinson (1989) have argued that social class more strongly relates to educational attainment levels than ethnicity does. However, to more accurately measure the impact of ethnicity itself on educational performance, one would need to control on class by comparing the performance of pupils of different ethnic groups but of the same social class backgrounds.

Another approach to understanding levels of educational performance relates to the family life of ethnic minority groups. For example, Afro Caribbean families have traditionally comprised far higher proportions of single parent female headed families than any other ethnic group. Evidence has indicated that generally pupils from single parent families perform less well educationally. Common explanations for the poor performance of children from single parent family backgrounds have often pointed to a negative effect of the absence of a male breadwinner role model and authority figure. Poorer educational performance associated with this family type, perhaps itself at least in part influenced by teacher stereotypes of the above common explanations, has therefore impacted more heavily on Afro Caribbeans and been seen by teachers as explaining to a casual attitude to learning and indiscipline in the classroom and apparently substantiated by high levels of school expulsion recorded for this group.

Explanations may also be couched in terms of ethnic subcultural values. Two such approaches will be mentioned here with one tending to attribute blame to ethnic minorities and the other not. The first explanation looks to place the blame on negative or anti-educational values argued to be held by an ethnic group and has in the past sometimes been used to explain the poor educational performance of Afro Caribbean boys. Similar explanations have been used in explaining the poor performance levels of white working class boys who are members of deviant school subcultures.

The second type of explanation, taking a lead from the ideas of Bourdieu, looks at poor achievement in terms of cultural deficit. In this explanation, the education system is shaped by the ability of the middle and upper classes to impose their culture as the framework by which assessment and achievement is measured. Thus, just as the working class may be disadvantaged by a lack of middle and upper class cultural assets, so may ethnic minorities. Even though parents within these groups may be just as highly motivated as any others for their children to do well at school, they may lack the cultural assets to be able to help as much. Even so, the parental response is not necessarily a passive one, as witnessed by examples of the setting up of Saturday schools by ethnic groups to improve the performance of their children.

More explanations can be found by focussing on aspects of the school environment. For example, one may question the extent to which the high level of exclusion of Afro Caribbean boys from school is simply a measure of particularly challenging behaviour of this group, often explained in terms of lack of a father figure in the family, or is at least to some extent a consequence of negative labelling by teachers based on this very stereotype, whereby similar behaviour by pupils from other ethnic groups that teachers hold a more favourable stereotype of is less likely to lead to expulsion. This interpretation is supported by the research of Wright (1992) who found that in the primary schools that she studied, Afro Caribbean boys tended to be singled out for disciplinary treatment when similar behaviour conduct by white boys did not lead to similar levels of disciplinary response.

The Swann Report referred to negative stereotyping of Afro Caribbeans by teachers. Research conducted by the Runnymead Trust (1997) found that teachers often used negative stereotypes in the way that they related to ethnic minority students, and research by Connolly (1998) found that at the primary school level teachers differentiated their judgements of Afro Caribbean and Asian pupils in negative and more positive terms respectively in relation to their general stereotypes and views of the supposedly different family life of these ethnic groups. Clearly, teachers' treatment of students based on ethnic stereotyping can lead to a self-fulfilling prophecy in the performance of pupils. However, research findings by Fuller (1984), Mac an Ghaill (1988) and Mirza (1992) into the performance of black ethnic minority girls offers a cautionary reminder that groups may resist negative stereotyping and perform well. Whilst the girls exhibited a defiant attitude toward their learning experience, unlike the white working class boys in Willis' research they did not adopt an anti-learning culture and in recognizing the practical importance of obtaining qualifications worked hard to achieve them.

The Swann Report also found that Afro Caribbean pupils experienced high levels of placement in schools for the 'educationally subnormal'. It highlighted the inappropriateness of this provision when in the many cases the difficulty was more to do with the language used rather than innate backwardness, and that youngsters could be better supported through other specialist provision which took this into account. Furthermore, the view that linguistic variations from standard English are necessarily intellectually inferior can itself be highly questioned.

The school environment and curriculum may be experienced as alienating, especially to recent migrants, if it provides little or no consideration of their cultural heritage. This ethnocentrism, linked to the immigrant / host viewpoint and emphasis on assimilation, can lead to a disconnection of pupils from the education process through the excessive emphasis of British culture in such subjects as English literature and history. Ethnic minorities can feel alienated if the implication is that their cultural background is worthless.

Developments in educational policy:

We have seen that during the post-war years up to the 1960s, there existed between Labour and Conservative governments a degree of consensus on the importance of extending state education in such a way as to enhance meritocratic opportunity. The socialist tinge in Labour ideology emphasised the importance of enhancing equality of opportunity by which more children of working class parents may through educational achievement experience social mobility. The Conservatives, tending to adopt a 'one nation' approach, placed greater emphasis on competition and the incentives of inequality of outcome, but conceded to attempts to improve equality of opportunity in the interests of social harmony and stability. These differing emphases became clearer in the dispute over the retention of the selective tripartite system, generally supported by the Conservatives, and the promotion of comprehensive education by Labour governments. However, both parties tended to share the view that state intervention in education was an important part of a broader process of social engineering guided by an ethic of social justice and thus subscribed to what we have previously referred to as a social democratic approach to education.

1. New right (neo-liberal) policy – the promotion of diversity and choice

In the context of Britain's waning economic performance, debate from the mid 70s was increasingly focussing on the appropriateness of educational provision to cater for the needs of employers and the broader economy. This issue was raised to prominence in 1976 by the Labour Prime Minister James Callaghan in his Ruskin College speech. In sociological terms, concern across the political spectrum was emerging about the effectiveness of the education system in performing its economic function. This was compounded by a period of growing labour unrest which culminated in the widespread industrial disputes that marked the 'winter of discontent' during 1978 – 1979 that brought down the Labour government.

When the Conservative government came to power in 1979, they were intent on reforming education with the aim of improving economic efficiency and competitiveness and re-imposing social order within an increasingly challenging global environment. A greater emphasis was placed on vocational training and education with, for example, the introduction of the Youth Training Scheme which was aimed at providing work related skills for school leavers, and NVQs to provide occupationally related training and qualifications. Further, their general approach to educational reform signalled a break from the social democratic model pursued by previous Labour and Conservative governments. The issue of enhancing social justice by promoting equality of educational opportunity with reference to social class background tended to be downgraded, with greater concern being placed on raising overall standards. From a new right perspective, it was argued that this could best be achieved by 'marketising' the education system - introducing reforms into the public sector to create a competitive environment similar to that of the private sector in which individual schools would be run like competing businesses to attract consumers.

The old tripartite versus comprehensive battle was eclipsed by a policy promoting greater diversity of schools and enhancing (parental) choice. As things stood, selective education was allowed to continue in those, mainly Conservative, areas that had retained grammar schools. Many local authorities were in the process of converting to comprehensive provision, whereas in some localities grammar schools coexisted alongside 'comprehensives' which were therefore strictly speaking not comprehensives at all for their catchment area. Most schools were coeducational, but some had single sex intake. Faith schools, partly funded by churches, offered further options in many local authorities.

New right reforms extended this diversity. City technology colleges, funded by both central government and business and specialising in science, technology and business subjects, were established in a small number of urban localities. Schools could also elect to become 'grant maintained'. These schools 'opted out' of local authority finance and control, were funded directly from the government, and were run autonomously by boards of school governors that included parents. Some introduced highly selective intake procedures, whilst others did not. The government also introduced the Assisted Places Scheme. This provided means tested support for able children of poorer families to enter independent schools.

Alongside this growing diversity of provision, uniformity of assessment within the state sector was enhanced through the introduction of the national curriculum and periodic standardised testing. This uniformity formed the foundation of publicly accessible information on academic achievement. On the basis of standardised information compiled in the form of published league tables, it was intended that schools would have to become more publicly accountable for their performance and that parents would be able to make enlightened decisions on the best schools for their children to attend. Schools needed to be more competitive as intake quotas were no longer guaranteed and funding followed their ability to attract pupils. All this meant that schools had to become better at marketing themselves within a competitive environment.

Another element of educational diversity remained in the independent school sector. Independent schools, as privately run charitable organisations, rely heavily on parental payment of fees for their children to attend. Within this sector, the more exclusive and prestigious schools are referred to as public schools. At secondary level, public schools usually have an entry age of 13, which coincides with completing private preparatory school, and pupils are required to have passed the common entrance exam. Many public schools offer boarding facilities and a number have retained single sex intake.

A degree of power was taken away from the teaching profession and local authorities (the providers of education) and the system was more centralised through the introduction of the national curriculum, standardised testing and Ofsted inspections. On the other hand, power was diffused down to consumers of education, particularly parents in the case of school children, through their greater involvement in choice of school, opportunity to vote for a school to be transferred to grant maintained status, and involvement on boards of school governors. However, an opening up of the selection process to parental choice arguably also enhanced a process of covert selection by social advantage whereby some parents with greater economic, social and cultural capital were more able to get the most for their children from the choices available.

So did new right reforms improve educational standards? There is clear evidence if one takes GCSE and A level grades as the benchmark that performances have improved year after year through to the early twenty first century. However, two important questions will be raised at present. Firstly, because the market test is set in terms of qualifications and grades, there are pressures to 'teach to tests'. Therefore, improvements in results may be gained by retreat to a narrowed experience of education by pupils. Secondly, improvement in grades may in part be a consequence of 'grade inflation' – the view that the standards by which grades can be achieved become watered down over time.

2. New Labour policy – no return to the social democratic model

When New Labour came to power in 1997, they were faced with an increasingly fluid globalised world market where inward investment needed to be attracted. It was argued that to successfully compete in this global market, the state had a key role to play in providing the infrastructure and skilled workforce that was necessary to attract business investment. A 'magnet economy' had to be created in which, through the expansion of education and training, businesses would be prepared to invest and offer high wages to highly skilled workers. In effect, forces of globalisation were encouraging a more instrumentalist educational culture by which could be detected an increased emphasis on education taking the form of training for vocational utility.

In many respects, Labour followed the neo-liberal reforms of the new right era. They were as determined as the Conservatives had been to promote diversity and competition within education and to impose a demanding inspection regime, all to promote high educational standards. In fact, the passage of their reforms sometimes relied on Conservative support in Parliament. Although admissions within the state secondary system became largely non-selective, in contrast to the policy of previous Labour regimes the government did not actively promoted the abolition of the remaining grammar schools but left decisions to local democratic processes. Whilst grant maintained schools reverted back to local authority funding, with most becoming foundation schools, their governing boards retained a high level of decision making autonomy from local authorities. City technology colleges that were established by the new right joined the ranks of city academies, set up by New Labour to improve educational performance in deprived and underachieving inner city areas by replacing comprehensives. City academies were run as self-governing trusts, which were partly supported by private funding and expertise. Specialist schools, allowed to select up to 10% of their pupils in terms of their specialist ability, were set up with such varied emphases as sports, modern languages, technology and the arts. Comprehensives, once favoured by Labour, were encouraged to become specialist schools and the formation of new faith schools had government support.

The Labour government required all new schools to operate as self-governing trusts, organisations partly supported by charitable foundation partners and run by their own boards of governors. In the long run, all state secondary schools were expected to become either specialist schools or academy trusts. Overall, local diversity and autonomy, market competition, parental choice, and the driving up of standards, measured by examination performance, remained central features of government policy on education.

New Labour even took the use of private finance within the state education system further than the Conservative new right had. Private finance was used to help re-equip schools with the latest technology and even provide capital for building new schools. In the case of the latter, the taxpaying electorate was saved the burden of the up-front payment for the provision, but interest rates were to be paid by the government over a contracted period of time.

Other reforms held more social democratic credentials. Pre-school and nursery provision were substantially expanded, Education Action Zones were established to inject more funding from government and private enterprise into inner city areas of deprivation and poor educational performance, and financial support of up to £30 a week for students from poorer backgrounds and aged 16 to 19 was introduced through the Education Maintenance Allowance. Also, resources from the winding up of the Assisted Places Scheme were redirected toward reducing the size of primary school classes.

Two issues will be raised at this point. Firstly, Brown and Lauder (1996, in Ball ed. 2004) have suggested that New Labour's broad economic approach places too much faith in the superior magnetic attraction of the home economy to achieve inward investment. It is argued that other countries within a competitive global environment, some with lower labour costs, will be pursuing similar policies and will likewise be developing their infrastructure and human resources to attract inward investment. Thus, whilst the government may be able to enhance people's employability through enhanced education and training, it may not be within their control to deliver full employment of the educated and trained.

Secondly, although examination performance continued to improve under Labour's watch, there were far less impressive findings in terms of social justice. Commenting on a 2006 Organisation for Economic Co-operation and Development survey which looked at literacy and numeracy skills in 29 member countries, Green and Unwin found that in England the impact of social background on educational performance was the fifth most severe (Chitty, 2009, p.250). Chitty went on to comment that 'for all of the political rhetoric about raising educational standards and furthering opportunity, English schools do more to lock in intergenerational inequality than to promote social mobility' (Chitty, 2009, P.250).

3. Coalition policy – adding to diversity

Since the election of a coalition government headed by the Conservatives in 2010, the market competition approach to education has very much remained in place. The government has strongly pushed toward more schools becoming academies, with the assumption that most new schools will be of this type. However, in distinction to the emphasis under New Labour of using academies to improve educational performance in deprived and underperforming areas, it is now schools that have achieved outstanding performance that can be fast tracked to academy status and in some cases schools have been forced to make the transition.

To further the mix of schools, a new type has been introduced in the form of 'free schools'. Like academies, these schools are run independently of local authorities and are intended to strongly reflect local needs. Free schools can be set up by parents, community groups, charities or teachers. Through the utilisation of buildings that can be converted to schools, these schools have provided a cost saving advantage on building at a time of budget cuts. As in the case of academies, free schools do not necessarily need to employ fully qualified teachers or heads, they are not required to abide by national terms of pay and conditions of employment, they allow greater freedom of teaching styles and curriculum and do not have to adhere to nutritional standards guidelines in the provision of meals.

There have been some high profile cases of free schools failing to reach acceptable standards, linked to inadequate teaching and leadership, even leading to cases of closure. As some free schools are faith schools, they have also been criticised as promoting segregation. In some cases, schools have failed Ofsted inspections following claims that Islamification has led to a narrowing of the syllabus and differentiation in the teaching of boys and girls according to Islamic strictures. Furthermore, some have been established in areas where there already exists a surplus of local authority school places, with many of these schools already performing at good to outstanding levels. A strong case can therefore be made that in such areas available resources are being wasted.

Overall, the government's preference for academies and free schools has been criticised for eroding national terms and conditions of employment and pay levels, further fragmenting the educational 'system' in England, and its propensity for segregating children along religious and social class lines.

The Education Maintenance Allowance introduced by Labour to support students from poorer backgrounds has been replaced by a more restricted and tightly targeted fund. However, the introduction of the Pupil Premium has retargeted funds to schools dependent on the numbers of pupils that claim free school meals.

In higher education, tuition fees that universities can charge have had their ceiling raised to £9,000. Although overall this does not appear to have had a detrimental effect on higher education applications from students of poorer backgrounds, there is evidence that they are tending to choose institutions closer to home and with lower fees. This may include enrolling on HE vocational courses provided at local FE institutions.

Contemporary developments in education:

1. An emphasis on examination performance:

Grade inflation?

Educational performance is conventionally viewed as synonymous with achievement grades and certificates. This allows ease of statistical measurement of performance across the student population and the establishment of trends of change. In a more personalised way, examination performance is annually symbolised in the media by students receiving their (usually high grade!) results.

Such statistics provide the appearance of factual data on achievement levels that positivist minded sociologists might prefer to work with. However, there are various reasons why caution is necessary in the use of such statistics. Firstly, one needs to be aware of the different baselines from which measurements are taken. These can lead to slightly different conclusions. For example, if we were considering performance at GCSE level, some statistics will be in the form of the percentage of students who have achieved grade C or above in at least five subjects, whereas an alternative measurement may simply relate to the proportion of grade Cs and above in relation to the total number of subjects sat. Other measurements may focus on the proportion of A and A* grades achieved. Data may or may not include other equivalent level qualifications. Even with awareness of factors such as these, it is important to establish whether the statistics refer to just England or the UK. In the latter case, figures for Northern Ireland and Wales would be included but it would need to be clear whether or not figures for Scottish equivalent qualifications were. Moreover, the most up to date information that is provided after results are released is usually provisional and may require revision in the future due to the outcome of appeals.

A second area of difficulty arises around the issue of the continuity of standards or otherwise over time and the difficulty of making realistic performance comparisons when subjects are 'toughened up' or the qualification or grading system changes.

Let us first look at some statistics at face value to see what they suggest. One of the most remarkable trends has been the opening up of a gender gap in GCSE and A level as the attainment of girls improved more rapidly than that of boys. Since the replacement of the GCE with the GCSE qualification in 1988, the performance of girls had moved ahead of boys in each year up to 2002 with the exception of 2001. As a result, the overall GCSE United Kingdom (excluding Scotland) figures for August 2002 showed that 62.4% of girls' entries achieved a grade C or above compared to 53.4% for boys. 5.9% of girls' entries achieved an A* grade compared to 4.1% for boys. Likewise, at A level, girls were consistently outperforming boys in overall pass rates. What changed was an overhauling of the achievement of boys at the level of A grade passes. During the early 1990s, boys slightly outperformed girls in the achievement of top grades. However, in August 2002, 21.9% of girls' entries achieved an A grade pass compared to 19.3% of boys'. This represented a threefold increase in their lead compared with 2001 figures.

On a subject by subject basis, girls during this period extended their lead in performance in those areas where they have more traditionally outperformed boys (in the arts and humanities) and were increasing their participation and often moving ahead of boys in most of the traditional male subject areas (in science subjects). The latter advance was arguably assisted by the impact of the national curriculum, which required all students to study sciences, and the use of less gender biased texts.

In the light of the above figures, attention was focussed on the problem of relative male underachievement which has been usually explained in terms of laddish culture and behaviour, especially amongst those from poorer backgrounds. On the other hand, it has been suggested that a greater proportion of coursework assessment has favoured females who tend to be more methodical in their application to their studies and better in the presentation of their work.

The performance figures for girls and boys for 2006 and 2007 indicated that the gap opened up by girls over boys was closing. Thus, at GCSE level in 2006, the achievement gap in A* and A grades narrowed compared to 2005 by 0.5%, but still remained at 7.7%. This gap narrowed by a further 0.2% by 2007 and the A* to C grade performance gap narrowed by 0.6% between 2006 and 2007. At A level, between 2005 and 2007, boys closed the gap on girls slightly in the achievement of A-E passes, but between 2005 and 2006, girls had increased their lead over boys in achieving A grade passes.

One explanation for this brief reversal of the previous trend is that a number of schools had selected more adventure and action based texts for study which boys tended to find more appealing – an interesting reversal of past feminist crusades to make texts more female friendly at a time before the opening of the gender gap in favour of girls.

However, provisional data for 2013 shows that at GCSE A* and A grades, in aggregate grades girls still excelled over boys by 7.2% and within the range of A* to C grade passes their performance was superior by 8.6%. Interestingly, there has also remained a very pronounced gendered pattern of subject preference. For example, at A level contemporary data shows that boys comprise 80% of physics and over 60% of maths entries, as well as significant majorities in economics and computing, whereas girls strongly outnumber boys in pursuing English, psychology, biology and art.

The performance of ethnic minority pupils has generally improved more rapidly than that of white students. This has sometimes been from a relatively low base of achievement. For example, in GCSE grades A*-C, the performance of black Caribbean students improved by approximately 6% over the two years leading up to 2006 to reach 41.7% and black Africans by 5% to 48.3%. At the higher end, the figure for Chinese students improved in the year up to 2006 by 6.8% to reach 74.2%.

When figures are broken down in terms of ethnicity, gender, and living in poverty, the poorest performers appear to be white boys from poor backgrounds. Research conducted by Cassen and Kingdom (2007) for the Joseph Rowntree Foundation found that 62% of white boys who take free school meals appear in the bottom 10% of performers in education (18/6/2014, p.14), a figure far higher than for equally poor Afro-Carribeans. The research identified an anti-education culture amongst classmates and at home a poor learning environment and limited language communication as part of the problem.

Certain ethnic minority groups have achieved superior performance to that of whites for some time, and most other groups are at least closing the performance gap. The fact that achievement at GCSE level is compared at the age of 16 may generally underestimate the performance of ethnic minority groups whose children are more likely to stay on until 17, sometimes to retake their exams. They also have a comparatively high likelihood of entering higher education, although to date are conspicuously thin on the ground in the most elite universities.

Regarding the performance of ethnic minority groups, the Statistical First Release figures for England use a slightly different measurement in terms of achieving at least 5 GCESs at C and above, including within the definition English and maths or International GCSEs. By this measure, Chinese pupils still performed the best, exceeding the national average by 17.6% in 2012, (20/11/2013) but given their very high performances in previous years, their lead over the national average had decreased by 4.1% compared to that of 2008. Other notable points were that the performance of Indian pupils was not far behind that of the Chinese and that Banglsadeshi pupils had improved their performance to such an extent that they had risen from below the national average in 2008 to above it in 2012. Afro Caribbean performance has improved between these dates, but has remained the lowest of the ethnic minorities. Data on traveller communities shows extremely low performance and only slight improvement.

The overall performance figures for 2002 indicated an improvement on those of the previous year. At GCSE level, A-C passes increased from 57.1% to 59.9% and A-G level grades reached 97.1%. Additionally, the number of students fast tracking to take GCSE exams at the age of 15 or under was more than double that of the previous year. A level passes (grades A-E) showed the largest annual increase, climbing from 89.8% to 94.3% of all entries.

The general trend in examination performance remained an upward one. By 2006, A-C grade passes at GCSE reached 62.4% of all entries and the number of A* and A grades increased by 0.7% on the previous year's figure to 19.1%. The figures for 2007 had further improved to 63.3% and 19.5% respectively, whilst the proportion of fast tracked students (fifteen year olds or under) had reached 14% of all entries. The 2006 A level figures for A-E grade passes reached 96.6%, and A grades achieved improved by 1.3% on the figure for the previous year to reach 24.1%. By 2007, A-E passes improved further to 96.9% and the proportion of A grades awarded increased by a further 1.2% to reach 25.3%. By comparison, the A grade figure for independent schools rose from 41.3% of entries in 2002 to 47.9% in 2006 and remained almost unchanged at 47.8% in 2007.

What are we to make of this data which on the surface indicates a continuous improvement in standards from the 1980s through to the early twenty first century? Much debate has emerged over the question of standards and the problem is that approaching this issue is difficult to reduce to a purely technical matter. It is quite possible that enhanced competition within the system has improved the focus and effort put in by both teachers and students. It is also possible that given their concern about league table placing, schools have become more cautious in their selection of pupils for exam entry. Additionally, the introduction of AS levels has enhanced the process of filtering through self-selection. By taking AS levels after one year, students are able to make decisions on which subjects they will drop and which they will continue to study through to A level. The fact that the largest annual increase in A level performance has coincided with a 6% drop in entrants following the introduction of AS levels appears to offer confirmation of these effects of self-selection.

An opposing argument is essentially that the improving statistics can only come from an erosion of qualification standards. Those who adopt this view tend to maintain that innate ability follows a standard distribution curve for the population as a whole and does not significantly advance over time. This position often lies behind the criticisms of those who identify with the political right. It is argued that the evidence suggesting annual improvements in success bears little relationship to real improvements in performance or overall levels of intelligence and can only be achieved through the erosion of standards. Ruth Lea, of the Institute of Directors, has used the term 'grade inflation' – the watering down of performance required to achieve higher grades and give a statistically misleading suggestion of improvement - to express this position.

But how might this happen? Ironically, the finger of blame is usually pointed at competition. Whilst schools have to compete for league table places, exam boards are also in competition for exam entries. In this toxic mix, schools search for 'softer' exam boards that they think will maximise their success rates and exam boards compete to oblige.

In reality, however, it is quite possible that both grade inflation is taking place and student performance is improving.

During and since the summer of 2003, a number of universities expressed concern regarding problems of differentiating student performance. As more students were passing A levels with top grades, concern was raised over the growing difficulty of using these grades to separate out the most able students. Students themselves were increasingly finding that top grades were no guarantee of gaining access to popular and competitive courses and the most prestigious universities. As a consequence, more universities started to set their own entrance exams and looked to alternatives to A levels which would better differentiate levels of student ability and performance.

Within schools, one response was an increasing uptake of the more demanding Advanced Extension Award which replaced special level papers from 2002. This exam, aimed at the top 10% of A level students, required the demonstration of a deeper level of subject understanding. Universities occasionally made the Advanced Extension Award part of an offer. The government also became involved in piloting a toughening of A level questions with the aim of introducing more challenging A levels from September 2008. The changes introduced included a movement away from structured exam questions and the requirement of more extended answers, as well as an A* grade for those who achieve 90% or above in their final exams. In measuring differentiation at the top end of achievement, the introduction of the A* grade from 2010 led to the virtual withdrawal of the Advanced Extension Award.

A further development has been an increasing take up in schools of the International Baccalaureate Diploma which combines core and optional elements into a broad education. This offers highly differentiated outcomes ranging from certificates in individual subjects for those who do not pass the diploma overall to a top end of achievement equivalent in UCAS points to that of six grade A A levels. A leading examining board also piloted a baccalaureate type qualification which added to three A levels a paper in general studies, critical thinking or citizenship and a piece of extended essay or project work.

An enhanced measure of GCSE performance and preferable foundation in choice of subjects for progression on to A levels and university was proposed by the Russell Group of top universities. This would constitute achievement in terms of an English Baccalaureate combination of GCSE subjects (the EBacc, not to be confused with the later ill-fated English Baccalaureate Certificate, the EBC, that was to replace GCSEs). From 2010, this more demanding measure of success comprised grade C performance or above in a core of the following subjects: English language, mathematics, history or geography, two science subjects and a modern language. Data for 2010 showed that significantly fewer students eligible for free school meals took the Baccalaureate combination than those not eligible (8% as opposed to 24%) and of those entered, a smaller proportion were successful (4% as opposed to 17%).

Grade deflation?

Some attempts were being made, then, under the New Labour government to provide more challenging measures of achievement. A greater proportion of more able students were also hot housed to enter GCSE exams before the age of 16. Following the general election of 2010, a coalition government was formed with the Conservatives as the senior partner. Michael Gove, as Secretary of State for Education, clearly took on board the message of the grade inflation camp. His aspiration to return more fully to traditional 'O' level type exams was blocked by Liberal Democrat coalition partners. Gove conceded that his intention to replace GCSEs with an English Baccalaureate Certificate (EBC) was a step too far, at least in the time span envisaged, but already more students were choosing subjects which led to English Baccalaureate GCSEs and which included less internal assessment and a greater emphasis on final exams. The proportion of students choosing these subjects increased from 22% in 2010 to 48% in 2012. This has reversed a decline in the number of students studying history, geography and modern languages at GCSE level.

Against the backdrop of a climate of scepticism regarding the academic value of GCSE and A level qualifications, various changes introduced or planned to toughen up standards include the following:

In terms of curriculum and learning, a more facts based approach to reciting 'correct' information is being adopted. Opponents have criticised this change as narrowing the experience of education toward that of memory recall at the expense of considering alternative viewpoints and encouraging critical thinking.

There has been a substantial increase between 2012 and 2013 in the entry of under 16s (by 39%) for GCSE exams and a smaller (9%) increase of post 16 entries, both groups of which perform significantly more poorly than 16 year olds at grades C and above and the highest grades.

Following the highly publicised shifting of the grade boundaries in English Language between January and June 2012, with the outcome of increasing the difficulty of passing at grade C, there was a significant increase in multiple exam entries for the same subject, for example GCSE English and International GCSE English as schools attempted to protect their position in league tables. This practice has not been confined to the subject of English.

Science GCSE subjects were toughened up between 2012 and 2013. This led to a collapse in entry, with fewer than half the number of 16 year olds that entered in 2012 put in in 2013. C and above grades for 16 year olds fell in all of the sciences (but not in mathematics), the greatest fall coming in science from 64.7% to 47.9%, whilst in physics, chemistry and biology the increase in the numbers of under 16s performing more poorly than 16 year olds in was between two and threefold.

It is planned that GCSEs will be reoriented away from coursework assessment and toward assessment of performance in final exams. One anticipated consequence of this is the likelihood of a narrowing of the achievement gap between boys and girls.

A further change is planned for the GCSE grading system, to be operative from 2016. This is to extend the number of grading categories to nine, with grade nine being the highest achievement level and one being the lowest, with the purpose of increasing the achievement stretch. A grade nine will be twice as difficult to achieve as the current A* grade.

The changes referred to above have at present put into reveres of decades of improved performance data at GCSE level. Provisional data published by the Joint Council for Qualifications (28/11/2013) indicates that, in terms of all entries for GCSEs, for 2013 there has been a drop in achievement across the United Kingdom (England, Wales and Northern Ireland) of C and above grades from 69.4% to 68.1% and A and A* grades from 22.4% to 21.3% compared to 2012. Further, the 2012 results for A and A* grades were down on those of 2011.

Other aspects of the school environment that can affect performance are the effect of cautiously made decisions on early streaming which can ultimately lead to restriction to lower tiered entry at GCSE in certain subjects.

The standard measure of deprivation that is frequently used in educational studies is that of eligibility for free school meals. By this measure, the performance gap with reference to achieving at least 5 GCSEs at C or above had narrowed from 26.7% in 2008 to 16.5% in 2012. However, the definition of this category had been broadened from 2012. Previously, it comprised those pupils who were eligible for free school meals in the spring census. In 2012, the measure was changed to include all pupils who had been eligible for free school meals at any time during the previous six years. One would expect, given the difference in performance between those eligible for free school meals and those that are not, that broadening the category may by itself have reduced the measured difference between these groups. Nonetheless, the performance gap has consistently narrowed in the years before the classification change.

Of pupils classified as having special educational needs, the poorest performing group were those having behavioural, emotional and social difficulties whilst those with visual impairment were amongst the highest performing groups, nevertheless performing substantially below the national average.

Provisional data on A level results for the United Kingdom for 2013 supplied by the Joint Council for Qualifications (28/11/2014) shows that 7.6% of all entries achieved A*, 26.3% A* or A, and 98.1% a pass. Compared to grades in previous years, the overall pass figure is up by 0.1% on the figure for 2012 and continues a long term upward trend stretching back over three decades. However, the figures for the two A grade categories showed a second year of decline, the respective figures being 27% in 2011, 26.6% for 2012 and 26.3% in 2013.

Broken down by gender, girls performed better than boys in the A* and A categories (26.7% as opposed to 25.9%), but compared to the previous year the gap was closing as male performance was only down by 0.1%, whereas that of females declined by 0.5%. Girls used to outperform boys at A* level, but for the last 2 years, boys have outperformed girls, the figures for 2013 being 7.9% and 7.4% respectively. When broken down into subjects, boys' A* performance is most ahead in maths, with a 3.3% lead over girls. However, girls' performance is ahead of boys in English.

Regarding changes in subject choices, the influence of the GCSE English Baccalaureate as an indication of university subject preferences appears to have filtered through to A level to increase student take up in mathematics, the sciences and geography, but not in languages which tended to be down on the previous year. As with GCSE, the best A level performance was in Northern Ireland, where, for example, 30.7% of students achieved A* and A grades.

We have seen that the coalition government bought into the argument that grade inflation has watered down educational standards and has responded with attempts to toughen up on the criteria for achievement. However, an alternative interpretation to this toughening up has been proposed by Allen (19/6/2014). This questions whether globalisation has brought about the highly skilled and paid jobs that were expected, suggesting instead that relatively low skilled, low paid and casualised work has been created. Employment opportunities for the young have been particularly hard hit and opportunities for social mobility have gone into decline. As a result, particularly with the expansion of higher education, very many youngsters find themselves overqualified for the work that is available or unemployed. From this vantage point, the toughening up on educational standards, ostensibly for the purpose of tackling grade inflation, can be interpreted as an attempt to limit aspirations and levels of educational achievement in order to establish a new correspondence between education and limited employment opportunities.

2. Types of illiteracy

There may be marked generational differences regarding definitions of literacy. As new generations are brought up amidst new technology and introduced to relevant technological skills from a young age at school, they are often far more familiar and comfortable with using technology both at school and in their everyday lives that older generations. The latter would appear to them to be technologically quite illiterate; a type of 'new illiteracy'.

On the other hand, older generations may view youngsters as linguistically illiterate in the in the use of abbreviated forms of expression which accompany the use of new technology, for example in the form of commonly acceptable standards of communication by e mail.

3. The expansion of higher education

Higher education in Britain has witnessed massive expansion in terms of student numbers since the early 1960s. For example, during 1962-3, approximately 216,000 students were in full-time higher education. By 1997-8, the figure had risen to approximately 1,200,000, with 34% of all 18 to 19 year olds entering higher education. The percentage has continued to rise slightly since, with 36% of 18 year olds going on to full-time higher education in 2000. However, different rates of access for those of different social class background have remained remarkably entrenched. In 1991-1992, when 23% of 18 to 19 year olds were entering full-time higher education, 55% from professional background gained access whilst from unskilled manual background only 6% went on to higher education. By 2001-2002, these figures had risen to 79% and 15% respectively. Yet when one looks at entry in terms of gender, there has been a massive increase in female participation to the point where females are now entering higher education in significantly higher numbers than males.

The pressures of global economic competition have been a key driving force in the expansion of higher education, a phenomena which is particularly evident in most rapidly developing countries. The expansion of student numbers and the provision of new technology places a massive increase in the cost of the provision of education. However, as capital investment becomes more globally mobile, there is pressure for governments to reduce the taxation of corporations as they are likely to favour low tax economies and countries compete for inward investment. For example, the British government plans to reduce corporation tax by a further 1% in the tax year of 2015. This would result in a 20% rate compared to the 28% that was in place when it came to office, now joint lowest amongst G20 economies.

Student finance has changed to accommodate increased participation. Up to the mid 1990s, students in higher education were supported by local authority grants. These grants were means tested in that parental income was taken into account. Students whose parents were on modest incomes would receive the full grant, whereas those whose parents earned higher salaries would have their grants reduced by an assessed amount of parental contribution. Higher education fees were also paid by local authorities. By the late 1990s, grants had been phased out and replaced by low interest loans and charges for fees were introduced. The latter initially were paid up front, but repayment has since been deferred until a certain level of income is obtained through employment.

From the start of the 2006 academic year, top up fees were introduced. This allowed universities to increase fees from the old flat rate of £1,100 per year up to £3,000 per year. Most universities imposed the full increase. At the time it looked as if the cost may have had a detrimental effect since the number of students enrolled fell by 3.6% compared to 2005. However, closer scrutiny suggests that the decreased numbers for 2006 followed a surge in entry in 2005 as many students who would have otherwise taken a gap year, knowing of the proposed future fee increase, went straight to university to avoid paying the higher fees which a delay would incur. This interpretation is born out by the 6.4% increase in applicants to British universities for 2007. Of these applicants, 221,523 were female and 173,784 were male. Unsurprisingly, subjects which attracted the greatest increase in applicants at this time were vocational subjects such as business and administration (a 25% increase) which offer the prospects of a quicker clearing of student debt. Such financial pressures have therefore encouraged students to choose courses most obviously linked to the economic function of education.

From September 2012, the government raised the fee ceiling to £9,000. Early evidence suggests that applications to British universities by British students have significantly dropped since 2012, perhaps by over 10%, arguably due to the combined effect of the substantial fee increases and the deep and protracted recession.

Despite this recent dip in higher education applications and a degree of downward pressure on A level and GCSE grades, it remains the case that given the level of qualifications being achieved at all levels of the education system, their value in the labour market swamped with qualifications has tended to decline and more or higher level qualifications are required for particular jobs. This phenomena is referred to by the term 'credential inflation' and means that individuals are under pressure to obtain more qualifications to just stand still in the labour market. At the same time, to pay for this expansion in provision, a higher level of burden is passed from governments, keen to limit public expenditure, down to individuals and families.

4. Meritocracy – advance or retreat?

The concept 'meritocracy' has been previously introduced and refers to a society in which achievement is based on individual effort and ability alone. As well as being central to the debate between major theoretical perspectives, this is a term which has been applied positively by politicians to our educational system. As an exercise in sociological thinking, we should now be able to apply this concept systematically to scrutinise educational opportunity. The following points would appear to be salient:

1) In terms of educational achievement at GCSE and A level, entry to higher education and success in higher grade degree passes, it would appear that there have been significant advances toward a more meritocratic educational system for females. However, there is more doubt, as can be seen in the chapter on social stratification, about the extent to which this translates sufficiently into equal opportunity with males for occupational success.

2) Regarding the enhancement of market forces in the school system, a key issue is that of social class differences in utilising the system. In an increasingly diverse system, there is strong evidence suggesting that

middle class parents understand it better, know how to get the best from it, and are better able to prepare their children for success, for example through paying for private tutors. Working class parents are more likely to accept sending their children to a local school which may include poorly performing schools in run down areas. Therefore, if parents are given greater choice in the schools attended by their children, this would appear to enhance class related differences in children's educational opportunity and suggest a retreat from meritocracy as family background life chances play a greater role in educational access again. This is not necessarily a reflection of more negative attitudes toward education by working class parents, but rather supports the argument of Phillip Brown that marketization spells a retreat from meritocracy (selection in terms of how the child is able to perform) to that of 'parentocracy' (selection in terms of what the parent is able to do to assist the child).

3) The massive expansion of higher education may at first glance appear to further meritocracy within education as more people are offered the opportunity to pursue their studies. However, increasing access may not advance meritocracy when to do so a new funding system has had to be introduced in the form of the replacement of student grants with loans, coupled with substantial increases in the level of fees. The loan system introduces financial hardships and pressures which are unlikely to be experienced uniformly across the social classes. Those of working class background who are considering entering higher education may be faced with a painful costs / benefits analysis in which the calculation of future debt can be of overriding importance and off-putting. Of those who enter higher education, the greater financial pressure that some students are likely to be under and the consequent temptation to combine paid work with study is likely to undermine a more level playing field of academic achievement.

Research conducted in 2005 by the Higher Education Funding Council for England appears to bear out these concerns. It was found that students from poor and ethnic minority backgrounds were under greater pressure to work during term time. Figures showed that about 30% of these students worked for twenty hours a week or more. Many felt under pressure to skip lectures and give in poor work. Evidence indicated that students who devoted fifteen hours a week or more to work had only a 62% chance of achieving a first class or upper second class honours degree compared to those who were able to devote their time fully to their studies. Furthermore, there was evidence that students of working class background who completed their studies were likely to end up with bigger debts. It could therefore be argued that although the grant based system could only support a smaller HE intake, and in that sense was more elitist, it operated more meritocratically in that it enabled a more level playing field of academic competition.

Furthermore, the higher education sector is not an undifferentiated one. The higher status universities tend to charge fees at the top level. At the end of the day, given the academic, financial and cultural barriers of entry to elite universities for those of working class background, it is hardly surprising that even if they enter higher education it is more likely to be at a lower status university closer to home and charging lower fees or even a vocational HE course run at a local FE institution.

4) Part of educational diversity has been the retention of the independent sector. At the pinnacle of this sector reside the prestigious public schools, entry to which is essentially based on social connections and parental ability to pay high fees. These schools offer enhanced access to elite universities and the exclusive higher echelons of the top professions. Whilst politicians of the major political parties have been keen to refer positively to meritocracy, they usually prefer to remain silent on this vestige of privilege which flies in the face of meritocracy. It may be suspected that this omission is an attempt to discourage the layman from engaging in joined up thinking in this area. By contrast, sociology encourages us to think systematically and follow where logic leads us when applying such concepts to our educational system. In so doing, assertions by politicians about meritocracy in education may turn out to look superficial and unconvincing.

Contemporary sociological perspectives on education:

Postmodernism – the liberating potential of education

According to postmodernists such as Lyotard, contemporary societies are entering a stage which is very different from past traditional and modern societies. A hallmark of traditional or pre-modern society was the predominance of religious dogma and superstition. Religion provided an all embracing metanarrative which claimed to provide a single truth and education reflected this. However, during the eighteenth century, Enlightenment thinking, in the form of scientific and rational criticism, undermined religious dogma and promised the realisation of intellectual liberty and human progress through applying rational thinking to social intervention. The development of modern education was the product of this Enlightenment optimism of the modern period.

Postmodernists argue that the promise of science has disappointed as modern society substituted one claim to a single truth, the metanarrative of religion, by another, the metanarrative of rational analysis and the methods of science. In terms of application, it has failed. Thus we have seen that education policy in the post-war era was aimed at engineering an educational system which improved social justice by opening up life chances and social mobility opportunities to those from less privileged backgrounds. However, we have also seen that 1) social class related differences in educational achievement remained quite obstinately entrenched and that 2), as explained in the social stratification chapter, the modest improvements in social mobility experienced by the time that children of the post-war generation entered the work place were more to do with changes in the occupational structure than rationally engineered educational reform.

Moreover, postmodernists claim that rational and scientific thinking itself became repressive by imposing its logic and methods on society and education as the only criteria of truth. It is also argued that compulsory attendance within educational institutions has been used to shape and control populations. For example, within the English state system central control has been enhanced through the introduction of the national curriculum and Ofsted inspections, and a strong emphasis has been placed on skill acquisition as opposed to other possible purposes of education. Postmodernists argue that with the emergence of contemporary postmodern conditions of social and cultural diversity, faith in a single and indispensable foundation for certain knowledge will collapse and along with it the modernist metanarrative.

For postmodernists, contemporary societies entering the postmodern era become increasingly pluralistic and comprise diverse cultural and consumer interests. Education must reflect this by moving away from belief in the absolute truth of science and rational thinking and the imposition of a standardised system. Education under postmodern conditions needs to become diverse in provision and relativistic, questioning the ascendancy of any single type of education and the idea of a single absolute truth. Rather than moulding, controlling and restricting individuals, education should be a diverse resource that can be utilised by people to cater for their disparate and changing needs. Whether pursued for purposes of lifestyle image, general interest, personal fulfilment or the acquisition of work skills, there should be no single standard against which any of these purposes can be deemed universally superior.

For proponents Usher and Edwards, postmodernism challenges the favoured status to work related skills and the emphasis placed by governments that education should be organised primarily along such lines. Contemporary educational provision needs to be part of a society of growing variety of choice and lifestyle as it becomes increasingly utilised by individuals who - as in the case of other products they consume – may use it to seek status and convey an image. There is nothing intrinsically superior in formal classroom teaching and learning in which the teacher is the lecturer and fount of all knowledge. Instead, the teacher should be the guider and facilitator of student learning in which, assisted by advanced technology, a broader range of approaches and settings are becoming available. For postmodernists, only by such varied and flexible provision and a relativistic view of knowledge itself can education become truly liberating.

High modernism – education for adaptation

One of the leading high modernist theorists is Anthony Giddens. For Giddens, rational thinking associated with the Enlightenment is viewed in a more positive way than by postmodernists. The high modernist view is that in contemporary society science and rational thinking can still demonstrate superiority over other forms of knowledge. It is still the basis for understanding society and guiding progress, albeit under more challenging conditions of social complexity, globalisation and rapid technological change.

High modernists view education in the context of rapidly changing high tech knowledge economies. In this context, constant updating of work skills is a vital element of education as societies compete to attract inward investment in a global competitive market. Governments need to play an active role in encouraging individuals to update their skills through retraining. Individuals cannot expect to complete their education at a fixed point in life but must be prepared to engage in lifelong learning.

Britain's New Labour government tended to follow this line in promoting a more flexible culture of education in globally competitive conditions. People have been encouraged to embrace advances in technology and constantly update their work skills, benefiting both themselves and the economy. New computer technology has both required the mastery of new skills and enabled learning to occur in a diversity of settings, including people's own homes through an expansion of distance learning made possible by the internet, and the development of outreach centres.

These challenges both offer opportunities and introduce strains and burdens into people's lives as they struggle to respond to a rapidly changing world and risk getting left behind. In addition to preparing for work related skills, a key purpose of education must be to equip members of society with the skills to adopt a reflexive approach to life, a requirement against which the recent coalition government emphasis on a return to factual learning seems to be somewhat at odds.

7 // Power and Politics

Abstract

There are various levels at which it is possible to view politics. One, often adopted by the general public, is that which focuses on political parties, governments and elections. Sociologically, this is a relatively restricted view. In this chapter, the reader is encouraged to adopt a broader and more systematic approach to politics. This will be based on tracing the workings of power in social relationships. Definitions of power and other central concepts in the sociology of politics are introduced to assist the reader in that analysis.

A range of established sociological perspectives on power and politics, particularly with regard to representative democracies, are reviewed. These comprise functionalism, Marxism, the approach of Weber, elite theory and pluralism. Each of these theories apply sociological definitions of power systematically to social relationships. They offer differing analyses of the sources and distribution of power in liberal democracies, who holds power and to whose benefit it is used.

In a further section, a review is undertaken of a range of sociological perspectives on the scope and impact of the state in liberal democracies.

A more restricted outlook on politics is adopted in the sections on voting behaviour. However, the approach remains sociological in the sense that attempts to understand voting behaviour are related to social influences and broader social changes. The question of the decline in the influence of social class on voting behaviour and the consideration of alternative influences is of central importance in this section.

The study of politics in a more contemporary light requires an understanding of the ways in which globalisation is reshaping the political world. Some alternative interpretations of the effect of globalisation on the political landscape are considered. Foucault's approach to surveillance and political control is sketched and globalisation is related to postmodern and high modern approaches. These perspectives point to fundamental changes taking place in society and raise challenging questions for both a sociological understanding of contemporary politics and, regarding *high modernism, the guidance that sociology can give for the fashioning of political institutions appropriate for the current age.*

Reference is made to the emergence of new social movements and how they can be related to the influence of globalisation.

An attempt is made to draw connections between Giddens' approach to high modernism, his transformationist position on globalisation, and his advocacy of 'third way' politics which provided an underpinning for New Labour. To complete the chapter, a sketch of the reasoning behind the civic Conservatism of the senior partner in the post 2010 coalition government is provided.

The sociological challenge

At one level, politics can be seen to be about formal political party institutions and governments. This view focuses on the policies of political parties, general elections, Parliamentary processes and the policies and actions of government. Encouraged by certain sections of the mass media, our interest may also focus on the deeds of politicians in their professional capacities and private lives. Viewing politics at this level alone, our involvement is likely to be limited to participation in general elections when the aforementioned preoccupations become heightened.

Otherwise, we are often preoccupied with issues and problems of our immediate personal world. We may not consider these matters to be of a political nature and, as C. Wright Mills has maintained, we may tend to individualise problems rather than link them to broader public issues.

The study of politics in sociology requires us to break away from the vantage points identified above. In sociology, the study of politics is about the concentration, distribution and exercise of power at different levels within society, between societies and globally. Looked at sociologically, power, briefly defined, is to do with the capacity that some people have to exert their will over others. This concept of power can apply to any social situation. Following this view of power, a focus on political parties, the formal institutions of government, and political personalities, is too restricted and may hide more about politics than it reveals. Instead, a sociological view can reveal the power and therefore political nature of organised groups such as trade unions or the capital of employers. Power can be exerted through military or paramilitary means. Playground bullying can be viewed as political as can the use of patriarchal (male over female) power in a variety of contexts. Even the language that people use in everyday social encounters to negotiate with others and attempt to persuade them or impose their meanings and viewpoints can be seen as political.

The tendency to individualise the relationships and problems of our personal lives is likely to blind us to their connections to broader social and power structures. Intimate relationships can be regarded as political in terms of the above definition of politics, even if we often do not see them as such. Furthermore, we should be prepared to recognise that the political influences acting on even our most immediate social world do not necessarily stop even at the recognised borders of nations! Decisions made by people at great geographical distance from us to move investment and businesses between countries can affect people's employment opportunities, standards of living, capacity to take political action, quality of life and relationships within families. Migration can bring about a range of different relationships between ethnic groups and cultures within a society. The fact that political issues can be global in origin takes us into the area of global political responses in terms of transnational pressure groups such as Greenpeace and supra-national governmental organisations like the European Union.

The difficulty that we may face in trying to adopt a sociological view of politics can be in putting more conventional and limited preconceptions about its nature and scope to one side. We will need to understand the precise use of sociological concepts and how applying them systematically may open up new vantage points on the origin and distribution of power. In so doing, it will become apparent that politics surrounds our daily lives. We may even gain insights which suggest why it is convenient to certain others that our view of politics should remain restricted.

Definition of main concepts

Establishing a clear meaning and use of key concepts is a necessary platform for developing a sociological approach to politics. So how does sociology approach politics? Politics is to do with the use of **power**. Power can be defined as the capacity that individuals or groups have to exert their will over others in social encounters. The inclination or capacity for resistance will depend on other features of the power relationship. If power is exerted in the form of **coercion**, it is experienced as an oppressive force exerted, from the viewpoint of the oppressed, without effective justification. In such situations, those with power are likely to be opposed by the oppressed should opportunities arise. However, if those exerting power are able to justify their use of it to others, they are able to claim **authority**. As the exercise of authority is backed up by justification, it is likely to realise a degree of willing compliance form those over whom it is exerted. In this case, the use of power is recognised as **legitimate.**

The term **ideology** has more than one application. More conventionally in politics, ideology is related to the different value systems that distinguish the political parties. These value systems provide particular interpretations of the world and offer ideal images of beneficial directions of social change. Appealing as much to emotions as the intellect, party ideology is important to attract voter and activist identification to the cause.

But the concept of ideology is also used in sociology in a more all-embracing way. The justifications by which authority gains its legitimacy may take the form of ideology – a term used particularly in Marxist theory to refer to the systematic distortion of reality for the purpose of gaining the compliance of a subject class. From this perspective, ideology, dominant political institutions and economic forces may work in a complementary way to powerfully support ruling class power and project a view of the prevailing institutions of capitalism as natural. The term **hegemony** had been used to define this situation but also express the fact that the capacity for consciousness domination of the subject class will never be total whilst worker's direct experiences contradict the distorted image of social reality.

Nations of the world are bounded territories governed by **states.** Institutions of the state include the government, regulatory apparatus such as the civil service, the armed forces, the legal system, welfare and educational institutions and local authorities. We will later see that some theorists would define the state even more broadly than this. States hold **sovereign** power over national territories in their exclusive right to make and apply laws, guarantee citizens' rights and impose the rule of law. **Citizenship** denotes individual rights held by members of a society, but states hold a monopoly of the legitimate use of force within their territory and establish compliance through the courts, the police or the military.

In reality, contemporary societies have found it beneficial to relinquish some sovereignty to supra-state bodies such as the European Union for economic benefit, political allegiance and tackling a range of problems and risks which do not stop at national boundaries.

Legitimacy may not always be easily maintained. If the behaviour of authorities falls conspicuously short of the values and standards by which it is justified, as, for example, if political corruption becomes evident, the authority of those in power, or even the entire social and political system, may face a loss of legitimacy. This can prove to be a fertile ground for the spread of counter ideologies and opposition movements. Under such circumstances, a government may be faced with a breakdown of social order and resort to coercive methods in an attempt to retain control.

Societies involve conflicts of interest. How these conflicts are managed by government will vary with the type of political institutions. In **authoritarian** states, power is imposed oppressively to limit the rights and freedoms of the subject population. If elections take place, it is with the purpose of legitimising single party rule.

In **representative democracies**, the population in the form of the electorate can periodically choose its government from rival political parties. Whilst the precise nature of political institutions and electoral systems varies from society to society, success in the electoral process gives government a **mandate** to introduce policies deriving from the manifesto that it was elected on for a term of office without the need to regularly re-consult the electorate.

The matter of legitimacy is however not always straightforward in the real world. Governments in representative democracies legitimise their policies and actions through acquiring power by democratic means and as such hold authority. However, consider the situation whereby through popular vote a government came to power pledged to nationalise certain industries. Whilst it would derive legitimacy and authority to do so from the electorate, implementing nationalisation could be viewed as a coercive act by representatives of private industry and therefore non-legitimate. The problem here would be a conflict of legitimacy based on the will of the electorate as opposed to the legitimacy of the ownership of private enterprise.

The term **fully participatory democracy** is reserved for systems in which those whom any decisions will effect must be consulted and allowed their input into the decision making process. Although arguably an unworkable form of democracy in complex modern societies, examples of participatory democracy on a smaller scale include Israeli kibbutzim as originally constituted and workers co-operatives.

The use of power may not be as transparent as these introductory definitions suggest. Various **faces of power** have been identified by

Steven Lukes. At the most obvious level, a measure of power may simply be the ability some people have to impose decisions on others. However, power can include the capacity that some groups have to avoid the raising of certain issues in the first place, thus precluding political debate and decisions in these areas. Lack of debate over the privileges of public schools may be an example of the use of this type of power. Furthermore, power can even involve the capacity that some people have to persuade others to make or accept decisions which could otherwise be shown to be against their interests. The abandonment by many workers of trade unions in Britain during the 1980s could be seen as an example of the use of this face of power.

Founding sociological perspectives on power and politics:

Sociological theory applied to politics attempts to address a variety of complex problems. Classical perspectives offer differing analyses of the origin and distribution of power in society, how it can best be measured, who holds it, and how they use it. These perspectives differ over the extent to which social relations are viewed as essentially harmonious or rooted in conflict, what the basis of harmony or conflict is, where lines of conflict are likely to occur, and how fluid they are. They also attempt to address such fundamental questions as the relationship between people's position in the social structure and their political consciousness and political action.

Despite fundamental differences between the classical perspectives, a key feature which they have in common is the tendency to view societies as if they are bounded entities. It will later be shown that more contemporary approaches increasingly question the validity of this position and, in some cases, even the degree to which political awareness still exists.

Functionalism – representative democracy and the use of power in the collective interest

The founding social context of functionalism can be traced back to the aftermath of the French Revolution and the writings of Auguste Comte. Developed by Comte as a reaction to the social instabilities in France following the Revolution, functionalism has retained an emphasis on gradual change, social order, hierarchy and stability as being both the natural and desirable social condition. Societies are seen as like systems or organisms. Although tending to self-regulate toward equilibrium, they can experience rapid and disturbing changes. For Comte, the forces of change of the French Revolution were rapid and fundamental in sweeping aside the institutions of feudalism, but left disarray in their wake. A new social and political order needed to be established, and Comte argued that this could be assisted by rational social analysis.

Following in this tradition, Durkheim maintained that a key practical aim of scientific sociology should be to assist in the fashioning of new social institutions to replace those that had been swept away with feudalism, for the purpose of assisting modern democratic societies to adjust to a new state of social stability.

Talcott Parsons developed the functionalist perspective within the modern American context. For Parsons, modern industrial societies are viewed as complex and highly differentiated social structures. For their efficient operation, and in contrast to traditional societies, positions of command must be allocated in terms of individual ability and expertise rather than through birthright. Modern capitalist society should operate as a meritocracy and to synchronise with this reality the values of a meritocracy would provide the most appropriate basis for social consensus. To motivate individual competition, a highly differentiated reward structure of occupations is necessary. Against the background of individual aspiration and materialistic values, high on the list of shared social goals by which governments can be judged is the enhancement of material living standards.

The institutions of representative democracy allow judgement of government to be expressed by the populace in the form of an electorate. Access to universal suffrage and choice between competing political parties enables the population to grant power on trust to the government to mirror collective sentiments and pursue shared social goals. The winning party, legitimised through the electoral process to pursue common goals, will have to face future elections at which its performance will be again judged by the electorate. Their consent, if necessary, can be withdrawn and power transferred to an alternative political party whose programme better expresses the will of the electorate. This process ensures a relatively smooth transfer of power.

As a consensus theory, functionalism focuses on the power 'of' society – led by government – measured in terms of its capacity for achieving common goals. The power of society can therefore grow with technological development, improved efficiency and minimal social conflict. From this healthy social condition, it is argued that members of society generally will benefit.

Marxism – representative democracy hiding the power of the capitalist class

A weakness of functionalism is clearly its inability to explain persisting levels of conflict and instability in capitalist societies. Most other sociological perspectives, and particularly Marxism, pay more attention to divisions and conflicting interests within society. However, the works of Marx and Engels are so extensive that different emphases have been detected in different works and varied interpretations of the 'inevitability' of revolution and role of the state have been proposed by those who follow in the footsteps of Marx.

The basic Marxist position is that social relations are fundamentally shaped by economic class relations. For Marx, political power derives from ownership of economic resources – especially the means of production. Power is firmly located in the employment relationship between employer and employee and this is a social class relationship. Ultimately, political power is as concentrated or distributed as is the ownership of the means of production. Under capitalism, economic and political power is concentrated in the hands of a minority capitalist class whose wealth depends on the employment of workers. Marx viewed this relationship as one of class exploitation and conflict of interest.

However, productivity and the wealth it creates can only be fully effective if workers are industrious and compliant. Since conflict of class interests is built into the capitalist system, how can such compliance be brought about?

From a Marxist perspective, conflict of class interests is generated in the economic sphere. Marxists refer to this domain as the infrastructure. This conflict is managed by the dominant institutions and ideas of capitalist society, together referred to as the superstructure. The institutions are primarily those of state control. The key controlling institutions of the state, such as the legal system, the police and the military, can suppress resistance by coercive means if necessary. However, these institutions of control are vested in legitimacy and authority by appearing to represent the common good rather than, Marxists claim, primarily serving ruling class interests.

This takes the analysis on to another level of control. The willing compliance of the subject class can be most effectively furthered by the manipulation of the way that they see society, referred to by Marx as the promotion of false consciousness based on a distorted (ideological) view of reality. For Marx, religion and the political institutions and values of liberal democracies comprised a potent means of such control. Religion softens the pain of suffering by holding out an illusion of hope in the form of paradise in an afterlife to those who live a good life of compliant application. Liberal democracies claim to offer freedom of choice and the prospect of meaningful political change through the ballot box. Marxists have come to focus more on the controlling impact of education and the mass media, and some even the family. All of these institutions and the values that they enshrine are seen to play a political role in the broad sense of the term as defined earlier in this chapter – the capacity that some people (in this case a dominant social class) have to exert their will over others. Against this backdrop, the focus here will be on what Marxists view as the real political significance of the political institutions as more narrowly defined – political parties, general elections and the policies and actions of elected governments.

The political institutions of capitalist representative democracies convey an image of accountability of political leaders to an electorate. Government, and the political system itself, are legitimised through giving citizens access to an electoral system in which they are free to choose between rival political parties by casting their vote at elections.

From a Marxist perspective, such legitimacy is based upon illusion and serves the purpose of ideological control. The primary purpose of the political institutions of capitalist liberal democracies is to maintain the smooth working of the capitalist system. Reducing politics to the outcome of an aggregate of individual voting decisions for the transfer of power assists this process. Whichever party wins an election has to govern through the state apparatus and within the constraints of the capitalist system. Therefore, the appearance of significant choice between political parties turns out to be quite narrow when they enter government. For example, it could be argued that changes in policy when New Labour replaced the Conservatives as the party of government in Britain from 1997 were not great and that the replacement of a discredited government by a fresh government with a strong electoral mandate was beneficial to British capitalism.

As power in capitalist societies actually originates in ownership of the means of production, the view that it rests with democratically elected governments fosters the illusion that the electorate has significant political power in its capacity to change governments and provides the government with its necessary legitimacy in the eyes of the electorate. From a Marxist perspective, whatever debate and acrimony takes place within Parliament, it is essentially a talking shop which restricts the image of politics to that of elected government and through the appearance of representation emasculates more radical and direct political action. Despite the veneer of democratic choice, government is effectively little more than through a single party state, as whichever party governs will be more attuned to the power and interests of the 'hidden rulers' than that of the electorate.

For Marx, genuine democracy would need to be more fully participatory. This would require the diffusion of political power. However, as political power derives from economic power, its diffusion could only come from acquisition of the means of production into common ownership. As the capitalist class were unlikely to give up wealth and power without a struggle, meaningful democracy was only likely to be achieved through the revolutionary overthrow the capitalist class and the capitalist system.

There are, however, different Marxist interpretations regarding the degree to which revolution is inevitable. A straightforward economic determinist view emphasises that 1) economic polarisation between working and capitalist classes is built into capitalism and 2) this is exacerbated during periods of inevitable economic depression. These economic forces are likely to act as a trigger for the emergence of class consciousness and revolution. Here, revolution is the outcome of powerful social and economic forces with actors following the roles in an historical script.

Writing early in the twentieth century, Antonio Gramsci picked out a different emphasis from Marx's works. He argued that the state governed through the use of both coercive force and ideological control and referred to the complimentary dominance of economic and political institutions and ruling class values as hegemonic control. However, ruling class dominance can only gain sufficient compliance from the subject class if timely concessions are made to it. There is therefore room for political manoeuvre by the subject class. Furthermore, worker's direct experience often contradicted the picture given by the dominant ideology. Awareness of this contradiction offered an opening through which class consciousness could emerge, providing space for the actions of radical political parties, trade unions and intellectuals to foster class consciousness, challenge ruling class hegemony and engage workers in direct political action.

At the centre of the state apparatus in capitalist societies are senior politicians and civil servants, the upper echelons of the military, the legal profession and the established church. The exact relationship between the state and the capitalist class is open to some debate within Marxist theory. An instrumentalist interpretation, advocated by Ralph Miliband (1973), emphasises that the key positions of state are manned by a privileged group, at least in part comprising those directly representing powerful business interests, all of whom tend to share a common elite background and outlook. The views of a capitalist class prevail and capitalist interests predominate. Therefore, the state is effectively headed by a ruling class rather than an elite (for an alternative perspective, see the elite theory section).

An opposing Marxist interpretation is provided by the structuralist theorists Louis Althusser and Nicos Poulantzas (Poulantzas, in Blackburn ed. 1972). Here, in contrast to Milband's position, the social background and motives of state officials are of little importance. The structural position of the state imposes on officials service to the interests of capitalism, regardless of their social class background. A degree of autonomy between the ruling capitalist class and the governing political class is necessary for the more effective regulation of the system. This distancing allows the state to occasionally act against particular capitalist interests (for example through passing anti-monopoly legislation) or offer timely concessions to the working class (for example through welfare reforms) enhances its capacity to promote the long-term interests of the capitalist system. It can rise above any factionalism within the capitalist class which would be damaging if they directly governed. Furthermore, the appearance of the state as acting neutrally and for the benefit of all can be more effectively conveyed.

For all of its valuable insights into power and control in capitalist societies, the Marxist perspective, developed around the middle of the nineteenth century, has faced a number of fundamental challenges in recent decades. Firstly, when communist societies did emerge in the twentieth century, they took the form of repressive single party states, run by party elites, not the fully democratic societies that Marx predicted would eventually emerge. Secondly, the collapse of Eastern Bloc communist systems between 1989 –1991 has led to the virtual global spread of capitalism – a historical trend (outcome?) operating in reverse to Marx's predictions. Thirdly, within capitalist societies, economic class as the key configuration of political divisions has arguably evaporated rather than advanced. For example, in Britain although economic inequality has grown since the 1980s under both Conservative and New Labour governments, class consciousness appears to have declined and more fractured interest group politics advanced. Fourthly, it is a new challenge for Marxists to show how their perspective can be applied to a modern service and information economy as opposed to the industrial capitalism of Marx's day.

Weber – representative democracy versus bureaucracy

As explained in the social stratification chapter, for Weber social conflict is not essentially reducible to class conflict. Modern liberal democratic societies are arenas of conflict between status groups and interest groups as well as classes, all of which are likely to defend or attempt to enhance their power. In societies that are representative democracies, as in societies with other formal political systems, those who hold power usually attempt to retain it at the expense of others. To understand how power is legitimised to enable rulers to claim authority, Weber emphasised that legitimacy must be understood in the context of prevailing cultural values and belief systems. Weber developed 'ideal types' to assist this understanding. Ideal types are intellectual models which highlight the essential features of a society. Their purpose is to assist in the understanding of highly complex social phenomena and to classify different types of society. However, Weber's typology of authority types was not just a static classificatory system but part of a theory of social change. The essential types of authority that Weber identified were traditional, rational-legal and charismatic.

Traditional authority is prevalent in pre-industrial, particularly feudal societies, and societies earlier in history. In feudal societies, life is largely tied to agriculture and the routines of the seasons. It is lived out in small communities which comprise well established hierarchies with people experiencing little geographical or social mobility. Religion and custom prevail in people's thinking and actions. Tradition – the justification of present ways through reference to things having always been that way – tends to be accepted in its own right. In such a society, leadership is a privilege of inheritance. Obedience to one's 'social betters' is often justified by recourse to such ideas as superior social breeding – the notion that demonstration of a family lineage of leadership denotes the inheritance of leadership qualities. The credibility of authority justified in this way can be related to social settings where people are familiar with livestock breeding.

For Weber, the advance of rational thinking, science and technology undermines tradition. This process of rationalization promotes the quest for efficiency and the need for change. These forces prepare the way for industrial capitalism which eventually comes to develop large scale and impersonal organisational structures. Life becomes more freed from the traditions and routines of nature and agriculture and is dominated by the man-made routines and formal relationships within factories and offices, the latter referred to by Weber as bureaucracies. In such a society, authority in the workplace is justified by achievement and merit. Selection is a formal process in a system of rules and laws that require people to impersonally compete for occupational position. The formation of government through a system of representative democracy takes place through political party competition within the formal rules of a democratic framework for election to office. Weber referred to this type of authority, framed by standardised and formal procedures, as rational–legal.

Authority is not intrinsic to the person but derives from one's position within the organizational hierarchy. Contrary to a number of more recent organisational theorists, Weber maintained that bureaucracy is the most efficient form of social organisation. This efficiency stems from the way that formal selection matches skills with position, the top down imposition of authority through the machinery of a tiered formal organisational structure and the conformity of functionaries to orders, rules and regulations. Weber argued that competition between organisations and the drive for efficiency inclines modern complex industrial societies to become bureaucratised throughout.

Weber harboured grave concerns for the human condition in such a bureaucratized society in which slavish adherence within the workplace (and outside) to rules and regulations would reduce individuals to the position of being like cogs in a machine. Furthermore, with the growth of a far reaching modern sophisticated state apparatus, Weber was concerned that democratic accountability would become choked as decision making and power fall into the hands of un-elected bureaucrats and experts, and that the political participation of citizens may decline. Could anything check these consequences of the relentless march of bureaucratization?

Weber maintained that capitalist liberal democracies offered more potential of some resistance to this process than socialist systems would. Firstly, contrary to Marx, Weber argued that the state was not simply an instrument of the capitalist class but the product of a lengthy process of rationalization and bureaucratization. The owners of capital may thus be in a position to offer some resistance to the bureaucrats. Secondly, a well-established multi-party representative democracy in which civil servants are accountable to politicians who themselves are accountable to the electorate may help to restrain the power of unelected officials.

For Weber, to overthrow capitalism and representative democracy by revolution and take the means of production into public ownership would not lead to the fully participatory democracy that Marx had predicted, but the antithesis in the form of top down bureaucratic regulation. This is because, contrary to Marx, power does not flow exclusively from ownership of the means of production but can be concentrated in the means of state administration. State ownership of the means of production would thus concentrate bureaucratic and economic centralisation of power. Consequently, a revolution in which the means of production become commonly owned would lead to a single party state of party bureaucrats with little check, in the absence of private capital and choice of political party, on the advance of bureaucracy and the concentration of power in an unaccountable state apparatus.

Charismatic authority, Weber's third type, differs from traditional and rational-legal in that it derives from the perceived exceptional qualities (real or otherwise) of an individual leader in the subjective consciousness of devoted followers. Viewed historically and sociologically, such leaders are most likely to come to power during times of social crisis when significant sections of the population are more primed or susceptible to follow a person who is believed to have mystical qualities or intuitive genius. This type of political authority is the least rational and political decisions are likely to be justified through belief in the special insight of the leader. It is therefore often the most mercurial use of authority. Leaders are likely to engender strong emotional identification from followers, almost a hypnotic charm, and often adopt an authoritarian leadership style. Napoleon and (after Weber wrote), Stalin and Hitler each exemplify this type of rule arising from social crisis. However, charismatic authority, which may break out from predominantly traditional or rational-legal settings, is usually relatively short lived. Given its emotional intensity and personal nature, charismatic authority is by definition difficult to institutionalize and is likely to lapse with the fall of the leader.

Elite theory – representative democracy, fine as long as it does not amount to much!

Classical elite theorists, developing their ideas during the late nineteenth and early twentieth centuries, also strongly contested Marxist theory. They agreed with Marxism only at the most general level – that power in society is concentrated in the hands of a small minority who attempt to retain exclusive access and control. However, for elite theorists, rule by a small superior minority is a necessary and inevitable feature of all societies. That minority will comprise those who occupy key positions in society and especially the state, including senior politicians, civil servants, ambassadors, judges, and high ranking military officials. It could include owners of private business, but not exclusively, and there is no reason why power should specially emanate from ownership of the means of production. In their criticism of the economic determinism of the Marxist model, classical elite theorists argue that Marxists pay insufficient recognition to the political and cultural sphere as a source of power. The identification of rulers as an elite rather than a ruling class emphasises this key point. By contrast, for Marxists, as we have seen, even though elites rather than capitalists may man the state, the influence of the capitalist class, openly or behind the scenes, on these elites is so substantial that it is justified to refer to a state ruling class.

Classical elite theorists argue that a feature of societies throughout history is that their populations are divided into elites and masses. For Vilfredo Pareto, this universal feature relates to the social distribution of personal or psychological qualities. Following his distant predecessor Niccolo Macchiavelli, Pareto distinguished two main types of leadership quality: stealth and cunning, and the ability to take decisive action. Pareto argued that people with these leadership capabilities will always be in short supply in any population. The majority, lacking the qualities necessary for political leadership, will need to be and even prefer to be led by others. Indeed, Pareto went as far as claiming that the masses were by and large deficient in rational thinking and that elites can intelligently manipulate the masses by appealing to their instincts, sentiments and emotions. On this basis, elite rule is inevitable and democratic accountability to the masses is far from being equated with progress.

Members of an elite often act as a cohesive group to protect their interests and privileges. Denial of access by other groups is common as circulation takes place within elites who interchange between privileged positions and are able to pass privileged access to elite positions down the generations. There can arise, however, threats to elite dominance. Pareto recognised that the style of elite rule must be suited to the social needs of the time. As social circumstances change, elites must either adapt so as to enable themselves to retain political control or they are likely to face a challenge from other aspiring elites, counter-elites, more suited to rule in these conditions. Such a challenge may take the form of a military coup or revolution, which if successful brings about a circulation of entire elites with counter-elites assuming power. Moreover, although the masses are considered to be generally lacking in leadership qualities, an elite that becomes too socially closed off risks becoming decadent, out of touch and vulnerable to challenge. Some degree of social mobility of the able few from the masses may therefore be desirable so as to replenish an elite and deny the masses potentially capable leadership, thus enhancing the longevity of the elite.

Pareto's analysis of the distribution of power was similar to that of Gaetano Mosca, to whom he owed unacknowledged intellectual debt. However, Mosca did recognise that the qualities of elites may be acquired more through inherited social advantage than superior innate qualities. He also appreciated that elites that govern within the institutions of representative democracy can serve the general interest, especially if not drawn exclusively from privileged backgrounds. Mosca further recognised the importance of a growing sub-elite organisational stratum comprising, for example, managers, engineers and intellectuals, who contributed to the effective governance of modern society. However, both theorists held the view that the masses were generally unworthy of exercising power and should be excluded from doing so. And, even further, for Pareto in particular, it is in the best interests of society that in a representative democracy elites can use their political abilities to effectively manipulate the masses into believing that they are being consulted rather than meaningfully consulting them.

Robert Michels, in his work 'Political Parties', reached a similar position to that of Pareto and Mosca but built his analysis on society's organisational requirements. Like Weber, he argued that bureaucracy, a top down form of organisation, was necessary for any large organisation or modern society to operate efficiently. Hierarchical organisation inevitably leads to rule by the few – otherwise known as 'oligarchy'. Michels argued that representative democracy is the only form of democracy which is feasible for the efficient political organisation of large populations. In this form of democracy, electorates are only occasionally consulted and political leaders govern for the vast majority of time on their behalf. It is impossible for populations to be regularly involved in the decision making process (a situation akin to fully participatory democracy). Instead, full-time bureaucrats and political leaders are required to take key decisions and implement policy on an ongoing basis. For Michels, a disillusioned ex-Marxist, however radically democratic the policies of a party may have been when in opposition, once established into power, they have to govern. To govern efficiently, regular consultation with the masses is not possible. The consequent tendency is then for political leaders to become disengaged, acquire privileges and in time develop a vested interest in protecting their own position more than representing the populace who may have bought them to power. The assumption of power even by radical parties therefore ultimately equates to elite rule. Even in representative democracies, oligarchical structures headed by relatively unaccountable elites are inevitable – a process for which Michels coined the phrase the 'iron law of oligarchy'.

From the classical elite theory perspective, Marxism is not the scientific theory of social change that it claims to be, but just a utopian ideology. As an ideology, it is a system of thinking which distorts reality and can itself be used by an aspiring counter-elite to engender the support of the masses against a ruling elite. Marxism is utopian because the fully participatory democracy that it promises for the future cannot be realised. Any revolutionary party that gains power will need to govern a modern and complex society. In such a society, fully participatory democracy, if attempted, would lead to massive inefficiency associated with the necessity for regular consultation of the populace. To tackle this, direct leadership would need to be asserted. Thus, even out of communist revolution, a new oligarchical structure must emerge with leaders becoming increasingly detached from the lives of the led. A revolutionary party, in gaining power, gives rise to a new elite which will protect its power and privileges by controlling the masses through both coercive means and myth or ideology rather than the impossible reality of communist fully participatory democracy.

If Michels is correct, in the interests of efficiency, fully participatory democracy is an unworkable type of political system, and even representative democracy will amount to little in terms of meaningful consultation. Governments in representative democracies, of course, have to periodically face the electorate. Whether a particular change of government is a change of elite or a change within an elite is a matter of analysis. However, oligarchical structures will remain in place. The detachment of leaders from led which oligarchical structures brings can become particularly evident when governments that have been in power for a long time display a growing tendency, when facing the potential accountability of media questions, to not have ministers available for comment.

Other sociologists have taken elite theory in a more radical direction. From this position, elite rule is not regarded as preferable or inevitable.

Instead, it is lamentable that many modern societies that masquerade as democracies can be better understood as being controlled by elites who are by and large un-elected. An early exponent of this position was C. Wright Mills who argued in the 1950s that America was dominated by a single and largely unaccountable power elite comprising a network of personal contacts and occupational exchanges across the upper reaches of business corporations, the military and the governmental apparatus.

More contemporary sociologists use insights from elite theory to raise a number of points. There are certain key occupations in society, positions at the top of which confer great power, status and privilege to people in these positions and include the armed forces, the church, the legal profession, the civil service, government and large business corporations. The top occupational positions within these institutions tend to be held by people of similar privileged social and educational background. These people often know each other and share a similar elitist social outlook and membership of exclusive clubs. There is much movement across the top of the occupational structure. For example, business leaders may move into top governmental positions or vice versa and individual politicians may hold interlocking directorships (be directors of a number of companies). All of this takes place across what John Scott calls a 'web of connections' at the top of society.

Great power resides in the hands of senior civil servants who invariably will have an Oxbridge or public school background. Many operations of the state take place behind closed doors and most institutions are not directly accountable to the public. Allegations of abuses involving elites are often historical, and the destruction or 'loss' of potentially incriminating documents may look suspiciously self-protective. If public pressure leads to the setting up of an inquiry, the government sets the framework and appoints a figure from the elite as head. Further, it has been argued that, through consumerism and growing affluence, general populations have become depoliticised and politically apathetic.

Amongst the political elite, the evidence available suggests there to be a modest long-term decline in the proportion of MPs with a public school educational background, but that substantial differences remain between the main political parties. For example, figures provided by Bilton et al (1985) indicated that in 1966, 76.6% of Conservative MPs in Parliament came from a public school background as opposed to 19.5% of Labour MPs. At the pinnacle of government power, it was found that in the 1963 Conservative cabinet, 63.6% of members had attended one of the top six public schools, and the figure for the Labour cabinet for 1967 was 15.8%.

Research by Criddley indicated that in 2001 the proportions of MPs with public school background had declined to 64% of Conservatives and 17% of New Labour members. Two out of 412 Labour MPs had attended Eton whereas 14 out of 166 Conservative MPs had. However, New Labour achieved a large majority in the 2001 general election. With such marked differences in privileged educational background between the parties, the overall proportion of public school and top public school educated MPs and cabinet members is likely to fluctuate with a change of government, sometimes bucking the more modest long-term downward trend. Thus, following the 2010 general election and the formation of a Conservative headed coalition government, 19 out of 306 Conservative MPs had been educated at Eton alone and 62% of the coalition cabinet and 54% of Conservative MPs (compared to 7% of the general population) had been privately educated.

Regarding their previous professions, information from the House of Commons Library (12/8/2013, p.45) shows that only 4% of MPs (predominantly Labour) had been manual workers, whereas 35% held professional and 25% business backgrounds, the latter spread disproportionately between 41% of Conservative MPs and 8% of Labour MPs.

Pluralism – representative democracy as a balancing of diverse interests

Classical pluralism, which has strong roots in American political theory of the 1960s, adopts a position which is strongly critical of the power concentration models of both Marxist and elite theory perspectives. By contrast, it adopts a self-congratulatory view of the virtues of modern liberal democratic political systems as dissipating power down to individuals and across to numerous competing interest groups. This structure Dahl refers to as 'ployarchy' (many hierarchies). It is the hallmark of a healthy and vibrant liberal democracy that a broad variety of interests can be fed into the political process and, through contest and compromise, interest groups can, to a greater of lesser extent, influence the political decision making process and government policy. It is up to citizens to actively pursue their interests in this political arena and government to act as an 'honest broker' between the parties and guardian ensuring that participation takes place according to the rules of the game. It must then have the power to implement policies which are the outcome of this democratic process.

From this perspective, representative democracies are complex societies which comprise a broad spectrum of interests. Individuals have their own range of interests which they may want to register into the political decision making process. People are free to voice and pursue their interests through pressure group activity and can come together to do so with other individuals who agree on specific issues. In the competitive process of influencing political decisions, all interests can have an input, although the involvement and influence of groups will vary over time and according to the issues contested. As new issues evolve, new pressure groups will emerge along with new configurations in the dispute of interests.

For pluralists, it is possible to empirically test this model by studying which groups are involved in the political arena are, the processes taking place in their engagement, the outcome of these processes and the degree to which the interests of different parties have prevailed. In support of this model, Dahl (1961) used empirical evidence from his study of New Haven politics to show that across a range of issues the decisions arrived at gave no single interest group a monopoly of influence and that group influence varied from issue to issue.

A cornerstone of representative democracy is the competition between political parties by which, at elections, voters periodically hold governments and local politicians accountable. Political parties offer viable options to a universal electorate, allowing them to have their say in the formation of government. To attract the support of voters, political parties must keep a careful eye on the state of popular opinion. To this end, voter opinion surveys are regularly conducted and parties may need to change their policies or political position in their bid to retain or acquire power. The power of the vote therefore gives the electorate the power to shape policy and to replace political parties in government. Thus, from a pluralist position, in contrast to a Marxist interpretation, that it was not the constraints of the capitalist system which forced the British Labour Party to 'modernise' between 1983 and 1997 and acquire office, but the opinion of the electorate which they had to satisfy to gain their adherence.

Pluralists emphasise that whilst voters are free to vote for a party which most closely reflects their range of interests, pressure groups enable people to fine tune their influence on decision makers regarding more specific issues and on an ongoing basis. Government is therefore not just about becoming elected but responding to the pressure of different organised interests and seeking compromise. By such means, in representative democracies the process of democratic accountability is a more continuous process than the periodic contesting of elections.

Where, then, do the boundaries of legitimate pressure group activity lie? Traditional pluralists tend to have in mind a model of pressure groups as hierarchical organisations whose representatives engage in regular contact with local and central government decision makers. These organisations have been referred to by Wyn Grant as 'insider' or conventional pressure groups. In Britain, such groups may include the Confederation of British Industry, Age Concern and the Automobile Association. Their representatives have meetings with government officials and they operate within the law and the rules of the political game. Their influence can also be extended by the fact that the government relies on them for information and expertise in helping to shape policy in their specific areas.

Other types of pressure group may employ the tactic of rapid response and direct action and operate on the margins of or outside the law. Their actions are likely to make these 'outsider' groups to the political establishment. Within this category would be included the Animal Liberation Front, Fathers for Justice, and some environmental pressure groups. Against such groups, the traditional pluralist position is that state power may need to be rallied to ensure that the law is not subverted and, in the extreme, the very institutions which safeguard the freedoms of law abiding individuals are not threatened.

A further type of political influence open to people is the use of their consumer spending power. Contrary to Marxism, which emphasises the relative powerlessness of the employee, pluralism focuses on the power of the consumer. Classical pluralists argue that in a system of private enterprise and competition in the pursuit of profit, businesses must respond to consumer demand in order to flourish or even survive. As well as the need to satisfy customers with particular goods and services, businesses, along with political regimes, will be concerned about their ethical image since if viewed as disreputable they may face concerted action in the form of consumer boycotts. Consumer action against the apartheid regime in South Africa during the 1980s and more recent boycotting of genetically modified crops offer good examples of the potential impact of such movements combining consumer and pressure group influences.

How does pluralism compare to the other political theories introduced in this chapter? Like functionalism, the pluralist perspective recognizes the importance of commonly agreed values. However, these are more of a backdrop to social diversity and particular conflicts of interest which can be pursued within the agreed rules of the political game. For pluralists, the closest approximation to the common interest comes as a result of compromise within this conflict and no single sectional interest can consistently prevail. Contrary to the Marxist model, the interests of private enterprise (if such a uniformity of interests exists) do not hold a monopoly of power and the ability to continuously shape political decisions in their favour, but are checked by various other interest groups. Neither is there an undifferentiated working class who use class as the main basis for political action, since in complex contemporary societies divisions of interest break up the formation of any significant cross cutting common class interest. Unlike classical elite theory, classical pluralism does not maintain that liberal democracies are or should be governed by a single ruling elite, nor does it emphasise the inferiority and manipulated compliance of the masses. Power is diffused down to an enlightened and active citizenship.

Elite pluralism or fragmented elites?

Pluralism, a particularly influential theory in the United States from the 1960s, provides, indeed, a highly self-congratulatory view positing the widespread distribution of power in capitalist liberal democracies. But just how accurate is this model? A number of questions, including the following, have been frequently raised. Are all sections of society adequately represented? Are some groups substantially over-represented in the power that they can exert in relation to their numerical composition? Are pressure groups themselves always internally democratic? Answers to such questions have led some writers such as J. K. Galbraith toward a refocusing of pluralism in the direction of elite pluralism (sometimes referred to as neo-pluralism) (Heywood, 1999, pp.78-79). Although retaining the pluralist perspective as a touchstone, advocates of this modified position acknowledge that some groups in society, in particular large business interests, are likely to have a disproportionate influence on political decisions, especially in the economic sphere. On the other hand, the needs of other sections of society, such as the homeless, tend to get overlooked. It is also often now emphasised that there has been a degree of reconfiguration of pressure group activity away from a focus on national governments, as political problems and the means of tackling them have become more globalised. Furthermore, as hierarchical organisations, conventional pressure groups are often not very open to democratic influence by members from within but are effectively run and represented to government by elites. Overall, power may not therefore be as evenly spread, focussed on national government, or as diffused down to active participants as classical pluralism once maintained. From this modified perspective, liberal democracies are sometimes referred to by elite pluralists as 'deformed polyarchies'.

From the other end of the scale, there have also been criticisms of and modifications to the classical elite theory position. The idea of 'fragmented elites', adopted by Ian Budge et al, argues that rather than a single cohesive elite acting with a unified purpose and sense of direction, there exists different interests which elites strive to pursue. The interests of business elites may diverge with that of government elites, for example over taxation and anti-monopoly legislation. The elite of the judiciary can come into conflict with government elites over sentencing policy. There may even be fragmentation within each of these elites. For example, it is doubtful, other than at a very general level, whether there exists a single business community interest between elites in manufacturing, banking and retailing, and within government career civil servants may have different interests to politicians and different spending departments often have to compete for limited resources. However, although fragmented, from the above perspective these elites may share a similar general background and outlook and often experience little popular control.

Taking into account these variations, elite theory and pluralist positions can be represented as follows:

Continuum of Elite Theory and Pluralist Perspectives				
Classical Elite	**Fragmented Elite**		**Elite Pluralism**	**Classical Pluralism**
Single ruling elite exists with a shared interest. This is necessary, beneficial and inevitable. Masses need to be led and should not have power.	Elites rule, but not as a single cohesive group. Despite similar background and outlook, there are divisions of interest.		Popular participation in interest groups may be limited as leaders represent interests. Some groups have disproportionate power.	Diversity of pressure groups involves members in active and effective participation in pursuit of their interests. Influence of groups varies with issues.

Society and the state

A general definition of the state can usefully take a lead from Max Weber who defined it in terms of a community of persons with the capacity to impose power through authority or coercion over a given territory. To quote Weber, the 'state is a human community that (successfully) claims the *monopoly of the legitimate use of physical force* within a given territory' comprising 'a relation of men dominating men, a relation supported by means of legitimate (i.e. considered to be legitimate) violence' (Gerth & Mills, 1977, p.78).

The nation state is viewed to hold sovereignty over its territory – that is, the right to pass laws and enact policy within its territory, recognized by international law and supported by powerful national symbols. It will also confer to members of society as citizens certain duties and rights.

The state uses its powers through various institutions at its disposal. How may we more specifically define the scope of the state? There are more or less obvious components to it, depending on the breadth of definition applied. Even a relatively narrow and formal definition of the state would include the institutions of political parties and government, the civil service, the judicial system, the armed forces, the police, the apparatus of local government, a variety of regulatory bodies, the National Health Service and the state education system. These both regulate and protect the lives of citizens.

Some social theorists view the institutions of the state more inclusively. For example, the Marxist Poulantzas also includes in the state the mass media and even the family as these form part of the means of ideological control.

In the various sociological perspectives on power and politics covered in this chapter, it can be noted that the state is viewed as deeply rooted within the broader social context. For most of these perspectives, this engenders a 'society focussed' view of the state which relates it to surrounding social forces rather than a 'state focussed' approach which emphasises its power and influence on society as an entity in its own right.

For functionalists, the state can be seen as a rational directing power, utilising the ability of experts appointed on merit to intervene in society to promote social order and integration for the common well-being. It therefore performs the key function of engineering the smooth functioning of society. To this rational dimension can be added the importance of state ceremonies and rituals which convey to individuals, through powerful state symbolism, a collective consciousness and feeling of national identity. These latter issues will also be picked up on in the chapter on religion.

By contrast, as a basic recipe, Marxists view the state in capitalist societies as shaped by relationships of class power and representing the interests of an economically dominant ruling class. There is, however, some debate within Marxist circles as to the extent to which the state is simply a direct instrument of the ruling class (an instrumentalist view) or whether it has to act more autonomously. We have seen that an instrumentalist position was adopted by Miliband who regards the state as run by an elite but controlled by a capitalist class. The capitalist class is therefore a thoroughly ruling class. However, Poulantzas has adopted the position that for the benefit of the long term continuity of the capitalist system, the state must avoid such direct class control which would simply reproduce in the state any divisions which exist within the capitalist class. From this Marxist perspective, greater autonomy from the capitalist class enables the state to both act as a more cohesive representative of capitalist class interests and to offer concessions when necessary to the subject class. For example, from this position and that of Gramsci, if the capitalist class ruled too directly through the state, it is questionable whether the welfare state would have developed to the extent that it has. However, the welfare state could be seen as the worthwhile ransom price that needs to be paid for social harmony and the continuity of capitalism, especially if the main beneficiaries of welfare state provisions are also the main financial contributors. A degree of state autonomy thus enables the state to institute reforms to perpetuate the system from which the capitalist class are the prime beneficiaries and to save them from themselves.

For Weber, the growth of the nation state is part of a more general process of bureaucratization in which social relationships become formalized. However, his approach tends to be a more state centred one than others in this section since it focusses on the rational decisions and actions of actors within the machinery of state and how these are imposed on the population through the bureaucratic apparatus.

In contrast to Marxists, elite theorists view the state as a separate political entity from the economy. It is an oligarchical instrument of rule headed by a privileged minority ruling in the interests of an established elite and manipulating the masses through the facade of democracy. State oligarchical structures are inevitable, even if one elite should replace another.

Pluralists tend to view the state in liberal democracies as a relatively innocuous entity in terms of the limited imposition of institutional power. It acts as the arbiter of competing interests, all comprising the means by which political decisions are arrived at through a broad process of democratic participation. It then implements the outcomes of the decisions arrived at within the rules of the game. Neo-pluralists, such as

Galbraith, have developed the pluralist model in a way which recognises the distorting effect of corporate power on this decision making process. Another variant of pluralism is the post-war corporatist state model in which government brings representatives of the interests of labour and capital into the social and economic planning process to seek their co-operation and agreement to compromise their aspirations in the interest of social harmony and economic stability. Such an approach was last attempted in Britain though the Labour government's 'social contract' of the mid 1970s.

Noam Chomsky locates the American state as both an instrument of powerful economic interests and a powerful economic and military entity in its own right. As such, he provides a scathing condemnation of America's democratic credentials.

For Chomsky, American politics in recent decades has been dominated by a neo-liberal free market philosophy. Powerful supporters of this approach argue that free enterprise capitalism and free trade for all enhances democratic freedom and the standard of living throughout the world. However, Chomsky argues that in reality American social policy is shaped by and caters for the needs of large corporate interests and the rich. Democratic accountability is thus undermined as policies which may benefit the majority, such as welfare reform, become undermined as the taxation necessary to implement them clashes with the economic self-interest of the rich and powerful who provide the funding that is necessary for political campaigns. The policy difference between the major political parties is therefore negligible. Furthermore, the media tends to restrict the scope for political discussion and stifle genuine debate through generating a climate of fear of political enemies of America. The United States is therefore not democratic even in the rather restricted sense of the pluralist model.

Further, despite claiming to be the advocate of democracy throughout the world, America's priority is always the self-interested one of maintaining its political and economic power. To do so, it has intervened to subvert the outcome of democratic elections which are viewed as a threat to its interests (for example, the CIA assisted overthrow of the Marxist sympathetic and democratically elected Allende government in Chile and its replacement by the Pinochet military junta who favoured free market reforms) and supported undemocratic regimes by which America benefits (for example in oil rich Saudi Arabia).

In terms of international trade, the principles of free trade are also distorted through economic self-interest. For example, poorer countries find that loans from the World Bank and the IMF invariably have strings attached that require them to open up their economies to free trade from which wealthier countries such as the United States are the main beneficiaries, whilst in America agricultural subsidies are used to protect farming interests.

Society rooted approaches to the state are not the only focus which has been adopted. An alternative position regards the state as a powerful and separate entity in its own right with the capacity to shape society according to its own goals, if necessary against resistance. This position is well exemplified in the works of Theda Skocpol. In her analysis of the French, Chinese and Russian Revolutions, she argues that the key animating force of change may appear to have been the revolutionary movements, but more decisive was the incapacity of those who had commanded the state to rise to the challenge of changing international conditions. The success or otherwise of revolutions is related to the strategic strength of the state, the international circumstances in which it is operating and its capacity to respond based on the choices taken by rulers. We might further illustrate this with the example of Japanese modernization. Japan managed to avoid revolution because the elites, learning from the example of western destabilisation of China, restricted western intrusions and forced reform from above through state directed modernization.

Whatever the differences between the theories of the state so far examined, there is at least agreement that it is a sovereign entity governing a nation. We will later see that this basic assumption has been increasingly called into question, especially through the impact of globalisation.

The vote – more an index of power than power itself?

Universal franchise – the extension of the vote to all people over a certain age bar limited prescribed sections of the population – is a fundamental feature of contemporary representative democracies. Having access to the vote opens up a degree of choice and political power to the electorate; just how much choice and power is open to debate and is an issue which is disputed from various theoretical perspectives such as those introduced above. Moreover, viewed sociologically, power, as previously defined, is potentially an element of all social relationships. Prior to the study of voting behaviour, it is therefore important to appreciate that the acquisition of universal suffrage can itself be placed in the context of political struggles between groups within society for a say in the formation of governments. In this context, the restriction or extension of the vote itself provides a barometer of changing power relationships within society.

Groups that have used their power to acquire access to the vote have sometimes attempted to exclude its extension to others. By so doing, they try to promote social closure. In Britain in the early 1830s, the extension of the vote to a broader category of male property owners reflected the growing social power of the middle classes following the Industrial Revolution. At the time, the exclusion of non-property owners was justified on the ideological basis that a more open social structure had emerged in which property acquisition by the self made man was proof of industriousness and the capacity to make sound judgements. Property ownership was therefore argued to demonstrate proven worthiness of the capacity to make sound political judgements and the criteria of deservedness for access to the vote.

At various times and in different societies, other ideological justifications, including those based on racism and sexism, have been used by some groups to exclude other sections of the population from acquiring full access to the vote. Thus, although universal suffrage is the hallmark of modern liberal democracies, it has been fought for by chartists, suffragists, supporters of civil rights, and anti-apartheid movements, etc.

In Britain, through legislative reforms responding to the growing organisation and power of the industrial working class and the suffrage stage of the women's movement, all males over 21 had gained access to the vote in 1918, and females, on an equal basis to males, in 1928. Legislation passed in 1969 brought the minimum voting age down to 18 and there has also more recently been talk of a possible further reduction to the age of 16.

Sociological approach to voting behaviour

Academic sociology is parcelled into different topic areas to assist in the focus of analysis. Politics, and more specifically voting behaviour, is part of this process of academic specialisation. However, the real world is interconnected. To reflect this, sociologists need to be able to make interconnections within their subject. Hence, to understand voting behaviour sociologically requires a sociological understanding of surrounding social conditions and changes within which evidence of patterns of voting behaviour can be interpreted. The reader is therefore encouraged to relate an understanding of voting behaviour to sociological analysis in other chapters, especially the one on social stratification.

A post war baseline – voting behaviour and social class

During the post war years and up to the early 1970s, voting in Britain appeared to exhibit quite a stable pattern. Voters tended to retain loyalty to their chosen political party from one general election to another. Swings in party support between elections were modest. The beneficiaries of this stability were the Labour and Conservative Parties, who between them regularly obtained over 80% of the vote and took their turns in government.

Explanations of this stability tend to emphasise the long term and cumulative effect on people of political socialisation within a relatively stable social structure. Such explanations have been referred to as 'primacy' explanations (Coxall et al, 2003, p.101). At this period in time, social class appeared to be the primacy influence of overriding importance. It was argued that social class was the basis of partisan party identification and alignment in voting behaviour. Partisan identification refers to a high level of voter commitment and loyalty to a particular party, often based on commitment to a set of ideological values and the pursuit of a cause. Partisanship therefore often entails a high degree of emotional commitment from the voter, who may not necessarily have a detailed knowledge of issues and policy across the political parties. Class alignment emphasised a link between a person's social class and the tendency to vote for a party which is perceived to represent that class interest. Seen as combined, these influences are referred to as partisan class alignment. In a stable class structure, with limited opportunities for geographical and social mobility, the impact of family socialisation and class identification – reinforced, according to Butler and Stokes (1969), by the type of neighbourhood lived in, school attended and work environment – provided a class differentiated pattern of socialisation which produced a strong predisposition toward class based voting behaviour. According to this explanation, a strong bond existed between being manual working class and voting for the Labour Party and being white collar middle class and voting for the Conservatives. Social class alone provided the best indicator and predictor of voting behaviour.

The impact of working class community life on political consciousness and voting behaviour was picked up on by Parkin (1967). Parkin argued that the dominant ideological culture of the state and the privileged and wealthy social orders is more attuned to the political outlook of the Conservative Party. If the impact of this dominant culture were all embracing, working class support for the Conservatives would be high. However, the characteristics of working class communities and socialization, as suggested by Butler and Stokes, provided a degree of insulation from the impact of the dominant political culture and provided support for an oppositional culture with a degree of class consciousness and support for Labour as the party of the working class.

Detailed evidence to support partisan and class alignment was not abundant in the post war years, since sophisticated electoral surveys in the form of exit polls only date from 1964. However, supporting circumstantial evidence was strong. This included low levels of net voter volatility between elections, comparatively high electoral turnout of around 75%, and the dominance in politics of two major parties, Labour and the Conservatives, reflecting a society of two main social classes, the working and middle classes.

However, evidence also indicated that a significant proportion of voters in each class did not conform to the dominant voting pattern. For example, research conducted by Ivor Crewe (1983) established that in the 1959 general election approximately 1/5 of non-manual workers voted Labour and about 1/3 of manual workers voted Conservative. An important concern during the 1960s and 1970s was therefore to explain the reasons behind these levels of 'deviant voting' or 'class defection'. Some of these explanations are briefly summarised below.

Firstly, social classes are not uniform blocks; different occupational sectors exist within social classes which may encourage different political outlooks. Within the working class, Goldthorpe and Lockwood argued that agricultural labourers and coal miners tended to adopt opposing political attitudes which were based on their differing views of the social structure. Such differences were related to distinctive occupational and community influences. For example, the dangers of coal mining required high levels of co-operation between workers who also lived in tightly knit community networks around the pits. This life encouraged a view of the social structure as divided between 'us and them' – a view which promoted strong identification toward Labour as the party of the working class. By contrast, agricultural workers, who worked and lived in smaller scattered groups and communities and had more regular contact with their employers, were more likely to view the social hierarchy as a justifiable order. Associated traditional attitudes of deference to social superiors would incline many of these workers toward voting Conservative as the party of natural leaders.

Secondly, there is the question of how social class is defined and measured and who is defining and measuring it. If people are designated to a social class by sociologists through the use of traditional occupational scales alone, their own subjective interpretations of their social class position are being ignored. Butler and Stokes found that where people's subjective judgement of their social class did not agree with that allocated to them by researchers, there was a higher tendency for them to be deviant voters in terms of sociologists' class definitions, whereas if their subjective views correlated with sociologists' definition of their class they were very likely to be class conformist in their voting. Personal perception of their class was therefore of some importance to a person's voting decisions and when taken into account could help to explain levels of so called deviant voting.

Thirdly, voters experiencing cross class social mobility may, through the continuing effect of earlier political socialisation, remain loyal to the party of their class of origin, thus becoming deviant voters in their class of destination. The upwardly mobile may therefore remain loyal to Labour – as discovered by Goldthorpe and Lockwood in the case of the sons of affluent blue collar workers who became white collar workers. Likewise, those downwardly mobile from the middle to working class may retain adherence to the Conservative Party.

Fourthly, although the impact of social class was arguably very powerful, other social factors can cut across and to some extent break up its overriding influence. For example, Anthony Heath has shown that within the working class, private home owners were more likely to vote Conservative than council house occupants.

Another cross cutting influence is that of religion. In England, Catholics have traditionally tended to vote Labour whereas those who identify with the Church of England (the religion of the establishment) are more likely to vote Conservative (seeing it as the party of the establishment). For example, Heath found in 1992 that of middle class voters who identified with the Church of England, 72% voted Conservative, whereas only 47% of middle class voters who held no religious beliefs voted Conservative. Moreover, the intensity of the impact of religion is likely to vary alongside levels of religious identification in different parts of the country. Since locality, gender, ethnicity and age all show some influence on voting behaviour, they also provide potential for breaking up the single influence of social class.

However, even during the 1960s, there was evidence emerging of a changing relationship between the electorate and the political parties that they supported. For example, Goldthorpe and Lockwood (1969) found that although 80% of affluent blue collar workers in their research had voted Labour at the 1959 general election, their identification was based less on strong party loyalty and an ideological commitment than was thought to traditionally be the case for working class Labour voters. Although these affluent voters still tended to see themselves as working class, their greater affluence and home centeredness encouraged a more isolated lifestyle and instrumental attitude toward trade unions and political parties, support for which became more contingent on the furtherance of their standard of living. As affluent workers comprised an expanding section of the working class, there was a possibility of potential desertion from voting Labour by a growing section of blue collar workers in the future if Labour failed to deliver.

Some similarity to the above trend but with reference to the nature of attachment to voting Conservative was argued by McKenzie and Silver (1972). Goldthorpe and Lockwood, and long before them Walter Bagehot, had argued that a substantial proportion of Conservative support, including that from working class voters, was based on a deferential social outlook toward those perceived as natural superiors. However, McKenzie and Silver argued that the deferential outlook was declining whilst of increasing importance in voting Conservative was a 'secular' outlook which focussed more on party policy and assessed the practical implications for a voter's standard of living.

From the mid 1950s, a number of changes were affecting working class community life. These included: the start of a long term decline in employment in traditional industries such as steel working, shipbuilding, and dock work, followed by a later dramatic decline in coal mining, and with this a decline in the possibility of working class nepotism; geographical movement required with the demolition of slums and re-housing or the search for new types of work; and some improvement in opportunities for social mobility. In these developments can be seen the undermining of community life and a thinning out of the boundaries of class formation which were likely to diminish the impact of social class on working class social and political outlook and voting behaviour.

Whatever direct influence social class was likely to retain on voting behaviour, if, as Dahrendorf has argued, class decomposition was taking place, it should be expected that likewise a pattern of decomposition in voting behaviour would follow. This and the decline of the traditional working class already signalled long-term problems for the Labour Party it if relied on appealing to the working class voter.

The decline of social class based voting?

Signs of how these underlying social changes were having a significant effect on voting behaviour were first observed in the February 1974 general election. In this election, the Liberal vote increased substantially to 19.3% from a 1951 low of 2.6% and a level of still only 7.5% in the 1970 election. This increase was at the expense of the combined Labour and Conservative vote which fell from 89.4% in the 1970 election to 74.9% in February 1974 (and this later declined to 65% in the 2010 election). After falling back a little in the 1979 election, the 'Liberal' vote surged again in 1983 when the Liberal SDP Alliance polled 25.4% of the vote; only about 2% behind the Labour vote. This decline in the two party monopoly, at least as far as proportion of the vote is concerned, suggested a significant move away from the two party partisan identification and class alignment model of voting behaviour. Of much debate since has been the question of how fundamental this change has become and what other social factors may be emerging to influence voting behaviour at the expense of social class.

Of some significance to the debate has not just been the increase in the 'Liberal' vote (the parties of the Liberal SDP Alliance merged in 1988 and eventually settled on the new name of Liberal Democrats), but also the nature of its support. Until well into the 1990s, the Liberal Democrats had retained the Liberal tradition of being fairly centrally positioned on the left to right political scale between the Labour and Conservative Parties respectively. Their supporters have been amongst the most fickle section of the electorate, with only a minority remaining loyal over two consecutive elections. Instability in voting behaviour, although not only concentrated here, appears to have become an increasing feature of British general elections. There is also clear evidence of a significant decline in voter turnout in recent general elections: 77.7% in 1992, 71.4% in 1997, just below 60% in 2001, just above 60% in 2005 and 65.1% in 2010. This trend would appear to offer evidence of declining partisan identification by the electorate.

It is against the backdrop of such evidence that arguments over dealignment in terms of both party loyalty and class identification have emerged. An early advocate of the interpretation that a fundamental dealignment was taking place in voting behaviour was Ivor Crewe who headed the British Election Studies of 1974 and 1979. He argued that voting was becoming less based on feelings of loyalty toward a particular political party – a process referred to as partisan dealignment. An effective way to measure this is to look at the strength with which voters identify with political parties. To this end, research conducted by Crewe and Thompson found that whilst 44% of voters identified very strongly with a political party in 1964, this figure had fallen to 16% by 1997, and later, according to Saunders et al, to 9% in 2005.

Furthermore, evidence suggested that social class, based on occupation, was becoming a poorer indicator of voting behaviour – suggesting that class dealignment was also taking place. General election figures provided by Saunders show that during the1960s, Labour and the

Conservatives held steady class based monopolies of the vote at the expense of the Liberals. The Liberals then made some inroads in 1974. Over the four elections between 1979 and 1992, Labour were the main casualties of dealignment with the Conservatives regularly polling between 35 and 36% of the manual workers' vote. However, in 1997, dealignment worked against the Conservatives with Labour becoming New Labour and capturing 40% of the non-manual vote.

Anthony Heath (who also headed a number of the British Election Studies) had been initially more sceptical of the long-term impact of dealignment. He acknowledged that there was research evidence indicating a decline in partisan voting, but cast doubt on the extent and lasting effect of class dealignment. Much depends on how social class is defined. Heath made more specific distinctions than between middle class and working class and when focussing on the voting behaviour of powerless blue collar workers, found an unchanging pattern of support for Labour through the 1960s and into the 1980s. Overall, for Heath, changing patterns of voting behaviour were tending to reflect changes in the class structure itself with a declining size of the working class disadvantaging Labour. However, Heath argued that growing inequality under the Conservatives could reverse any class dealignment and lead to the re-emergence of class as the major social factor in voting behaviour.

It is very doubtful, however, whether a process of realignment has transpired. As inequality was increasing under the Conservatives, class consciousness may have been simultaneously declining. A more individualistic culture had been promoted by the new right. Many blue collar workers were turning away from trade unions who (still strongly associated with the Labour Party) were blighted with unpopularity following the 'winter of discontent', and were looking toward the potential individual benefits from Conservative reforms such as the promotion of home ownership. There is therefore not necessarily a straightforward causal relationship between occupation and economic factors and class consciousness. Furthermore, an important component of New Labour's landslide election victory in 1997 was a substantial shift toward Labour support from sections of the middle class, whilst in their defeat in the 2010 election, it appears that it was amongst skilled manual workers that a major desertion from Labour took place.

Could patterns of voting behaviour still be explained in primacy terms? Could they be better explained by reference to an overriding social factor other than social class? Dunleavy and Husbands (1985) thought so in their sectoral politics model. Central to this explanation is the view that a closer fit with voting behaviour than social class division appears in the division between the public and private sector. This model predicted that the more that people were involved in the public sector in their employment position, consumer capacity and housing situation, the more likely they were to vote Labour whatever their occupational class, whereas the more they were implicated in the private sector, the greater likelihood that they would vote Conservative, again largely irrespective of social class. In terms of consumer capacity and use of services, important areas of the pubic and private divide would include housing, educational provision, health provision and pensions. This model suggested a shift from class to status as a major influence on voting behaviour. And given the changing balance in favour of private commodity and service as opposed to state provision and the declining numbers employed in the public sector during the 1980s, each brought about by Conservative reforms, it is clear that if this analysis is correct, the Conservatives were building a substantial social basis of long term support that Labour would need to respond to.

Another possibility is that no single primacy (long term) or structural factor can any longer adequately explain voting behaviour, but that a fluid combination of influences may be coming into play. Religion, region and neighbourhood, age, gender and ethnicity all show some impact on voting behaviour. However, it may be suspected that higher levels of volatility are associated with the impact of more short-term influences. These have been referred to as 'recency' influences (Coxall et al, 2003, p.105) and tend to be associated with a more instrumental and individualised approach to voting in which individuals reflect on political issues and make rational decisions based on the calculated impact of policy on their personal well being, especially on their standard of living, in contrast to necessarily following class, family and community traditions. Amongst these influences may be leadership image, the econometric or 'feel good' factor and the impact of the mass media. Indeed, as the latter enables the electorate to acquire up to date intelligence on the state of the parties through the findings of opinion polls, effective tactical voting (usually taking the form of switching to a party which has a perceived better chance of defeating a disliked party than voting for one's party of first choice in a constituency) becomes more of a possibility. This arguably both presupposes and promotes a decline in partisan voting and further assists volatility.

Leadership image arguably played an increasing profile in the British 2010 general election as for the first time televised debates between the leaders of the three major parties were held. Extensive polling suggested that, following the first debate on 15 April, Liberal Democrat support surged from about 20% to 30%, at the expense of Conservative and, to a slightly lesser extent, Labour support (House of Commons Library, 12/8/2013, p.69). This was by far the most marked opinion shift of the campaign and, according to an Ipsos MORI poll, 60% of respondents claimed that the debates were an important factor in influencing who they would vote for (House of Commons Library, 12/8/2013, p.73).

A further aspect of voting behaviour relates to the ideological and policy positioning of the political parties themselves. For example, in the 1983 general election, there was clear polarisation between the Labour Party and the Conservatives both ideologically and on a range of issues including privatisation and nuclear disarmament. The Conservatives won the election and attracted the vote of 35% of voters in manual occupations. The wide gap in the middle of the political spectrum enabled the Liberal / SDP Alliance to occupy a position from which their percentage of the vote peaked. Labour had since become rebranded as 'New labour' and in distancing itself from its historical connections with trade unions and the imagery of being the party of the working class, and accepting many of the Conservative reforms, had moved into the political middle ground. In doing so, New Labour successfully managed to broaden its appeal across society to the extent that in the 1997 general election it obtained about 40% of the middle class vote.

A narrowing of party positions around the centre of the political scale is likely to make it more difficult for voters to make clear cut ideological distinctions between the parties. It has been argued that they will therefore be more likely to base their vote on judgements of how they think that the different political parties will tackle particular issues that they deem to be important, a phenomena referred to as 'issue salience'. Of high priority, but not necessarily determining election outcomes, is the electorate's assessment of a party in managing the economy and raising standards of living. This was clearly an important factor in the 2010 election which took place in the wake of the banking crisis and economic recession, with polls conducted by the British Election Study showing that the Conservatives had a substantial lead over Labour in the electorate's views of who could best manage the economic situation going forward.

However, politics arguably remains as much about the manipulation of subjective perception by political parties and the ideological filtering of information as it is about debate over objective facts. As things stand in the spring of 2014, the Conservative led coalition government are able to provide the electorate with evidence of sustained economic recovery whereas Labour are questioning who the main beneficiaries of this recovery are. The appeal of the arguments put forward is still likely to relate to people's position in the social structure, the ideological filtering of the messages and the degree to which they remain committed to a particular party.

The classical sociological perspectives differ in their evaluation of the political impact that the electorate can have in shaping policy and bringing about political change. This should be quite apparent in a comparison of classical pluralist and Marxist perspectives on the sources and distribution of power in capitalist democracies. For Marxists, the electorate can only appear (but for the main beneficiaries of capitalism it is important that this appearance is kept up) to have significant say in the complexion of government in capitalist societies. In reality, much of the power to influence policy is concentrated in the hands of a capitalist class and serves the interests of capital.

The pluralist model, by contrast, has been argued to effectively explain the impact of recency influences and instrumental attitudes toward voting. This model, put forward for example by Himmelweit (1985), suggests that social class and party ideology have little impact on the decision making of voters because they adopt a pragmatic consumer based approach to voting. They shop around and rationally compare the benefit to themselves of the policies on offer in a similar way to that in which they choose from a range of products before deciding on a purchase (or not) when casting their vote (or not). Political parties must compete in packaging their policies to attract the votes of political consumers who are thus able to shape party policy. This approach explains the preoccupation that political parties have for conducting political opinion polls in search of policy proposals that will promote their appeal to the broadest audience of voters. It also suggests that in the competition to do so, the range of political party options will tend to narrow and usually seek support on the centre ground of politics. Thus, just as the Labour Party had to reposition itself from the left of the spectrum in the early 1980s toward the centre of the spectrum under New Labour to win the 1997 general election, the Conservatives were successful in the 2010 election, becoming the main party in a coalition government with the Liberal Democrats, by repositioning themselves in a more moderately right position and promoting a more caring and consensual image under the leadership of David Cameron.

A growing concern amongst the political parties, though, is that a substantial proportion of the electorate do not appear to be buying into party politics, if the turnout at recent general elections is anything to go by. It is with this concern in mind that various alternatives to people having to turn out to the voting booth, such as the expansion of postal, electronic and telephone voting, are being considered. In the next section, it will be suggested that the process of globalisation appears to be having a significant effect on national and electoral politics.

Contemporary sociological perspectives on power and politics:

Important contemporary developments in power and politics involve debates concerning the nature and extent of globalisation and the responses advocated, on whether contemporary societies can best be explained in terms of postmodern or high modern conditions, and what the social implications of these analyses are. A central issue in this is how power in the contemporary world may be becoming reconfigured and what the opportunities are for new types of political action and control.

Globalisation – the erosion of the power of the state and national government?

The traditional role of the state related to the rational planning of the economy and the exercise of sovereign political power within the prescribed territorial area of the nation. This role was exemplified in the Keynesian model of judicious government intervention to regulate the economy and protect members of society from the ravages of mass unemployment which had been suffered during the pre-war years. An underlying assumption of this model was that such interventions can be effective within the territorial confines of the nation state. The virtual abandonment of the Keynesian approach from the mid 1970s can be traceable to a number of internal and external factors.

When the new right Conservative government came to power in Britain from 1979, a period of industrial strife and poor economic performance that they inherited was laid at the door of excessive government interventionism through Keynesian and corporative approaches. It was argued that through competition for the popular vote, pressures were built into the system toward pledges to the electorate for more government intervention. This was leading to government overload and governments were becoming overstretched in their regulatory role. Excessive intervention, especially in economic matters, arguably brought inefficiency.

In response, there has transpired a 'hollowing out' of the state through a combination of internal and external pressures. An internal dimension of these processes involved the privatisation, marketization and the contracting out of services pursued by the Conservative governments during the 1980s and 1990s and continued by New Labour. The external processes impacting on the state, which also provide a broader framework for the internal reforms, relate to globalisation, the main subject of this section.

Globalisation is a complex set of processes, the extent and impact of which as well as suggested responses have been hotly debated. What most analysts would agree is that fundamental changes have taken place in the global environment which are having a profound effect on the role of the state and democratic politics.

Processes of globalisation can be overviewed in terms of the emergence of networks of information, economic relations and political and cultural processes that cut across national boundaries. There is little doubt that these processes have extended their range, speed of operation and mobility with the advance of high tech global capitalism. Satellite, internet, and mobile phone technology allow instantaneous communication of information around the world. Masses of information can be exchanged. Social protest movements can more easily communicate and operate across national boundaries. Global financial movements can instantly take place based on access to the latest financial intelligence. Businesses can readily move their production between countries to take advantage of cheaper labour and / or more profitable activity. As nations have become increasingly enmeshed in this maelstrom of activity, governmental processes have had to adapt. But how?

A number of issues and questions, including the following, can be raised with reference to globalisation and politics. Just how fundamental and wide ranging is the impact of globalisation? What are the benefits and risks involved? What are its consequences for national governments? Are they losing power to forces of global capitalism and if so how and to what extent? How may globalisation be changing the activities of the nation state and national democratic politics? What responses are emerging to globalisation, and what new types of political institutions may be necessary? Are governments able to retain a monopoly in the use of power in their prescribed territories? And to what extent is it necessary, or possible, for national governments to beneficially reconfigure their use of power by a degree of devolution downwards to regional and local levels and by passing some sovereignty upwards to supra-state organisations? Such questions are being debated across a range of positions adopted on globalisation.

For purposes of classification, the author will be guided by a system devised by David Held (2000a & b). One position is labelled 'traditionalist'. This emphasises that despite evidence of extensive internationalisation, the impact of globalisation has been overstated. Whilst states have had to adapt to changing international conditions, they remain strong and powerful political entities. Toward the other extreme, a second position emphasises that the forces of globalisation are profound and irresistible, fundamentally weakening the power of the state. This position is sometimes referred to as 'hyper-globalist' and adopts a positive and optimistic view of the benefits of global free enterprise, especially for consumers. However, whilst agreeing with the profound effect of global capitalism, there is also a far more pessimistic interpretation which emphasises the ravages brought by large corporations and a transnational capitalist class. In between the traditionalist and globalist positions lies the 'transformationist' position. Transformationists agree that profound forces of globalisation are at work and contend that they bring both benefits and risks. This stance is cautiously optimistic. For transformationists, although difficult, it is possible and necessary to steer the globalisation process through utilising various levels of governance from the local through to the global, working with national governments so as to enhance benefits and minimise risks which are emerging.

Hirst and Thompson are proponents of the traditionalist position. They argue that a distinction needs to be made between multinational businesses (with a headquarters fixed in one country and operations in other countries) and transnational businesses (which can move between countries much more freely). Multinationals provide an index of internationalisation but only transnationals are truly global organisations and these do not predominate. Hirst and Thompson use economic data to argue that the differences in levels of international trade in the contemporary world and that which existed in previous conditions of colonialism around the turn of the twentieth century are not that great. International trade was then well advanced and national economies have not since become disembedded and integrated into a single global economy, due to the limited impact of transnational corporations. Instead, they are integrated into an international economy, with some divisions into trading blocks, and where multinationals with headquarters in nations where they are subject to control are the key business organisations. Hirst and Thompson tend to adopt the 'state as container' view of politics, which maintains that control of national boundaries remains relatively intact and nation states retain strong control within their territory and remain a very powerful political influence in the world.

The above position now tends to be a minority one. Most analysts recognise that modern technology has compressed time, sped up the pace of change and reduced the barriers of distance. Finance, financial institutions and high tech industry, a growing element of advanced economies, create light economies in which productive forces are much more mobile than those of traditional manufacturing and extractive industries. Continuity of access to information is part of the new global environment. As communication is global and instantaneous, events happening in different parts of the world and communicated globally are received in countries at their own local time. At the cultural level, long gone seem the days (the early 1980s) when most people in Britain had access to only three television channels, each of which went off the air late at night, with the BBC airing the national anthem.

The effects of globalisation are arguably varied and penetrating. Change and innovation are vital to the survival of businesses in a competitive global environment. National governments are likely to find it increasingly difficult to operate as bounded sovereign entities in the face of world financial markets, business investment decisions and flows of information. Faced with these dynamics, workers have to be prepared to retrain or relocate and governments need to support this process, as well as keeping down rates of corporation tax, if they are to attract and retain inward investment. As countries open up to attract investment from overseas, they tend to also be open to its potential withdrawal.

Kenichi Ohmae adopts the above mentioned hyper-globalist position and argues that the forces of free enterprise global capitalism are both irresistible and beneficial. Left to itself in a free market globalised world, he argues that business finds the most advantageous places for its activities and sales of goods and services. According to Ohmae, such freely operating globalised business and trade enhances overall prosperity and should therefore be embraced. In complete opposition to the 'state as container' view, Ohmae argues that national governments should tend to shed their functions of economic regulation as the forces of globalisation bring about a 'borderless world'. Attempts to erect national trade barriers or introduce protectionist subsidies would distort the beneficial effect of the global free market and thus be backward looking and counterproductive. By contrast, the natural role of government in a globalised world is to promote conditions of flexibility and free markets for both businesses and workers, and their main interventionist role is to provide adequate infrastructure and well educated and trained employees. Power becomes increasingly transferred to consumers who benefit from massive diversity and choice in global markets. From this perspective, there would be little role for supra-national governance apart from guaranteeing a framework for the operation of global free enterprise. Ohmae claims a further benefit of globalisation to be a reduced risk of war between nations. This is because as the capital of organisations is increasingly global, wars between nations would destroy abroad the resources of home based businesses.

Critics have suggested that Ohmae's position is reminiscent of the ideological arguments adopted by mid nineteenth century liberal economists on the civilising and wealth creating benefits of free trade. As such, it attempts to justify those processes which primarily benefit a few by emphasising that the benefits are widespread.

The availability of cheap goods may be attractive to consumers. However, cheap goods often originate from countries where cheap labour is available. Given the high mobility of capital compared to labour, in a competitive global free for all it may be very difficult for many workers to resist pressures toward a deterioration in their terms and conditions of employment when they face the possibility of unemployment that can come from the threat to move capital investment to lower wage economies. Governments that try to restrict the mobility of capital investment are likely to find it difficult to attract inward investment in the first place and traditional trade union action to protect wages and conditions of employment is likely to be ineffective or even counterproductive as businesses are more freely able to utilise cheap labour that is available in developing countries.

Leslie Sklair adopts an opposing stance on globalisation to that of Ohmae. He takes evidence of the growth of transnational corporations as an index of globalisation. Sklair argues that the driving force for expansion of these organisations is a transnational capitalist class whose primary aim is maximisation of shareholder profit. It is not the consumer with whom power lies under global capitalism but, via the spread of cheaply available mass media throughout the world and the indoctrination of people into the ideology of consumerism, the real beneficiaries are the corporations and their shareholders. Otherwise, the effects of global capitalism are largely negative in two interconnected areas. Firstly, it is claimed that globalisation brings about growing inequality between and within nations, and secondly it is ecologically destructive. Driven by consumerism and the quest for profits, transnational corporations hold little concern for the sustainability of resources or the needs of indigenous populations.

The transformationist position on globalisation will be scrutinised in more detail in a later section as it tends to be aligned with high modernist sociological analysis. Held and McGrew favour a transformationist perspective. From this position, in the context of an increasingly complex and quickly changing world where events can have long range impacts, the forces of globalisation need to be politically steered to minimise new associated risks and maximise beneficial outcomes. To do so, national governments will need to become reconfigured to work with supra-national political and organisational bodies, non-governmental organisations and local political bodies, and trade a degree of sovereign power to enhance overall political control. This is part of a complex and changing world of democratic politics which may raise questions about the capacity of national governments to reflect the will of their electorates and lead to more political activity through 'new social movements'.

New social movements

Whilst there is some disagreement on the extent to which the issues and strategies of 'new social movements' are that new, the main hallmark of these movements is their capacity to organise and engage in rapid and often direct action protests with remarkable speed and often on an international scale. Direct action protests are not themselves new; witness the 1932 mass trespass in the Peak District to acquire access rights for walking the countryside and the Jarrow March of unemployed workers in 1936 during the Great Depression. However, from the late 1960s direct action protests in terms of growing scale and global impact were really making their mark. A new generation, socialized into a society of relative prosperity following the post war austerity, were seizing on issues of liberation and identity in protest movements for civil rights and women's rights and in opposition to the Vietnam War. These types of protest movement were arguably a stepping stone to the new type.

Technological advances have assisted the process of globalisation. New means of communication, for example in the form of satellite communication and the internet, have extended the range and immediacy with which large sections of the population can receive information about events throughout the world. Such communications technology, especially the internet and mobile phones, becomes a key force at the disposal of new social movements offering instant global communications networks for sharing information and mobilising action. The outcome has been an array of global protest movements including those on environmental issues, against hunger and starvation, against global capitalism generally and against the Gulf war and the Iraq war. And even protests which are more locally focussed, as, for example, those opposing the expansion of particular airports or road building programs, often take their lead from issues of global relevance such as damage to the environment.

The mass media has also been used to assist in organising on line petitions. The potential speed by which a response can be mobilised is illustrated in a petition initiated in May 2014 which received over 100,000 signatures to pressure the American authorities to resume their search for the crew of a yacht that capsized in the mid-Atlantic within about 48 hours of their decision to call off the search.

How do these movements contrast with politics more conventional to the industrial age? Evidence suggests that labour movements emerged and declined alongside the era of industrial capitalism. This era witnessed the growth of trade unions, established to protect the interests of industrial workers, and it was from the trade union movement in Britain that the Labour Party was established to represent workers' interests in Parliament. Labour thus became the party of significant sections of the working class and it is argued that voting was often both partisan and class aligned. Social and political divisions were shaped by battles for resources and the achievement of material security in a relatively class conscious society. Political engagement was thus allied with industrial and class struggles and was channelled largely through the formal organisations of trade unions, employers' associations and national political parties.

What social and political changes have undermined this traditional model? We have previously reviewed arguments that following the post war years a decomposition of the class system has been accompanied by a decline in class alignment and partisanship in voting behaviour. From this it can be concluded that the class attachments of the past have become of less significance in rallying contemporary voters.

Furthermore, low turnout rates in national elections can be argued to be indicative of growing apathy or disillusionment in national politics. One reason for this could be the lack of range available to voters in liberal democratic political systems, where the battle for the mass vote tends to narrow the position of the political parties toward occupancy of the centre ground. For example, in Britain since the 1980s, Labour and then the Conservatives have moderated their positions in an attempt to maximise their appeal to the mass electorate. However, this can mean that parties find it difficult to establish clear policy and ideological battle lines and increasing proportions of the electorate come to feel that there is little clear choice available to them. The repositioning of the Labour Party in Britain has been particularly instructive. Once adopting a position on the political left and advocating an alternative model to free enterprise capitalism, New Labour became far more attuned to the interests of business and global capitalism. Those opposing these forces might feel the need to become involved outside of party politics to make their mark.

As problems and attempts to politically manage them are rising to a global level, new political infrastructure of supra national organisations have emerged. These include the European Union, various regional trading blocks, the United Nations and the World Bank. Agreements have been made between governments on issues such as restricting greenhouse gas emissions. States have thus had to surrender a degree of national sovereignty for the common good in the face of global problems. The view that conventional national politics cannot offer solutions to problems of global scale, along with the perception of the declining national sovereignty and thus also the declining impact of the electorate on the policies of national government may also be part of a political reconfiguration process which sees more people turn to the politics of new social movements.

In an age of affluence and social class decline in western democracies, the political agenda has moved more toward ethical global issues and new arenas of protest. New social movements have broadened both the view of politics and the types of political involvement. Protest does not have to be organised through established political hierarchies but can take place through wide ranging networks. The protest movements themselves often enshrine anti-bureaucratic and anti-hierarchical values and can form broad alliances of groups under such general umbrellas as anti-globalisation and anti-capitalism. Peace movements, environmental protection movements and protests against rampant capitalism can take the form of global social movement responses coinciding with international forums of politicians established to reach agreement on global issues but which appear to protestors to be protecting the vested interests which are part of the problem. Widespread access to communications technology has therefore arguably enhanced and enlivened the democratic process and as well as extending communication, globalisation has extended opportunities for geographical mobility.

Action has included protests outside the World Trade Organization meeting in Seattle in 1999 in which protest groups on a wide range of issues, from various countries and adopting a variety of strategies, protested under the general umbrella of opposition to global capitalism. It was the direct action of some in the form of damage to property which grabbed the news headlines globally. Anti Iraq war demonstrations in cities throughout the world, culminating around the 15 – 16 February 2003, provide an example of the mobilization potential of new social movements with the largest gathering in Rome estimated to have attracted about three million people.

Despite their global nature, how new social movement protests play themselves out in different countries can remain quite variable. This suggests that there can remain a significant degree of national framing to political responses. For example, research by Koopmans (Porta (ed) 2009) into protests against the Gulf War in January 1991 compared the protest movements in Germany, France and the Netherlands. Despite global transmission of sanitised and standardised images as a result of military censorship, Koopmans found vastly different levels and types of protest in the three countries which he related to different political opportunity structures and cultural and historical interpretive frameworks.

Theoretical contributions to the study of new social movements include those of Castells, Giddens and Beck. Castells sees the emergence of information network societies as providing a new arena of conflict between oppressors and oppressed replacing the old social class opposition of industrial capitalism. Under conditions of fluid global capitalism, governments compete to attract and hold onto inward investment for the benefit of employment and tax income. This leads national governments to a dilemma. Business and investment will be particularly attracted to those countries with the lower corporate tax rates and welfare costs. However, such a situation may be unattractive to large proportions of their national electorate who find that they have no party to champion the welfare state and protect workers' rights.

Both Giddens and Beck analyse the emergence of new social movements in terms of new risks associated with an increasingly globalized world. For Giddens, risks of war, environmental destruction and financial instability are not new. However, the extent of our vulnerability to them has been exacerbated by the advance of global interconnectedness, whilst national governments appear increasingly ill equipped to tackle them. For Beck, the emergence of new social movements in the context of globalisation represents both the death of old and birth of new democratic politics. The advance of globalisation brings with it the major bi-product of new and unexpected risks which are of a global nature and cannot be resolved by national governments. The attempt to manage risks must therefore be global and new democratic politics takes the form of globalisation from above and globalisation from below. Globalisation from above sees the emergence of transnational structures of governance, forums and international treaties which bind national governments to commitments. Globalisation from below takes the form of social movements that operate in an ad hoc way, outside of formal political and party structures, to influence political decision making.

Foucault – the power of discourse

For Foucault, the term 'discourse' refers to ways of thinking and talking that relate to the use of power. The advance of the Enlightenment promoted the discourse of science – the view that science and rational thinking can be used to ameliorate the social condition. This Enlightenment discourse heralded new approaches to the problem of social control in the form of a transition from punishment of offenders through the imposition of bodily pain, to confinement, treatment and surveillance. From the perspective of the Enlightenment discourse, this was viewed as an advance in humanitarianism.

Foucault challenged this interpretation. Instead, he argued, the Enlightenment discourse has helped to shape an acceptance of control by scientific professionals in the treatment of those who do not conform to moral norms. Experts grade and classify behaviour and refine appropriate punishment or treatment for non-conformity. The general trend has been toward a 'carceral society' of rationally regulated thinking and behaviour in which the state and various social institutions have developed in the capacity to oversee populations as a means of imposing discipline and control. Indeed, self-reflection on the possibility of surveillance makes self-control all the more effective, but through the capacity that people have for evasion control is never total.

Consider, for example, the surveillance threat of possible inspection at any time which is designed to control the performance of teachers. Although acting as a powerful constraint on performance and behaviour, like people in other situations where control is imposed through the constant threat of surveillance, teachers are not helpless in employing tactics of resistance or evasion.

Discourse brings deviance into being. For example, homosexuality was once regarded as sinful behaviour in the context of religious discourse. As such, it was either suppressed or perhaps owned up to in the privacy of the confessional. It subsequently became seen as a deviance and illness in need of scientific treatment to suppress and cure, continuing similar moral judgements but now through the control of a substituted scientific jargon. From a Foucaultian viewpoint, on the one hand liberalisation of the law and the more recent availability of gay civil ceremonies and marriages appear to be libertarian and humanitarian reforms resulting from challenges to the dominant discourse of sexual deviance. However, one could also argue that reforms have enabled greater surveillance of sexual preference by making the choices available more open and thus more visible.

According to Foucault, prior to the Enlightenment, the mad were viewed as relatively harmless and left to go about their lives unhindered. Foucault argues that the advance of the discourse of reason accompanying the Enlightenment brought into sharp relief the danger of madness and the need for confinement, control and treatment to bring the person to reason. The development of the sciences of treatment, especially psychiatry, in a sense create deviances for purposes of intervention, institutionalisation and control. They claim a truth in their scientific diagnosis, but the claim to scientific truth is in reality more a claim to the control of deviance. For Foucault, treatment of the mad does not represent the commonly accepted advance in humanitarianism, but is part of broader surveillance society of regulation and discipline across a range in institutions in which people become the objects of power in the form of scientific discourse.

Postmodernism – the illusion of politics

The effects of globalisation, especially with reference to the mass media, are an integral part of postmodern theory. For postmodernists, the positive connotation of modernity associated with the eighteenth century Enlightenment was the idea of progressive human liberation from control by fear and superstition through the application of science and rational thinking. Faith in the application of science to society brought the prospect of social improvement through social engineering. For Bauman, this metanarrative (all embracing system of beliefs) became associated in the twentieth century with the political metanarratives and collectivist ideologies of fascism and communism which were adopted by totalitarian regimes through which states controlled their populations through fear and repression. In Britain, the post war creation of the welfare state was seen by Bauman as another example from the modern period of the state attempting to engineer policy based on a single set of ideals.

Thus, in modern society, the state intervened into the personal sphere to deliver universal policies. Intervention was guided by political metanarratives such as social democracy, liberalism or Marxism and faith in the application of science. Metanarratives provided people with ontological security – a feeling of the comfort of certainty – which also related to social structures that provided fixed identify and lifetime projects.

Postmodernists maintain that the crisis that confronted modernity was the abject failure of social engineering shaped by political metanarratives to deliver the progress that it promised. With this failure collapsed the modernist metanarrative and from it postmodern society, devoid of an overarching metanarrative, and experiencing a fragmentation of state power, was emerging. Arguably, the watershed of this change in Britain was the emergence of new right anti-collectivist politics during the 1980s when the promise of improvement for the poor through social engineering gave way to policy of general improvement through opening up free market forces. Abroad, the failure of social engineering was dramatically evidenced in the collapse of the Eastern Bloc regimes from the late 1980s. For Bauman, in the postmodern global environment, collective projects and actions collapse and the state retreats from being a focal point of both power and political protest. The politics of control by or fear of the state give way to a new type of fear that people experience in having to make choices in situations of massively enhanced individual autonomy.

Those who argue that a postmodern condition has emerged emphasise that belief in singular moral codes and universal truths has collapsed, as has social structuring and identity in terms of class, gender and ethnicity. Within this context, ontological security has to be continuously sought and reinventing personal identity becomes an essential skill.

Postmodern societies are media, information and high tech societies. The condition of the cultural environment is thus seen as coming to play a more important role in life than economic factors. In such societies, according to Lyotard, knowledge loses its monopoly as an all embracing truth, used by the state to engineer social control. Instead, people apply knowledge for its usefulness in a society of diverse interests. Through this relativistic and pragmatic use of knowledge, power becomes dispersed down from the state to various pressure groups and businesses who use information to advance their different interests.

The postmodern world is one of social fragmentation and fluidity, one in which metanarratives will not form useful guides to thinking and organising one's life. Participatory democracy loses its vitality as life has become individualised. Fewer people participate in conventional politics and civic activities; politics has become personalised and perhaps trivialised as an activity of individual status aspiration and, especially for the younger generation, more often takes on the form of direct action new social movements of post material politics focussing on ethical issues.

Baudrillard takes the postmodernist position further and argues that in a media dominated society, politics recedes to the manipulation of symbols to convey political messages which have no necessary connection to any underlying political events. As political messages rely on endlessly back referenced media images, neither truth nor authentic reality can be substantiated and politics collapses into the realm of illusion.

High modernism and risk society

Ulrich Beck, like Anthony Giddens, is more cautions of the celebratory effects of modernisation than many nineteenth and early twentieth century thinkers, but not as critical as postmodernists of the achievements of modernism. Neither do they view the modernist era as finished and becoming replaced by postmodern society.

Beck recognises three key historical stages: 1) pre-modern, 2) simple modern and 3) reflexive modern. Thus 'just as modernization dissolved the structure of feudal society in the nineteenth century and produced the industrial society, modernisation today is dissolving industrial society and another modernity is coming into being' (Beck,1992, p.10). The simple modern stage is the classical industrial society which is organised around the principle of the distribution of goods and structured into social classes. The reflexive modern society is one of new and enhanced risks created by the advance of industry and science in which various scientific specialisms have developed to manage these risks. However, people working within these specialisms act as technical experts who are often alien to people directly affected by the risks and have frequently been able to overpower lay contributors by imposing unreflexive scientific boundaries on public debate.

For Beck, reflexive modernisation heralds a stage in the modernisation process whereby further progress requires a new type of political involvement to overcome the culture of scientism (the cultural belief in the unassailability of science) that accompanied the earlier modern stage. He argues that more genuine reflexive negotiation needs to be engaged in between scientists and technical experts, who study the risk effects of our interventions in society and nature in terms of laboratory knowledge, and lay people who hold the knowledge of their direct experience. This requires the political engagement of the latter in the political task of more effectively managing risk.

The break in the first (classical industrial) and second (risk industrial) phases of modernity has brought new insecurities into people's lives.

The breakdown of constraining but supporting social structures and the advance of individualism has transpired at the same time that the effects of scientific and technological advance have increased the risks that are consequent on their growing capacity for intervention in society and nature. First modernity opposed tradition with science and rationality. During this modern industrial stage, an emphasis on the creation of wealth and progress predominated with risks seen in terms of side effects. However, second modernity takes modernisation to a new level. At this level, the extent of technological and economic intervention by highly developed productive forces has raised the consequent production of risk to a position of primacy over production itself. The key task is now managing the risks created but this cannot be achieved within the circle of science alone that created them. A fundamental change in politics is required.

In early modern society, a system of representative democracy had developed in which politics was about democratic rights of the governed to give their consent to the formation of governments. During this stage, business was seen as a non-political private sphere in which enhancement of the standard of living and progress which it brought protected it from criticism regarding its negative consequences. Beck argues that this separation of the spheres of politics and non-politics was operative up to the first half of the twentieth century. However, the separation first blurred and then tended to switch over. Frenetic changes in the 'techno-economic system' during the latter decades of the twentieth century led to growing discontent with the sphere of politics conventionally defined. At the same time, the risk consequences of the techno-economic system were enhanced and the protective trust in progress undermined. New social movements, such as green politics, emerged to refocus politics into this previously non-political area. Industry had thus had to increasingly work within a new political and moral framework where the consequences of its interventions can be checked and monitored.

High modernism – transformationism and the reconfiguration of political power

Social theorists who adopt what can generally be called a high modernist position argue that postmodernists go too far in their analysis of the decline of politics. Whilst it is recognised that globalisation has led to fundamental social changes, high modernists argue that the modernist task of rational understanding as the basis for social intervention should not be abandoned. They tend to adopt what Held refers to as a transformationist approach toward globalisation. This position shares some common ground with globalists in opposing the 'state as container' view held by traditionalists and acknowledges that global processes are intruding into national politics. However, for transformationists, unlike hyper-globalists, this does not mean that state power is in substantial decline. They argue that governments can and have to respond to the impact of globalisation through reconfiguring their power and legitimacy alongside that of other institutions. This provides the governance to enhance globalisation by steering the process at appropriate levels. For transformationists, this means that national governments must be prepared to share some sovereignty with international (for example the United Nations), transnational (for example the European Union) and sub-state organisations (for example non-governmental organisations).

Both Anthony Giddens and Ulrich Beck draw attention to new levels of risk which emerge with globalisation. The risks themselves are manufactured rather than natural risks – they are a product of technological advances, including those which were aimed to control other risks. Manufactured risks are often of global magnitude and include environmental damage, the consequences of global warming, reliance on internet computer systems which are vulnerable to computer virus and cyber attacks, possible economic destabilisation through rapid and vast currency movements, polarisation of rich and poor nations, and international crime and terrorism.

Giddens points out that people in mature democracies appear to be losing faith in the capacity or will of national governments to tackle global problems as they can see global forces cutting across domestic democratic politics. In Britain, for example, a steady decline in turnout at recent general elections may reflect a growing lack of confidence that national government has the political purchase on events in a globalised world that it once had. Furthermore, faith in politicians can be undermined as more open information societies are likely to provide knowledge of misdeeds and corruption in politics.

On the other hand, there is evidence of increasing involvement, especially by young people, in global pressure groups on issues such as world trade, poverty and the environment. These movements are usually less hierarchical than more traditional pressure groups and utilise modern technology for people to communicate and organise quickly, sometimes at a global level. Against high tech new social movement networks, government, which tends to operate top down, can be slow footed.

For high modernists, new and more appropriate institutions, guided by contemporary theory, need to be developed to help obtain political purchase on events in the face of new global risks. It is argued that we cannot be resigned to the intellectual anarchy of the postmodernists and the economic anarchy of the global free marketers. Instead, guided by the insights of a transformationist and high modernist analysis, political institutions need to be refashioned and sufficiently sophisticated to respond to new challenges in a rapidly changing world. This relates particularly to the need to develop supra-national institutions which can operate to combat global problems and risks more effectively than states can individually.

What practical guidance can theory provide to improve governance in a globalising world? In Runaway World (2002), Giddens argues that democratic political institutions are the only ones that can be sufficiently equipped to respond to a dynamic global environment. Democracy therefore needs to be enhanced. For Giddens, improved responsiveness to people and processes requires a deepening of democracy. He emphasises the following dimensions:

1) Democratic institutions need to be devolved below state level to regions, localities and pressure groups which national governments should work closely with.

2) The expansion of voluntary and self-help groups requires the nurturing of a civil culture of responsibility. Free market reforms are not enough. They can damage the social fabric by leaving a void between the individual and the state, as experienced in the reforms introduced in Russia following the collapse of the Soviet Union.

3) The development of a range of democratic institutions above the state are essential to cope with global matters. These may include international

organisations such as the United Nations, which have limited power over the sovereignty of state members, or transnational organisations such as the European Union, whose member states pool a degree of their sovereignty to engage more effectively at a transnational level. In organisations of the former type, it may be beneficial for member states to cede more sovereignty, whilst regarding the European Union, a case is put for greater democratisation.

Deficiencies of supra-national organisations

A number of criticisms have been frequently made against supra-national organisations. Some organisations, such as the World Bank and the World Trade Organisation, were set up to promote the development of poor countries. A strong criticism is that grants, loans and debt cancellation usually have attached to them the requirement of liberal market reforms which arguably have often worsened the life of the poor in the recipient countries.

A related criticism is that wealthy nations are the main beneficiaries of free trade, yet they have the power to oppose free trade agreements when it suits them. An example here is the deadlock faced in free trade negotiations following the 2001 World trade Organisation meeting on such sticking points as the refusal of the United States to relinquish payment of subsidies to its farmers.

Both the World Trade Organisation and the G8, which represents the world's leading eight industrial nations, have often been perceived as being only concerned with the interests of powerful capitalist nations. As a result, the meetings of both organisations have encountered massive protests, the most notorious being at the WTO meeting in Seattle in 1999. A related issue is that these organisations are also sometimes seen as out of step with issues of concern to their own populations. For example, at the 2006 G8 meeting at St. Petersberg, attention was focussed on co-operation on energy and combating global terrorism, whilst opinion polls conducted amongst people in the member states indicated that they wanted issues of global poverty, human rights and combating infectious diseases discussed.

A further issue is that some supra-national organisations, such as the United Nations, lack binding controls over member states. For example, although the UN General Assembly can pass resolutions, these are not legally binding and cannot override national sovereignty. Furthermore, national sovereignty again prevails vis-à-vis the UN International Court of Justice in relation to which only about a third of member states, notably excluding the United States, accept its jurisdiction.

Against the backdrop of such criticisms, several pointers toward institutional reform of supra-national organisations have been suggested by J. Lloyd in 'The Protest Ethic' (2001). Firstly, he argues that global institutions need to be based on a broadly agreed global ethical basis without appearing to be an imposition of the west. Secondly, it is likely that new and more powerful supra-national organisations and agreements will need to be established to form a binding obligation between nations if some of the most pressing global problems are to be tackled. Thirdly, institutions need to be established in a form which is more responsive to challenges than traditional bureaucratic hierarchies are. Fourthly, these institutions must not be too remote but need to be in touch with issues of concern to citizens. Fifthly, governments will often find it beneficial to set up cross-national organisations sharing surveillance and intelligence to deal with problems such as the global dimension of criminal activity and terrorism.

High modernism, transformationism and third way politics

Anthony Giddens offered a broad analytic basis for New Labour politics and has been open in his intellectual association with 'the third way' approach in the text of that title (2000). Applied in the context of British politics, he argued that the politics of the traditional Labour left and the old new right Conservatives have failed and are increasingly inappropriate approaches for the current age of globalisation. By demonstrating the intellectual foundations of third way politics, Giddens argues that the radical nature of this centre ground position will become clearer.

The politics of the old left regarded the motives and actions of private enterprise as suspect and in need of regulation. The traditional left distrusted the free market as a means of allocating goods and services. Instead, faith was put in state bureaucratic centralisation in economic planning and the nationalisation of strategic industries. Egalitarianism was to be promoted through redistributive taxation and welfare services delivered through the public sector. Top down planning was imposed to control the anarchic features of free enterprise capitalism. Politics following this model was adopted by the post war Labour government and, the author of this text would add, more reluctantly by post war Conservative governments.

The economic failures of the 1970s led to a resurgence of free enterprise thinking and the coming to power of the new right Conservatives in 1979. State regulation and an over bloated public sector were blamed for the economic sclerosis and social breakdown of the 1970s. The response of the new right was to cut down bureaucracy, pursue privatisation and reinvigorate the free market. With successive election victories in 1983, 1987 and 1992, anti-collectivist policies were followed.

For Giddens, the fluidity and interconnectedness of the new global world has rendered both positions inappropriate. On the one hand, the central control and planning approach of the old left is too top down and not responsive enough to the needs of quickly changing modern global markets. The suspicion of and restrictions on private enterprise are not necessarily well founded and would be counterproductive to investment and employment in a global environment of mobile capital. On the other hand, it is argued that relinquishing social responsibilities and allowing free market forces to rule is very dangerous to social stability in the fluid conditions of global capitalism.

So what is the alternative? For Giddens, the high modernist approach coupled with a transformationist view of globalisation leads to third way politics. This is not just about politics in Britain but, as part of a modernising response to globalisation, Giddens argues that it is necessary for all governments to take heed of contemporary challenges and cooperate in developing supra-national guidelines and institutions. Although sovereign powers of nation states remain, there needs to be some pooling of sovereignty for the benefit of all nations.

Capitalist markets cannot be banned or overregulated. At one extreme, the collapse of the old Eastern Bloc command economies shows that such central planning cannot cope with globalisation. At the other extreme, however, left to their own devices, free markets will wreak havoc. Giddens suggests that markets need to be improved by governmental action, but not by a centralist approach. Instead, more institutions both above and below the state need to be developed to improve the workings of the free market and offer safeguards against its negative effects. For example, world economies are now so integrated that the impact of financial crises could be swift, major and extensive. This does not mean turning away from global capitalism but setting up institutions for both surveillance and fast response.

Man's impact on the environment is bringing global changes. This again does not mean turning away from modernisation and shackling businesses. Often technology provides solutions. Thus, waste is now increasingly becoming a resource and the knowledge economy produces more with less resources. However, the increasingly global nature of risk does mean that globally agreed political responses with teeth and based on science need to foster ecological responsibility in both producers and consumers.

New Labour – the radical centre?

There was much debate over the policies and ideology of New Labour. Had it betrayed the values and goals of the old Labour Party? Was it bereft of ideological guiding principles and preoccupied with pragmatic decision making? Was it little different from new right Conservatism but with a limited added social dimension? In this section, a brief account of New Labour policy and its intellectual basis will be offered.

The 'third way' tag and official re-branding of Labour as New Labour emphasised a break from the old ideologies of the post war political left (collectivism) and more recent new right approach to conservatism (anti-collectivism). Respectively, these ideological positions prioritised the state and public sector or the deregulated private sector as superior models for organising society. Unlike the new right, New Labour retained the view that there is such a thing as the common good, but just what this common good is and how it can best be achieved marked New Labour off from traditional Labour.

Given the high tech nature of the contemporary economy, the break up of the old class structure and the decline of class politics, New Labour had not put itself forward as a party of the working class. Rather, it had managed to broaden its appeal to attract electoral support from people across a range of occupations.

Reform of the public services was central to Labour's modernisation agenda and exemplified its third way approach. It was argued that whilst the goal of providing good quality public services remained, the means of achieving this needed to be more flexible. The old model of state provided and top down planned public service provision was argued to be insufficiently responsive to user needs and modernisation. By contrast, an emphasis on the free market, privatisation and contracting out had arguably damaged public services. New Labour's position was less ideologically fundamentalist than either of these approaches. It relied on breaking down boundaries and the ideological divide between public sector provision and private sector provision. It may be that in a number of cases, the resources for public services could be maximised by public and private partnership arrangements. The exact configuration for the provision of different public service projects would be a matter of analysis in each case.

New right reforms placed emphasis on the individual and tended to neglect 'society'. A criticism of this emphasis was that a social void tended to be left between the state and the free market. Reminiscent of Durkheim's earlier suggestions for engineering a more integrated society, an emphasis was placed by New Labour on the need for more intermediate level institutions such as voluntary groups to help bind civil society and encourage people in civic responsibilities.

For New Labour, it was the role of government to help create the conditions for both business and workers to adapt to global change. Given the enhanced challenges of global competition, the government attempted to work with the grain of capitalism by promoting a flexible labour market underpinned by retraining to encourage economic competitiveness and inward investment. This was referred to as the creation of a 'magnet economy' of skilled labour in which the government attempted to combine the economic competitiveness of a market economy with social justice goals of fairness through such safeguards as the minimum wage.

On the question of opportunity, New Labour attempted to enhance opportunity of the many by maximising opportunities for participation in work to those who may otherwise have been excluded (for example the unskilled and single parents). In doing so, it balanced the left derived principle of rights with the right orientated principle of obligations. This meant that the government provided schemes, including retraining and child care, to help people to become self-supporting, but emphasised that it is their responsibility to take advantage of such opportunities.

On the question of equality, New Labour dismissed the conception of equality of outcome as a relic of old Labour which would be completely inappropriate in a market driven global world. Instead, equality should be seen primarily in terms of opportunity. There were problems here however, which tended to get side stepped. For example, Giddens has pointed out that the diverse outcomes of equality of opportunity for one generation can lead to inequality of opportunity for the next generation. Little was said by Giddens or New Labour on whether or how this can be countered. Furthermore, society had itself, by some measures, become increasingly unequal in the distribution of income, not just during the period of new right government but also during the time that New Labour was in power. In this context, the Labour government had been remarkably quiet on the issue of executive and director pay packages and massive city bonuses, all of which were way above the settlements that lower paid workers have had to accept.

It could be argued that those who opposed the third way and criticise it as an amorphous compromise with no real compass bearing tended to do so if they were rooted in the old left or right ideological opposition and models of the past. For Giddens, by abandoning these redundant positions, it could be appreciated that politics of the third way had a dynamic cutting edge necessary for coming to terms with and managing the challenges of globalisation where past approaches would fail.

Civic Conservatism

New Labour was defeated in the 2010 General Election and replaced in government by a Conservative-led coalition with the Liberal Democrats. David Cameron had been leader of the Conservative Party since 2005 and had engaged in a process of modernizing the Party image and ideology. This process was influenced by a number of important factors. Firstly, Cameron wanted to develop an alternative form of conservatism to the free market model of the new right and to distance the modern Conservative Party from its past reputation as the 'nasty party' of greed and heartless individualism and move in the direction of a more caring image. Secondly, he needed to retain Conservative opposition to the tendency for growing state intervention which had taken place under New Labour. Thirdly, he had inherited an economic crisis which had to be managed following the banking crisis. Fourthly, his party had to find sufficient common ground for working with their Liberal Democrat junior partners in a coalition government.

Much of the intellectual basis for a Cameron's new conservatism is traceable back to the work of David Willetts in the mid 1990s. Willetts developed the idea of Civic Conservatism. This approach looked to involve people in various voluntary and local groups to deliver some of the services of the state. It was argued that (despite talk of greater civic involvement) the growth of the state under New Labour had undermined people's sense of civic responsibility. Civic Conservatism maintained that by transferring some of the burden on the state to civic organisations, citizen involvement and community integration would be enhanced. This anti-state strand of new conservatism opposed what was viewed as New Labour's state centralized approach and to that extent worked with the anti-collectivist heritage of new right conservatism. However, there was also a more collectivist element to Civic Conservatism which picked up on traditional conservative values of promoting local communities to help bond individuals to society and combat the destructive effect on community life of the excessive individualism associated with the free market approach of the new right. Civic Conservatism argued that civic responsibility must be promoted by encouraging people to become involved in local civic organisations which stand in between the state and the individual to deliver services. This approach thus claimed to expand society (hence Cameron's reference to the 'big society') not through the power of the state but through displacing downwards to communities some state activities.

Local civic groups could include residents associations, church groups, political parties, pressure groups, new social movements and numerous charitable organisations and self-help groups. A good example of civic group involvement stemming directly from government policy has been the introduction of free schools. Although taxpayer funded, these institutions are set up locally by such participants as parents, teachers or religious groups and operate independently from local authorities.

Time will tell how far civic involvement will develop. Given the government's priority of deficit reduction through sending cuts and rebalancing the economy in the direction of public to private sector, economic policy does not appear that dissimilar to policy once pursued by the new right and critics may suspect that the notion of the 'big society' provides a cloak of respectability to cutting back state expenditure.

8 // Sociology of Religion

Abstract

The study of religion offers one of the most testing challenges of the need for the sociologist to suspend personal beliefs so as to approach the study of the subject area dispassionately. Sociology does not attempt to answer questions about the existence of a god but analyses religions as belief systems and their influence within society. To do so, the reader will need to be prepared to consider different and unfamiliar ways of defining religion, some of which go beyond religion as conventionally defined.

Some of the key terminology utilised in the sociology of religion is explained, followed by a study of the role of religion in society from the vantage point of the modern founding sociological perspectives of functionalism, Marxism, phenomenology and social action theory.

The question of secularisation is addressed. Secularisation is defined as the assertion of the declining importance of religion and related to the process of modernisation. The secularisation debate is introduced as strongly influenced by Enlightenment thinking which pitted rational scientific thinking against religious belief systems, an influence which fed strongly into the thinking of the founding sociological theorists. The question of secularisation is initially discussed in terms of the reliability and validity of data and touches on methodological disputes between positivists and phenomenologists.

Contemporary disputes within the church in terms of tradition versus reform reflect debates within society. Those touched on here will be the issues of gender equality (the ordination of women priests) and sexuality (the ordination of gay priests).

The issue of secularisation is returned to with reference to the question of a possible resurgence of religion. This is approached in different ways. One approach is simply to consider various forms of evidence such as the emergence of fundamentalist movements and new religious movements, especially in the context of globalisation. Another way of viewing the possible revitalisation of religion is through considering new approaches *to its study. Those introduced here, located mainly in an American setting are ration choice theory and resource mobilisation theory.*

From a more European context, postmodernist and high modernist theoretical perspectives on religion are finally considered. Postmodern theory characterises contemporary society in terms of diversity of belief systems which consumers are free to choose from and move between as lifestyle options. This may be more accommodating than founding theory to recognising the persistence of religion. For high modernists such as Giddens, a world of diversity, rapid change, and uncertainty holds the risk of attraction to the certainty of religious fundamentalism as a source of potential conflict.

The sociological challenge

Religion can be one of the most sensitive of topics to approach sociologically. Its study raises a number of obvious and less obvious problems for the layperson to confront. An obvious problem is that the study of religion can tap into a person's profound beliefs, feelings, emotions and deeply held convictions. The individual may not even be that aware of holding such beliefs. If this is the case, perhaps the greater is the risk of value judgements unknowingly intruding into analysis.

Measuring the extent of religious belief in society is itself a complex issue. However, people's personal beliefs may predispose individuals toward viewing evidence differently or disagreeing on what even counts as evidence. The prospect of a decline in religious belief may elicit from a person with strong religious beliefs the tendency to dismiss it or lament a presumed associated decline in moral standards. Alternatively, to an atheist, such evidence may be welcomed as indicating progress from the grip of dogma and superstition. Atheism, though, is just as much a belief system as are religions. The challenge for the sociologist is to step back and attempt to suspend judgements.

To analyse religion sociologically, we must also be prepared to break away from trying to answer theological questions over the existence of a god or gods. This is not a question tackled directly in sociology but one for theologians and philosophers. Sociological analysis is on a different plane; religions are viewed as systems of belief which serve human and social purposes. Sociologists are thus interested in studying religion as providing systems of meaning which sanctify moral values and guide behaviour. A socially focussed approach can lead to an expansiveness in the definition of religion from traditional ones that we may be more familiar with. This is because belief systems not conventionally viewed as religions, for example political ideologies, may be argued to perform similar personal needs and social functions to those of traditional religions. These belief systems have been referred to as 'quasi religions', providing a broadening of the definition of religion which one who adheres to traditional religious beliefs may find difficult to accept.

Neither is it the role of sociology to compare the plausibility of different systems of religious belief. If sociologists are to compare religions, it is in terms of their impact on behaviour and society. From this vantage point, key questions include the following: to what extent do religions tend to promote social harmony or conflict? In what ways do they primarily support tradition or help bring about social change? What opportunities do their organisations offer or exclude to different social groups such as men and women? What is the relationship between religion and politics in terms of controlling people's lives? How do different religious organisations relate to the state?

A further issue relates to disagreements over the extent to which science can lay claim to a different and superior way of establishing the truth to that of religion. This can lead, within sociology, to the need to be prepared to examine certain assumptions about the nature and practice of science.

Religious belief systems also raise the question of ethnocentricity. Socialisation into a particular religious tradition through family, community or broader cultural influences may incline the believer to view the religions of other cultures as strange or incredible, bizarre or inferior compared to what one is familiar with. But it is a salutary lesson to remember that this outlook is likely to be reciprocated – a similar view is likely to be applied by those of other religious and cultural traditions to our beliefs. The sociologist must be prepared to step back from adopting an ethnocentric stance and partisanship and examine religious belief systems as part of different social and cultural contexts and the different ways of life that they sanction.

A problem which is quite acute in the sociology of religion relates to the use of certain terminology. In their classification of types of religious organisation, sociologists have traditionally employed the terms sect and cult to smaller religious groups. To many people, these terms carry highly negative connotations from which it may be difficult to insulate their use in sociology. Sects and cults have often been viewed with suspicion and hostility and held in low status as deviant communities. It is therefore particularly important that sociologists are able to adopt a degree of value neutrality in the use of such terminology. Indeed, in the face of invasive pejorative connotations, sociologists seem to be abandoning reference to the terms sect and cult in preference for the more neutral alternative of 'new religious movements'.

Definition of main concepts

A **belief system** comprises an integrated and self-contained set of ideas which give a community of adherents a shared understanding of the world. The interconnection of ideas can make belief systems self-reinforcing and resistant to criticism or even change. Ultimately, belief systems rely on followers retaining faith in the basic principles and values upon which the system is based. Religions are classic cases of belief systems, but there is debate in sociology as to how different they are to other systems of thinking, in particular the sciences.

Defining **religion** is problematic. Attempts to provide a definition may vary in emphasising the importance of such different aspects as institutions, rituals, beliefs, sacred texts, and the existence and influence of supernatural beings. For example, it has been suggested that a universally applicable feature of all religions is their claim that supernatural beings have a governing effect over events on earth. This definition derives from the work of Ronald Robertson. Anthony Giddens regards the universal features of religion to include the existence of sacred symbols which elicit a feeling of reverence from a believer; engagement in ritual activities by a community of believers; and places separated from everyday activities in which ceremonies can take place. In so doing, he adopts a definition of religion close to that of Durkheim.

Disputes within sociology regarding the pervasiveness of religion in society and its effects are partly related to the application of such different definitions. Some definitions can be criticised as being too exclusive – being rather narrow, they would exclude some belief systems which others would argue to be religions. Robertson's definition of religion, for example, would exclude Confucianism on the grounds that it lacks belief in a supernatural being. By contrast, other definitions may be so broad and inclusive that they could include as religions some belief systems which many would discount. For example, if religion includes any system of beliefs through which followers acquire an answer to ultimate questions of life, as emphasised by phenomenologists, it is possible that Marxism could be included as a religion. It is important to be aware in this chapter of the variable scope of definitions applied by different sociologists, especially as it may be suspected that definitions employed, the types of evidence sought and the way in which that evidence is interpreted may be used to provide support for desired conclusions. In such a heated area, normally expected scientific procedures may be vulnerable.

It is not always easy to distinguish whether certain beliefs or activities should be referred to as religion or magic. As used in sociology, religion tends to relate to matters of general public wellbeing and the engagement in ritual to these ends by a community of believers. In usually recognising the existence of supernatural powers or beings, the attitude of believers is likely to be one of conciliation and humility toward these powers in the hope of benign intervention bringing beneficial outcomes.

By contrast, **magic** tends to be practiced in small groups or by individuals. According to Goode, magic comprises beliefs and practices in which supernatural forces can be harnessed in a more instrumental and manipulative way to bring about specific desired outcomes for the individual. For Malinowski, magic is pre-scientific in the sense that it is likely to be turned to in cultures where scientific understanding of and technological intervention in life are too limited as a means of effecting desired outcomes. In this context, magic can include the belief that occult forces can be manipulated by a specialist, such as a magician, to cast a spell on certain others, often to perform harm. Voodoo or vengeance magic would provide good examples of such beliefs and practices. If a cult claims to be able to call up supernatural powers, offered in service to individual customers, as in the case of spiritualism, this practice could according to the above definition be classified as magic rather than religion. The fact that it often isn't highlights some of the definitional problems which abound in this area of study.

Magic may also include the belief in fortune telling or individual acts of ritual which are thought to bring good luck. The rituals that some sports people engage in, in the hope of continuing their sporting success, may, although seemingly trivial, be examples of magical superstition. Likewise, a student may place a lucky charm object on their desk when facing the uncertainty and importance in life's fortunes when sitting an exam. The evolutionary anthropologist E.B Tylor referred to the existence of such rituals and beliefs in the contemporary context as 'survivals'; they survive, somewhat out of context, into the modern scientific age as a relic of more primitive times where their original purpose can be more clearly apprehended.

Distinguishing between religion and magic is therefore not always a clear-cut matter and can be fraught with the problem of pejorative judgement.

As well as in the form of belief systems and ritual, religion can be studied sociologically in terms of organisations which can be classified into types. The approach traditionally used classifies **religious organisations** as churches, denominations or sects. At present, these organisations will be defined but the shortcomings of this classification system should be noted. Firstly, it is a western derived typology which may make little sense if it were attempted to be applied to religion in non-western societies. Secondly, the classification of specific religious organisations in terms of this typology may not be clear cut. Thirdly, confusion can arise when these and other terms are used loosely in everyday contexts and applied inconsistently by sociologists. Fourthly, definition and classification should only be a starting point for assist analysis, not an end in itself.

A **church** is a large and formal religious organisation, run by a hierarchy of professional theological specialists and support staff. Church 'membership' is inclusive; it is open and loose in the sense that people are seen to be born into an established church which they are free to opt out of if they so decide. Membership is conducive to full participation in mainstream social life. A church will therefore need to balance the extent to which it adapts to changes in the values and culture of society with moral guidance based on adherence to traditional teachings. It can impose sanctions on behaviour. An example would be through withdrawing sacraments, as, for example, in refusing to marry divorcees. An established church is usually closely allied to the politics of the state. In England, for example, high dignitaries of the Church of England are involved in state ceremonies and bishops sit in the House of Lords. Being part of the political establishment, it tends to be closely identified with by the upper echelons of society. Like the Conservative Party (the Anglican Church has been referred to as the Conservative Party at prayer) it nevertheless relies on support from all levels of society and particular bishops have at times spoken out against the government on such issues as poverty. This evidence of autonomy between church and state and the declining support that the Church receives are sometimes regarded as demonstrating that it is developing denominational characteristics.

The concept of **denomination** was developed by the theological writer Niebuhr. Denominations form part of a pluralistic culture that recognises the legitimacy of a number of religious organisations. They have been particularly noted as a feature of the American religious landscape in which there is no single dominant church that claims inclusive representation and acquires privileges from the state.

Denominational religion is conducive to a free market consumer society in which people may switch between denominations as a form of free choice. It is an intermediate level of religious organisation between that of church and sect, and takes the form of a relatively open institution which may appeal to those dissatisfied with a mainstream church. The organisation is more likely than a church to use lay preachers and allow a more fervent style of preaching. It will be more removed from close identification with state policies than a church and is likely to find less support from the upper classes. A denomination does not tend to place restrictions on members' full participation in mainstream society but may be a little more particular in providing its guidance to followers on its expectations regarding a good way of life. It is also likely that its places of worship will comprise smaller and simpler buildings than those of the established church. As in the case of nineteenth century Methodism, a denomination may grow out of a smaller and more radical group, a sect, which had originally broken away from an established church but over time 'cooled down' in fervour, compromised its strictures and grown.

The term **sect** was used by Weber to denote small religious groups who adhere to an intensive body of beliefs and forming religious communities which usually originate as dissenting breakaway groups that have become dissatisfied with what they perceive as the laxity of churches which they condemn as having compromised their teachings. They therefore often claim to uphold pure religious beliefs to which they expect from their followers close adherence. Sects are likely to put in place strict entry requirements for membership and close monitoring of demanding lifestyles. They will attract larger proportions of people who oppose the state and the ways and values of mainstream society than other religious groups. This type of religious organisation therefore faces a high risk of being viewed as deviant or worse by those who adhere to mainstream religions and lifestyles. To uphold their differences, sects may sometimes erect protective barriers between their group and broader society in the form of geographical distance, distinctive ways of behaving or speaking, and distinctive dress. Methodism at the time of the Wesleys in the eighteenth century was a fiery religious sect and the Quakers during the time of the Restoration of the monarchy in the seventeenth century adopted a defensive sect posture to separate themselves from the more radical levellers. Both sects have since developed in the direction of denominations by growing in size and 'cooling down'.

Membership of sects can be highly exclusive and may require of the potential entrant proof of a conversion experience, the undergoing of initiation ceremonies and the expectation of a deep level of commitment. Members may therefore claim the exclusivity of being part of the initiated superior few. Their relatively small size means that a prescribed way of life can often be closely monitored. Authority and control is not likely to work through a bureaucratic hierarchy but more likely through a charismatic leader.

Unfortunately, within sociology one can find definitional and classificatory inconsistencies in the use of the terms sect and **cult**. Both are small scale organisations which may reject the ways of mainstream society. The term cult has been used by Wallis to define a sect like but less inclusive religious organisation which may not form a cohesive community with a collective place of worship or have a clearly established membership count. For Stark and Bainbridge, the distinguishing feature of cults is that their ideas are either created anew or refashioned from imported traditions, often resulting in eclectic belief systems. The distinction between cults and sects is not always an easy one to apply though. For example, on this basis should Transcendental Meditation, a derivative of Hindu religious beliefs, be referred to as a sect or a cult?

Cults tend to be more deviant from the belief systems of orthodox religions. Some are highly ritualistic and through their own signs and symbols contain esoteric knowledge which they attempt to keep secret to their followers, but many may require little collective ritual and have little clear sense of membership. A diversity of belief systems and degrees of organisational intensity, ranging, for example, from a token interest in astrology to life within a total institution dominated by a powerful personality, requiring close adhesion to prescribed beliefs and subject to precise behavioural controls, as in the Heaven's Gate movement, have been referred to as cults.

The cult type can therefore be subdivided. When Stark and Bainbridge constructed their typology of religious cults (Hunt, 2002, pp.143-144), an interest in astrology would have provided an example of an **audience cult** and Heaven's Gate that of a **cult movement**. In between these extremes they located **client cults** which offer services, such as the technique of Dianetics provided by Scientology, to help people make adjustments to cope with the difficulties of contemporary life. This type is therefore compatible with successful life within mainstream culture. It closely resembles Wallis' world affirming type and would seem well adapted to the needs of a consumer society.

Millenarian movements are religious groups which anticipate fundamental world change through supernatural intervention and are sometimes referred to as revolutionary religions. Such intervention invariably offers salvation to followers and punishment to others who are seen as corrupt. Millenarian movements therefore can appeal to people who have been marginalized in mainstream society and who feel oppressed or have experienced painful personal circumstances or social change. These religions may predict a specific date of reckoning or read into signs foretelling apocalyptic events. However, Chomsky argues that for their teachings to be attractive to followers, the prophesied events need to be within their lifetime. These groups usually take the form of sects or cults, although more mainstream religions may also include millenarian dimensions. The Jehovah's Witnesses provide an example of a millenarian movement.

It is not surprising that many sociologists have decided to stop using the terms cult and sect which are laced in everyday language with sinister meaning and in sociology are susceptible to inconsistent usage. Instead, the more neutral sounding term **new religious movements** has grown in common usage. The term refers to a diversity of small-scale alternatives to established religion which usually originate in cults. These movements often take the form of more loosely organised cults. Moreover, the term 'new' can imply the decline in support for traditional religious organisations and the emergence of novel alternatives, much in the same way as new social movements may indicate a turning away from conventional party politics.

A classificatory scheme for new religious movements has been devised by Roy Wallis. The basis of the classification is the movement's relationship with mainstream society. He identifies **world rejecting** religions as those which are highly critical of the beliefs and ways of broader society. Such movements usually establish a clear psychological and sometimes spatial divide between themselves and conventional society through their own intensive community life and may be referred to as introversionist. Members are likely to have turned their back, at least temporarily, on the outside world and may be expected to renounce contact with broader society, including their family, and undergo a process of conversion to the strict theological dogma and life of the movement. This can include the giving up of past identity, giving over possessions to the movement, acquiring new names and wearing uniforms. In such extreme and rare cases as the Heaven's Gate movement (see box 1), intense control of group members combined with millenarian beliefs has led to mass suicides.

It is through examples of groups at this extreme end of the scale that the labels cult or sect have generated public hostility. Yet the conventional wisdom that cult and sect members are disproportionately drawn from poor backgrounds and are passive and brainwashed victims is not born out by broader evidence.

Box 1

The Heaven's Gate religious cult – a case study of a world rejecting cult

Leaders
Heaven's Gate was a world rejecting cult community. It was established by Marshall Applewhite and Bonnie Nettles in 1975. Within the group, Applewhite took the name of 'Do' and Nettles the name of 'Ti'. When Ti died, Do became the exclusive group leader.

Claims
Do claimed that he had been sent to earth on a mission from the 'next level', as had Jesus, to save souls. The purpose was to save those who could be saved from base human ways, since the day

---

of reckoning was at hand when those who adhered to such base ways would be 'recycled'.

Belief system and opportunity

The belief system was explained through a gardening analogy. Do explained that from the level above human, occasional contact with humans was made. On such occasions, souls from the level above human enter pre-prepared human bodies. Do and Ti were themselves incarnated into human bodies to spread the message – an identical process and purpose to that of Jesus 2000 years ago.

At the time of contact, only some individuals receive souls. This gives them an initial capacity for growth to a higher level, but only under the guidance of the incarnated representative, Do. Do's purpose was to nurture souls, taking followers on a difficult path of renouncing base human ways, a path which only some would be able to follow.

According to Do, each 2000 years, base humans, like weeds, are 'spaded under' and a new cycle of human existence starts. The purpose of the human body in this is to grow souls. Those who are able to follow the rigors of working toward this new level of knowledge and consciousness will ascend to the next level at the day of reckoning. This point in time is immanent and joining the group offers a window of opportunity.

Lifestyle

The group took the form of a highly controlled total institution in which salvation could only be possible through following the tutorship of Do. All members were given new names. Since the next level to which members were aspiring to graduate was sexless, within the cult sex was banned and sexual thoughts had to be guarded against as forms of base human ways. Females had their hair cropped, unisex clothing was worn and some males were castrated. The higher level was able to add to its members through the process of metamorphosis which members were being guided to achieve. Any slippage toward sexuality had to be admitted.

A list of regulations prescribed behaviour in great detail. Exact recipes and procedures had to be followed in the cooking of meals. Occasional fasting was required to cleanse the body. Even the process of shaving had to follow specific instructions. Members were watched over by check partners.

Since Do was convinced that the cult were being watched by the authorities, he devised deception techniques. The community were often on the move, and where they were established, only a limited number of members were allowed outside the building in an attempt to deceive the authorities as to the size of the community.

Behind such controls there was always the threat that the cult offered members their last chance of salvation, to which Do was the only one who held the key.

Science
The imagery of science took numerous forms. It was claimed that Do and Ti had arrived on earth in UFOs. A group member explained that to rise to the next level of consciousness was just like reprogramming a human computer brain with next level knowledge. Web sites were frequently used to propagate the cult's message. The appearance of the Hale-Bopp comet was taken by Do as a sign from Ti that a spaceship was arriving to evacuate the group who would be saved from the spading under process. Even the costumes that group members wore on the goodbye video had space insignia on them.

Evacuation
On 22 March, 1997, in preparation for evacuation, the 39 group members took their lives, mainly through the ingestion of pain killer mixed in apple sauce. The scene of the mass suicide showed the bodies laid out in a highly organised fashion in an attitude of serene countenance.

By contrast, **world affirming** religions focus on developing the spiritual powers of individuals to cope within society. Techniques for coping are aimed at enabling individuals to achieve their full potential. These religions therefore enable followers to positively embrace mainstream society rather than turn away from or against it. They tend to be far less intrusive into lives of followers than are world rejecting religions and may not require participation in a place of collective worship. World affirming religions usually actively market themselves, sell their services and seek widespread participation. They therefore tend to coincide with Stark and Bainbridge's category of client cults. Clients may include high profile celebrity figures, as in the case of the attraction of the Beatles to Transcendental Meditation (a derivative from eastern religions) and Tom Cruise to Scientology, as they offer means of achieving peace of mind and the capacity to cope within a world of stress through the use of a technique. Given their therapeutic dimension, world affirming religions can come into conflict with mainstream psychiatry, as has been the case of the practice of Dianetics within the Scientology movement.

World accommodating religions can be distinguished from each of the above types in that they are neither driven by alienation from broader society nor the enhancement of success within it. Instead, the attitude toward the ways of the world tends to be one of indifference. World accommodating religions may become established through process of breakaway from churches or denominations in the quest for religious and spiritual purity which it is believed the parent organisation has compromised. They therefore tend to to have the characteristics of sects as earlier defined and are likely to focus on improving the inner spiritual life of followers through participation in collective worship, but otherwise make little imposition into the everyday lives of their followers.

An example of a world accommodating religion is Neo-Pentecostalism which is an American Christian revivalist denomination that emphasises the importance of the personal experience of closeness to God rather than dogmatic adherence to religious strictures and the instilling of such experience in others through lively participation at religions meetings. Another is the Atherius Society which combines influences from Christian and eastern religions with the belief in contact from extra-terrestrial intelligences.

Despite evidence of the growth of new and non-western religions in western societies in recent times, an enduring debate in sociology surrounds the question of **secularisation.** Secularisation is the view that the process of modernisation brings with it a decline in the significance of religion. Its advance is often related to the progress of scientific knowledge and industrialisation which are accompanied by rational explanation of and control over the world. It is argued that the advance of rational thinking inclines behaviour toward efficiency and change, which, along with the application of logical scrutiny, undermines tradition and religious beliefs. This suggests that science and religion are opposed ways of thinking and are inversely related – the more there is of one, the less there is of the other. The key sociological theorists who established the foundations of the discipline during the modern period were writing against the backdrop of the Enlightenment and were convinced that forces of secularisation were powerfully at work. Some contemporary theorists have however become far more cautious of the view that religion is in terminal decline.

Founding sociological perspectives on religion:

Functionalism – the social utility of religion

Functionalism is a theory of social utility. In the case of religion, it therefore focuses on how religion benefits society or promotes social well being. This perspective adopts a holistic approach; religion is seen as giving sanction to a single body of values that provide constrains on individual behaviour, thereby integrating society.

Early functionalist approaches to religion were heavily influenced by the social destabilisation of the French Revolution of 1789. Auguste Comte, writing between the 1820s and 1850s, was pained by what he saw as the anarchy of the times, but believed that a new stable social order was on the horizon. From Comte's theoretical perspective, the condition of society is largely determined by the prevailing condition of knowledge about society. For example, the Catholic Church had provided social stability through the Middle Ages because Catholicism was a coherent doctrine that bound the individual to society in a series of religiously sanctioned duties which provided powerful moral constraints on behaviour. However, throughout the eighteenth century, Enlightenment writers were attacking the dogmatic teachings of the Catholic Church with rational, scientific and atheistic critiques. This period of intellectual criticism advanced ideas of individual rights as opposed to religious duties. According to Comte, this intellectual attack on the integrated belief system of Catholicism undermined the religious consensus which had upheld the old social order of feudalism, and helped to precipitate the French Revolution which was followed by a protracted period of social destabilisation.

Comte argued that the re-establishment of a stable social order required a new and positive coherent social doctrine to bind people to society. He maintained that as knowledge progresses, theology can no longer do this job. Science must replace religion in this constructive role. In this future 'positivist' society, experts would use social science to analyse and organise society and science would operate as a new integrating body of beliefs for the populace as religion once had.

What was the basis of Comte's certainty about this future? For Comte, the driving force for social change was change in dominant systems of thinking. He believed that he had uncovered laws of progress in human thinking from which he was able to anticipate the immanence of the positivist society. These laws he referred to as the law of the three stages and the hierarchy of the sciences (see also Chapter 2).

The law of the three stages posited that all areas of knowledge progress sequentially through three different types of thinking: the theological, the metaphysical and the scientific. In theological thinking, the behaviour of phenomena is explained in terms of the volition of powerful gods. Metaphysical thinking explains phenomena in terms of mysterious abstract forces (such as nature) inherent in the phenomena. Eventually, through rigorous observation, notions of mysterious forces give way to the establishment of concrete scientific laws which explain the behaviour of phenomena in terms of causes.

Comte maintained that all phenomena actually operated according to scientific laws which were of different levels of complexity depending on the phenomena concerned. The hierarchy of the sciences represented this ascending order of complexity. The complexity of the phenomena affected the pace at which scientific knowledge could be established in different subject areas. For example, our knowledge of the physical realm could be more easily and quickly reduced to scientific and mathematical laws. The metaphysical beliefs of astrology and alchemy could therefore make the transition to the sciences of astronomy and chemistry respectively, but the understanding of the most complex area to explain in scientific terms – society – had for the longest time remained at the theological level. However, the study of society had progressed to the metaphysical stage during the Enlightenment where critical philosophy had undermined religion. It was now necessary and inevitable that social scientific understanding would emerge to form the basis of a new stable social order.

Comte's attitude toward the Enlightenment was ambivalent. Although as a rationalist he acknowledged the great divide between religious and scientific thinking, he argued that the social purpose of each was much the same. The certainty involved in a coherent scientific understanding of society would form the basis of social regulation by leaders and a climate of faith for the masses appropriate to the modern age.

In his later works, Comte came to argue that although intellectually theology had become surpassed and positive social science would guide the political process, religion still had a vital function to play in promoting altruistic feeling and binding individuals to society. The most appropriate form of this religion would have a secular focus. For Comte, the 'religion of humanity', celebrating the greatest individuals throughout human history, would perform this role.

Following in the tradition of Comte, Durkheim's functionalist approach views religion in terms of its social utility. However, he maintained that as societies evolve and grow in size and complexity, the essence of religion from a sociological viewpoint can get lost. For Durkheim, establishing the essential functional utility of religion suggested that the difference between belief systems themselves was not of great importance. He argued that to understand the fundamental nature of religion, it should be studied in its most primitive but still existing form. For this purpose, Durkheim based his theory of religion on the study of Australian Aboriginal clan society.

In Aboriginal society, clans were social groups which claimed a common ancestry. However, bands comprised the smaller social units in which people lived out their daily lives. Each clan was distinguished by its symbol which took the form of a specific natural feature such as a plant or animal. These distinguishing symbols operated as totems – they took the form of sacred symbols with imagined special powers demanding respect and veneration from clan members and acting as rallying points for bands to come together and participate in collective ritual and worship. When engaging in collective ritual in the presence of the totem, individuals often experienced religious ecstasy and felt themselves to be in contact with a superior force. Durkheim wanted to rationally examine what was the source and social function of these activities and experiences.

He argued that the purpose of religion is to assert the primacy of a powerful sense of group being - the collective consciousness - over self-interest for the benefit of society. This requires symbols representing the group to be perceived as having sacred significance. As such, individual consciousness and conscience is impressed through the experience of ritual participation within the group with respect for the community whose codes of conduct are given sacred sanction. In primitive societies, with a low division of labour and much common experience, the capacity for the collective consciousness to overwhelm the individual was immense.

What fundamental truth about religion did Durkheim claim that this analysis revealed? He argued that religion must have some substance given its universality. But that substance is not the same as that imagined by those who engage in collective worship. For Durkheim, religion acts as a unifying social force. All that can be rationally established is that when worshipping what they experienced as the superior force of a god, group members are in effect worshipping the personification of the superior force of society imposing itself over the self-interest of individual members.

Sociologically, the question of the truth of people's religious beliefs is of little importance. From this perspective, individual conscience is a social product. Through the socialising experience of group participation, focussed upon powerful sacred symbols, the individual internalises the sacred nature of social guidelines demarcating acceptable and non-acceptable behaviour. Durkheim emphasised that this function is particularly important in modern industrial societies in which enhanced size and individual differences brought about by an extended division of labour required the effect of powerful integrating forces to act against the potentially socially damaging impact of excessive individualism.

From the study of religion in primitive social groups, Durkheim claimed to have identified a universal and indispensable function of religion, equally applicable therefore to religion in the contemporary world. What, then, if the advance of rational thinking undermines faith in the supernatural? Adherence to religion thus defined must surely decline with damaging consequences for social integration. Durkheim's answer was that a religious type function is indispensable to any society.

> 'There is something eternal in religion which is destined to survive all the particular symbols in which religious thought has successively enveloped itself. There can be no society which does not feel the need of upholding and reaffirming at regular intervals the collective sentiments and the collective ideas which make its unity and its personality. Now this moral remaking cannot be achieved except by the means of reunions, assemblies and meetings where the individuals, being closely united to one another, reaffirm in common their common sentiments; hence some ceremonies which do not differ from regular religious ceremonies, either in their object, the results which they produce, or the processes employed to attain these results' (Durkheim, 1976, p.427).

As secularisation takes place in the sense that belief in worshipping a god declines, new belief systems with their powerful symbols of allegiance are necessary to keep the collective consciousness alive. For Durkheim, faith based on reason must have as its object humanity.

From a Durkheimian perspective, nationalistic and patriotic belief systems hold a religious type significance. Symbols associated with these belief systems, in the form of national flags and anthems, are kept alive in the minds of individuals at such occasions as political and state ceremonies and national sporting events which convey common feelings of national identity. These belief systems have been subsequently referred to as 'quasi religions' – they are not religions in the conventional sense but perform a similar and necessary social function.

As for Comte and Durkheim, Parsons' functionalist approach to religion focusses on its positive attributes and necessity. Religion provides a sacred source for shared values and social norms and an umbrella of abstract beliefs and meanings. These translate into more specific guidelines and recipes for behaviour which are shared by a community and are vested in the ultimate sanction of religion. It therefore promotes social order. However, for Parsons, rather than the secularisation of religion, traditional religion was argued to be undergoing a revival. Firstly, as well as social needs, there are perennial individual needs which must be catered for and which only religion can satisfy. Individuals will always have to face the death of loved ones, illness, unforeseeable events, misfortune and injustice. Religion is uniquely placed to sooth, help in coping and motivate where rational responses alone are inadequate. Secondly, religion has itself been purified in this role through the process of structural differentiation. This refers to a process whereby as societies grow and modernise, new institutions develop to perform increasingly specialised social functions. Old institutions, which once provided a broad range of functions, lose some of these functions. Religious institutions are no exception, and they have had to disengage from many areas of life that they were once involved in as other institutions take over. This enables religious institutions to concentrate on furnishing the profound meaning that individuals require and providing a sacred aspect to shared social values. In America, despite its religious denominationalism, its culture and values are Christian, and often more specifically Protestant, in their origin, hence the capacity for the creation of a general value consensus.

Parsons' theory thus combines a recognition of individual with social needs. Serving profound individual needs contributes toward the maintenance of social harmony. Furthermore, in the phenomena of the counter culture of love from the late 1960s, Parsons detected the emergence of religious values not dissimilar to those of early Christianity.

Marxism – religion as political control

The term 'economic determinism' is often applied to Marxist theory. This means that social ideas and institutions and the consciousness of people are shaped by economic forces. For Marxists, the most important economic factors are the means of production – the means through which production takes place. Where these are privately owned, a system of social class dominance inevitably exists. To perpetuate class inequalities for the benefit of the class owning the means of production, the ruling class, ideas that explain social reality also systematically distort it. The effect of distortion is control and in this process religion is strongly implicated. It acts as a highly conservative force; it distorts reality so as to encourage in the exploited class, who work in the employment of the owners of the means of production, an attitude of application to work and acceptance of its position in the social structure. Religion, as a product of the need to control the majority which originates from economic inequality, is a form of 'epiphenomena' – it has little other purpose of its own.

Important to understanding religion from a Marxist perspective is the concept of alienation. From this perspective, alienation is experienced under capitalism by workers in the form of powerlessness, meaninglessness and lack of fulfilment which accompanies the use of one's labour as an object of others' profit in the productive process. It is the dehumanising experience of being an appendage to a machine under the discipline of the factory work regime. Against these circumstances, religion provides a belief system which fills this meaning vacuum. For exploited workers, it offers solace to a hard life but also promotes resignation to it. Belief in god is therefore a man created phenomena which responds to a socially induced need but comes to control. For example, Christianity creates the image of paradise in an afterlife which awaits the righteous (or eternal suffering for the wicked). Some austere ascetic sects even elevate worldly suffering to a virtue. Millenarian religions prophesy the world being put to rights only by process of future supernatural intervention. In various ways, then, religion stupefies the believer and distracts the attention of the exploited from the socially created situation of their exploitation and the need or possibility of improving life in this world through direct political action. It acts as the opium of the masses and gives supernatural sanctity to the prevailing social structure.

Moreover, religion has often sided with the forces of order and repression. When it teaches that human nature is essentially sinful or wicked, it provides a backdrop against which repression can be justified as necessary for the maintenance of social order. Marxism challenges this highly 'conservative' ideological component of religion. Marx adopted a view derived from the Enlightenment that the condition of human nature is in fact not fixed, but is a product of the social environment. Human wickedness or 'sinfulness' is itself a product of the social conditions of

461

oppression and exploitation rather than a fixed condition. From a classical Marxist perspective, it is therefore by recognising and eradicating the conditions of exploitation that we can improve social conditions to the benefit of human nature and strive to realise utopia on earth in the form of communism in which the conditions of the need for religion will disappear.

Within the Marxist perspective, belief in supernatural forces guiding events on earth is viewed as false consciousness. Notions such as 'divine providence' draw a veil of mystery over the real laws of social change. For Marx, social change can be understood scientifically by adopting a materialist view of history. From this viewpoint, the driving force for change is the development and ownership of the means of production and class relationships. To believe in god is to remain in an infantile state of believing in a benign supernatural power when the alternative of social scientific knowledge in the form of Marxist analysis is available to guide mature and responsible action to bring about the full realisation of Christian values on earth through direct political action. The creation of an environment in which the potential for good in human nature can be fully realised will be a communist system which spells the end of religion and is the true realisation of Christian values.

To sum up, Marxists agree with functionalists that religion tends to integrate society, but thereafter their analyses are diametrically opposed. Whilst Comte argued that the driving force for social change and economic development was the progress of systems of thinking, Marx argued that systems of thinking are largely determined by the economic system. Whilst functionalists relate religion to the promotion of social integration for the benefit of all, Marxists view religion as propping up exploitative social systems for the benefit of a minority. Whilst Durkheim related religion to the positive integrative function of promoting the collective consciousness, Marx referred to the containing effect on class conflict of religion through promoting false consciousness. Although both perspectives explain forces of secularisation, for Marx, religion can only become redundant with the advent of communism, whereas functionalists argue that 'religion' will always be of functional necessity even though, particularly for Comte and Durkheim, the form it takes is likely to become increasingly secular. Consequently, from this perspective, even atheistic communist societies, such as the old Soviet Union, would require their own totems (as in the statues of leaders), flags, anthems and celebrations which integrate society, and a communist belief system, all of which perform the task of a quasi religion.

Weber – religion and western capitalism

The social action approach adopted by Weber emphasised that action could only be understood with reference to people's motives. Therefore, although sociology uses broad categories to frame an understanding of social action, the springboard for action is in the individual's subjective consciousness. However, to understand individual's motives for action, the broader meaning systems that they relate to and how individuals interpreted them must be studied. Amongst the most potent of meaning systems for orientating action can be systems of religious belief. But for Weber, in contrast to Marx, systems of meaning are not necessarily the just product of economic systems. Cultural meaning systems can have their own dynamics and effect on social action independently of and even influentially over economic change. Weber was therefore countering what he believed to be the excessive economic determinism and materialism in Marxist theory.

Of special interest to Weber was the relationship between religion and social change. As a result of comparative and historical studies of world religions, Weber felt that he was able to demonstrate that a relationship existed between religious belief systems and the propensity for social modernisation or relative stagnation. In particular, he was interested in explaining why England was the first country to industrialise and what shaped the value system of western capitalism. Through comparative analysis, he believed that he had identified a key influence (but not a singular cause) in the form of a religious ethic which was more strongly present in England prior to the transition to capitalism than in many other countries. This was seventeenth century Calvinism, an ascetic protestant belief system similar to that of puritanism, which came to instil in believers a powerful work ethic.

To fully appreciate Weber's explanation, it is important for the reader to make a psychological leap to a time in history when religious beliefs may have profoundly affected in many people a deep sense of self and their actions. Calvinism was preached by the charismatic John

Calvin in the sixteenth century as a salvationist religion. For Calvinists, only an 'elect' few are chosen by god to enter heaven. Although this choice was predetermined and fixed by god, individuals could not know whether they were one of the elect. Weber argued that this created in the mind of the believer a great tension which he referred to as 'salvation anxiety'. This drove believers to attempt to psychologically resolve the following tensions. Actions on earth could not change predestination. Yet believers questioned whether god could have predestined an elect who disobeyed his commandments and thought it to be likely that he would have chosen those who live by his commandments. From this position, for the Calvinist believer, following an upright life of sober dedication was a necessity. But by what observable and measurable sign could one take that god had chosen them as worthy? The answer arrived at was that god favours the elect with material prosperity. In a logically contradictory but psychologically satisfying way, this now put the answer to the question of predestination in the hands of the believer. A life of asceticism (industriousness and single minded application to hard work and a simple life of moral rectitude) guided the believer in the resolution of salvation anxiety and the resultant achievement of economic worldly success could be taken as a token of one's worthiness to enter heaven.

Weber argued that there was a conspicuous similarity between this religious work ethic, which channelled salvation anxiety into application, and the values of what later became western capitalism – the one was conducive to the emergence of the other. Driven by their religious beliefs and anxieties, many ascetic protestants were industrious and enterprising in their values and behaviour in a pre-capitalist age. Calvinism was therefore a religious belief system originating in pre-capitalist society which promoted action in the believer that would be conducive to capitalist modernisation. Worldly success could be measured in terms of profit derived from application. Profit maximisation required abstinence from luxury or squandering one's hard worked for gain. To the believer, time and money should not be wasted on idle pursuits, but profit should be relentlessly ploughed back into one's business. Calvinist salvation religion was therefore a powerful driving force for believers to live a simple, dedicated and industrious lifestyle. Furthermore, it tended to promote rational and innovative decision making at the expense of following tradition for its own sake since profit maximisation required careful calculation of the comparative returns from different courses of action and necessitated the development of rational accountancy.

A number of important points emerge from this perspective:

1) Weber was able to show that a religious belief system was an important factor in the process of modernisation along the lines of western capitalism. Ascetic protestant beliefs sanctioned dedicated action and domination of the environment as a route to economic success and salvation. By contrast, eastern religions were more contemplative. They tended to emphasise in the believer the importance of escapism to spiritual experience, contemplation and harmony with the environment. These eastern societies, many of which were once scientifically and technologically advanced compared to the west, did not in this religious and cultural environment tend to generate an internal dynamic of capitalist modernisation. Ascetic Protestantism did not contain this barrier to the development of modern rational capitalism.

2) Comparing western societies, the prominence of Catholicism in a society was not conducive to early capitalist modernisation. Catholicism did not readily provide an ascetic based work ethic. The church conveyed an image of splendour and luxury, fostering the view that it was acceptable to idle one's time in comfort from any money made. Furthermore, Catholicism offered an outlet to the continuous anxiety regarding individual salvation experienced by the Calvinist that was absent in ascetic Protestantism – its use of the confessional by which the believer could acquire forgiveness for straying from the straight and narrow. Ascetic Protestantism was also more of the 'real world' than monastic as in the case of Catholicism.

3) Although indicating their great potential influence, Weber did not regard religious belief systems as a single determinant of social change or stagnation. Maintaining a multifactoral view of change, Weber recognised that religious belief systems would be one of a number of factors of varying importance in different societies at different times in history. For example, another favourable factor to the creation of industrial wealth in England was that as part of an island, less wealth creation was diverted to supporting standing armies than was necessary in a number

of European countries that shared borders with potential enemies. For Weber, capitalist modernisation was influenced by a contingent mixture of circumstances, an important one of which was the presence of an ascetic protestant belief system.

4) For Marx, the economic arrangements of capitalism preceded and largely determined the nature of religion which acted back as a conservative social force. Weber challenged this economic determinism and materialist approach to religion. In his study of the emergence of capitalism in England, he argued that conducive religious beliefs tended to precede the economic arrangements of capitalism and promoted the dynamic action which helped to bring it about. But Weber did not challenge the materialism of Marxism with a similarly one-sided idealist account which would emphasise that ideas always determine economic matters. For Weber, the question of causality was always open to detailed analysis. He also recognised that the different positions that people occupy in the social structure may incline them toward different religions beliefs.

5) Weber proposed a powerful theory of secularisation. He argued that over time Calvinism proved to be a religious ethic that undermined religion. The rationality and quest for profit maximisation that Calvinism helped set in train, even though driven by the quest for salvation, had focussed action on this worldly business endeavour. Over time, the values and organisation of modern capitalism that had been set in motion were able to become self-sustaining, enabling rational action to increasingly became a secular orientated end in itself rather than a means to an end in an afterlife. Thus, in time, the cultural belief system of the work ethic remains, but the religious roots wither. The forces of modernisation which Calvinism helped to unleash were creating an increasingly spiritless and disenchanted world which was dominated by the achievements of scientific and rational thinking and efficient bureaucratic organisations at the expense of the mysteries of more religious and magical belief systems. Ascetic protestants had made their own decisions to constrain their lives to relentless work. Without the purposeful intention of bringing it about, Weber argues that the rational and bureaucratic structures of emergent western capitalism have become external impositions from which there is now no escape.

Phenomenology – religion and ontological security

Phenomenological approaches to religion focus on its crucial importance in the construction of meaning. The meaning systems provided by religions are of profound importance as they relate to ultimate questions regarding the meaning of life itself.

A leading exponent of this perspective is Peter Berger. In similar vein to Durkeheim, Berger recognised in religion the powerful impact of the sacred in commanding awe and respect as a socially constructive feature of religion. But to this, Berger supplements a phenomenological dimension by explaining that religion provides a 'sacred canopy' of protection against meaninglessness, which he referred to as the terror of chaos, to which we would be vulnerable in its absence. It provides individuals with 'ontological security'.

Central to the phenomenological perspective is the distinction between the human and animal condition. Unlike animals, human behaviour is not highly pre-ordered by its biological makeup. However, human intelligence includes the capacity and desire to impose meaning on the world. Society is the product of this active creation of shared meaning and provides the civilising influence of the ordering of behaviour.

Berger (1969, Ch.1) identifies the main components of this process as externalisation, objectivation and internalisation. Externalisation refers to the projection of meaning onto reality. The communication of shared meaning and understanding provides a social environment of belief systems and institutions. These develop an independence of their own and become experienced as it they were an external objective reality – the process of objectivation. Reacting back on its human creators, this shared social world becomes internalised into the subjective consciousness of individuals. As a result, the actions of individuals take place within the constraints of society as a human product. The creation of meaning and the imposition of order thus act as a shield against social anarchy and in particular the terror of intellectual chaos that would otherwise be experienced by the lack of biological ordering of behaviour which is part of the human condition.

Within society, through shared meaning, humans rise above the rest of nature. The capacity to ask ultimate questions about life requires answers to which only religion can provide a satisfactory meaning system. It plays a key strategic part in maintaining social and intellectual order. This is because it offers an ultimate legitimisation of social meanings and institutions by providing sacred sanction and locating them within a cosmic frame of reference. Religion assists human activity to operate within humanly constructed social constraints which nevertheless appear to have inevitability and provide a necessary framework of security.

For Berger, religion provides the comfort of a single universe of meaning. However, he argues that this becomes undermined as modern societies pluralise into a number of belief systems and religion loses its plausibility. Modern societies thus become deficient in satisfying the human need for ultimate belief.

Modernism and secularisation

In sociology, the term 'secularisation' refers to the assertion that religion is being undermined by forces of modernisation. Key features of the modernisation process include the advance of scientific and rational thinking and their application to understanding an increasing range of phenomena, the development of technology and industry, and the enhanced capacity of humankind to predict and control its environment. Rationalists tend most strongly to recognise and identify with such changes which have been closely linked to the idea of progress. Developing within the climate of eighteenth century Enlightenment, the rationalist tradition viewed science as a progressive force toward the establishment of truth in the face of religious obscurantism, dogma, and superstition. Through theory, prediction, observation, measurement and testing, rationalists argued that science provided a superior means of achieving certain and grounded knowledge compared to religion that is based on superstition and revelation. The advance of the rationalist attack on religion opened up a 'great divide' between religious beliefs and scientific method.

Viewed this way, science and religion are incompatible and completely opposed ways of thinking. They can also be seen as essentially inversely related – the more there is of one, the less there is of the other. Therefore, as science, which employs logical method and fact based explanations, provides demonstrable knowledge to explain a growing area of reality, its progress tends to erode understanding derived from religious faith. As Steve Bruce has put it, as the spread of science and technological advances enhances the ability of humankind to exert increasing prediction and control over the world, the need to resort to supernatural explanations of events or to appeal to supernatural forces for benign intervention decreases.

Rationalism and the Enlightenment were a powerful influence on the emergence of sociological thinking in the nineteenth century. Advances in the physical sciences held the prospect and kudos of the extension and application of science to the understanding of society. This was the aim of positivism – the understanding of society through observation, measurement and the rational analysis of data. Such understanding could assist judicious intervention in society in the form of social engineering. The most influential founding social theorists adopted a rationalistic approach to the study of society. Their personal convictions tended to be atheistic and their theories claimed to show that social forces were leading to a decline in theological belief systems. The works of these thinkers provided a powerful impetus for secularisation theory in sociology thereafter.

Secularisation tended to be viewed in unilinear (single line) terms, suggesting that there is a trajectory of social change in the direction of the progress of scientific and rational thinking, setting in motion a cumulative decline in religion, which all societies in time would tend to follow. Rooted in western thinking, this approach suggests that modern secularising western societies hold a future image for the 'less advanced' societies. Others, particularly phenomenologists such as David Martin, have questioned the extent to which this unilinear view is correct, cast doubts on its extent and postulate the possibility of a resurgence of religion.

The secularisation debate – seeming victory for the rationalists?

The study of secularisation in sociology is a highly contested area. By the 1970s, much of the secularisation debate revolved around theoretical and methodological positions in which phenomenologists, such as Peter Berger and David Martin, studied religion in terms of meaning systems and, respectively, either lamented or were more sceptical of the decline of religion, whilst others, such as Bryan Wilson, sometimes adopted more positivist methods of using statistics on institutional participation, as clear evidence of secularisation. Wilson nevertheless also viewed the decline in religion as one of great loss.

Both religion and secularisation can be viewed as multifaceted. Religion has various dimensions – personal faith, belief systems, collective participation, ritual, and sacred objects etc. – and may be viewed in traditional terms of specifically relating to established institutions (in particular churches) and belief systems, or may be applied to a broader variety of phenomena as in the case of quasi religions. Facets of secularisation could include assertions of a decline in thinking regarding a supernatural realm and an afterlife and a growing preoccupation with the material here and now of this world, the retreat from involvement of religious institutions in people's lives, declining participation in religious services and a decline in the status of religion in society. Larry Shiner and David Martin, both sceptics on secularisation, raise the issue of the varied and imprecise use of the term within sociology. Overall, the problem is that there is sufficient room for sociologists to define both religion and secularisation, seek evidence and interpret it in such a way as to selectively support one side of the argument or the other. And the suspicion is that this is the case.

One way in which sociologists may attempt to measure religious belief is through behavioural indicators. This approach is in the positivist tradition of looking for hard observational evidence. An obvious source of such evidence is the availability of organisational statistics showing the extent of public involvement in religious institutions. Those who work in the positivist tradition tend to regard this evidence as reliable (it is standardised and accurate) and valid (it measures what it claims to measure – the extent of religiosity) evidence by which to measure secularisation. For purpose of analysis, official statistics, particularly on church and denominational attendance and membership, are readily available. In Britain, the sources of statistics on church attendance in a range of Christian 'churches' go back to the 1851 Census on Religion and include more recent church censuses. This data can be studied to establish trends of change over time. Overall, these statistics indicate a long-term decline in regular Sunday attendance from almost 40% of adults in 1851 to now little over 6% by the early twenty first century.

Statistics for church membership closely follow this trend although are usually between about two to five percentage points higher.

Using Sunday attendance provides measurement with a degree of historical standardisation. However, given that work and leisure activities are now commonplace on Sundays (itself possibly evidence of secularisation), a more contemporary measure of church attendance on any day of the week would seem to be justified. But even by this measure, the figures for the late twentieth century would only be closer to 8% of adults, although according to Brierley they indicate a levelling out during the early twenty first century from a long term period of decline. There is evidence of a significantly higher level of occasional attendance, such as at seasonal church ceremonies, than weekly attendance figures.

According to official statistics, the numbers of baptisms, confirmations, church weddings and burials have significantly declined throughout the twentieth century. For example, marriages in the Church of England comprised 56% of all marriages in England and Wales in 1929 and fell to 37% in 1973. Following the extension of the availability of non-church marriages to approved premises other than register offices, by 2009 total church marriages fell to about a third of all marriages.

On the surface, these figures would appear to offer compelling evidence to support the secularisation thesis. However, there are reasons to be cautions. Firstly, some exceptions to these general trends can be revealed when looking at the United Kingdom figures in a little more detail on a regional basis. For example, in Northern Ireland, figures on attendance and membership have held up at a remarkably high level. Over 70% of the adult population were members of Anglican, Roman Catholic or Presbyterian churches in 1995, with total membership figures slightly up from those of 1980.

Secondly, whilst attendances have declined amongst the main Christian churches and denominations, membership of a number of non-trinitarian religious organisations has shown significant growth. These 'churches' can be distinguished from the established Christian churches on the theological ground that they do not believe in the unity of the father, son and holy spirit in one god. Although the profile of change in non-trinitarian church membership shows variation between different religions, the overall pattern is one of sustained expansion. Survey figures provided by Brierley show that The Church of Jesus Christ of the Latter-day Saints (the Mormons) and the Jehovah's Witnesses have the largest membership in this category of religions in Britain and their growth in membership has been around 70% between 1980 and 2010. These are organisations with global followings and have shown themselves to be highly effective in resource mobilisation to recruit new members. The smaller non-trinitarian Church of Scientology has seen its membership approximately quadruple over this time period. In total, membership of non-trinitarian churches as a proportion of all Christian church membership is relatively small but growing, the figures for 1995 and 2000 being approximately 8% and 9% respectively.

Thirdly, membership in the United Kingdom of world religions other than Christian has likewise shown a variable pattern of change but an overall sizeable increase, in this case of over 70% between 1980 and 1995. The most significant increase has been amongst Muslims and Sikhs, together roughly doubling their membership between 1980 and 1995. Since then, followers of the Muslim faith have shown the greatest rise. In terms of the more general measure of percentage of the population, estimates for 2005 put followers of non-Christian religions at about 6% of the population. However, attendance and membership figures for these religions tend to be a higher proportion of followers than those of the main Christian religions.

Fourthly, the phenomena of 'new religious movements' must be taken into account. There have been definitional problems regarding this category, but at present the term will be applied to diversity of small contemporary religious groups which may otherwise have been referred to as sects and in particular cults. New religious movements often eclectically utilise ideas from a diversity of sources including eastern and pagan religions. They are usually very loosely organised and often require little formal commitment from their followers. Therefore, precise statistical evidence on 'membership' or participation (attendance would often not be an applicable term as there may not be formal church gatherings) is largely lacking. Whilst probably becoming an increasing feature of contemporary societies, many movements are relatively short lived and it will be shown that the interpretation of their significance in contemporary society is highly contested by participants in the secularisation debate.

Overall, the figures indicate a decline in religion if religion is measured in terms of church attendance and membership. However, they also indicate a changing balance in which the monopoly of the main Christian churches has given some ground to a greater diversity of religions. This partly reflects the growing ethnic diversity of Britain's population composition but may also be evidence of a more general process of religious fracturing which is taking place. The case made for secularisation therefore is not just about numbers but also has to take account of evidence of divergent patterns of change and greater religious pluralism.

So far, we have taken church attendance statistics at face value. One area of contention is the questionable reliability and the validity of these statistics. For example, on the issue of reliability, different churches use different attendance and membership criteria upon which to construct their statistics. There may also be distortions in the statistics resulting from the vested interests of those who produce them. Fears of church closure may encourage the inflation of Anglican Church attendance figures whereas the payment of taxation based on congregation size is likely to have the opposite effect on figures provided by Catholic churches. Regarding both reliability and validity, different religions vary in the importance that they attach to regular institutional participation. For example, in its emphasis on church hierarchy and ritual and sacraments, the Catholic Church arguably places greater importance on attendance than the more liberal protestant tradition of the Anglican Church. Further, given the growing diversity of religious life, it is important to consider the different emphases on attendance or what membership actually means between the different religions. Does attendance and membership therefore really provide a comparable statistical basis of measurement between the different religions, especially given the unknown extent of new religious movement adherents?

Disagreements over measurement of religion can relate to differences between different opposing theoretical approaches to the subject. Quantifiable data on institutional participation as a measurement of religiosity is likely to appeal to positivist inclined sociologists. By contrast, phenomenologists emphasise that establishing the extent of religious belief is more important than measuring action, and question the assumption that belief necessarily correlates highly with participation. From this position, David Martin has argued that the relatively high rates of church attendance recorded in the nineteenth century were partly attributable to the quest for social status which attendance gave people at this time. As a greater proportion of people were attending church for such secular motives, Martin argues that the validity of the figures as a measure of genuine religious belief must be questioned. The extent of secularisation since this period derived simply from a decline in the figures may be exaggerated due to the misleadingly high historical reference point.

In taking a longer range historical view, it can be argued that a strong case for secularisation can be made by contrasting the Middle Ages as a golden era of religion in terms of strong religious cultures and communities and high rates of participation against the take it or leave it religious culture and low participation rates in much of Britain today. However, the validity of this interpretation can be questioned since the image of a past golden religious age has been questioned as being no more than an unsubstantiated caricature of the past. In this vein, Larry Shiner questions exactly when and where this golden age was and suggests that firm evidence for its existence is lacking. Moreover, K. V. Thomas suggests that views of the pervasiveness of religion during the sixteenth and seventeenth centuries are excessively influenced by an image left by elites of the time with regard to established religions and tell us little about the beliefs of the general population. Furthermore, at the contemporary end of the historical spectrum, greater credence has been given to the importance of religion which is more likely to be freely chosen rather than externally imposed with the expectation of outward expressions of faith as Martin argues was likely to be the case in the Middle Ages.

Another source of quantitative measure of religiosity is through the use of social surveys of religious belief. Surveys regularly indicate that belief is far more widespread than implied by measurements of institutional involvement. For example, a 1991 British Social Attitudes Survey found that 62% of respondents could be classified within three religious belief categories ranging from having no doubt about the existence of god to believing at some times but not others. Whilst such surveys may offer a challenge to the validity of measuring religious belief through church attendance rates, even these relatively high figures may support rather than undermine secularisation when taken from a number of surveys over time. Comparing survey findings from the late 1950s, Steve Bruce found that there was evidence of a decline in religious belief. This trend has appeared to continue as the Social Attitudes Survey of 1998 found that only 58% of respondents fell into the same categories of believers as identified above in the 1991 survey. Moreover, the decline was concentrated in the two strongest belief categories.

The use of social survey evidence also raises a number of methodological issues. One is that when asked about church attendance, Hadaway et al (1993) found that respondents in the United States tended to claim higher levels of participation than is substantiated by official figures provided by religious organisations. We have already questioned both the reliability and validity of official figures on church attendance. Now, it is suggested that the reliability of survey information regarding actual attendance levels can be questionable; both methods of quantification can be cast in doubt. However, there is also a more profound question which relates to the choice of the social survey in terms of research methodology. For Wilson, it is no coincidence that those challenging secularisation use social surveys of religious belief to demonstrate its extent and to question the validity of declining church attendance rates as a measure of secularisation. Surveys of belief might record much higher measurements of belief than attendance rates suggest but they use a methodology which just provides an aggregate measurement of individual belief, devoid of measuring what Wilson argues are the key dimensions of religion – those of participation and community.

In relation to the discrepancy between church attendance rates and the extent of religious belief measured in social surveys, an argument which cautions the extent of secularisation is the view that church religion still has much following but that religious 'participation' is taking a more privatised form. Bradley, for example, points to the high figures for television audiences watching religious services. These people, many of whom do not attend church, are expressing an interest in religious matters. For Bellah, pursuing religion as a more private activity allows greater freedom of choice and thus provides a strong index of belief. However, there are problems with this interpretation. One criticism is that if religious belief is being pursued more privately, by its very nature it is difficult to be sure of its extent. And a further point, raised by Wilson, is to do with his preferred definition of religiosity. If people are becoming privatized believers, belief is becoming separated from belonging, which for Wilson is further evidence of secularisation as religion retreats to the private sphere and in so doing becomes deficient.

Bryan Wilson defines religion simply in terms of 'invocation of the supernatural', thereby defining out from consideration belief systems which others might regard as functional equivalents to religion in which belief in the supernatural is absent – referred to as quasi religions. For Wilson, the characteristics of a religious society tend to be couched in traditional terms, arguably assisting the ease with which his case for secularisation can be made. His view of a religious society is one of common participation in which religion is rooted in communities. Belief must be complemented with belonging and at societal level a religious society shares one predominant faith which provides social stability and unquestioning authority. From this point of view, declining participation rates within the major churches and denominations provides clear evidence of secularisation. The decline of local communities through the process of urbanisation and heightened levels of geographical and social mobility undermines the continuity of religious beliefs across the generations. Moreover, the expansion of a diversity of new religious movements is regarded as evidence that religion has fractured into a scattering of minority cult pursuits which require little commitment, and sects, which suggests that religion is becoming consigned to the margins of mainstream secular society. A plurality of religions undermines the capacity of religion overall to provide the basis for a single moral order. And it could be added that as well as the relative superficiality of many new religions, the question of which religion to choose raises the further question of whether to choose religion at all, thus further assisting the process of secularisation.

Others have argued that religious pluralism is compatible with a religious society. For example, Greeley points out that as some sects in particular and denominations to some extent require a higher level of commitment, intensity of belief and degree of sacrifice from their members than is usually required from churches, religious pluralism may be deepening and reviving religion – a process which he refers to as resacrilisation. Furthermore, it should be noted that religiosity, measured in terms of attendance rates, is very high in the United States – the most religiously pluralistic society - compared to other western societies.

Phenomenologists Berger and Luckmann disagree in their interpretations of diversity of belief systems. Peter Berger argues that in their everyday lives, people need an ordered sense of reality – they devise meaning systems which give them the certainty required for action. Berger adopts a holistic view of religious meaning systems and looks negatively on the fracturing of world views in an increasingly secular and pluralistic world, doubting whether they can provide the ontological security that a single religious world view can.

However, for Thomas Luckmann, the definition of religion is broadened out and a sense of ontological security can come from within a diversity of meaning systems such as political ideology, support for a football team or following a particular genre of pop music. Whether or not meaning systems derive from religion as conventionally defined, it is argued that they still perform a necessary and similar purpose to that of religion in enabling people to make sense of the world.

The issue of religious pluralism is one that is taken up in a further section on secularisation.

Wilson appears to offer convincing evidence of secularisation. Like Weber, he closely aligns secularisation to the process of rationalisation but Wilson gives greater emphasis to the influence of scientific advance than ascetic Protestant sects such as the Calvinists. However, there are many dimensions upon which secularisation can be appraised and reasons why some caution may be necessary in assessing the extent of its advance.

The question of 'American exceptionalism' raises other issues regarding the secularisation debate. There is evidence to show that 'church' attendance rates in the United States are as high as about 40%. According to Finke, church membership in the United States increased from about a third of the population in 1850 to two thirds in 1980. More precise figures from the 'Yearbook of American Churches', show that church membership between 1940 and 1957 increased from 49% of the population to 61%. This evidence would appear to pose a fundamental inconsistency regarding the secularisation debate. Since secularisation is supposed to be intimately connected to the forces of modernisation, why were these membership figures increasing at the same time that

American was modernising and how is it that the most industrially and technologically advanced nation shows such a high measure of religiosity in terms of church attendance rates compared to Britain and other European societies? Based on this data, is America more religious than European countries?

One early attempt to explain of this phenomena was provided by Will Herberg. According to Herberg (1956), in essence, religious institutions adapted to change more effectively and took on a more secular emphasis in the United States, and so, compared to the retention of old medieval dogmas and beliefs in European churches, were able to retain greater plausibility for followers. America experienced high levels of immigration up to the mid 1920s. Settlers faced with an unfamiliar environment adopted high levels of religious participation for two complementary reasons. Firstly, continuing or taking up religious participation within their ethnic communities provided a sense of ethnic tradition and continuity in a new land, and secondly, participation corresponded with church going as a requirement of being a good American citizen. Herberg argues that this necessity declined in the second generation of immigrants but re-emerged in the third generation (corresponding with the time period of the membership figures cited above) who were searching to re-establish their cultural identity. The reasons for the pursuit of religion were therefore strongly influenced by secular purposes. By contrast, the medieval heritage of the European churches created a plausibility gap between its teachings and the needs of a secular orientated population.

Looking beyond the question of church membership and attendance, there is little dispute that, over the long term, the involvement of the church in different areas of British social life has declined. This process is sometimes referred to in terms of 'disengagement' between the church and broader society. In this sense, compared to its deeply embedded involvement in European societies during the Middle Ages, the church in contemporary society has retreated from involvement in many areas of daily life, including politics (where although it still retains important state ceremonial roles, in Britain the Anglican Church has occasionally expressed criticism of the social consequences of government policy), health care, the provision of welfare for the poor, education, and as a major patron of the arts. The modern state has taken over as a main provider of these services. This process has arguably been accompanied by a degree of separation of church from the state, a cooling of relations between these institutions and a growing secular influence in these areas.

General agreement on the process of disengagement has been met with alternative interpretations regarding the implications for secularisation. For Wilson, this retreat of the church from its rooting in social life provides further evidence of religious decline through its marginalisation from everyday life. For Steve Bruce, secular state provision in people's lives has expanded and church provision has declined. The secular state has grown in power and largely sidelined the church from the process of political decision making and thus the influence of the church and religion in society has waned.

By contrast, David Martin argues that the distancing of church from state may have assisted the cause of religion. This is because in the Middle Ages, the church could be more easily corrupted by its involvement in politics. Detachment from politics has enabled the church to specialise in becoming the source of more purely religious ethics and enhanced its social status.

The disputes over secularisation covered in this section have shown that despite much supporting evidence, the issue has not been entirely clear cut. In a later section, more contemporary theory and evidence will be introduced that raises the issue of a possible revitalisation of religion.

Contemporary developments with reference to religion:

1. Tradition and reform – gender and sexuality

Contemporary society has witnessed reform toward gender equality in the workplace, improved educational opportunity and achievement levels for females, and changing roles within the domestic sphere. Compared to these advances, there is substantial evidence available to those who regard religion as an essentially conservative force which perpetuates traditional gender inequalities. In most religions, male figures or symbolism have come to predominate. Within most religious institutional hierarchies, women have traditionally been excluded from power by being confined to low level positions. Moreover, religion has often supported the subordinate position of women to men in the family and in society. The major religions may therefore be seen as reflecting and legitimising male power throughout society.

In recent decades, though, opposition between liberals and traditionalists on the question of the ordination of women has arisen in the Anglican Church. From the late 1980s, the Church sanctioned the opportunity for women to become deaconesses and later opened up access to the priesthood. The response of a number of male and female traditionalists has been to convert to the Catholic Church which had remained staunch in its opposition to such reforms. Nevertheless, for many, reform within the Anglican Church appeared slow, as demonstrated by the acrimony which resulted from the failure of the passage of a measure to allow women to become bishops to gain the necessary two thirds majorities in all three Houses of the Church Synod in 2012. A new vote in July 2014 resulted in the necessary majorities throughout the Synod for women to have access to the post of bishop – with arbitration available within parishes that object.

On the issue of sexuality, homosexuality has ceased to be a criminal offence in Britain since 1967 and from December 2005 secular ceremonies allowed same sex couples to enter into civil partnerships. Legislation has since been passed allowing same sex partners to achieve married status within religious organisations that are prepared to officiate, but the legislation formally excludes this option within the Church of England.

An issue which has ignited much feeling and debate within the Anglican Church is that of the ordination of gay priests. In England, Jeffrey John, a priest who admitted to having a past gay relationship, stood down from his appointment as Bishop of Reading as a result of much opposition from within the church. The ordination of a practicing gay priest in the United States has been the focus of much attention in the Anglican Church throughout the world. Opponents have been forthright in quoting from the scriptures, whereas supporters have looked to such reforms in terms of promoting a feeling of inclusivity for all members of the Church.

2. Secularisation revisited:

Up to the 1970s, the secularisation debate within sociology was largely a methodological one between supporters of rival camps of positivists and phenomenologists in which positivists tended to be the main providers of strong evidence demonstrating the process of secularisation and phenomenologists struggled to put persuasive counter arguments. This era was the main focus of a previous section which analysed some of the academic arguments. However, major political changes have seen the collapse of atheistic political systems. Furthermore, the religious landscape has changed significantly in recent decades with advances in very different forms; fundamentalism on the one hand and new religious movements on the other. These changes have arguably raised a significant challenge to the once persuasive case for the relentless march of secularisation. They have also moved the debate on from being of largely academic and methodological interest within sociology to matters of more practical and political concern at a global level.

a) The collapse of communism

The collapse of the atheistic regimes of the Eastern Bloc communist states dates from the late 1980s. In many of these states, the Catholic or Orthodox Church had been highly influential in pre-communist times. During the decades of communist rule, religion had been largely driven underground by the state. However, as these regimes came under challenge from reform movements during the 1980s, churches were often allying themselves with the forces of change. A good example of this was the growing prominence of the Catholic Church in Poland during the growth of the free trade union movement 'Solidarity'. As communist regimes collapsed, many societies witnessed a revived influence of Catholic or Orthodox religions.

These political changes offer a fundamental challenge to the secularisation thesis, but the extent of religious revival or desecularisation is difficult to ascertain. This is because although religion revived openly, there remains uncertainty about the extent to which religious belief and practice were secretly maintained by people under the old communist regimes. However, the re-emergence of religion can be interpreted as providing support for the phenomenological viewpoint of Berger who argued that only religion can adequately respond to the need for ontological security which is part of the human condition, thus making the revival of religion always a distinct possibility.

b) The rise of fundamentalism

A further change of great magnitude has been the rise of religious 'fundamentalism'. This term is fraught with both definitional problems and emotional overtones. It has been questioned whether it provides an equally valid description of the reassertion of traditions when applied to different religions and in different settings and sometimes the less pejorative term of 'neo-traditionalism' is preferred. However, for Bruce, fundamentalism is a valid concept which includes the following components. Fundamentalist approaches to religion emphasise the importance of referring to a source of beliefs which is claimed to be free from error, for the purpose of supplying strict moral guidelines for behaviour. The social significance of tradition as opposed to changes which are regarded as compromising is therefore asserted. These changes may have affected the social status of those to whom fundamentalism is more likely to appeal and an image of presumed past pure religious conditions is held up as something to return to. Yet despite strong opposition to the eroding effects of modernism, fundamentalist movements are not usually averse to the use of modern technology by which to communicate their message. Thus defined, evidence of reversion to fundamentalism poses a major challenge to exponents of secularisation.

The emergence of religious fundamentalism has been explained in terms of crisis theory. Explanations under this heading view the appeal of fundamentalism as a response to various aspects of modernisation as crisis. Fundamentalism has therefore provided, in response, a coping mechanism. For example, the rise of Christian right fundamentalism in some parts of the United States during the 1970s and 1980s can be viewed in the social context of a reaction by the so called 'moral majority' to the growing permissiveness of the late 1960s. American Christian fundamentalists believed that Christian teachings had liberalised too far and in so doing compromised from correct and non-negotiable moral and religious strictures deriving from a literal interpretation of the Bible. The issues that they raised shared some common ground with the political right which came to prominence in the United States (and in Britain) during the 1980s – in particular, the need to return to such basics as the sanctity of family life and sexual restraint outside of marriage. The measures that more extreme factions have been prepared to take have included direct action in the form of threats and extreme violence against practitioners at abortion clinics. Other fringe groups organised themselves as militias in preparation for the coming collapse in the social order – a type of apocalyptic vision of the future.

The actual impact of Christian fundamentalism on mainstream culture in the United States is quite debatable though. For example, for Bruce, the prominence that it acquired is out of proportion to its geographically and numerically restricted appeal and the attention that it caused should be seen as a measure of the largely secular background against which it so clearly stood out.

In Britain, religiously inspired resistance in the 1960s and 70s to the permissive society took a relatively mild form. For example, it emerged in the moral pressure group the National Viewers and Listeners Association which was influential in having films with what was argued to be content offensive to Christian religion banned and sex shops closed down. During the new right governments of 1980s and early 1990s, 'back to basics' was formally more a political than religious campaign, especially aimed at supporting traditional family life. However, more recently, controversy has been sparked by the inclusion of creationist teaching, applying literal interpretations of the Bible to explain creation, in a small number of mainly independent Christian schools. Although hardly fundamentalist, New Labour policy encouraged the establishment of faith schools, even though they require more liberal entrance criteria on religious grounds than some religious organisations would prefer. Under the coalition government, a small number of free schools have been opened, some promoting Islamic and other religions of non-western tradition. In some instances, schools have been put under the spotlight for their alleged application of hard line Islamic principles.

The rise of Islamic fundamentalism can be viewed as an attempt to return to literal and uncompromising teachings from the Koran in the broader historical context of the perceived corruption of an Islamic culture in retreat from the influence of westernism – especially the United States - and Christianity. A momentous example of this religious and cultural re-purification process was the Iranian Revolution of 1979 which overthrew the modernising and pro-Western Shah of Iran. The emerging state was effectively a theocracy – a society ruled by religious clerics in strict accordance with religious strictures. The rule of the Taliban in

Afghanistan between 1996 and 2001 provides another example of rule according to fundamental Islamic principles. Such societies in the grip of resurgent Islamic fundamentalism have been strongly resistant to the political institutions of contemporary western democracies.

The impact of Islamic fundamentalism was brought home most dramatically by the 11 September 2001 attack on the twin towers in the United States. These events, the reasons behind them and the response of the west would seem to indicate the opening up fault lines between Christian and Islamic civilisation and a heightening of religious awareness at a global level following the collapse of the communist empire and the ending of ideological opposition between the capitalist west and the communist east. Reversion from political to religious opposition on such a scale could be taken as strong evidence of desecularisation.

c) New religious movements

Reference to 'new religious movements' raises problems of definition and classification within sociology. It can include a full range of sects and cults of more contemporary times in western societies and now tends to be the preferred terminology in avoiding the pejorative judgements which often accompany the use of these terms. However, the characteristics of alternative religious groups in western liberal democracies are arguably changing within the context of an increasingly free market environment. It would appear that world affirming client cults (and to some extent world accommodation audience cults) are prospering as well suited to this environment. Therefore, without ruling out the other types, the definition of new religious movements applied here will be tilted in that direction with reference to the following distinguishing characteristics. Firstly, they are not just new in the sense of being relatively contemporary, but that they are usually quite original or they select ideas from religions of other times or cultures which are interpreted and recombined in novel ways. Secondly, organisation and membership are relatively loose, unstructured and non-hierarchical, in contrast to world rejecting cult movements. Thirdly, although cult like, the term movement tends to suggest that they have grown in size. However, an exact measure of membership is often difficult to establish. Fourthly, the values of some new religious movements may provide common ground with new social movements. A good example of this would be that of New Age religion which, on environmental issues, may much in common with environmental protest groups and although the latter are primarily political they may also be viewed as quasi religious movements.

Sociological explanations for the attractiveness of alternative religious groups have been varied and include the following.

1) One approach is specific to the conditions of the late 1960s and early 1970s, especially in America, which arguably provided fertile ground for the emergence of counter cultural values and new religious movements. These conditions can be documented as a reactive response to the experience of bureaucratisation and spiritless materialism and the Vietnam War, growing escapism to drug taking culture and an increase in the activities of missionaries of eastern religions.

2) Alternatively, Glock (Furseth & Repstad, 2010, p.148) explains attraction in terms of the experience of deprivation. Deprivation may here be viewed economically but could also be seen in terms of other dimensions such as not feeling valued. In these cases, some cults or sects may provide an answer in denigrating material aspiration and enhancing the self-esteem of the member.

3) If a search for fellowship amidst the decline of community in the contemporary urban world and the need to find meaning and identity in a world that is experienced as cold and bureaucratic may turn people to religion, why may they not turn to the more established churches? Stark and Bainbridge argue that in a rapidly changing world, more established religions have left gaps in the market that new movements are better suited to fill.

Alternative religious movements have often had to contend with hostile public reaction, viewing them in a common stereotypical way as authoritarian total institutions, led by charismatic personalities who brainwash vulnerable individuals to become mindless followers. Eileen Barker demonstrated in her study of the Unification Church that such perceptions that had been applied to this movement were not well founded. In reality, the broader evidence available suggests that very few groups, more likely to be of the world rejecting cult movement type, conform to this caricature. Followers of most new religious movements tend to be young, well educated and of middle class background. Rather than passive victims, they often make active decisions to experiment with an alternative way of life and rather than becoming manipulated, brainwashed coerced and hooked in, will make as active decisions to leave as they did to enter the group.

Richardson (1993) suggests that hostility toward and misperception of new religious movements can stem from a number of vested interests. For example, sections of the mass media have an interest in focussing on any group that can provide sensational stories and maximise their sales or viewers. In cases where family breakdown has preceded members joining a religious sect, family members may be keen on moving the focus of attention away from family problems and on to the persuasive techniques of the movement to explain what has happened. And professionals may have a vested interest in providing therapeutic deprogramming help for the indoctrinated that leave the sect.

But what are the consequences of public hostility to minority religious groups? In his study of the Scientology movement in Britain, Wallis (1993) applied the deviance amplification model – an approach which has been effectively used by labelling theorists to study the dynamics involved between the general public, who feel themselves to be custodians of moral good, and groups labelled as deviant. For Wallis, the initial public reaction to the Scientology movement was one of hostility framed by the perception of their deviation from conventional social norms. Social hostility generated a siege mentality within the movement and led to attacks on its detractors. This response was taken by the press as evidence to confirm that the initial hostile public assessment was correct. The mass media constructed and projected to the public a negative stereotypical image of the movement and a moral crusade which induced a public panic reaction against the movement emerged. In Britain, this ultimately led to legal and governmental denunciations of the movement and the refusal to recognise it as a religion or provide charitable status.

When debating secularisation, those who retain a traditional view of religion, which provides a specific definition of what religion 'is', invariably including reference to the supernatural, are likely to find evidence of secularisation in the process of modernisation. Much depends on how far one is prepared to broaden out the definition. For example, traditional definitions may or may not (but probably not) enable one to classify certain UFO cults in which salvation to believers is promised through messages sent by superior beings as religions. However, the potential for a more broadly embracing recognition of religion is usually substantially enhanced by those who apply a functional approach which defines religion not in terms of what it is but in terms of what it 'does' – for example, it provides a body of sacred beliefs that tie people into a community of shared values. Definitions of this type are more likely to recognise the continuance of religious functions in new quasi religious forms, possibly comprising secular belief systems. These may have their own spiritual dimension such as health fads and environmentalism, or in the case of supporters of football clubs revered club symbols, tradition, ritual, collective gatherings and the worship of footballing icons. Perhaps the issue has become more one of change in the form of a fracturing of single world views, growing pluralism of belief systems and diversity of choice than secularisation, since sociologically it could be argued that in the case of quasi or secular religions the social functions and psychological needs of religion are still being met.

Contemporary sociological perspectives on religion:

In light of the issues raised in the preceding sections, contemporary social theorists are often more cautious on the question of secularisation than the founding theorists or sociological commentators in the early 1970s were. In fact, there is a tendency in contemporary theory to acknowledge a rejuvenation of religion. How is this change in outlook explained?

Globalisation – religious cosmopolitanism or fundamentalism?

There is much debate about the exact nature and impact of globalisation, but to many the world can now be less effectively understood in terms of nation states as relatively closed territorial units with distinct boundaries. Countries are becoming increasingly intertwined as economic, technological, political and cultural forces operate across national boundaries. It is possible that, through growing contact between people of different societies and cultures, these processes can generate greater understanding and tolerance of diversity. Both Giddens and Beck consider this optimistic possibility to which Giddens applies the term 'global cosmopolitanism'.

However, it is also possible that globalisation may bring about intolerance and new conflicts. For example, the growth of global capitalism can lead to western (particularly American) values, culture and ways infiltrating and being perceived as imposing themselves on the cultural traditions of the societies that they are seen as 'invading'. Although non-military, such an invasion may nevertheless be experienced as pervasive. In response, in some cases a rise in nationalism and religious fundamentalism can result. Thus, we have seen that the 1979 Iranian Revolution can be viewed as a response against western cultural and political influence brought about by the reforms of the Shah of Iran. The response took the form of a resurgent Islam which took a fundamentalist form.

Within this global context, for S. P. Huntington (1993), enhanced civilization consciousness is providing such new fault lines of conflict at a global level. The cultures of civilisations are closely linked to the religious traditions of the major world religions. Civilization consciousness and religious fundamentalism are important ingredients in the heightened tensions which have emerged between Islamic and Christian civilization. This new global configuration, it is argued, is taking the dangerous form of a 'clash of civilisations'.

Adopting a more economic and politically based viewpoint, Karen Armstrong views Islamic fundamentalism as a reaction to forces of rapid social and economic modernisation experienced in a number of Muslim countries. She argued that these strains tend to undermine moderate religious traditions and give rise to fundamentalism - a response which blames the west (often especially the USA) as the cause of changes which it reacts against. Hatred of America by radical groups derives from its perceived arrogance as a superpower and supporter of the main beneficiaries of change – the corrupt feudal oil rich dynasties which they oppose. In this context, terrorist sacrifices against America and the west can come to be raised to that of religious duty. Furthermore, the global mass media now offers these groups the impact of a global theatre for sensational actions.

However, evidence of growing religious fundamentalism is not confined to that of the Islamic religion. At times in recent decades there has been evidence of a rise in Christian fundamentalism in the United States and orthodox Judaism in Israel. America is seen in many Islamic states as biased in its dealings toward the state of Israel, an enemy occupying Muslim land. For its part, following the Islamic Revolution in Iran and later the collapse of the Soviet Block, in the late twentieth century and particularly within the Republican Party, the United States has come to view Islamic fundamentalism as the new religiously inspired threat to the west. Overall, a process of desecularisation has arguably been taking place at a global level.

Theories of the revitalisation of religion

Altogether new approaches to the study of religion have emerged in the United States and in Europe which are refocusing some of the issues in the secularisation debate. The common context is the development of societies which have become highly consumerist and diverse. European thinking has tended to take as its theoretical context postmodern or high modern approaches which will be discussed later.

In America, rational choice and resource mobilisation theory have become prominent approaches in which religion is placed within the broader context of a free market environment of supply and demand for goods and services. America is a pluralistic society and plurality applies as much to religion in a society where constitutionally there is no established church as it does to pressure groups. Rational choice theory studies this diversity mainly in terms of demand and choice whereas resource mobilisation theory focusses more on supply. These approaches suggest that what appeared to be a steady linear decline in religion was in fact the downward phase of a longer term cycle in which we are now entering an upward phase of religious rejuvenation and reinvigoration.

Rational choice theory was pioneered by Stark and Bainbridge. Their model locates religion within rewards and costs analysis. For Stark and Bainbridge, rewards are desirable outcomes which individuals crave but carry costs in their realisation. Such rewards can include wealth, status, good health and the quest for immortality. The simplest positive choice is in deciding to pursue rewards where it is calculated that the benefits outweigh the costs incurred in their achievement. However, some rewards, though highly desirable, may be very distant, difficult or uncertain in their realisation or not achievable at all. Moreover, the costs in their pursuit may seem too high. This is why religion satisfies a perennial need; it provides 'compensators'. Compensators are key aspects of religious belief systems. They provide a surrogate reward for those desired rewards that may not be achievable or painfully costly in their pursuit. Religion is regarded as uniquely placed to fill this role as compensator. It is the only type of belief system which can provide powerful enough compensation for the costs incurred to achieve rewards, providing faith for motivation and answering ultimate questions which science and ideological belief systems cannot fulfil. This can be demonstrated in the quest for the ultimate reward of immortality which only supernatural belief in an afterlife can satisfy.

Stark and Bainbridge argue that a perennial quest for compensators follows from the psychological needs of individuals to pursue challenging rewards and answer ultimate questions. They therefore provide a response to the psychological need for a belief system that acts as a prop in doing so. Different types of religious belief system offer different types of compensator. For example, audience cults are only likely to provide relatively weak compensators, whereas those of cult movements are stronger and need to be quite all embracing. Choosing between belief systems and their compensators may be a rational one, but the belief systems themselves must include reference to the supernatural.

From the position of rational choice theory, national churches are regarded as like any other nationalised monopolies in that through state support and privileges, they are likely to lose their competitive vibrancy. By contrast, religious denominations, sects and cults are organisations that compete to satisfy the needs of religious consumers and provide a competitive market of free choice amongst this diversity of religious belief systems. This means that religious organisations are vibrant and through free choice religion becomes resurgent. This 'new voluntarism' makes religion stronger, not weaker. In the free market of the United States, religions adapt to satisfy individual requirements, compared to the less responsive state religions in European societies which, as a consequence, lose support. Furthermore, from this viewpoint, whatever the religious participation rates were in the Middle Ages, this period cannot be viewed as a golden age of religion since often participation was not willingly chosen but instead the result of powerful social impositions.

At a general level, religion, which provides supernatural belief of reward in an afterlife offers the ultimate compensation for hardships experienced in this life. Religion will therefore prevail and it is only a question of the forms that it takes. Any tendencies toward secularisation will be self-limiting and religions which neglect the supernatural will decline as they cannot provide adequate compensators for rewards that may be very distant and difficult to achieve. From this viewpoint, rather than dismissing new religious movements as superficial phenomena in a largely secularised world, they are seen as part of a vibrant religious revival. As a free market in religion, America is regarded by Stark and Bainbridge to be a truly vibrant religious society.

In criticism of this approach, Bruce suggests that the rational choice between religions presupposes the fact that society is essentially rational at the expense of religion in the first place. Wilson goes on to suggest that the high participation rates in the United States belie the secular and shallow nature of religion as mainly providing a choice of recipes for good citizenship. And a further criticism of new religious movements is that theological guidance deriving from divine imposition is being replaced by religion as a type of plaything in the pursuit of gratification and this worldly experience.

Resource mobilisation theory approaches the free market of religion in terms of how religious organisations effectively use resources as a means of survival and grow by supplying and stimulating demand. This approach has been adapted from pioneering work by Tilly et al. into new social movements. Like other organisations in a competitive environment, religious organisations must work hard for their success by maximising their utilisation of the resources at their disposal to win and retain adherents by adopting rational organisational strategies. These resources will include leadership skills and effective organisation, the support of activists, effectiveness in fund raising and capacity to adjust to a changing broader social environment. This framework has been used to explain the remarkable success of such movements as the Unification Church (or Moonies) in America, the Church of Jesus Christ of Latter-day Saints (the Mormons) and the Jehovah's Witnesses.

The processes and features of modernisation identified by the founding sociological theorists included the spread of rational thinking and science,

491

and the associated belief in the certainty of its explanations and solutions. A highly secularised, rational and scientific society would be the end point of historical progress. However, the implication that modernisation necessarily leads to religious decline has been questioned on many fronts. In American sociology, rational choice theory has provided a prominent explanation of resurgent religion.

In European sociological thinking, postmodernist and high modernist theories have had more impact. At a general level, both perspectives place religion within the context of contemporary societies in which the individual is seen as set free from the social constraints and intellectual certainties of the past. In such a society, the dominance of churches and optimism in the ability of science to claim a monopoly of truth and control the world for human benefit are argued to be giving way to a growing diversity of belief systems, including sciences, religions and quasi religions. Against this general backdrop, there is dispute between supporters of high modernist and postmodernist positions as to the exact nature of life in contemporary society and how fundamental this change from the modern period has been.

Postmodernism – religious and cultural diversity

For postmodernists, in postmodern society individuals are free from the imposition of traditional or modern metanarratives (all encompassing belief systems) which once offered all-embracing truths as well as guidelines and constraints on behaviour. Dominant religious metanarratives in traditional society (for example, feudal society of the Middle Ages) engulfed thinking in religious dogma and superstition which provided an essentially non-optional belief system for moral guidance.

The modern period (industrial) witnessed the emergence of a new metanarrative of rational and scientific truth which promised liberation from the constraints of religion and the guidance of behaviour through rational intellect, but which imposed its own certainties and iron cage of thinking.

What is distinct about the postmodern world is the collapse of all metanarratives and with it a collapse in the perception that there are single universal truths, religious or scientific. Individuals are therefore set free to search for intellectual and moral guidance from a diversity of belief systems and lifestyles, offering bewildering choice in a market in which they are the consumer. Change is relentless and choice of beliefs may take more the form of fashion or status statements as people freely move through different belief systems and lifestyles. In such a society, culture is fragmented and a diversity of new types of religion will emerge as recipes for living which will replace the discredited metanarrative of rational and scientific certainty of the modern period. Religion will thus tend to lose its role as the conveyer of tradition, a situation which traditional churches will find it difficult to adapt to.

There is arguably some evidence to support this process of fragmentation in the form of a growing diversity of 'new religions'. Such religions may appeal to those turning away from institutional religion in a search for greater spiritual meaning in more intimate settings. They may also be chosen as fashion accessories and status symbols, something which has been referred to as 'spirituality shopping'. In Britain, although in aggregate new religions appear to have a minimal following, this following may be increasing, especially if quasi religions are also included. Overall, such belief systems offer evidence of growing diversity and choice in religious beliefs as adherence to mainstream Christian religions appears to be declining. As David Lyon argues (Flanagan & Jupp ed., 1999, Ch1) freed from the grasp of metanarratives, people still require some form of more micro narratives by which they can choose to orient their lives and even frequently change.

In his postmodernist writings, Zygmunt Bauman claims that advanced contemporary societies have reached a stage which is fundamentally different from modern scientific and rational society. For Bauman, the modern metanarrative had enabled individuals to evade moral responsibility in their choice of action through the justification of rational and institutional framed behaviour to achieve ends. This had led to many of the disasters of the modern era.

Individuals in the postmodern world have to act more autonomously. They have to seek 'self-determination' and 'self-construction' in a social world without single clearly prescribed models for behaviour. People have to relate to a rapidly changing environment 'reflexively' – they have to engage in constant self-reflection and self-evaluation, processes which enhance moral self-awareness. Consequently, ethical debate becomes heightened and religious type agencies specialising in moral values may gain attractiveness. Ultimately, this diversity and choice places moral responsibility in the hands of the individual.

High modernism – fundamentalism as an escape from reflexivity

Anthony Giddens prefers to refer to contemporary societies as having entered a high modern stage. Unlike postmodernists who view society as collapsing into a state of moral and intellectual relativism, Giddens argues that rational criteria can still be applied to distinguish between the viability of different intellectual and belief systems to assist in enlightened social intervention. However, high modern societies face new challenges in applying rational understanding in an increasingly complex and rapidly changing globalised world. Although society is still driven by rational calculation, the application of scientific advances generates unanticipated and unwelcome consequences, creating a new environment of manufactured risks which offer unprecedented challenges. These include the consequences of global warming or the possibility of economic meltdown.

It is this rapidly changing world of new risks and uncertainties that individuals have to navigate through. They have lost their anchorage in local communities which reinforced social positions, identity and beliefs. This breakdown of traditional social constraints offers unparalleled opportunities for individual self-construction. Faced with diversity and choice of ways of life and belief systems individuals have to relate to life reflexively – they need to constantly examine their beliefs and life strategies in an ever changing environment in which the risks from action need to be factored in as best as possible. One's life becomes a project of self-creation for which one is responsible. The search for their own belief systems to escape the experience of meaninglessness becomes a continuous and daunting task in which liberation can be troubling.

In traditional societies, religion provided relatively fixed belief systems and moral imperatives within quite closed social structures. The transition to modern societies undermined pervasive religion and promoted secularisation with the advance of logical thought and the testing of truth through empirical observation. However, Giddens argues that the personal doubt and insecurity which is the product of high modernism leads to a resurgence of religion, for example in new and diverse forms or more dangerous fundamentalist varieties.

In 'Runaway World' (2002), Giddens expresses concern that against the experience of openness in a high modern risk society, some people will feel the need to retreat to tradition as far as turning to religious fundamentalism. He argues that the security of tradition that fundamentalism provides takes the form of certainty and intolerance against a world of rationalism and uncertainty. Furthermore, what many manufactured risks associated with high modernism and globalisation have in common is their cataclysmic nature. As such imagery is also common to religions, the experience that the world is running out of control can encourage responses in the form of religious revivalism.

9 // Developments in Sociological Theory

Abstract

The purpose of this final chapter is to pull together some developments in sociological theory which were signalled at the end of the second chapter and built upon at the end of subsequent topic area chapters. These developments are taken a little further and others introduced.

The emergence of contemporary sociological theory is related to conditions of a rapidly changing social world, for example in the form of technological advance and the role of information and the mass media in society. It is emphasised that such changes bring about new opportunities and problems and with them a desire for the development of new theory to assist in their understanding. Key conceptualisation and theories through which sociology is attempting to understand the contemporary world include globalisation, postmodernism and high modernism.

A definition of globalisation is built up and technological, economic, cultural and political dimensions are brought out. Explanation of different positions on globalisation, based on the writings of David Held - globalist, traditionalist and transformationist - is then provided as a framework of analysis. This is rounded off with a broader overview which emphasises the complexity of globalisation and summarises some implications for sociology of the above mentioned positions adopted.

Linked with the question of globalisation is the emergence of postmodern and high modern perspectives. Important social changes and associated social thinking in the form of post-industrial society, post Fordism and neo Marxism that lie behind the emergence of these broad approaches are introduced. Some of the key features of postmodern theory are explained and related to the social conditions behind its emergence. The idea of social control through discourse is introduced with reference to the thinking of Foucault and queer theory is explained as providing a new approach to gender identity within a postmodern context.

It is shown that whilst postmodernism offers little hope of certain knowledge and positive rational intervention in society, high modernist approaches retain faith in our potential to understand new challenges that confront us and the capacity of renewed sociological theory to assist in rising to these challenges.

In trying to explain a rapidly changing world of extensive and immediate communication, some of the theory touched on in this chapter, such as informational society, hybrid society, manufactured risk and post-social world is at a relatively formative stage of development. The reader may therefore find it more useful in terms of the questions and insights that it raises rather than the more firmed up analysis of the founding perspectives.

Introduction – a rapidly changing world

In chapter two, it was shown that sociology emerged as a response to the major social changes which formed the transformation from traditional pre-industrial to modern industrial societies. Theories were developed to explain the characteristics of the main social types and the processes, dynamics and direction of change. These theories explained how traditional societies, characterised by local communities and rural life, relatively closed social hierarchies, and the prevalence of religious thinking, were giving way to urban development, more open social hierarchies, greater geographical mobility and the advance of science. The development of social theory can be viewed in terms of a response to the need for 'ontological security' – the need to structure understanding of society brought about by times of unprecedented change.

To many contemporary observers, it appears that fundamental changes at least as profound as those involved in the emergence of modern industrial society are again afoot in the world. These changes are posing new challenges to our understanding of society. Sociologists who adopt this view are arguing that new forms of conceptualising society are needed. There is, however, much debate on the nature of this society and how it can best be conceptualised, with the most radical positions asserting that society no longer exists.

Recent decades have been marked by the development and mass uptake of new technologies. Most notable of these are satellite television, computers, tablets, access to the internet and mobile phones. Computers have rapidly advanced in their speed of operation, capacity and their mobility - the latter in the form of lap tops. Mobile phones can now have internet facilities and the capacity to take and send pictures. Video conferencing enables the supplementation or replacement of face-to-face meetings by 'bringing together' participants who remain spatially separated and the possibilities of holographic technology to transport talking images of people has been demonstrated. In schools, the internet is now both an educational aid and its use an essential skill for the workplace. We are living in a world in which, through the medium of advanced technology, it is increasingly commonplace that communication is both becoming instant and overcoming past barriers of distance.

How is the use of new technology affecting peoples' lives? It can help to provide more efficient private and public services. However, our reliance on modern technology is particularly evident when systems struggle to cope with the job for which they were designed. This was evident in the case of problems encountered with computer systems installed for the London Ambulance Service and Air Traffic Control.

Modern technology also gives organisations access to information about us as consumers and citizens and the authorities are equipped with improved surveillance techniques. There is more information stored on us than ever before. On the other hand, advances in technology have also enhanced people's capacity to organise direct political action by establishing networks of rapid and flexible communication. In the case of the direct action taken by farmers and lorry drivers in Britain in response to high fuel duty prices in 2000, the use of internet and mobile phone facilities initially seemed to catch the government on the back foot. Other forms of direct political action made possible by the use of modern communications technology have included more global based protests such as those timed to coincide with G8 summit meetings.

The prevalence of new technology raises issues of freedom and security. It has been used by governments to monitor communications between people and to store official secrets. Important issues of state security, public interest and freedom to know have been raised when some of this information has been accessed and made publically available. Technology can be used as a weapon of sabotage through sending computer viruses and by terrorist groups recruiting and organising through the internet. Mobile phones have been used both to detonate explosives on a public transport system and also to track terrorists.

For all of its promise, modern technology introduces new risks into our lives. Such risks include the uncertain but potentially catastrophic effects of global warming and concerns regarding the introduction of genetically modified crops. Against these challenges, a key question is the extent to which technology may both help provide solutions and introduce further problems and risks in the process.

From this brief introduction, the broader question to be considered in this chapter is the effect that recent changes are having on both society and people's lives. Whilst sociology can help to address these questions, it should also become evident that to do so sociologists must reflect on the theories and concepts that have been inherited from the period of the inception of the subject and be prepared to develop theories and concepts better able to shed light on contemporary conditions. It is in this context that some of the debates surrounding globalisation, postmodernism and high modernism will be reviewed in this chapter.

Conceptualising globalisation

Globalisation is a term that became commonplace very quickly, both in everyday usage and in academia. Its common usage says much about a general awareness of powerful global forces. However, in this context the term has often been used loosely and applied uncritically, sometimes eliciting evaluations of it being a wholly good or bad process. In academic circles, there has been much debate about the nature and extent of globalisation, but most sociologists agree that the processes involved are highly complex and the outcomes uncertain. It is therefore particularly important that both the term is defined and the processes examined as carefully as possible.

The writings of David Held (2002) offer a valuable starting point for defining globalisation. Held has identified the key features of globalisation as 1) the stretching of social relations, 2) the intensification of flows, 3) increasing interpenetration and 4) the emergence of global infrastructure.

1) Social relations are stretched when they are able to cut across and transcend prescribed national boundaries or geographical regions. Stretching can be evidenced by an increasing range of migration and labour movement and the improved retention of communication that people are able to maintain with their location of origin.

2) Flow refers to extent, intensity and fluidity of communication which increases the volume of stretched interaction. It may involve the volume of migration flows or information flows as communication (relationships?) can be detached from the limits of geographical space and time through immediate high tech global communication.

3) Interpenetration refers to the complex relationship between the global and the local which can promote on the one hand global uniformity and on the other local diversity. This dynamic has been summed up by the term 'glocalization', a phenomena regarding which many examples can be provided. The impact of global uniformity can be illustrated by 'McDonaldization' – the setting up of McDonalds fast food outlets and its associated symbolism across the world. The tendency toward global uniformity in this instance is easy to recognise. However, McDonalds has had to improvise its product to cater for different cultural tastes. Moreover, as many different food traditions also become extended globally through food transportation, travel and migration, the overall crisscrossing effect is likely to add to local diversity.

Different cultural settings can form the context for variations in consumer tastes. Large global corporations thus have to balance economic pressures for standardisation with the satisfaction of different tastes and requirements in different countries and localities. Some financial institutions have picked up on the imagery of glocalization in appealing to customers as institutions of multinational power and local expertise.

Environmental movements also provide examples of glocalization by emphasising that action at the local level is important in tackling global environmental issues. Thus, consumer preference for locally produced foodstuffs may be encouraged to help combat global pollution resulting from long range transportation.

4) Finally, global infrastructure refers to the emergence of networks and institutions which may interface with and effect the policy options that are available to the state. This infrastructure could involve the power of transnational corporations to influence labour relations policy, the emergence of supra national organisations of global governance designed to tackle new global problems, or the influence of non-governmental organisations such as Amnesty International to globally monitor abuses of human rights which arguably even the most secretive states would now find it difficult to hide.

Overall, for Anthony Giddens, the world is becoming more interdependent. A key feature of globalisation is time-space distanciation. Through the speed and reach of contemporary communications technology and transportation systems, past barriers of time and distance fall down and the world is experienced as if shrinking. There is little doubt that we are becoming socialised into seeing the world as a much smaller place than people just two generations ago would have, let alone those who lived in pre-industrial times. An important consequence of advancing time-space distanciation is that decisions directly affecting people, for example corporate investment decisions, can be made at ever increasing distance. The impact of such decisions can sometimes be destructive of local communities and opportunities, with decisions made from afar 'disembedded' from those who are affected.

Analysing globalisation is thus a very complex process. As a preliminary exercise, different dimensions of the social - the technological, the economic, the cultural and the political - will be separated out for purposes of definition and illustration. In the real world, of course, these categories overlap, but it may also be that globalisation is taking contradictory paths in the different areas. These dimensions will later be reviewed in the context of a classificatory system of rival interpretations of globalisation developed by Held.

Dimensions of globalisation

A key aspect of globalisation is the advance of **technology**. Technological advance has enabled the high-speed transfer of information within and across national boundaries. This makes it possible for financial institutions which are globally linked to transfer money from place to place instantaneously. It allows news events to be instantly communicated globally and other mass media information to be broadly disseminated. Modern technology has enabled call centres, servicing people in western countries, to be set up in countries such as India where the advantages of cheap labour can be utilised. In developed and even increasingly in developing countries, the technology of the internet is a commonly used means of access to information and communication. Rapid means of personal transportation over great distances are now accessible to more people as witnessed in pressures for airport growth.

Technological changes have also often generated new problems, one of which is the vulnerability of computer systems of individuals, organisations and governments to security breaches or attacks. Some of the changes brought about by technology generate opposition, as in the case of protests against airport expansion or consumer dissatisfaction with the use of overseas call centres. Furthermore, it may be asked to what extent technologically mediated communication is authentically social and what influences its spread may have on people in their daily lives and psychologically.

A measure of **economic** globalisation is the emergence of industrial and service enterprises, often giants, with a base in more than one country in the form of multinationals and transnational corporations. Following definitions employed by Hirst and Thompson, multinationals can be viewed as international organisations that have a home based headquarters in one country and are thus subject to regulation by their home government. Transnational corporations differ from multinationals in that they can move their operations and even headquarters anywhere in search of the most favourable conditions of operation. They are relatively light and nimble footed and this mobility can influence the policies of national governments who want to attract and retain inward investment.

For Hirst and Thompson, whilst multinational corporations point to an international economy, it is really only the activities of transnational corporations which are indicative of truly globalised economic relationships. In reality, though, the difference is often unclear and more a matter of degree. However classified, corporations such as Toyota, Coca-Cola and General Motors operate as global organisations.

Global communications enable businesses to utilise up to date intelligence on the state of markets and adapt innovatively to changing conditions and opportunities. In this environment, they tend to employ flexible production techniques in which they can change specialist runs of products based on the latest consumer demands in different parts of the world. Employees therefore have to be increasingly prepared to respond to change in the form of retraining and new working practices as well as the possible threat of redundancy or unemployment. Global corporations may be attracted to a location by low wages or the availability of certain labour skills, restrictions on trade union activity and low rates of corporation tax. Some have even, through the practice of internal transfer pricing, managed to effectively transfer profits made in one country of higher corporation tax to another where the rate is lower, thus engaging in legal tax avoidance in a country where the profit was made.

In sociology, **Culture** refers to an environment of meaning. It is conveyed through language and symbols and can be located in local environments and communicated by process of face-to-face contact. Culture is the means of conveying national traditions and heritage and it shapes people's values and understanding of the world. Following Ritzer (2008, pp.579-589), key questions here are whether in a globalising world the integrity of traditional cultures can be maintained, whether cultural convergence is taking place or whether new hybrid cultural forms are emerging. Moreover, culture arguably also has an increasingly technologically related aspect to its formation through the output of the mass media. A key question here is the degree and nature of the impact of a mass media culture of global range on national or local culture. Is it likely to erode national cultural differences, perhaps into a global mush, or is its impact relatively superficial in the face of millennia of rooted cultural traditions? May it help to promote an enhanced cosmopolitan outlook and tolerance throughout as people's knowledge of different cultures is enhanced? Or may it provoke cultural reactions in the form of assertions of national traditions or even the appeal of fundamentalism?

The position of Samuel Huntington is that cultural differences will be retained but between civilisations. Civilisations are cultural heritages which straddle individual nations and provide a very broad sense of identity which is often related to religious traditions. For Huntington, certain historical civilisation differences became temporarily submerged beneath the economic, political and ideological animosity between the communist east and capitalist west during the post-war cold war era. With the collapse of communism, global fault lines have reconfigured to those between civilisations. He goes on to argue that the most dangerous element of this is the 'clash of civilisations' between the Christian west, which has attempted to universalise its culture, and the resurgence of Islamic culture. Similar animosities may also emerge within multicultural societies.

An alternative interpretation of the effects of globalisation is that of cultural convergence. This view suggests that globalisation is changing all cultures toward something similar. Convergence may well be driven by economic factors to do with the standardising effect of global capitalism. If this is the case, the convergence is likely to lean strongly in the direction of the values of western or American capitalism. In the strongest assertion of this position, it may be seen as 'converging' completely in this direction in the form of 'cultural imperialism'.

Arguably, 'hybridization' provides the most optimistic interpretation of the effect of globalisation on culture. A hybrid culture is a unique and creative outcome of the interplay between various cultural influences coming into global contact with each other. More societies are therefore experiencing a growing cultural mix throughout the world that can lead to novel outcomes in such forms as popular music and religious belief systems – a recipe that chimes well with postmodern theory.

Politics is about the institutions of government but it is also about the distribution and use of power locally, nationally and globally. Traditionally, the key institutions of government have been associated with the nation and the state. The sovereignty of the state gives governments the right to legislate and form policy at national level as well as the legitimate use of power within its own national boundaries. A number of questions bearing on national sovereignty arise with reference to globalisation. To what extent may governments have to modify their policy to accommodate the wishes of global corporations? How can governments co-operate to respond to international crime and terrorism? How can governments work together in response to global environmental issues?

In a globalised world, there are many pressures on governments to compromise a degree of national sovereignty, ideally for the mutual benefit of their societies in tackling global problems. For this purpose, various supra national institutions have been created. One of these is the International Monetary Fund which provides loans for economies in trouble. In this case, when one looks at the playing field within which this institution operates, it is one of the imposition of conditions of free market reforms. Thus, Greece had to compromise a degree of national sovereignty by forcing through unpopular austerity and privatisation reforms as part of an economic bailout deal in part supplied by the IMF to avoid its own economic collapse and the contagious effect that this would likely have on other economies in a globally interlinked world. This raises questions regarding implications for its own internal democratic processes and the response options available to its citizens.

Held's classification of approaches to globalisation

Sociological analyses of the nature and extent of globalisation are varied. Following a review of a broad range of sociological contributions on the subject, David Held (2000a & b) has devised a classification system of positions adopted. This classification system will form an organisational reference point for the ideas of some key contributors to the debate and reference will be made to the above dimensions of globalisation.

Held applies the term **globalists** to those who view the process of globalisation as profound and inevitable. Globalisation can be measured in terms of the growing extent and frequency of flows of information, communication, trade, capital etc. To varying degrees, those who adopt a globalist position emphasise the eroding effect of these processes on national boundaries and the sovereign power of the state.

Globalists can be differentiated into optimists, who adopt a positive stance toward global capitalism, and pessimists who recognise the effects of global capitalism but are critical. A highly optimistic position is taken by Kenichi Ohmae who advocates the merits of global free enterprise capitalism leading to the complete opening up of national borders to the free flow of trade and finance. By such means, it is argued that businesses and consumers can take maximum advantage of local specialisation in the production of goods and services through which when traded the total global creation of wealth can be maximised. Consumers are therefore regarded as the main beneficiaries of unbounded globalisation. Ohmae argues that in an increasingly borderless world economy, governments need to go with the grain of global capitalism, enhancing the competitive edge of their workforce by encouraging employee flexibility and supporting retraining. It is argued that the wealth created will in time trickle down to poorer sections of society and to the poorest countries so long as free market reforms are embraced. This is quite an extreme globalist position which Held has referred to as 'hyperglobalist'.

At the cultural level, the massive expansion of commercially funded satellite and cable television and the internet can be taken as a measure of globalisation. A positive slant was put on the emergence of a global media by Marshall McLuhan as far back as the 1960s. McLuhan emphasised that communications revolutions are the driving force for social change and that the electronic media revolution held the potential for bringing the world together in a 'global village' of shared information to which our sensory perceptions would adjust. More recently, Ohmae sees the emergence of a common global enterprise culture accompanying the triumph of global free enterprise capitalism as positive change, with rampant consumerism buoying up global capitalism.

In the realm of politics, the forces of globalisation, as argued by Ohmae, render national governments relatively powerless to control their own economies. The mobility of capital tends to pressure states toward open market friendly policies by which they can benefit by attracting inward investment. For Ohmae, government intervention in the form of the erection of protectionist barriers to free trade in a globalising world would be damaging to the process of global wealth creation by distorting the beneficial effect of free markets to allocate production to the cheapest and most efficient locations.

A critical stance toward global capitalism is adopted by globalists taking a neo-Marxist slant. Although the global spread of free enterprise is recognised, here globalism is viewed in terms of the imposition of the interests of western capitalism and a capitalist class throughout the world. The result is a deterioration in the terms and conditions of employment experienced by workers in the face of profit maximising mobile capital and increasing polarisation of levels of income and wealth both within many societies and between the richer and poorer nations.

Tunstall views global media in terms of the cultural imposition of western capitalist values on developing countries. From this perspective, the mass media has the power to impress on populations an external culture of consumerism against which an indigenous culture has little defence. This cultural imperialism is a new form of external domination that does not require armies for its imposition.

Leslie Sklaire also adopts a neo-Marxist position. He points to the growing economic turnover of transnational corporations as powerful evidence of a globalised world in which national boundaries are being eroded by the emergence of a transnational system that has risen above nation states. At this general level, there is some agreement with Ohmae. However, for Sklaire, the main beneficiaries of this process are not consumers but a broadly defined transnational capitalist class including corporate executives, professionals, pro-globalist politicians and bureaucrats and mass media producers. The almost complete global reach and pervasiveness of the mass media promotes an 'ideology of consumerism' – a powerfully dominant view that consumerism is natural and desirable. This ideology extends an appetite to consume from a growing array of goods and services that are available, with the effect of maintaining the buoyancy of transnational capitalism.

Sklaire argues that global socialism may ultimately emerge out of global capitalism. This is because the consequences of transnational capitalism are the crises of economic polarisation between and often within societies as well as the ecological damage caused. In response, anti-capitalist and environmental movements come to adopt an increasingly global stance of opposition to transnational capitalism and some governments are engaging in protectionist measures to defend their environment and ways of life.

In contrast to globalists, **traditionalists** adopt a sceptical position on the extent to which the forces of globalisation have really advanced. They are keen to differentiate between globalisation and internationalism, the latter taking the form of trade and communications between states. Hirst and Thompson, for example, maintain that the case for globalisation has been overstated. They argue that state power and national culture within national boundaries remains substantial. In terms of economics, they point out that there is little new in the nature and extent of international trade. For example, Thompson offers evidence that the trade to GDP ratio for many countries in 1995 was little changed from that of 1913. Moreover, he maintains that most international corporations are multinationals. With their headquarters rooted in one country, these organisations can be controlled by national governments. Very few businesses are strictly transnational corporations that can move freely between countries and call the shots – the true index of globalisation.

Whilst governments are keen to attract inward investment, they may be more protectionist in terms of major corporate takeovers from an external source. For example, in 2014, the American pharmaceutical giant Pfizer, which had previously closed a major plant in England, launched an attempt to take over the British pharmaceutical company AstraZeneca, prospectively becoming the largest takeover of a British company. At the time, the government claimed to be looking at whether the move would satisfy the public interest, which it defined in terms of British jobs and science. Whilst this might suggest evidence of national government resistance to unbounded economic globalisation, the capacity of the government to override the decision of shareholders if 1) the government decided that a takeover was against the public interest but 2) shareholders nevertheless voted for the takeover (which they didn't) would have provided an interesting test case between the perspectives of traditionalists and globalists.

A traditionalist position on culture emphasises that national cultures are rooted in national traditions and are quite resistant to the more ephemeral effects of the global media. Information crossing national boundaries is mediated through the prism of a national culture and mass media, especially where national public service channels such as the BBC operate.

For traditionalists, the focus of political power remains strongly with national governments. Governments retain the ability to pass legislation, control their own economic and social policy and, where inclined, to defend the welfare state. Moreover, it could be argued that the development of modern technology in the form of information gathering and surveillance techniques has actually enhanced the power of the state. Governments retain their own armies, police and intelligence services and can maintain their own borders. Indeed, the issue of immigration control figured prominently in the May 2014 European elections, with the success of parties of the political right sending a strong message to a number of national governments.

Transformationists adopt a position somewhere in between that of globalists and traditionalists, but in certain respects closer to the former. They maintain that profound globalising changes have been taking place but, unlike globalists, they see no single and inevitable direction to these changes which are very complex and can work themselves out differently in economic, cultural and political spheres. For writers such as Giddens and Beck, although the challenges and risks associated with globalisation are great, sometimes new, and solutions uncertain, global governance is emerging and needs to be developed to help manage these problems. The state remains a powerful entity but must increasingly work alongside a plethora of global, regional and local institutions to go with the grain of globalisation but also to tame its excesses.

Those who adopt this position recognise some of the economic changes that have been highlighted by globalists, but do not view them in terms of unmitigated success or disaster as optimistic and pessimistic globalists respectively tend to. Although the global economy is capable of producing great wealth, it is argued that if left unchecked it could lead to a further polarisation between winners and losers within and between nations. However, for Giddens, the main losers are countries which have been marginalised by the globalisation process. Writers in this tradition tend to emphasise that it is possible and necessary to rationally intervene to tame global capitalism in such a way that international and national security and justice can complement the benefits of economic efficiency and the creation of wealth.

For transformationists, the impact of globalisation on culture is complex. Unlike neo-Marxists, transformationists argue that cultural flows from the mass media are not simply top down one-way influences of cultural imperialism and ideology of consumerism which are uniformly imposed on and passively absorbed by populations. Different readings of standardized media output are likely to form in the context of different cultures. Thus, although in the 1980s the television programme 'Dallas' achieved massive worldwide coverage, its messages regarding the American wealthy were read differently by audiences in different political systems and cultures. From the transformationist position, it is argued that detailed research is necessary to establish the dynamics involved in the different readings of media output in different cultural contexts.

Transformationists such as Giddens strongly emphasise the need to develop new institutions of 'global governance' to tackle problems that have taken on an increasingly global dimension such as inequalities in the distribution of wealth, international crime, the risk of destabilised financial markets and global economic collapse and environmental damage. Governments must be prepared to cede a degree of national sovereignty to global institutions for the common benefit. Giddens sees the European Union as an important model in the direction of global governance, but one which needs to improve the democratic accountability of its institutions.

Globalisation – an overview

Many issues can be raised regarding globalisation, a small number of which will be touched on here.

Firstly, just how new is this process? For example, it has been suggested that there have been early historical episodes of mini-globalisations, such as the reach of the Roman Empire two thousand years ago, which subsequently faltered (Holton, 2011, p.19). As with so much in sociology, the answer to such questions depends on definitions. If taken literally to mean the interconnectedness of the entire globe in the form of political and economic infrastructure and instantaneous global communication, it would be reasonable to conclude that globalisation is a uniquely recent and still somewhat uneven phenomena, perhaps gathering apace with the emergence of international free trade organisations from the 1950s, satellite broadcasting from about the mid-1960s and the collapse of the Soviet Union and Eastern European communist states between 1989 and 1991.

A further issue is the question of the apparent relentlessness of globalisation. This has been questioned by writers such as Polanyi (Holton, 2011, p.228) who has argued that there are economically related phases of globalisation and deglobalisation. In this view, tendencies toward free market deregulation eventually lead to social crisis and the need for interventionary responses. This could be in the form of the protection of home markets through import controls to safeguard home employment, as during the inter war years. Ironically, however, recent economic support packages to save economies from the consequences of deregulated financial markets have been provided by global institutions which have required the countries in receipt of massive funds to pursue deregulation in the form of free market reforms.

It has been argued by supporters of hyper globalisation such as Ohmae that allowing globalisation free range would contribute to global peace as well as prosperity. This would be because as well as free trade, permeable national borders would massively enhance investment across societies. In this event, countries would be reluctant to go to war with each other as to do so would destroy some of their own resources abroad.

Arguably, however, this view of conflict has become somewhat dated in ways related to the very forces of globalisation. The permeable national borders and use of modern technology which enabled the 9/11 attack on the twin towers symbolised a new type of warfare which may not be limited by such constraints. Hatred of America or the west have led to terrorist attacks in which the loss of property has not been a limiting factor.

Globalisation is a highly complex process, working in different and unpredictable ways in the interconnected spheres of the economy, culture and politics and is not simply a top down macro process moving throughout the world in a single and inevitable direction. The thoughtful observer may adopt a varied response to globalisation as it affects different aspects of their life. For example, opposition to the power of global multinationals may sit alongside support for global regulatory apparatus designed to constrain their activities. Furthermore, whilst for poorer sections of society, as consumers globalisation may bring within reach cheaper products such as clothes produced by cheap labour in other countries, they may find that as producers their own terms and conditions of employment are eroded by the capacity of multi and transnational companies to easily withdraw resources in an open global market to such very sources of cheap labour.

Briefly returning to the above typology, it is possible to extract from the different positions different consequences for the nature and role of sociology. For hypergloblists such as Ohmae, there is little that planned social intervention can or should do to stem the headlong process of global capitalism. From this position, sociology would be reduced to little more than the handmaiden of free market economics. For neo-Marxists, sociology can have a political role to play in highlighting the nature of consumerist ideology to enhance oppositional movements to transnational capitalism. For traditionalists, a sociology similar to that developed by the founding theorists which conceptualises society in terms of bounded nation states remains relatively valid. For transformationists, there is both the possibility of and need for enlightened human agency to influence the conditions of global capitalism and social change. Sociological theories and concepts are needed to guide human action, but the new and highly complex conditions of globalisation require a creative reworking rather than the retention of ideas fashioned in a different age of earlier modernism. We will review this position in more detail in a later section.

Toward contemporary theory

In this section, consideration will be given to some key insights into social change that would later be taken to a new level in postmodern and high modern social theory. The first theory of major social change to be considered is Daniel Bell's anticipation of a post-industrial society. Bell, developing his ideas from the early 1960s, extrapolated changes in the American economy and society to construct an image of a future society in which profit motive driven free enterprise capitalism based on manufacturing would give way to a predominantly service and knowledge orientated white collar professional middle class society.

The culture of modern capitalism in the form of the profit motive had been shaped by the economic base; this culture comprised the core values of a business owning capitalist class. However, Bell argued that a new service and information society would require highly trained and educated managers, technicians and scientists to head flexible organisational structures and university research institutes to promote innovation. Business reliance on the skills of rational planners and the use of high technology would promote a managerial revolution in which the ownership of enterprises would be separated from their control, with a substantial transfer of decision making power from those who owned capital to those with knowledge and expertise. The latter would comprise the emergence of a new 'knowledge class'.

In the post-industrial society, universities would take over from businesses as the core institution of innovation and provide the skills necessary to run a service economy. The service economy would include the provision of health, educational, financial and leisure services. The knowledge class would be a service class whose decisions made would be based on an ethic of service to the community rather than prioritising the profit motive. Through change in the economic base and the transference of power, in post-industrial society this co-operative ethic would broaden out into a new more general social culture. Whilst private ownership of enterprises would remain, the whole basis for old ideological opposition and class conflict would cease to exist.

This optimistic tone was enhanced by the view that technological advances would allow the length of the working week to decrease, leading to a society of increasing leisure time and consumer affluence in which the Calvinist self-restraint and work ethic of early capitalism would give way to present time orientation and instant gratification through the availability of instant credit and mass consumption. In effect, post-industrial society would deliver enhanced affluence to depoliticised consumers.

Although based on a model of trends in American capitalism, Bell envisaged that the economic aspects of a post-industrial society were part of a broad process of modernisation. Thus, despite the diversity of cultures and political systems in different societies, he argued that common features of post-industrial modernisation would reduce the ideological opposition between capitalist and communist systems of the cold war period of the industrial era.

Focussing on production and organisation of the workplace, Michael Piori and Charles Sabel were early exponents of the view that a major transition had been under way in the latter decades of the twentieth century in the form of a change from Fordist to post-Fordist production.

The model for workplace efficiency during the mass production industrial era was typified by the Henry Ford production line of the early twentieth century. This approach followed closely Frederick Taylor's scientific management principles. Taylor advocated that it was the responsibility of management to train production line workers to achieve maximum efficiency through carrying out narrowly designed, low skilled and highly repetitive work tasks. This hierarchical and prescriptive approach took no account of workers' need for job satisfaction, nevertheless appeared to be an ideal work system for the mass production of standardised products and was often incentivised by a piece work reward system.

Post-Fordists argue that Fordist production methods are an inappropriate model for the workplace in the context of rapidly changing global markets and post-industrial conditions of the latter twentieth century. They are too inflexible and rely on the economies of scale through mass standardisation. By contrast, fluid conditions of rapidly changing consumer taste and demand require firms to be highly attentive to changing markets for both goods and services. They must adopt highly flexible and responsive production techniques which can accommodate short term production runs of specialist goods. Rather than repetitiously following a single work task, workers need to develop a breadth of skills, be prepared to regularly retrain and be flexible. Businesses must be highly innovative. This requires collaborative rather than hierarchical relationships between workers and management, with work teams pooling skills and ideas to solve problems. Workers therefore work more autonomously, experience higher levels of satisfaction and gain in social status.

In reality, it would appear that post-Fordist production methods are part of a broader mix of approaches rather than taking the place of Fordist methods. There is therefore more continuity amongst change, as witnessed by the Fordist type production line practices in thriving fast food chains and call centres.

Some accounts of change have adopted a neo-Marxist analysis which maintained that consumer capitalism had become the dominant means of social control and de-politicisation. For Guy Debord, a key figure in the French Situationist International movement of the 1950s and 1960s, modern technology, the media and advertising created product 'spectacles' which enticed consumers into a fantasy world of artificially created needs for the latest goods which were associated with images of happiness.

Situationists argued that in modern consumer capitalism, the world is fabricated by advertisements and images which entice people to live their lives through the objects of consumption. Goods are desired and acquired for their status value. Identification with stars and celebrities, who themselves help give spectacle to consumer goods, offers some compensation for the very shallowness of these consumer orientated lives.

From this theoretical position, people's awareness of the class divided nature of capitalist society, which emanates from work based relations, becomes hidden behind consumerism which addresses all equally. The image of happiness associated with luxuries and the latest goods is open to all. By such means, social control is raised to a new level. Aiming for such happiness fantasies, workers become trapped into working harder to spend. Through the 'false consciousness' of achieving happiness through consumption, workers are not just exploited in the workplace but as consumers they are also the ultimate payers of the cost of media advertising. A further tie and burden is that of the cost of consumer debt. This pervasive form of domination renders workers de-politicised. As consumers, they abandon the trade union for the shopping mall.

In contrast to the classical Marxist position, this and other schools of post-war Marxism tend to recognise a greater potency of the superstructure, especially in the form of mass media advertising, to encourage workers, as consumers, to embrace capitalism. The development of the mass media has provided an encapsulating effect beyond that envisaged by Marx. Thus, although retaining a Marxist perspective, such writers are often less certain than Marx was regarding the immanent demise of capitalism. Postmodernists have since taken on board and developed further such insights into the effect of the media on society but have largely abandoned the Marxist framework of analysis.

Postmodernity or high modernity?

There has been much dispute over the nature of contemporary society relating to the types of changes identified earlier in this chapter. A key line of distinction can be drawn between those who maintain that modern society is being replaced by conditions of 'postmodernity' (for example Lyotard and Baudrillard) and others who refer to change taking place within modernity through reference to such terms as 'high modernity' (Giddens), 'second modernity' (Beck) or 'liquid modernity' (Bauman). Some commonality exists between the two main approaches, each of which emphasise the fluidity and uncertainty of contemporary life and there is a grey area in which it is difficult to classify a theorist as squarely in the modernist or postmodernist tradition (for example neo-Marxists such as Jameson and Harvey), and some writers, such as Bauman, have changed their position over time. However, if one were to somewhat simplify matters at this stage, there is one fundamental difference between the various contemporary modernist theories and postmodern approaches. Whilst those who refer to conditions of advanced or high modernism believe that even in a complex and fluid contemporary global world it is possible to still rationally analyse social conditions with the assistance of sociological theory and beneficially intervene in society, the more radical postmodernists (such as Baudrillard) claim that truth statements about contemporary social reality are not possible, that authentic society ceases to exist, and that sociology as a rational quest for truth about society and as a guide to intervention is now redundant. The break between modern and postmodern society is thus sharp and fundamental.

Postmodernism and the periodisation of history

Before the nature of the social condition advanced by a diverse body of thinkers commonly bracketed as postmodernists is outlined, it is necessary to review how they tend to periodise history leading up to the postmodern stage. The stages identified by Jean-Francois Lyotard are traditional, modern and postmodern.

Lyotard, an early exponent of postmodernism, emphasised the importance of the cultural dimension, in particular the understanding of the world through narratives. A narrative is a story conveyed by a narrator in a situation of discourse with others which holds a claim to truth. The nature of narratives defines historical stages. In traditional societies, narratives took the form of fables, religious stories and legends etc., and the legitimacy of the narrative was judged in terms of the status of the communicator and their exclusive access to the truth. Others acceptance of narrative explanations reflected and was a source of social dominance and reinforced positions within a closed social structure. This situation pertained in one form or another up to the late Middle Ages.

The transition to modern society was paved particularly by Enlightenment thinking of the late seventeenth and the eighteenth century which applied rational criticism to attack traditional thinking. Especially important were French Enlightenment thinkers who scrutinised and undermined religious dogma through the application of reason (for example Diderot and d'Alembert) and challenged the veneration of antiquity and its thinkers (for example Fontonelle). For Enlightenment thinkers, reason held the prospect of liberation from the clutches of religious dogma and superstition and could be applied to establish universal truths, organise society and promote progress. Such thinking assisted the transition to modern societies by helping to create the intellectual conditions for scientific progress behind political and industrial revolutions.

Postmodernists refer to the single dominant system of scientific and rational thinking that came to accompany the modern era as a 'metanarrative'. A metanarrative is an all-embracing system of thinking. The modern metanarrative, derived from the Enlightenment, asserted that the establishment of scientific truth was superior to all other knowledge, was possible, was applicable to all areas of understanding, and was beneficial. It accompanied a more open social structure in which statements could be judged according to the universal, objective and impersonal criteria of scientific truth rather than from a person's privileged position in the social structure. Scientific understanding could now be applied to all realms of the world, including society, and those with scientific and professional expertise acquired the power and status to control people's lives. This is the social context of the birth of sociology in its positivist (pretensions to science) form in the writings of Comte, Marx and Durkheim.

For Lyotard, the dominance of the metanarrative of science in the modern era failed to achieve the promised liberation. Instead, it created a sterile world of clinical efficiency, deficient of emotional intelligence and moral guidance. Technological advances accompanied by social disasters undermined faith in the superiority of scientifically established truth and spawned the conditions for the collapse of the scientific metanarrative as the context for superior knowledge and the transition to the postmodern world. Zygmunt Bauman, during his phase of postmodern writing, pointed out that the metanarrative of rational thinking, emphasising organisational efficiency, is by itself devoid of moral guidance. Associated with the modern propensity to try and create social utopia through social engineering, it had been put to use by totalitarian communist and fascist regimes applying totalizing ideology with disastrous consequences.

According to postmodernists, the scientific metanarrative is collapsing and leading to 'societies' (the reason for the inverted commas will be evident later) characterised by a plurality of belief systems. Only in such a 'society' where the relativity of different belief systems as different approaches to knowledge replaces the metanarrative of science can liberation through choice amongst diversity of beliefs and lifestyles be more fully realised. This is the postmodern era. It is a high tech computer and internet world where knowledge becomes a battle ground for use (what it can do) rather than truth. The search for marketable knowledge eclipses the search for truth.

Radical postmodernism – the end of society

Jean Baudrillard depicts the postmodern condition as one in which high tech mass media promotes a fashion dominated populist consumer culture in post industrial leisure and information societies. Everyday life is characterised by the elevation of consumption over production. Furthermore, the prevalence of the mass media in an information and entertainment society has led to an explosion of signs and symbols to the extent that the exchange of symbolic meaning has taken over from the material production of goods as the dominant form of production. In 'societies' where the creation of wealth is no longer a problem to our survival, we are surrounded by consumer products and messages in shops and massive shopping centres which bring together products from many countries. This experience comes to dominate people's consciousness. Displays offer meanings to objects such as new lifestyle images and shopping experiences, rather than focussing on their individual utility, and combine objects with the aim of directing purchasing impulses toward networks of products. Objects once purchased for utility become more acquired for the status associated with brand image. This is the cultural dimension of consumerism. The products of consumption are from diverse parts of the world and with heightened obsolescence and rapidly changing fashion become abstracted from context, are part of a fluid and rapidly changing fashion and present orientated world, and give the feeling of a 'society' without history.

The sprawling mass media promotes a bewildering diversity of images and information. This brings about what Vattimo calls 'the dissolution of centralized perspectives'. A pluralistic world view undermines any notion of a single reality and a single truth and promotes the recognition of the contingency of all systems of thinking. In the postmodern world, in contrast to modern society, people reach emancipation not through scientific truth but from its singular dominance.

For Baudrillard, we are entering a postmodern stage in which a high tech mass media conveys self-referencing signs and images (simulacra) in which messages become interconnected and understood with reference to each other. Signs and images which once reflected an underlying reality to which they were connected have now exploded to such an extent that they have detached themselves from their material reference points and created a reality of their own. They no longer portray reality, but become a different type of reality – a virtual reality. They masquerade as reality and encapsulate people in a world where reality and truth are illusive. In this world, the 'real' is obscured by electronic images of simulated events and cannot be distinguished from the latter. This media generated world becomes the realm of experience to which Baudrillard applies the term 'hyperreal' which replaces the reference points of a 'real' world by media produced self-referencing signs. The 'hyperreal' kills the 'real' which it artificially resurrects through self-referencing signs, rather like creating a theme park reality to replace authentic reality. Having no other reference point, the 'hyperreal' (illusion) fills the void as the 'real' world is lost to systems of signs and images. When we watch events on the television, they reference other events on the television and in the newspapers, and so on. In this way, emphasises Baudrillard, the Gulf War was experienced, by those not involved, at a clinical distance, rather like a simulated exercise, as a surgical operation of high tech precision bombing! But what really happened?

Baudrillard argues that the phase of modern capitalism described in the economic determinism of Marxist theory, in which power derives from economic production, has been largely transcended. In the postmodern era, power resides in 'hyperreality' – one-way media generated communication to politically passive and privatised consumers. In such a 'society', cultural production is everything and truth and reality are impossible to substantiate. This spells an end to sociology as an attempt to establish scientific truth about society and as a guide to tackling social issues. Since reality cannot be grasped, we are now beyond the point at which it can be constructively changed. People become abandoned to their worlds of personal troubles, unable to meaningfully relate them to broader social structures as authentic society ceases to exist.

In summary, according to this position, images become free floating in a world of make believe, leaving people helpless in ascertaining whether they bear any relationship with an underlying reality in a world where the cultural realm becomes dominant and all embracing.

Alternatively, it could be argued that the culture of media images has become a froth through which it is difficult to see an underlying reality rather than becoming a new reality itself.

Or capitalism in crisis?

Whilst many sociologists believe that profound changes are taking place in society and the world, many do not agree with postmodernist accounts, especially those as radical as Baudrillard's. Neo-Marxists attempt to explain some of the cultural features identified by postmodernists but within a Marxist framework. For example, Frederic Jameson recognises the emergence of simulacra, cultural superficiality and fragmentation, loss of historicity and the intensification of innovation. However, these cultural features are viewed as the products of 'late capitalism'. Therefore, despite these cultural changes, there is an underlying continuity between the modern and the postmodern as the essential economic structure of capitalism remains predominant across this period.

For Jameson, the development of new technology has helped to reinvigorate a waning capitalism by extending consumerism and the range of commodities from the production of goods to the entire culture through the reproductive technology of computers and television. The disorientating effect of postmodern culture is therefore not an out of control phenomena in its own right but a consequence of adjustments within capitalism. In contrast to the resignation of postmodernists, this effect can be overcome if social theorists develop a neo-Marxist analysis which can provide people with 'cognitive maps' by which they can regain an understanding of the world, develop class consciousness and reacquire their capacity for political action.

David Harvey also adopts a neo-Marxist interpretation of postmodernity and relates social and cultural changes to the economic base of capitalism in crisis. According to this analysis, during the post second world war decades, capitalism had delivered growth through the application of production line systems. Workers had experienced rising living standards based on systems of mass production of standardised goods. These modern techniques of production, referred to as 'Fordism', operated within the confines of economies regulated by Keynesian economic intervention, comprising a Fordist – Keynesian period of capitalism referred to as 'organised capital accumulation'.

However, for Harvey, the oil crisis of 1973 brought a period of crisis to capitalism. The hiking of oil prices by the oil producer nations had a major impact on the economies of modern capitalist societies. Businesses had to be more inventive and dynamic in their quest for profit if they were to compete and survive. The model of organised capital accumulation was too inflexible to respond to these needs. New post-Fordist work organisation and production techniques were devised in which businesses became lean, flexible, high tech and responsive to specialised markets. Work practices were changed. For many, security of employment diminished, and, assisted by right wing governments in Britain and the USA in the 1980s, the power of trade unions was curtailed. Subcontracting and privatisation were further features of the post-Fordist approach to production within deregulated economies, ushering in a period of 'flexible capital accumulation'.

According to Harvey, the intensification of time and space through technological advances and tendencies toward globalisation were the result of an intensification of the work process as capitalist enterprises were driven by the quest for improved efficiency and profit in crisis conditions. Changing fashions were driven by free enterprise to buoy up consumer demand and achieve profitability by businesses showing superior versatility and innovation to that of their competitors. For Harvey, this economic imperative of the quest for profitability under new conditions of capitalist competition was the real dynamic behind the pace of life and cultural changes in terms of growing diversity of social fashions and interests which had been highlighted by postmodernists.

Adopting a neo-Marxist position, Harvey believed that the Enlightenment project of understanding and improving society by means of intelligent intervention remained possible. Indeed, his theory is a theory of the social conditions of emergence of postmodern theory explained from a neo-Marxist perspective which prioritised the effect of economic forces to explain cultural change rather than a postmodern theory per se.

The discourse of science and normative control

The work of Michel Foucault is not strictly postmodernist and certainly not high modernist. He is usually viewed as a post-structuralist who is critical of macro and structural theories such as functionalism and Marxism, regarding them as totalising theories that filter reality in conformity to their perspectives. He also opposes theoretical approaches which see history as unfolding in a logical direction which is viewed in terms of progress. This would include the progressiveness and humanitarianism built into Enlightenment thinking and the above mentioned sociological theories which followed in its tradition. This, and the centrality of discourse to his analysis, makes Foucault's position very close to that of the postmodernists. His work, though, is recognised as having evolved from more structuralist beginnings.

Central to Foucault's approach was the idea that knowledge and power are closely interrelated and that control operates in the context of discourses. A discourse is a way of thinking, writing and talking regarding a set of assumptions which are taken as the truth and forms a milieu of communication. In fact, discourses are the means by which power operates. Foucault was particularly interested in the way that discourses in the wake of the Enlightenment were implicated in new methods of social control rather than their professed humanitarianism and liberation.

These features may appear to be true on the surface as witnessed by changes in the treatment of criminals who in the Middle Ages suffered bodily torture and public humiliation to that of confinement and rehabilitation in modern societies. This self-evident view of improvement is because the discourses of the Enlightenment have their own inbuilt view of progress which appears to be natural to the participants of that era of discourse. But people are in fact prisoners of the discourse who are not conscious of their mental confinement. It thus takes a careful examination of history in terms of different discourses to help reveal what may otherwise remain invisible within the discourse of the current age.

For Foucault, predominant discourses change over time, but there is no single or purposeful direction to this change or means of establishing the superiority of one discourse compared to another. Foucault studies the discourses of different eras to show that in fact the heritage of the Enlightenment is an extension of control through the application of 'supposed' science to classify and distinguish the pathological from the normal and to extend interventions by professionals in the name of scientific based treatment to suppress the pathological and regulate social normalcy. In other words, what passes as science is a new finely graded and more invasive form of control which is essentially moral based. Against this background, Foucault studies changes in discourse and its consequences regarding the mad, criminals and sexual deviance.

The emergence of the discourses of the human and social sciences are themselves a product of the Enlightenment. These sciences provided a justification for classifying and controlling populations in the guise of treatment and help. New interventions and knowledge, in the name of science, are in the hands of professionals – doctors, educators, psychiatrists, prison officials etc. In fact, science is essentially moral in that through it professionals impose normalising judgements on the behaviour of others, differentiating the normal from the pathological and providing 'helpful' interventions such as treatment and rehabilitation which enables professionals to impose moral and social control on others.

This can be illustrated in society's view of the mad. In the Middle Ages, the mad were cast from society, left free to roam, but were regarded as relatively harmless. The advance of rational thinking was bound up with the eighteenth century Enlightenment. Viewing phenomena from an increasingly rational point of view accentuated the distinction between the mad and the rational thinking and emphasised the extent to which the former was a threat to the latter. The mad, along with the destitute, left free could become a social order problem in a rationally organised society and so these groups tended to become commonly incarcerated and later separated. The advance of the sciences included the human and social sciences of psychology and psychiatry. The incarcerated mad were now viewed in confinement as 'mentally ill' and 'mental patients' requiring treatment by professionals versed in what Foucault regarded as an 'assumed' science. He questioned the extent to which psychiatry is a science and suggests that its interventions are morally based since the purpose of confinement and treatment was in fact a matter of social control with the aim of 'normalisation' of the 'pathological'.

A change in discourse also had implications for the treatment of criminals. Foucault's historical study of changes in the punishment of prisoners is intended to shed new light on the use of discipline but also on the technology of surveillance and control that has come to pervade society. Foucault shows that up to the middle of the eighteenth century, punishment of prisoners sometimes involved torture and public humiliation. The treatment of criminals up to this period of time was viewed from the Enlightenment perspective as barbaric and became replaced by rationally judged periods of confinement and the application of prison rules. The common view from within Enlightenment discourse is one of progress to a more humanitarian regime in which punishment was rationalised and routinized. But for Foucault, the aim was in fact to punish more effectively and control criminals. Here, the disciplinary power of surveillance is very important. The very potential for constant surveillance whilst in confinement enables control to run very deep. As the individual prisoner can never be sure of whether they are being observed or not, the possibility of surveillance generates self-discipline. Foucault goes on to argue that surveillance becomes a strategy for imposing self-control in a range of institutions including schools, psychiatric hospitals, and workplaces and is part of what could be more broadly called 'carceral society' in which activities are brought into regulation and surveillance by functionaries and professionals for purposes of social control. This extension of external control and its intrusion into self-control runs counter to the Enlightenment view of the progress of individual freedom. Enlightenment thinking provides the self-contained delusion of freedom which is difficult to recognise when looking from within its own discourse.

Participants within institutions are judged by professional educators, psychiatrists, officers etc. as objects of knowledge. The discourse of the human sciences and the emergence of professionals enables power to be exerted by professional experts over others. It provided institutional discipline in the form of record keeping and surveillance. Rather than emphasising that the source of power, discipline and surveillance is uniquely focussed in the centralised state or a ruling class, Foucault emphasised that it is decentered into these numerous institutions with their own history and uncertain future trajectory of change.

Foucault also argued that the imposition of power can never be total but will always generate its own opposition and evasions. Discourse on sexuality provides a good example of this. With the development of psychiatry, homosexuality became designated as pathological sexuality which treatment aimed to cure. For Foucault, the apparent science of psychiatry that was applied in treatments to bring about a moral 'normalisation' of behaviour was not dissimilar to moralising control through religious confession. Nevertheless, counter action by this persecuted minority has led to effective political opposition to the above viewpoint and the acquisition of new rights.

Queer theory

The issue of gender gained increasing prominence in both society and sociology from the late 1960s with the emergence of the women's movement and feminist thinking. Feminists attacked the use of patriarchal power over women throughout society and argued for equality of opportunity between the sexes. At a theoretical level, they were highly critical of the Parsonian model which emphasised early socialisation into gendered roles whereby women were expected to use their affective skills in the upbringing of children and men their instrumental skills in supporting the family unit.

From a postmodernist vantage point, despite its radical criticism at the time, feminism, like functionalism, was also a product of the modern era and its use of universal categories. Thus, although feminists recognised the role of socialisation in the formation of gender identity, they still saw gender in terms of a 'binary division' between female and male identities with females commonly experiencing patriarchal power. This universal binary division approach was reproduced by symbolic interactionists who studied homosexuality as a form of deviance from sexual norms. Postmodernists such as Judith Butler have come to argue that gender identity can no longer be viewed in such unitary terms and regarded as the primary feature of a fixed self. Instead, within the context of cultural diversity, it is an individual accomplishment that is open to reflexive change. Sexual identity is influenced by culture and discourse which in contemporary times is fragmented, multiple and shifting. This approach to gender and sexuality has been referred to as 'queer theory'.

In the context of postmodern studies, queer theory is not used as a derogatory term nor is it a form of gay or lesbian studies. Although, like gay and lesbian studies, it puts sexuality at the centre of analysis, it is critical of such studies for putting gays and lesbians at the centre of enquiry from a standpoint position as this only emphasises a heterosexual / homosexual divide, oversimplifies sexuality as a fixed characteristic and legitimises heterosexuality as a norm. From the queer theory viewpoint, defining people in terms of a single collective sexual identity is inappropriate as this 1) silences a range of other characteristics of identity, all of which are 2) highly complex and fluid. Sexuality is not seen as a naturally embedded core of identity but something which is socially constructed and policed. Queer theorists bring this to light and emphasise that in the postmodern condition of diversity and tolerance of difference there is great subtlety and indeterminacy to sexual identity.

High modernist theories:

The term 'high modernity' is used here as a general umbrella for a group of like terms also including 'liquid modernity' and 'second modernity' that have been identified in previous sections. To this we can also add Habermas' modernist view of the stage of 'late capitalism'.

1. Extending life world rationality

The social theory of late capitalism developed by Jurgen Habermas draws from a variety of theoretical sources. His work originated within the influence of the Frankfurt School of neo-Marxists, but Habermas adopted a less pessimistic view than earlier representatives of this tradition (such as Horkheimer and Adorno) of the capacity of the masses to resist the impact of consumerist ideology and instrumental rationalism. Likewise, although he built into his theory Weber's ideas regarding rationalisation and bureaucratisation, he was less pessimistic than Weber regarding the dehumanising effect of an all confining instrumental rationalism. Into these macro dimensions which focus on the social system, Habermas integrates phenomenological insights regarding processes of life world communication. Combined in Habermas' approach, these perspectives provide a powerful defence of modernism and the capacity for rational thought to be utilised to serve the public good. Habermas is therefore highly critical of postmodern thinking which tends to adopt a nihilistic attitude toward the prospects of social improvement through the application of rational thinking.

What are the purposes or ends to which rational action is directed and to what extent are these ends open to political debate? These questions are of central importance in Habermas' theory. In incorporating the above perspectives into his analysis, Habermas analyses society in terms of 'social integration' and 'systems integration'. Social integration refers to the processes of the everyday life world in which consensus is built on discourse between actors who are able to engage in free and rational communication. System integration refers to the way that action is structured through the dominance of social institutions and the external imposition of rules, constraints and regulations. For Habermas, the public sphere is a contested realm of free communication and debate and systematic institutional impositions.

At both levels, the Enlightenment inheritance of rationality is evident, but tension is generated over the different types of rationality. In the sphere of system integration, action is directed by instrumental rationality. This type of rationality is evident in systems which operate through the efficient direction of practical action toward given ends which are unreflectively accepted. The motivating force here may be enterprises driven by the profit motive or the efficiency of government bureaucratic structures. The external imposition of systems which aim at achieving material wealth are key to realising standards of living. However, the way in which they operate is through the use of power and the imposition of sanctions.

By contrast, social integration refers to everyday communication which takes place through shared meaning in an environment of open and free discourse. This discourse takes the form of the application of reasoned discussion in which individuals attempt to convince others, resulting in negotiated consensus. Issues therefore are to do with individual interests, social ends and quality of life. This form of rationality is referred to as substantive rationality in which rational communication is formative of public opinion. For Habermas, late capitalism has come to increasingly generate conflict between the levels of system integration and social integration rationality. Why is this so?

The eighteenth century Enlightenment was a period of the opening up of free discussion of contemporary issues and the development of critical rational thinking in the public sphere and beyond the control of the state. Free rational discourse undermined tradition and promoted revolutionary change in the form of emancipation of people from the servitude of feudal thinking and institutions and enhanced the democratic political institutions of modern western societies. The essential point for Habermas, though, and the one general point of agreement with the postmodernists, is that as modern societies progressed, the freedoms of substantive rationality were closed down. This was because the rationality of free and open public discourse became invaded by the instrumental rationality of the modern system, leading to the increasing bureaucratisation of public life, control by experts, the power of private enterprises and a mass consumerist culture, for the benefit of efficient production and profitability.

In contrast to postmodernists, who are resigned to the inevitability of bland consumerism, Habermas argues that such conditions are a pathology of late capitalist modernisation, not an essential condition of a postmodern society. The excessive intrusion into the life world by the instrumental rationality of the system (referred to as colonisation), through, for example, sophisticated mass media techniques, has closed down the area of public debate. In doing so, it distorts life world communication to its needs, where issues of standard of living prevail over quality of life and people tend to become controlled and passive consumers. The outcome is a pseudo public sphere. And, under communist regimes, it was administrative structures and the state imposed ideology of 'sham comradeship' that invaded the public sphere to distort free communication and control criticism.

The key to regaining the emancipatory potential of the Enlightenment is for the emergence of resistance in the public sphere to system colonisation by pushing back the intrusions of instrumental rationality. The public sphere needs to develop the space to re-established open discussion and free discourse regarding society's ultimate values, undistorted by system imperatives. Only by so doing can rational public discussion freely debate issues of public good and develop a constraining criticism of the instrumental rationality of the system.

For Habermas, in these conditions of late capitalist modernisation, it is communication conflict between the two rationalities which has replaced class conflict of the capitalism of Marx's time. However, he is not as pessimistic as Weber that society will be engulfed by instrumental rationality. One reason for this is that the development of the welfare state has opened up areas of debate and interest group action regarding its operation and the constraints that it is under. Another is that however much it has been closed down, debate is necessary for the legitimacy of democracy and so there will always be an opening for more free discussion. Moreover, given the advance of technologically mediated communication, the possibilities for debate and organised resistance to system colonisation of the life world may have been enhanced, and new social movements raising issues of the quality of life have an important role to play here.

Habermas is relatively optimistic that late modern society can regain the full liberating potential of the Enlightenment. This requires a new balance of the life world and system spheres so that the fruits of prosperity resulting from the application of instrumental rationalism of the system can be enjoyed within societies in which open rational discussion generates effective public opinion regarding ultimate values of public good. The main exception to this optimism is the United States where Habermas believes that the colonisation of the public sphere by instrumental rationalism and culture of consumerism are so complete that the liberating potential of true free public discussion is unlikely to emerge.

2. Liquid modernity and disembedding

Zygmunt Bauman's early works adopted a neo-Marxist orientation. However, the growing individualism and diversity that he observed to be taking place in advanced capitalism enhanced his dissatisfaction with the economic determinism and social categories built into Marxism. In the 1980s, Bauman come to recognise the merits of postmodernist approaches. In Gane's 'The Future of Social Theory' (2004), Bauman explains that his past postmodern stance was itself only a stopgap position. For Bauman, postmodernism had performed an important task of showing that the world was unlike the grid mapped by modernist grand theory such as Marxism and it alerted us to new uncertainties. However, Bauman announced that he was now abandoning postmodernism. He signified his change of position thus:

> 'The 'postmodern' has done its preliminary, site-clearing job: it aroused vigilance and sent the exploration in the right direction. It could not do much more, and so after that it outlived its usefulness;

or, rather, it worked itself out of a job.....And we can now say more about the present-day world than it is *unlike* the old familiar one. We have, so to speak, matured to afford (to risk?) a *positive* theory of its novelty' (Gane, 2004, pp.17-18).

For Bauman, postmodernism was, on the one hand, too negative regarding the prospects of developing a coherent understanding of the contemporary world, and on the other, overly optimistic regarding the individual freedoms and pleasures enjoyed in contemporary consumer society.

Bauman now proposed a theory of 'liquid modernity' to explain the contemporary social condition. In using the term 'liquid', Bauman was referring to a situation of continuous fluidity in social relations, in signs and in information. How does he apply this concept of liquidity? For Bauman, the transition from traditional pre-industrial to modern industrial societies involved the rapid and far reaching change from one solid social structure, through temporary liquefaction, to another solid structure. The temporary period of liquefaction of social structures disembedded people (lifted them out) from the social constraints of a traditional society which had provided a fixed position in a hierarchy of feudal estates. Once emerged, modern industrial society, referred to by Bauman as a phase of 'solid modernity', re-embedded people (placed them back) into a class stratified system in which position was not so ascribed but where acquiring social mobility depended on people learning rules of class admission. However, contemporary societies had, by the late twentieth century, entered a state of continuous fluidity with no prospect of this ending. In the society of liquid modernity, the structures and constraints of the phase of solid modernity have broken down and life is becoming individualised. People have experienced disembedding from the confines of the old class structure, but they have been cut adrift into a void of ever changing rules with no solid social structure for re-embedding. This new freedom is one of abandonment and uncertainty, which generates in the individual anxiety in the relentless quest for security and the self-construction of identity.

The structured past modern world of solid modernity was the world of Fordist production methods, top down organisational hierarchies, controlled workers, surveillance and imposed identity, established career paths and lasting marriages. It was a rational survival strategy, argues

Bauman, to learn the rules and structure of society and adjust one's behaviour accordingly in the expectation that this would serve one's interests in the long term over which one could expect to continue in a line of work or plan a career. In the context of liquid modernity, attempting to apply this strategy would be detrimental. Survival in the contemporary situation requires an unending process of trials and errors, learning, unlearning and relearning, and the abandonment of the idea of a single occupation or life project.

During the phase of solid modernity, both workers and employers experienced relative immobility. Workers held a degree of power in this antagonistic relationship through their ability to disrupt the production process. However, under conditions of liquid modernity, capital had migrated to cyberspace. In doing so, it had achieved far greater freedom of mobility than workers who remained relatively tied to their locality, and with it the threat and power of possible disengagement of capital. Workers have thus become relatively disempowered, with old forms of stratification conflict eclipsed by 'space wars' in which the most globally mobile are the winners. Bauman thus argued that mobility or lack of it becomes the new basis for social polarisation. Contemporary societies are also arenas of 'identity wars' involving struggles to impose one's own and others' identity through whatever resources are available.

Referring, as Mills had, to the relationship between personal troubles and the broader social structure, for Bauman, in structured traditional societies, and to some extent in solid modern societies, the causes of private troubles were often obvious to the individual as they were experienced directly. For example, the cause of individual hunger was obvious enough – a lack of food – even though solution of the problem for them may not have been quite so straightforward. In contemporary liquid modernity, new socially generated risks, in particular globalisation leading to the dismantling of social bonds, safety networks, and collective projects and the effects of pollution, are not so directly seen or easily understood by the individual. The effects of individualization are those of growing individual uncertainty and anxiety, whilst at the same time an understanding of the processes bringing this about is less easy to recognise through individual experiences. Individualization in contemporary society increases the rift between private experiences of anxiety and the capacity to understand the broader and often distant social causes of it, promoting the tendency in individuals to retreat into a world of private concerns.

For Bauman, unlike postmodernists, rational sociological analysis and intervention can help remedy the situation. The current time is one of urgent need for a reinvigorated sociological imagination. Society has fundamentally changed, but sociology has been weighed down by the baggage of an earlier era. Detailed sociological understanding of the contemporary condition of liquid modernity is needed to help re-establish the connection between private experiences and their social causes and to guide remedial political action. This requires the creative development of new sociological theories and concepts applicable to the contemporary condition of liquid modernity, not the use of what Beck refers to as 'zombie terms' such as social class and the family which are more applicable to the conditions of past solid modernity.

3. Informational society

Manuel Castells has analysed the effect of the rise of new information technology, especially in the form of the internet, on contemporary life. He argues that the globalising impact of such technology is having a profound effect on both capitalism and individual identity. For Castells, capitalism remains the social driving force, but the form that it is taking is changing. A key factor in this change is the ever sprawling internet which gives rise to networked communication. Compared to old hierarchies of command, these high tech networks are flexible, adaptable and instantaneous in their global reach. In the face of such changes, old command economies have had to adapt, as in the case of China, or fall, as did the Soviet Union.

According to Castells, such technology is bringing about a new form of global capitalism, 'informational capitalism', in which the search for wealth shifts from an emphasis on industrial production to the maximisation of investment opportunities via instant access and response to the condition of global markets. Money has therefore to some extent become separated from production in a more impersonal world.

In the informational society, Castells sees social conflict becoming displaced from the class conflict of an earlier era. Under industrial capitalism, organised labour could sometimes check the power of capital as both were locked together and relatively immobile. Adopting a similar view to Bauman, for Castells, under informational capitalism, capital is global and mobile whereas labour remains more locally rooted. Labour has therefore become relatively powerless and conflict has been displaced from that between the classes of earlier capitalism to that of protest groups, themselves organised through the use of modern technology which generates a new type of capacity for opposition.

High tech informational capitalism is having a major effect on the capacity of the state to any longer act as a self-contained entity as viewed by the pioneering sociologists. For example, the capacity of states to protect their welfare programs tends to be undermined by the ease that informational capitalism provides for capital movement to gravitate toward the states with the lowest welfare costs. In the competition for inward investment, states have to adapt accordingly – there is overall downward pressure on welfare expenditure.

For Castells, the positive effects of informational capitalism include the creation of enhanced opportunities for individual enterprise and greater individual input into identity creation. However, a major concern is the capacity of the informational world to become an out of control automaton. In response, Castells adopts a modernist approach that through the application of human reason and will, the information revolution can be harnessed for human good, but time may be running out for our opportunity to shape its effects.

4. Hybrid societies and reconfigured relationships

The form taken by sociology in its formative period reflected the then close association between societies and nation states - sociology was the study of bounded societies. Founding sociological theory linked the social, society and human, and, even in positivist theory, established clear distinctions between the physical science of objects and the social science of societies. For John Urry, the impact of developments in technology have led to the emergence of new patterns of social life and communication, reconfigured humans and the need for a reconfigured sociology.

The advance of technological modernisation and globalisation have weakened the society / nation tie as new networks without centres, in particular based on the internet, have emerged to enhance communication across national borders. As well as a growing separation of the social from nation states, social 'relations' themselves are increasingly made up of a mix of human agency and material objects and technologies. Urry suggests that in this sense we cannot now talk about uniquely human societies but of 'hybrid societies' – networks of connection involving humans and technological objects which change the human experience in ways that we need to understand. Consequently, a change is needed in sociological focus to recognise 'reconfigured' humans – a reconfigured sociology is required to account for the impact of technology and objects on 'relationships' which makes them less authentically social.

The effect of technological developments on the senses can be illustrated through the simple example of the development of the automobile. The speed and insulation involved in travelling through a city by car provides a very different experience of the environment than one would have when walking, whilst the presence of traffic in the city will also affect the experience of walkers.

What form may a reconfigured sociology take? Urry speculates that what is needed is a move from the study of bounded society to the study of high tech globally networked communications as open and dynamic systems which cut across societies and can be analysed as structures and flows. Movement thus replaces location in the study of the social. Theories and methods need to be developed that enable the analysis of connections between human powers and material objects and that track the effect of communication flows through networks. As new technologies such as travel, the internet, and the mobile phone have accelerated the experience of time, analysis needs to take account of instantaneous time rather than the traditional exclusive preoccupation with clock time.

As globalisation enhances cosmopolitanism, it is likely that emerging global standards will effect how people think and behave. This will enhance reflective modernisation and sociology will need to reconfigure itself in a global and cosmopolitan way, making society a decreasing focal point of study.

5. Society of manufactured risk

This section will be focussing on theories put forward by Anthony Giddens and Ulrich Beck. Both of these writers tend to adopt a transformationist position on globalisation – they argue that globalisation is bringing about profound changes and new problems and risks, but remain optimistic that these changes can be rationally understood and that positive intervention to improve society is possible. This transformationist stance therefore links closely to their characterisation of contemporary society as 'high modern' or 'second modern' rather than postmodern.

Giddens, in 'Runaway World' (2002), periodises history into traditional, modern and high modern phases. Traditional societies were agricultural based. Life for most people was linked to working the land and lived out within small local communities. The tempo of life was dominated by the repetitions and constraints of the seasons and ritual played an important part in people's lives. Nature related work tasks at a local level moulded the measurement and perception of distance and time to season and locality.

The dawn of the modern era came in the seventeenth and eighteenth centuries with the Enlightenment. Science and rational thinking were applied to question the superstitions and social constraints of traditional societies. Faith in social progress was invested in the capacity of science to fashion a rationally based social order. Scientific advances included the development of mechanical devices that enabled time to be precisely divided up and universalised. With industrialisation, this standardised time became attached to new routines as work became extracted from the tempo of nature and the countryside and increasingly governed by man made tempo of the factory and the office. The effect of these changes was the experience of the compression of distance and time.

A process linked to the compression of distance and time was the disembedding of social relations. In traditional societies, social relations operated largely at a personal, face-to-face level within the context of small local communities. The development of impersonal institutions accompanied modernisation. These institutions mediated social relationships involving, for example, the exchange of news and money. News could be widely disseminated through printed materials and financial transactions mediated through the institution of banks. These changes allowed such exchanges to become extracted from direct involvement in social encounters between parties.

Giddens argues that the freeing of social relationships from the constraints of traditional society led to life becoming more 'reflexive'. Social relations in traditional societies held certainties in the sense that life was parochial and opportunities were limited. These certainties were upset by the processes of modernisation which brought change and opened up opportunity. Uncertainty encourages reflexivity – the need of people to continuously monitor and interpret their own behaviour and that of others as they make assessments of risks and possibilities that their environment offers. However, if tradition is viewed in terms of behavioural rituals and repetitions which give life form, modern society was also characterised by its own traditions. The need for reflexivity was thus limited.

For Giddens, what has transpired more recently is that change, uncertainty and risk have now reached a new level. The 1970s witnessed an advance in the interconnectedness of the world as advances in technology extended the range and speed of communications and travel. This further compression of distance and time was associated with globalisation and was the hallmark of a new stage in society which Giddens refers to as high modern. Now, accompanying globalisation, change, uncertainty and risk take on new dimensions. In an increasingly interconnected world, unexpected happenings in one part, such as currency fluctuations, can impact globally and heighten instability. For individuals, uncertainty and constant reflexivity are part of high modern globalised life which accompany an extension of individual autonomy.

Globalisation brings with it new risks. Giddens explains the changing nature of risk. Traditional societies were vulnerable to risks of nature such as drought, flood and storm. These dangers Giddens refers to as natural or 'external' risks. The drive and industriousness behind capitalist modernisation saw a leap in the imposition of human action onto nature, creating new problems such as pollution and contagious diseases associated with crowded and unhygienic living conditions in towns and cities. However, because life in modern society was still structured and constrained by traditions and routines, our knowledge of risks could be calculated and some degree of security could be made possible through insurance.

In the high modern global context, our level of intervention into nature has brought about new dangers in the form of 'manufactured' risk. Global warming and its likely consequences is one such manufactured risk and others include the unknown effects of genetic modification of crops and the possibility of economic meltdown. These risks are different from external risks in that there is no experience by which outcomes can be calculated and therefore against which insurance can be provided. We have created through our interventions in nature a fluid and uncertain environment which is at the 'end of nature' and traditions, and risks getting out of our control. Given the level of individual autonomy, risk and need for constant reflexivity in contemporary society, there is attraction for some in turning to compulsive behaviour or fundamentalist beliefs (phenomena which are both on the increase) as attempts to close down the uncertainties and anxiety of individual autonomy through retreat to forms of ritual and tradition.

It is to the challenge of this environment of man-made risks that new and enlightened responses and new policies and forms of governmental organisation are required. Reflexivity is necessary at a governmental and global level given the global nature of the risks faced. Difficult as it is, Giddens argues that appropriate new institutions and interventions can still be rationally guided by a sociology that is up to the mark. This development is an urgent social imperative.

Ulrich Beck's analysis of the contemporary social and sociological condition is a remarkably similar one to that of Giddens. Beck places the changing nature of risk at the centre of his analysis and divides modernity into two phases - first modernity and second modernity. Prior to first industrial modernity, the main risks to people, such as famine and disease, were a consequence of nature and largely beyond the control of man. Beck defined the first phase of modernity as pre-globalised industrialisation. At this stage of development, scientific advances such as the introduction of new farming techniques and medical treatments assisted in the control of natural risk. However, the creation of wealth through technological intervention in nature created new by-product risks such as pollution. Within this first phase of modernisation, risk, like society itself, remained relatively localised and calculable. The scope for uncertain consequences of human intervention was limited.

At the theoretical level, society of the first modernity was adequately explained in the Parsonian functionalist model in which separate societies as nation states operated as systems which adjusted toward equilibrium and institutions such as the family and the church imposed a degree of certainty into people's lives.

A key feature of the second phase of modernity is that uncertainty cannot so readily be reduced to calculated and controlled risk. This is because societies have reached the stage where scientific and technological advance and intervention has led to the creation of new manufactured uncertainties. An example here may be the health threats posed by the emergence of superbugs as a result of the use of antibiotics to combat diseases. And even technological developments attempting to solve manufactured risks introduce their own uncertainties or unanticipated undesirable consequences. As technological intervention in the context of globalisation has enabled an ever-increasing dominance of nature, the new risks created, such as radiation and global warming, take on a more challenging global dimension. The one certainty that we now have is that there will be as yet unknown future consequences and risks of our current interventions.

Whilst the institutions of the family, social class, local community and religion constrained the lives of individuals during first stage modernity, they provided structure, a framework of identity and stability to people's lives. In second stage modernity, individual freedom has advanced as globalisation and cosmopolitanism have eroded these institutions and structures. This liberation from past constraints leaves individuals vulnerable to new insecurities. For all of the benefits that contemporary society brings, risk also becomes a growing feature of this liberation. Overall, it becomes so much a feature of life that we can characterise second phase modernity as 'risk society'. Risk society is so open that individuals are increasingly conscious that they often don't readily know or control the consequences of their actions. This can affect the very possibility of predicting or controlling their own life trajectories in a world of high levels of marital breakdown and highly flexible labour markets. Actors have to navigate their lives in new social conditions in which risks and uncertainties are transferred to the individual who has no socially handed down playscript for guidance. Life becomes an ongoing act of 'reflexivity' in which individuals are continuously weighing up circumstances and available options and adapting response strategies to attempt to promote a degree of security. This may include weighing up how one's behaviour can be changed to reduce global warming, considering whether it is safe at a particular time to travel by plane or considering precautions to avoid contracting sexually transmitted disease.

In response to risk, a new type of globally and environmentally aware politics has emerged. But in attempting to manage risk, do we trust the judgements of experts? Their calculations of risk are based on laboratory knowledge which first-hand experience may challenge. Whose interests do experts serve and can we trust what experts and politicians tell us? Risk society has thus seen the emergence of direct action protest movements aiming to influence or challenge decision making with regard to the risks accompanying technological intervention, as, for example, in the recent case of protests against the practice of fracking – the fracturing of rock formations to extract oil and gas.

For Beck, the world has moved on since that adequately explained by Parsonian functionalism. Just as people's national experiences and perspectives have been eclipsed by global and cosmopolitan forces and perspectives, so sociology must move on from the 'methodological nationalism' of its founding fathers to 'methodological cosmopolitanism'. It can only do so through engaging in painstaking research across the world and developing theories able to conceptualise contemporary conditions. It must move beyond what have now become the 'zombie categories', such as the family, social class, career and the nation, that it has inherited from the first modernity. By so doing, sociology may be able to provide analytical assistance to guide reflexivity in response to risk at both individual and governmental level.

6. A post-social world?

Technology is increasingly becoming the medium of communication, often squeezing out the need for direct face to face social contact. For example, computer technology and electronic communication has enabled work to be conducted in increasingly 'virtual organisations' in which telephone and e mail are the main means of contact.

One's finances can now be conducted via internet banking and the use of cash machines. Furthermore, if one were to phone a bank or one of many other large organisations, it is often necessary to have to navigate through a system of automated responses, frequently encouraging internet contact, before possibly speaking to a person. Even transferring small amounts of money from person to person can now take place via mobile phone rather than the need for personal contact.

There has been a massive increase in online shopping where goods can be selected, ordered and delivered with personal communication reduced to the signing of a docket on delivery. If one shops at a supermarket, the only required contact is with a checkout assistant and even this can be avoided through the use of self-service checkouts.

Computer technology can open up the possibility of cyber contact with people that one has never met personally. This can lead to new opportunities to develop personal friendships and relationships but can also entail risks associated with deception.

Through the use of advanced technology, the reach of possible contacts may be vastly extended at the same time as the experience of personal loneliness. Sociology will have to develop an understanding of the effects of a world of communication which is increasingly mediated by technology.

Bibliography

Abbott, P. & Wallace, C. (1997) *An Introduction to Sociology.* London: Routledge

Abercrombie, N. & Warde, A. et al. (2006) *Contemporary British Society.* Cambridge: Polity

Aldridge, A. (2013) *Religion in the Contemporary World.* Cambridge: Polity

Allan, K. (2005) *Explorations in Classical Sociological Theory.* California: Pine Forge

Allen, M. (2013) *The Curriculum Great Reversal.* Available at: **http:// radicaled.wordpress.com/2013/05/01/the-curriculum-great-reversal/ (Accessed 19/6/2014)**

Alvesson, M. (2002) *Postmodernism and Social Research.* Buckingham: Open University

Andreski, S. (1972) *Herbert Spencer.* London: Nelson

Apple, M.W. et al (ed.) (2010) *The Routledge International Handbook of the Sociology of Education.* London: Routledge

Ball, S.J. (ed.) (2004) *Sociology of Education.* London: Routledge Falmer

Barrington Moore Jr. (1969) *Social Origins of Dictatorship and Democracy.* Harmondsworth: Penguin

Beck, U. (1992) *Risk Society.* London: Sage

Becker, H.S. (1973) *Outsiders.* New York: The Free Press

Berger, P.L. (1969) *The Social Reality of Religion.* London: Faber & Faber

Berger, P.L. (1974) *Invitation to Sociology.* Harmondsworth: Penguin.

Bilton, T. et al. (2002) *Introductory Sociology.* Basingstoke: Palgrave MacMillan.

Blackburn, R. (ed.) (1972) *Ideology in Social Science.* Fontana / Collins: UK.

Bottero, W. (2005) *Stratification: Social Divisions and Inequality.* Abingdon: Routledge.

Bristow, J. (2005) *Civil partnerships: let's get one thing straight.* Available at: **http://www.spiked-online.com/ Articles/0000000CAEB0.htm (Accessed 11/2/2014)**

Browne, K. (2006) *An Introduction to Sociology.* Cambridge: Polity

Bruce, S. (1995) *Religion in Modern Britain.* Oxford: Oxford University Press

Calhoun, C. et al. (ed.) (2002) *Contemporary Sociological Theory.* Oxford: Blackwell

Cassen, R. & Kingdom, G. (2007) *Tackling low Educational Achievement.* Available at: **www.jrf.org.uk/sites/files/jrf/2063- education-schools (Accessed 18/6/2014)**

Cheal, D. (2002) *Sociology of Family Life.* Basingstoke: Palgrave MacMillan

Chitty, C. (2009) *Education Policy in Britain.* Basingstoke: Palgrave MacMillan

Coser, L.A. (1977) *Masters of Sociological Thought.* New York: Harcourt Brace Jovanovich

Coxall, B. et al. (2003) *Contemporary British Politics.* Basingstoke: Palgrave MacMillan

Crompton, R. (2008) *Class & Stratification.* Cambridge: Polity Press

Cuff, E.C. et al. (2001) *Perspectives in Sociology.* London: Routledge

Dahrendorf, R. (1959) *Class and Class Conflict in Industrial Society.* London: Routledge & Kegan Paul

Devine, F. & Heath, S. (1999) *Sociological Research Methods in Context.* Basingstoke: Macmillan

Durkheim, E. (1964a) *The Division of Labour in Society.* New York: Free Press

Durkheim, E. (1964b) *The Rules of Sociological Method.* New York: Free Press

Durkheim, E. (1970) *Suicide.* London: Routledge & Kegan Paul

Durkheim, E. (1976) *The Elementary Forms of the Religious Life.* London: George Allen & Unwin

Engels, F. (1974) *The Condition of the Working Class in England.* St Albans: Panther

Flanagan, K. & Jupp, P.C. (ed.) (1999) *Postmodernity, Sociology and Religion.* Basingstoke: Macmillan

Flick, U. (2011) *An Introduction to qualitative Research.* London: Sage

Frankenberg, R. (1973) *Communities in Britain.* Harmondsworth: Penguin

Fulcher, J. & Scott, J. (2011) *Sociology.* Oxford: Oxford University Press

Furseth, I. & Repstad, P. (2010) *An Introduction to the Sociology of Religion.* Farnham: Ashgate

Gabb, J. (2010) *Family Lives and Relational Living: Taking Account of Otherness.* Available at: **http://www.socresonline.org.uk/16/4/10.html (Accessed 8/6/2014)**

Gane, N. (2004) *The Future of Social Theory.* London: Continuum

Gane, N. (2012) *Max Weber and Contemporary Capitalism.* Basingstoke: Palgrave Macmillan

Garfinkle, H. (1984) *Studies in Ethnomethodology.* Cambridge: Polity Press

Gerth, H.H. & Mills, C. Wright (1977) *From Max Weber.* London: Routledge

Giddens, A. (1976) *New Rules of Sociological Method.* London: Hutchinson

Giddens, A. et al. (ed.) (1995) *The Polity Reader in Social Theory.* Cambridge: Polity Press

Giddens, A. (2000) *The Third Way and Its Critics.* Cambridge: Polity

Giddens, A. (2002) *Runaway World.* London: Profile

Giddens, A. (2009) *Sociology.* Cambridge: Polity

Hall, D. & Hall, I. (2005) *Practical Social Research: Project Work in the Community.* Basingstoke: Macmillan

Hall, S. et al. (ed.) (1993) *Modernity and its Futures.* Cambridge: Polity

Haralambos, M. & Holborn, M. (2013) *Sociology Themes and Perspectives.* London: HarperCollins

Held, D. (ed.) (2000a) *A Globalizing World?* New York: Routledge

Held, D. (2000b) *A Globalizing World? Culture, Economics, Politics* London: Routledge

Held, D. (ed.) (2003) *The Global Transformations Reader.* Cambridge: Polity

[""]

Hesse-Biber, S.N. (ed.) (2012) *The Handbook of Feminist Research.* London: Sage

Heywood, A. (1999) *Political Theory, An Introduction.* Basingstoke: Palgrave

Holton, R.J. (2011) *Globalization and the Nation State.* Basingstoke: Palgrave MacMillan

House of Commons Library - **www.parliament.uk , Research Paper 10/36 (Accessed 12/8/2013)**

Hunt, S. J. (2002) *Religion in Western Society.* Basingstoke: Palgrave

Hunt, S.J. (2005) *The Life Course.* Basingstoke: Palgrave MacMillan

Jacobs, J. (1969) "Symbolic Bureaucracy": A Case Study of a Social Welfare Agency. *Social Forces* 47 (4): 413-421

Jantti, M. et al. (2006) *American Exceptionalism in a New Light: A Comparison of Intergenerational Earnings Mobility in the Nordic Countries, the United Kingdom and the United States.* Available at **http://ftp.iza.org/ap1938.pdf (Accessed 10/3/2014)**

Joint Council for Qualifications. (2013) www.jcq.org.uk (Accessed 28/11/2013)

Kirby, M. et al. (2000) *Sociology in Perspective.* Oxford: Heinemann

Lincoln, Y.S. & Denzin, N.K. (ed.) (2003) *Turning Points in Qualitative Research.* Oxford: Altamira Press

Livesey, C. & Lawson, T. (2005) *AS Sociology for AQA.* Abingdon: Hodder Arnold

Lloyd, J. (2001) *The Protest Ethic.* London: Demos

McCall, G.J. & Simmons, J.L. (ed.) (1969) *Issues in Participant Observation.* London: Addison-Wesley

McKenzie, J. (2001) *Changing Education.* Harlow: Pearson

McNeill, P. & Chapman, S. (2005) *Research Methods.* London: Routledge

Macionis, J. J. & Plummer, K. (2008) *Sociology, A Global Introduction.* Harlow: Pearson

Marsh, I. (ed.) (2006) *Sociology, Making Sense of Society.* London: Pearson

Marshall, G. et al. (1993) *Social Class in Modern Britain.* London: Routledge

Marx, K. (1973) *The Revolutions of 1848.* Harmondsworth: Penguin

Matthewman, S. et al. (ed.) (2007) *Being Sociological.* Basingstoke: Palgrave

McIntosh, I. & Punch, S. (2005) *Get Set for Sociology.* Edinburgh: Edinburgh University Press

McNeill, P. & Chapman, S. (2005) *Research Methods.* Abingdon: Routledge

Miliband, R. (1973) *The State in Capitalist Society.* London: Quartet

Mills, C. Wright. (1975) *The Sociological Imagination.* Harmondsworth: Penguin

Monahan, S.C. (ed.) (2001) *Sociology of Religion.* New Jersey: Pearson

Office For National Statistics. (2013) *Crime Survey for England and Wales.* Available at: http://www.crimesurvey.co.uk/ (Accessed 11/12/2013)

Office For National Statistics. (2014) *Divorces in England and Wales, 2012.* Available at: **http://www.ons.gov.uk/ons/rel/vsob1/divorces-in-england-and-wales/2012/index.html (Accessed 11/2/2014)**

Parry, M. "Harvard Researchers Accused of Breaching Students' Privacy", *Chronicle of Higher Education*, 2011 (57) Issue 41

Parsons, T. & Shils, E.A. (1951) *Toward a General Theory of Action.* Cambridge: Harvard University Press

Porta, D. (ed.) (2009) *Social Movements in a Globalising World.* Basingstoke: Palgrave

Pullinger, J.T. (2015) *Prophets of Progress Saint Simon, Comte and Spencer, Pioneers of Sociology.* Cambridge: Cambridge Academic.

Punch, K.F. (2005) *Introduction to Social Research.* London: Sage

Ritzer, G. (2008) *Sociological Theory.* Boston: McGraw-Hill

Roberts, K. (2011) *Class in Contemporary Britain.* Basingstoke: Palgrave MacMillan

Robertson Elliot, F. (1996) *Gender, Family and Society.* Basingstoke: MacMillan

Saunders, P. (1990) *Social Class and Stratification.* London: Routledge

Schatzman, L. & Strauss, A.L. (1973) *Field Research.* New Jersey: Prentice – Hall

Schutz, A. (1974) *The Structures of the Life-World.* London: Heinemann

Sclater, S.D. (2005) *Families.* London: Hodder & Stoughton

Seale, C. (ed.) (2004) *Social Research Methods.* London: Routledge

Seldon, A. (ed.) (2001) *The Blair Effect.* London: Little, Brown & Co.

Selfe, P. & Starbuck, M. (2003) *Religion.* London: Hodder & Stoughton

Slattery, M. (2003) *Key Ideas in Sociology.* Cheltenham: Nelson Thornes

Smith, A. (13/4/2009) *Can Marxism Explain the Financial Crash?* Available at: **http://socialistworker.org/2009/04/13/marxism-and-the-financial-crash** **(Accessed 26/ 11/2013)**

Stake, R.E. (1995) *The Art of Case Study.* London: Sage

Statistical First Release. (24/1/2013) Available at: **http://www. education.gov.uk/researchandstatistics/allstatistics/a00219200/ gcse-and-equivalent-attainment** **(Accessed 20/11/2013)**

Steel, L. et al. (2012) *The Family.* Basingstoke: Palgrave MacMillan

Stephens, M. & Becker, S. (ed.) (1994) *Police Force, Police Service.* Basingstoke: MacMillan

Stones, R. (ed) (2008) *Key Sociological Thinkers.* Basingstoke: Palgrave

Struass, A. & Corbin, J. (1998) *Basics of Qualitative Research.* London: Sage

Swingewood, A. (2000) *A Short History of Sociological Thought.* Basingstoke: Palgrave

Thompson, K. (1976) *Auguste Comte: The Foundation of Sociology.* London: Nelson

Tocqueville, A. de. (1966) *The Ancien Regime and the French Revolution.* Manchester: Fontana

Toffler, A. (1971) *Future Shock.* London: Pan Books Ltd

de Vaus, D.A. de. (1999) *Surveys in Social Research.* London: UCL Press

Weber, M. (1978) *The Protestant Ethic and the Spirit of Capitalism.* London: George Allen & Unwin

Weiner, J.W. (1981) *English Culture and the Decline of the Industrial*

Spirit. Cambridge: Cambridge University Press

Worsley, P. (1970) *Introducing Sociology.* Harmondswirth: Penguin

Yin, R.K. (2009) *Case Study Research.* London: Sage

Young, M. & Willott, P. (1974) *Family and Kinship in East London.* Harmondsworth: Penguin

Picture sources

Auguste Comte Facts, information, pictures, www.encyclopedia.com (Accessed 30 May, 2014)

Herbert Spencer Facts, information, pictures, www.encyclopedia.com (Accessed 30 May, 2014)

Karl Marx Facts, information, pictures, www.encyclopedia.com (Accessed 30 May, 2014)

Index

29996566R00333

Printed in Poland
by Amazon Fulfillment
Poland Sp. z o.o., Wrocław